KU-492-594

Conversations in Japan

Modernization, Politics, and Culture

David Riesman

Evelyn Thompson Riesman

ALLEN LANE THE PENGUIN PRESS

LONDON 1967

First published in the U.S.A. by Basic Books, 1967
First published in Great Britain in 1967

Allen Lane The Penguin Press
Vigo Street, London, W.1.

Printed in the United States of America

To Shigeharu and Hanako Matsumoto

Acknowledgments

In preparing our Diaries for publication, we have changed names and sometimes locales to minimize embarrassment to individuals. We have also done a great deal of cutting in order to concentrate on our discussions and interviews. We are deeply indebted to Nathan Glick, a discriminating editor, who made suggestions for further cuts and helped clarify some passages that had been opaque and cryptic. Dr. Robert J. Lifton and his wife, Betty, also went over the manuscript with such considerations in mind. Ernest and Marilyn Young, and Albert and Terako Craig have also read the manuscript and given us helpful suggestions in editing. And it was Nathan Glazer who, with his enthusiasm for the Diaries, encouraged us to consider publication, in spite of our doubts.

Finally, our thanks to our friend and editor, Irving Kristol.

Brattleboro, Vermont
April 1967

DR
ETR

Preface

Our two-month visit to Japan was sponsored by the Japan Committee for Intellectual Interchange, an intercultural program that invites a guest lecturer from a foreign country for a month or two each year. I was to give a few lectures and to hold a few seminars and discussions with Japanese academicians and intellectuals; my wife was to come along for as much of this as she wished.

On the Japanese side, interest in my coming reflected not only the fact that many of my writings had been translated and fairly widely discussed and criticized, but also some awareness of my preoccupation with nuclear disarmament and foreign policy, as reflected in my association with the Committee of Correspondence (no longer active), made up mainly of academicians who wanted the United States to take more positive actions for peace. At a time in 1961 when many Japanese intellectuals were anxious about the stepped-up American presence in South Vietnam and the drive for bomb shelters, those Japanese not committed to intransigent anti-Americanism were eager for contact with non-Communist Americans who could share their concerns as well as their devotion to an idealistic and anti-chauvinistic American tradition.

We on our side had had a long but amateur interest in Japan. Evey had followed its novels in translation and some of its contemporary painting, and both of us its modern architecture. I had been interested in a society which had become urban and industrial by a different route from that of the West. At Harvard, I audited the famous "Rice Paddies" course given jointly by Professors John K. Fairbank and Edwin Reischauer; when the latter left to become Ambassador to Japan, his place in the course was taken by Professor Albert Craig, a scholar in modern Japanese history, from whom I learned much. I also profited from the teaching and writing of another colleague, Robert Bellah, as well as from the work of American and British historians and social scientists who have helped interpret Japan to the West.

We went without a thought of writing anything, and said as much when asked by our Japanese friends. Evey has been an inveterate if erratic diarist since her teens, and at various times I have made notes on trips within America; however, what appear here as excerpts from my diary began as round-robin letters to several friends, but soon became a staple of my visit as, caught up in the excitement of discovery, I found that recording events was a way not only to capture but to clarify experience. Moreover, during my arranged discussions with Japanese intellectuals, many of them tape-recorded and published in Japanese journals at the time, Evey fell into the habit of making notes which both served us as a record and gave her a self-evident function. Only three years later did the thought occur to us that we might publish our diaries. We asked our Japanese friends about the propriety of doing so, for we had often talked with each other in freedom and intimacy—quite off the record. We were assured by everyone we consulted that, by changing names and eliminating a few items which might be hurtful to individuals, we could publish this material without violating the tacit understandings people had had when they talked with us. Our American friends, Professor and Mrs. Ernest Young and Dr. and Mrs. Robert Jay Lifton, went over our manuscript with the same concern in mind, and we are deeply indebted to them. With their permission, we have not disguised their identity when they figure in these pages, nor that of some other American and English friends we saw in Japan, notably Nathan Glazer, whose visit overlapped ours and with whom we had many enlightening conversations.

As a colleague at Harvard, Dr. Lifton had already helped stimulate our interest in Japan, where he had returned in 1960 to continue his investigation of individual psychology and historical change among Japanese youth. He served on the Intellectual Interchange Committee which met in Japan to plan our schedule, and he took part in a number of the discussions thus arranged. With his wife, Betty, a writer and student of Japanese folklore, he helped interpret us to the Japanese, and vice versa, and tried to save us from the errors of tact and understanding of the impetuous "barbarian."

Other foreign visitors also facilitated our understanding. At International House, we met Professor Richard Storry of St. Antony's College, Oxford, whose *The Double Patriots* and *A History of Modern Japan* we had admired. Newspapermen, Embassy people (notably, Ernest Young), social scientists such as William Caudill and Henry Rosovsky, Fulbright lecturers such as Karl Loewenstein and Foster Rhea Dulles, all shared interpretations with us during our stay.

We have not changed the names of Mr. and Mrs. Shigeharu Matsumoto, to whom this book is dedicated. Mr. Matsumoto is the head of International House, and without his persuasive invitation and interest we would never have pulled ourselves out of our American cocoon. (I am also indebted to Harvard for a two-month leave of absence, and to a small grant from the Ford Foundation.) Mr. Matsumoto and his talented staff—Mrs. Kako and Messrs. Tsurumi, Royama, and Tanabe—helped see to it that we met the gamut of individuals it would be instructive for us to see; these hosts opened doors for us so that, despite the shortness of our visit, our "conversations" in Japan were intense. Moreover, the beauty and quiet of International House itself, and the grace and considerateness of all its staff, provided for the larger part of our stay an enclave in which I could work on my lectures—or recover from them. Beyond this, Mr. Matsumoto helped interpret Japan to us, drawing on his own immense experience and wide contacts as a journalist, and as an unofficial political figure and cultural ambassador around the globe.

Another Japanese friend, Professor Hidetoshi Kato, a sociologist at the Institute for Humanistic Studies at the University of Kyoto, also devoted himself to making our stay a meaningful one. He had studied in the United States—at Harvard, M.I.T., and Chicago—and we had met him there. When we decided to come to Japan, he took two months off from his academic duties and from his even more onerous work of making a living as a free-lance writer and broadcaster to act as mentor and interpreter for us. Younger than us and close to the recent student generations, he and some of his colleagues introduced us to members of what they term "the third generation": young Japanese who are neither promoting nor resisting the post-Meiji modernization of the country, but who see this as accomplished and go on to other "post-industrial" tasks. This group is vitally curious about the rest of the world, but equally so about Japan at all levels, from folklore and popular culture to high art and high politics; we hope that the discussions in Kyoto reported herein may give American readers some access to the free-wheeling brilliance of these scholars.

The zest, the lack of anxious snobberies, the wide curiosity of this group attracted us, and undoubtedly influenced our understanding of Japan. However, many friends of different cultural outlook whom we met in Japan sought to redress what they regarded as too sanguine a picture of Japanese modernization and too complacent a dismissal of the possibility of a right-wing revival and heightened political instability. We ourselves, as privileged visitors, suffered not at all from the constraints and oppressions of Japanese society. On the contrary, I was temporarily and partially released from the polemics within America over bomb shelters and testing, Berlin and Vietnam, in which I had reluctantly immersed myself; in Japan my problem was not to defend a minority position on American foreign policy, but to avoid being exploited precisely because of my position, on behalf of the dogmatic Left and of anti-American prejudices. In any case, the diary provides a limited glimpse of the criticisms the most gifted Japanese scholars make of their own society.*

Our involvement with Japan was not that of foreigners who had a mission or had to make a living there or of anthropologists in search of deep understanding. Even during our stay, we realized that certain early interpretations recorded in our diaries were simplified or mistaken, but later ones are not necessarily more chastened. Indeed, as will be seen, the method of our interview with Japan, if it can be called by so rational a name, was from the outset to make interpretations as a way of organizing our experience, but hopefully not overorganizing it or defending ourselves against it. We would toss these interpretations out as tentative ideas, seeking correction and sometimes obtaining a closer approximation to correctness. However, in preparing this book for print we have let our observations stand in their original chronological sequence without correcting them on the basis of hindsight; we have merely cut repetitions and clarified obscure shorthand expressions.

We had the rare opportunity of meeting some unusual Japanese—members of a culture at least as preoccupied or bemused by self-scrutiny as are we Americans. We returned, naturally enough, more puzzled by Japan than when we came—but then, all complex, rapidly changing societies are awash with mysteries and discontinuities. This book should be taken as no more than a record of unsystematic, but open-ended, encounters.

David Riesman

Cambridge, Massachusetts
April 1967

* Notably, in the work of Masao Maruyama and a group of younger men he has influenced. In English translation, see, e.g., Masao Maruyama, *Thought and Behavior in Modern Japanese Politics*, translated in part and edited by Ivan Morris (New York: Oxford University Press, 1963); compare my own discussion in "Japanese Intellectuals—and Americans," *The American Scholar*, 34 (1964–1965), pp. 51–66.

Conversations in Japan

Tokyo, September 30, 1961 **DR**

We met this morning with some of the officers of the Intellectual Interchange Committee to discuss my program. This meeting was a long-drawn-out one—I had already written that the schedule, carefully arranged for us, was just fine, and yet we had to go over it item by item, savoring it, as it were, as a gesture of politeness and consideration on the part of our hosts.

It was clear at this meeting that our hosts, with excellent intentions, were eager for us to see the best sides of Japan and to meet representative people; we would not avoid Communists or other extreme left-wing individuals, but neither would we go out of our way to cultivate them. Similarly, we were gently discouraged from trying to see Nara at this time, one of the early capitals of Japan and a beautiful city, because much of it has been wrecked by the recent typhoon and nobody wanted visitors to go there until it has been repaired. Indeed, one of the things that has struck us most in reading about Japan is the apparent humility and defensiveness of the Japanese vis-à-vis the "barbarian" foreigners. In the late nineteenth century, Japan in large measure covered its nudity, apologized for its mixed bathing, and in other ways tried to make itself even more Victorian than England. Today, Japan is an extraordinarily prosperous country with a cosmopolitan and cultivated capital, and yet this sense of what the foreigner might think, reminiscent of America vis-à-vis Europe until recently—but much stronger—still seems to persist and not to be entirely politeness or mock humility.

Tokyo, October 2

There was a small dinner for us given by the Japan Committee for Intellectual Interchange, very elegantly done, with place cards, in a private room. Our hosts were the Matsumotos—Mr. Matsumoto is poised and polished, and his wife, who comes from a noble house, is a charming and intelligent hostess who speaks excellent English. She was on my right, and on my left was Professor Kawasaki, the honorary chairman of the Committee, emeritus Professor of American Literature at the University of Tokyo, a man of sweetness and delicacy but also, we were told, of great firmness and strength—at the beginning of the Occupation, he protested to General MacArthur over rapes and other brutalities of American soldiers, and these were brought to an immediate stop.

Another guest was Mr. Hayakawa, president of the Japan Institute of Labor, a man who had studied with the historian Charles Beard at Columbia University and who has been active in the International Labor Organization. There was also Miss Maki, president of a woman's college, a small woman at once sweet and severe, a bluestocking who had gotten her degree from Wells College. She reminisced that when there were no jet planes she had to come to America and stay for four years, spending her summers visiting college friends.

There was small talk during dinner. I asked Miss Maki what her girls ended up doing; she said many went into journalism, into social-welfare work, and (reluctantly) into teaching. Evey sat between Mr. Matsumoto and Mr. Fujikawa, former tutor to the Crown Prince, who had studied at the London School of Economics with Harold Laski, spoke with a British accent, and seemed very "British" in his formal yet hearty style.

I had wondered whether there would be toasts and was a bit anxious about that but was not prepared for Mr. Matsumoto's getting up after the dinner and making a speech in my honor from a typewritten manuscript. He spoke about the contribution he hoped I might make toward understanding, and perhaps even doing something about, the breach between the young and the old in Japan, between the "two camps" (presumably the Communists and the West), and other such marked divisions that hampered the aims of peace and friendship. Responding, I said among other things that I hoped there would be many more models of industrialization and modernization than the American one, and that I thought of the Japanese as one such model, especially for the poorer countries of Asia and Africa—a model more relevant to their situation than the United States. I also said I hoped there would be many more models of socialism in addition to the countries who now paraded under that label, so that there would be developed many roads to modernization. I concluded that I appreciated the courtesy and the welcome of Mr. Matsumoto; that some people were kind and some were intelligent and that Mr. Matsumoto was both.

When I had finished, Mr. Matsumoto called on Professor Kawasaki, who spoke with simplicity and modesty, saying that while he had read much of my work, he did not consider himself an expert in it, but wanted to quote a sentence which he hoped I would regard as not uncharacteristic of my thought. He then quoted a paragraph in which I had said that I would not be true to my calling as a social scientist if I did not believe in the truth or to my calling as an American if I did not think the truth would set men free; and then he said he hoped the cause of truth and freedom would be served by my coming to Japan. He was quite moving.

Following these ceremonies, there was general conversation. Mr. Fujikawa asked if I had known Veblen, and we got into a long discussion of Veblen, in which Mr. Matsumoto also joined. This surprised me, since Veblen is so little known outside America. Mr. Hayakawa then asked me if I had known Charles Beard. He had been a great admirer of the historian and apparently had once brought him to Japan. In 1941, when he was visiting in the United States, Beard had told him that their friendship must come to an end because of Japanese militarism. I said I felt that this was not right, that national enmities and personal ones should be kept distinct. Professor Kawasaki defended Beard by saying that perhaps Beard wanted to be able to criticize American action as he had done in the war against Japan and wanted not to be contaminated by knowing any Japanese; but I couldn't agree and said I thought one should never shoot the messenger who would not be a messenger if he were typical of his countrymen. Mr. Matsumoto said that when he was studying at Yale in the 1920's Beard had told him he shouldn't bother to study at that provincial place, but should come to the New School, where Beard was then teaching.

Mr. Hayakawa asked me if I would consider doing a favor to Japan before I left, by saying something about how conformity could be reconciled with democracy, that this was a great problem in Japan and that—if I wouldn't take offense—he gathered that it was something of a problem in my country also. He said that he thought that most people in Japan did what the others did. They were a lonely crowd. I responded that Japan was an enormously complex and interdependent society on a small territorial base in which 100 million people had to get along with each other and that the problem of the whole world was to reconcile this necessity for adaptability with individuality; that I thought democracy should be seen not so much in formal terms as in terms of the feelings of potency which individuals might develop, that people could learn that it was possible to influence their destiny. I added that I was interested in the Zengakuren, the Japanese youth movement, which did seem to affect events, but I wasn't sure whether the individual members felt that they did.

I had wondered how the evening would come to an end and felt that I should have inquired whose responsibility it was, whether Evey's and mine or that of our hosts. At this point Mr. Matsumoto looked at his watch. It was just 9:30, and he said that as a number of people had to travel six or seven miles to get home, it might be best to adjourn. There was much handshaking and bowing all around—we seemed to say goodbye to everyone at least twice before we left.

Tokyo, October 3

This morning Evey and I left the safe confines of International House and walked in the neighboring area. The absence of zoning and city planning makes this city a paradise for the stroller—except for the fact that there are almost no sidewalks and one has constantly to dodge the heavy traffic, which often clogs even the tiny side streets as taxis and trucks try to find a way around the jammed main arteries. Shops, residential areas, factories are all cluttered together and many streets are just too narrow, so that when cars or buses of any size meet each other one of them must back up. In spite of the amount of state control which developed the Japanese economy in the Meiji period, cities seem to have grown helter-skelter even more than with us. Tokyo seems to be a metropolis superimposed on a series of small villages, but since it was not built for the auto, there is a density that is pleasant, and the urban sprawl doesn't have the depressing qualities of Los Angeles and many other American cities.

In the streets, most people we see are in Western dress, very neat; one finds older women in kimono and occasionally a younger woman for some ceremonial or festive reason. Then there are the endless students in their uniforms—so far as we've seen them, going around in single-sex groups; many were traveling in buses on Sunday in the vacation territory where we spent the weekend.

My press conference was scheduled for 4:00 P.M., to be followed by a big reception for us. I thought the reporters would ask questions about disarmament and related matters that would reveal me at odds with the Kennedy Administration, particularly since Reischauer a few days ago had gotten into a fracas with the head of Gensuikyo, the somewhat fellow-traveling anti-bomb organization (there is another, "second Gensuikyo" which is more Democratic Socialist and not Communist). Thus I faced the press conference with some trepidation since I wanted neither to disguise my views, nor to be misunderstood, nor unnecessarily to embarrass my hosts.

It turned out in many ways to be more of a photo conference than a press conference—reminding us of Adlai Stevenson's remark that he had heard Japan was a democracy but now he saw that it was a photocracy. I asked Mr. Matsumoto whether I would have an interpreter and he said no, the papers would send English-speaking correspondents. I was introduced to a few of them while the dozen or more cameramen got ready with their flashbulbs and then the conference began. Far from a barrage of questions, there were only two of the Japanese journalists who asked questions, while a number scribbled vigorously, taking down, it seemed to me, much more than had actually been said. I mentioned at one point my interest in disarmament and foreign policy—I thought this would start a flood of questions, but it didn't. One man asked me what interested me in Japan; I explained that I was interested in alternative routes to modernization and the model that Japan might be for the developing countries. (I was told later by Bob Lifton that the young journalists, many of whom come out of the Zengakuren movement and are left-wing, are critical of any praise of Japan from a foreigner; I suppose they feel as an American highbrow would who encounters a Pakistani lavish with praise for American efficiency or automobiles. They take for granted the accomplishments of Japan, and the remarkable phenomenon of the Meiji Restoration is, of course, something they grew up with.)

In a long silence Mr. Matsumoto said that there were ten minutes left—the schedule had allowed for only half an hour—and were there any further questions. The man who had broken the ice to start with asked me why I was interested in higher education. I was puzzled by the question but responded that I was interested both in the impact of higher education on the country and vice versa, and I tried to give a sense of the variety of American educational institutions by referring to the great number of institutions in Tokyo itself, which has one hundred and thirty colleges and universities, pointing out that some American schools were perhaps almost as selective as the University of Tokyo while others took in everybody. Mr. Matsumoto then said that there was time for one more question, but none came and he adjourned the affair amid further popping of flashbulbs.

Later I talked to Professor Kato, the young sociologist from the University of Kyoto who has volunteered to be my guide and interpreter; he said that he thought the awkwardness in English of most of the newspapermen was the reason they didn't ask questions or understand what I said. One came up to ask me to autograph the Anchor paperback edition of *Individualism Reconsidered* but he had not said a word during the questioning. Kato said that he was surrounded by newspapermen who wanted *him* to tell them what I had said—this included those who had asked questions in English; and another Japanese sociologist said he had also been questioned about me by the newspapermen.

Thereafter, Evey and I went directly downstairs to the reception. There was a large table outside where several International House people gave guests their name tags and checked off their names. The Matsumotos and Evey and I stood in a reception line, and Mr. Matsumoto introduced people as they came up, giving not only their names but their connections. The majority probably were academic people: some elderly and distinguished deans and presidents; many young sociologists and a few psychologists; some political scientists and economists; some press tycoons from *Asahi* and *Mainichi*; the Indian Ambassador and his wife, the director of the Franco-Japanese Institute, and Mr. and Mrs. Boylan from the United States Embassy.

There were perhaps three or four women in kimono. One of these was Mrs. Yoshida. Professor Yoshida (a close friend of American friends of ours) said to me that he was a tradition-directed Japanese and that in the housing development where he lived he was the only one with a Japanese- rather than a Western-style house. I kidded a little with him about the wife being the one to bear the burden of Japaneseness and he said, half jokingly, that she was an obedient wife. I had originally thought that some of these women would wear kimono for ceremonial occasions, but apparently not—most wore quite high-heeled shoes, which must be very tough to navigate on Tokyo streets, but not many were actually chic or smart. Kato told me that in Kyoto many more of the women would wear kimono—this is Japan's Boston, as is sometimes said, and the most traditional city in the country. While I was talking with Mr. Ota, assistant professor of sociology at Tokyo, Professor Atagawa came over and said that he was the teacher of Ota and another young sociologist I was talking with—they were his "boys." Mr. Matsumoto kept bringing over men of particular importance or interest.

I talked to the Indian Ambassador. He had just seen a movie, *The End of the World*, apparently a Japanese film, which had moved and frightened him. We talked of the fact that there was very little interest in India among Japanese academicians. There was interest in China, but their main focus seemed to be on the West. In reflecting on the interest in *The Lonely Crowd* shown here, I have the feeling that the

Japanese want to have all the "neuroses" of the West and not be deprived of a single one.

Later in the evening in the bar we had a really exciting talk with Richard Storry, the British scholar whose book, *A History of Modern Japan*, we liked so much. He said that Japan was a country to which one couldn't be indifferent, and that one either loved or hated it, and that for him this often depended on his mood or his experiences from day to day. I asked him what he hated, and he said that he had recently been at the Congress of Orientalists in Moscow and had been struck by similarities between pre-war Japan and present-day Moscow: the same oppressive atmosphere, the sense of the omnipresence of the police, with intellectuals making diffidently critical noises about the regime, and yet there was overwhelming friendliness and receptivity; he went on to say that he didn't like the use of the word "imitation" for the Japanese but that receptivity was a much more appropriate word, since they always altered what they took over, or "adaptation" might be better still. I gather that he hated the falseness in much Japanese social life, the lack of intellectual structure or tough-mindedness, the vagueness. He concluded, however, that there was much more love than hate in his relation to Japan and that he envied us staying for two months since he had to go back in a week. He asked how the press conference had gone and I told him; he said he thought the Japanese newspapermen would not give me a rough time but would have a certain awe of me (though they don't have such awe of their own figures and certainly not their own politicians). He said he thought this was a moment when the relations between American and Western intellectuals and the Japanese had been restored with the coming of Reischauer.

I raised the question of the lack of Japanese influence in foreign affairs and we spoke of the fact that hardly any Japanese statesmen had the kind of presence and style of a Nehru or a Nkrumah or a Lloyd George; he said that they were all too consultative, too little individuated. But he also said that the language barrier was an enormous one, for it was actually a barrier of culture. The Japanese language reflects a concrete, untheoretical way of thinking which makes English very difficult for them. Moreover, the Japanese learned in the last century that to translate literally into English all the honorific words—the honorable car and so on—made them ridiculous; and so they stopped it but were intimidated because these were the words that came to their tongues. This extraordinary lack of fluency in English (and presumably in any Western language) is therefore part of a broader blockage against the styles of thought of the West. He said that if one travels east from Great Britain one comes eventually to Hong Kong, which seems extremely exotic and "Eastern," whereas Japan seems to be very "Western" in comparison; but that the Japanese mentality was far more alien than the Chinese, for the Chinese could think philosophically and logically and the Japanese could not—the Japanese mentality was unique, a kind of end of the line in the East, and the more he studied it, the more he was baffled by it.

In fact, I'm struck by the way in which the problem of understanding Japan tortures both natives and visitors, and as with America, and perhaps more so, remains an endless sort of speculation: "What is this new man, this Japanese?"

Tokyo, October 4

We went to the Press Club with the Liftons to have lunch with Abe Rosenthal of *The New York Times*, a man whose work in India and Poland and more recently in Tokyo I'd admired. He turned out to be an extremely alert, intelligent, youthful-seeming man who, like most American correspondents here, relies on an assistant to translate material from the Japanese press and to act as an interpreter. I brought up (a question which I had discussed with Storry also) his story of a few days ago on the Japanese lack of figures like Nehru or Tito who could play a role on the world stage; and we were inclined to agree that in some ways perhaps this was a good thing because there were no demagogues in Japan, none of the strutting leadership of a Nkrumah or Nasser.

We talked of resistance by Japanese businessmen and conservatives to the appointment of Reischauer as Ambassador. There was reluctance to have an ambassador who, because he knew the language, was married to a Japanese wife, and knew the country, would not depend solely on them for his contacts and interpretation of the Japanese scene. (We had heard from others that some people in the State Department were also unhappy about an academician from outside coming in whose contacts with the opposition and with other non-orthodox groups could not be readily anticipated.) Now, however, the Japanese conservatives have changed their attitude, and the Embassy staff itself is enthusiastic about its new boss. I raised with Rosenthal the question whether Reischauer could do more than he was doing to cultivate the Leftists in Japan who might some day become the government. But Rosenthal used the example of Korea to show how difficult it was for the American Embassy to have contact with an opposition, not only because they found it more comfortable to deal with those in power and to whom they were increasingly tied, but because in the State Department and elsewhere back home, contacts outside officialdom would be frowned upon—and of course knowledge of such contacts would get back through Japanese or American conservatives.

Rosenthal said that he had his offices in the Asahi Building (as do many other foreign correspondents and press agencies) and that he had been marvelously and generously treated by *Asahi* and given everything he could ask for. In view of differences in "guest culture" in the two countries, he wondered whether *The New York Times* in the United States would be as helpful to *Asahi* people as the latter had been to *Times* men: probably, Japanese newspapermen in the United States would be reluctant to ask for help from the *Times*, reflecting their deference—what the Japanese themselves call "low posture."

Matsumoto called for us at the Press Club in his car; like other well-to-do or important Japanese he has a chauffeur, but I must say that after driving around the streets of Tokyo a chauffeur seems essential if one is to be spared the worst horrors of driving; and, if parking is hard in the United States, it's hopeless in Tokyo.

We called on Mr. Nishimoto, editor of a leading monthly. A former New York correspondent of *Mainichi* joined us to act as interpreter, for while Mr. Nishimoto speaks clear and distinct English, he explained that he doesn't think fluently in English. He is a big man, solidly built and "Western" in his whole appearance and quality. By training he is an economist. His secretary or girl Friday, who remained behind a screen and answered the phone, brought us cups of tea which surprised us by being ice-cold—it is still presumably summer.

The occasion was defined as an effort to help me understand the Japanese press, and I asked Mr. Nishimoto about the intellectual tone of the three large chains, and how did he explain this. He said that the business boards of each of the papers was kept utterly distinct from the editorial side. Their job was to get circulation and ads, but unlike the situation in the United States—he said this apologetically—they had no say on the editorial side. I replied that this was *The New Yorker* pattern and also that of a few papers, but that the search for circulation in the American press was based on the desire not only for money, but also for power; so that editors often acted like businessmen even if they didn't come up through the business side. He said that Japanese editors also wanted power, but that they sought it by running a good newspaper—apparently one defined as good by the intellectual community. In fact he said *Asahi*, for example, was constantly being criticized for not writing in simple enough language, and there were many people among its readers who couldn't follow its editorials. He smiled and said that intellectuals like to be obscure and that there was a constant tussle between the desire to be readable and the desire not to downgrade the papers, which were constantly being criticized when they moved in either direction; he seemed to think that there was some natural happy medium between readability and over-complexity.

I asked him whether people from the business side of a paper ever had a career line that took them over to the editorial side, and he said no, these were distinct, and I gather were recruited from different universities. I was told later that *Asahi* is still controlled by two powerful Osaka families and that this gives it some of its freedom not to make demagogic appeals. Both *Asahi* and *Mainichi* were originally Osaka papers with small Tokyo editions, but as the result of a long development, the Tokyo editions grew larger and larger and the Osaka papers are now virtual copies except for a page of local news.

I asked Mr. Nishimoto to describe for me the different readerships of the three papers. He said that *Yomiuri* appeals to the lowest class. He put matters this way: if the three papers ran an advertisement for serious books or records, this would appeal to nearly 100 per cent of *Asahi* readers (I would guess an exaggeration), to 40 to 60 per cent of *Mainichi* readers, and perhaps 20 per cent of *Yomiuri* readers. He indicated that, despite the greater buying power of *Asahi* readers, the paper couldn't run all the ads that it got, because readers insisted on a balanced page and would not like it if there were too many advertisements in the paper—of course the papers are small by Western standards, being twelve pages, although the weekend editions are very large. *Asahi*, he said, had really two classes of readers: the intellectuals, among whom he included the larger proportion of the white-collar workers, such as teachers, lawyers, accountants, and so on; and the business community. The business community tends to be critical of *Asahi*—as it violently was at the time of the riots over the United States-Japan Security Treaty—but I gathered has sufficient respect for the intellectual community to read a paper largely written for and by the latter. (Bob Lifton thinks that it has been possible for top financial interests to clamp down on the press, and especially *Asahi*, after the riots, and that the press has since then been more cautious and "responsible.")

As we talked, I more and more felt that the relative lack of anti-intellectualism in the Japanese mass press reflected not only increasing and widespread literacy, but a desire for uplift among many of the urban, especially white-collar, workers—they wanted to be in touch with "higher things," rather than, as often in the United States, feeling that all that culture stuff wasn't for them; it was honorific to read a paper that they had difficulty with and didn't always grasp. In this connection, I asked Mr. Nishimoto whether I was right in believing that the Japanese press had far less to fear from television than any other mass press; and he agreed with my picture of a highly print-oriented population in which the word has great authority—possibly the fact that the Japanese language is so very difficult to learn burns it in in a way that is less true where the alphabet makes the task less onerous.

On the subject of United States foreign policy, Mr. Nishimoto said that the Americans were very jumpy and quick on the trigger and, as a result of hasty action, were constantly having to reverse themselves. It was his impression that on the one side the State Department and the scholars and intellectuals were for a less "shoot from the hip" foreign policy; they would take into account the long-run interests of the United States, while Congress and people at large were in favor of impetuous action. Such mistakes were all right when one was dealing with a small and inconsequential power such as Cuba, but were frighteningly dangerous when one was dealing with a monster such as the Soviet Union, which he feared would win out if the United States did not pursue a more long-range policy. He also said that the United States hemmed Japan in very much and did not give it any freedom of action in dealing with China. In all this he spoke as a wise conservative worried about the tempestuous actions of a headstrong child.

I replied only to some of the things he said. I pointed out that Congress was not only a swamp of demagogic politicians, but included many men of the Fulbright type, who were a minority not to be ignored. I also indicated that the academic and intellectual community carried perhaps less weight than in Japan. I agreed with him that public men feel the pressure on them to appear decisive and quick, and that this is dangerous. I thought to myself that Mr. Nishimoto, in his generally conservative and anti-Communist outlook, was probably quite at odds with many younger editors and journalists, temperamentally as well as in terms of political alignment: they would see him as the too solid citizen, the indestructible bourgeois.

Matsumoto asked as we left if we would like to go to see the *Asahi* plant nearby; we jumped at the chance. We were taken into the largest city room I have ever seen, where there was feverish activity—many telephones, errand boys running around with galleys, all divided into sections by subject matter. (There were no women, and I asked Matsumoto about this later—there had been only one woman at my own press conference; he said that the job of a reporter in Japan was so terribly driving that women could not stand the pace.) We saw huge Japanese typewriters where, by a kind of double-shift system, one could deploy 2,000 characters. I asked a very young man who seemed to be in his teens how long it took to be trained to run this typewriter and was told three months of intensive work. There were whole banks of such typewriters.

Then we were shown the facsimile machines by which the Hokkaido edition is published—*Asahi* was the first press to use facsimile. About 80 per cent of the paper is set by monotype and the rest by hand, and we saw a number of workers setting headlines and advertisements by hand—they worked with fantastic speed among the characters, composing a page. I was struck by the enormous attention to makeup, and the reporter showed me how black must balance black and one photograph another and so on—terribly hard to do, he said, under the pressure of time, and yet terribly important; some of the pages I saw seemed quite beautiful. Then we were taken into the room of the huge rotary presses, and Mr. Matsumoto murmured that all these machines were Japanese-made—as if I doubted it.

Late in the afternoon we had a memorable conference with Miss Yamamoto, referred to in our schedule as a "social critic," and Professor Yoshida, an anthropologist whom we had met earlier at the reception. Bob Lifton also joined us.

Our guests were both utterly charming and fluent in English. Yoshida, whose face is expressive and lively, has a manner and accent that are quite American; he had studied in the United States for a number of years. Miss Yamamoto, a handsome young woman, was in a kimono, and I asked her about this. She explained that when after the war she had first begun wearing a kimono she was called reactionary by her friends, but that now this charge was less common. She said she found a kimono much more convenient. One could never be sure on a social occasion whether one would be Western-style or on *tatami*, and on the latter silk stockings were always getting runs and Western-style dresses made sitting in the proper way difficult—Evey was relieved to learn that Miss Yamamoto herself suffered in this squatting position which Evey thought made only us Americans miserable! This led into a discussion of whether one thought differently on *tatami* than one did on chairs. There was some joking about whether on *tatami* thought was more curved and less logical. Miss Yamamoto said she liked to sit on *tatami* for sociability but preferred to work at a Western-style desk, while Professor Yoshida said he had to sit on *tatami* in order to think. Then someone suggested that it was harder for women on *tatami* since they must sit with their knees under them in very rigid posture, while men can have their legs out in front and altogether can be sloppier and more comfortable.

Miss Yamamoto then began to tell about a survey she was doing of attitudes of Japanese university students and their values. She spoke of some recent discussions with students that had shocked and troubled her. By way of introduction, she explained that there had been great excitement over the killing of the Japanese Socialist leader Asanuma a year or so ago by a seventeen-year-old Rightist, and there was concern as to what was happening to the seventeen-year-olds in general, a crucial age in Japanese lore and also crucial in the sense that people of this age were born at the end of the war and had no memory of the war. Miss Yamamoto said that in one group discussion, students had begun by saying how terrible the killing of Asanuma was and tried to work out logically why this illegal act was different from the illegality of the student demonstrations against the Security Treaty and the Eisenhower visit; they had concluded that the latter actions were directed only against things—for instance, cars that were overturned—but not against people, not against human life, whereas the killing had destroyed irreplaceable human life. They had all nodded sagely at this, but then one boy had said that he understood this logically, but emotionally he couldn't see anything wrong with killing. And then the group came around finally to his point of view, saying that they believed in nothing and only wished they could believe in something.

I asked whether they thought the killer "sincere," and Miss Yamamoto said that this was an important element in their feeling. (Yoshida pointed out that two recent killers had come from rural-based families, one with a father in the Security Forces and the other also from a military tradition, both typical of right-wing extremism.) I asked Miss Yamamoto whether these students had read Camus's *The Stranger* and she said she thought Camus had influenced them, and existentialism generally. Yet they wished that they could believe in something. She also spoke of another group of senior high school students who had been similarly nihilistic. She was angry at them for their lack of political concern. She said that in this younger generation there was a revival of interest in the war and in war movies and novels, and even in military toys, which had been unheard of in the period immediately after the war. I gathered that these were still incipient trends of which she made herself a monitor.

Miss Yamamoto also talked about the attitude and role of women in present-day Japan: she said that many mothers of the early feminist generation had passed on to their daughters their own frustrations and inability to lead independent and creative lives, and the daughters had the legacy of carrying out the mothers' unfulfilled wishes. Many women students at the present time have this task of acting out what their mothers would like to have done, but didn't quite manage or dare to do. This is a reversal of the ordinary Japanese tradition in which the mother is oriented toward her son, not her daughter—of course, that tradition still survives. Thus, one finds daughters who are rebelling against their mothers, and daughters who are trying to carry out their mothers' unconsummated rebellion, and these provide very different constellations of attitude.

Whereas Miss Yamamoto tended to generalize on the basis of particular encounters, Yoshida was constantly insisting on the demographic factors and the specific social brackets about which one was talking. In fact, I thought the range of his command of economic, sociological, and political factors in Japanese life was spectacular. He spoke of the 40 per cent of Japanese still engaged in primary production, as compared with 5 per cent in England and 15 per cent or 20 per cent in the United States. He had recently been in Hokkaido, the northernmost island which is Japan's "West," a poor country with very cold winters and hard conditions. He is doing a study of a village there and of social mobility—he was thoroughly at home in the work of Lipset and Bendix and discussed with technical acumen their conclusion that mobility in Japan was as great as in America. He pointed out that the Japanese who leaves the farm for the city changes his style of life radically into a middle-class cosmopolitan style, while the American farmer or working-class person is already "middle class" in his pattern of consumption and general outlook even before he moves, in terms of occupation or income, into the middle class. But he said that with the spread of television Japan was in this respect coming to be more like America.

I asked about magazines which carried styles of life to the women. Several decades earlier, these magazines had tended to be puritanical and to preach obedience to women, conserving the home, and so on. There had been a kind of true-confessions magazine which also told women how they should behave. But now there was much more circulation of material that was subversive of traditional values among women—not, I gather, really feminist literature, but rather more erotic and more concerned with consumption and urban styles of life. Yoshida and Miss Yamamoto were both eager to see content analyses done of these magazines and research into their impact.

Yoshida spoke of a school he had visited in Hokkaido which was based on severe and extremely anti-progressive principles. As young as seven or eight, children started work at five in the morning, studied until seven, when it was time to leave for the public school, and returned at three for further study. If they didn't do their lessons they were beaten by the headmaster. Yoshida had at first been quite shocked by this, but then, after talking with the headmaster, concluded that the regimen might be defensible; for Hokkaido was poor, the children going to public school could not hope to get into Todai (the University of Tokyo) or the other leading universities in competition with the urban, middle-class, and professional children of Tokyo and the other big cities, and this was the only way in which these provincial families could have their children compete without handicap in the national educational market. That market would seem to be about the toughest in the world; Yoshida said that after getting into Todai students were often completely knocked out for two or three years—there was no great problem of survival once one got in. Often they never recaptured their former spontaneity and vigor. Many had been *ronin* (the name given those who try again and again over a period of years to pass the exams), and finally when they made it were exhausted. The effort to get into the good Tokyo high schools as a way of getting into Todai was also enormous; so that the pressure was on at an earlier and earlier age.

Yoshida spoke of a brilliant high-school student journalist whose yearbook or classbook he had judged in a prize contest, a boy he thought already a genius at sixteen, who had spent so much time on high-school journalism that he failed his exams for Todai and disappeared from view into an anonymous university. Yoshida was sure he would never be heard from. Indeed, the pressure to get into the universities is destroying extracurricular activities such as journalism in the secondary schools, and many students who have practiced piano give it up in the last two or three years of high school and never return to it. Even the private universities, such as Waseda, which are not quite so hard to get into, are now also very stiff because of the immense number of applicants, and of course are out of the question for a poor boy. Moreover, many of the students have *arubaito*, the German word in romanized Japanese. Richard Storry had told us of a nineteen-year-old Todai girl who works from seven to eleven every night in a bar where she does snatches of reading in her specialty of Russian literature.

Part of the resentment these practices have built up is funneled into the Zengakuren.* Of course the students are better off than they were before the war, and the climate of prosperity is all around them. Yet the rising expectations exceed the actual achievement; the students take the prosperity for granted and their own miseries and problems weigh heavily upon them. In comparison with the United States, a large number read the newspapers and follow political events, even when they reject politics—they start reading the papers very young. Indeed, there are magazines for children from the age of about two or three onward, first picture magazines and then more serious ones. After graduation, many relax into a greater ease, a kind of regression. Yoshida also spoke of the way in which students were organized into extra-curricular groups and circles, both for purposes of comradeship and of pressure; in spite of democratization and modernization, there is little universalism in Japan, and personal ties (and feuds) would seem to be even more important than in the United States.

Yoshida and Miss Yamamoto are both brilliant, wide-ranging, and lively people—so much so that when Mr. Matsumoto came in later, he said that after this discussion he hoped the evening wouldn't set a false standard to which the rest of our Japanese experience couldn't live up. Yoshida had no fear of contradicting me, of bringing generalizations down to earth, being at once very professional in his knowledge of American sociology and uncompartmentalized in his style of thought. Bob Lifton observed later that Yoshida was also unusual in being singularly free of ideological obsessions and compulsions. Miss Yamamoto said she wanted to show me the questionnaire that she had done, even though she was very dissatisfied with it—of course, with the Japanese, one engages in endless rounds of self-deprecation (here too, Yoshida, with his directness, is an exception) just as one goes through endless ceremonials as to who goes first through a door, and who is seated first.

(In reflecting on this discussion, I am aware that my own tendency is to use even a very inadequate theoretical formulation in an effort to organize material and to ask questions; I'm quite willing to abandon the theory, but I need it to help select from the flow of possible facts

* All Japanese Federation of Student Self-governing Societies, the group that led the demonstrations in 1960.

and interpretations—well, I shouldn't say I'm eager to abandon it, since I often push it until I must abandon it and even then try to modify it to take account of new evidence and contradictions. Even where my knowledge is very slender, I draw on it in this way if engaged in any kind of dialogue.)

ETR

Tokyo, October 5

This morning by good chance at breakfast Mr. Matsumoto introduced us to Bernard Leach, a gaunt, tall Englishman with a mop of gray hair. He had just come back to Japan for a short visit. He told us how wonderful it was to be back in this country where art is such an important part of life. Of course, he said, Japan is not so beautiful as it was when he first came here fifty or so years ago. He described his shock when he returned after his first visit (this was in 1909) and found the city virtually ruined by telegraph poles.* He finally got around to speaking of his work in pottery: a potter is a conveyor of traditional values rather than an innovator; he takes from what is around him and makes something simple and beautiful and useful. In this sense, the potter's art is still a folk art. He spoke of how much he had learned of this art in Japan, how much he had learned from Hamada, who in his opinion is the greatest living potter. Hamada, he said, never signs any of his work because he feels it is not only his: it belongs to the folk culture and tradition of which he is a part. Bernard Leach said that this is the difference between the folk arts and the high arts, where the artist is straining to create something unique and extreme in order to be original. He said that of course the great artist is evident in whatever he does: Hamada's work is unmistakable, and therefore it makes no difference whether or not he signs his work. (The folk arts today are, of course, no longer created for a folk society; and so they have a quite new—highbrow—meaning which Leach perhaps romantically does not fully take into account.)

Then he returned to the subject of Japan. He spoke of the Zen monasteries where people retire to contemplate and empty themselves. In such a country, he said, the appreciation of art is still intensely strong, for these people cultivate fine taste and the love of beautiful things.

He seemed to enjoy talking and sat, leisurely, over his cup of tea.

* Of course there had been a telegraph system in Japan since the 1870's, but the poles were not in evidence until the spread of the telephone.

He spoke of buying, when he was a very young man and first came to Tokyo, some pots for his house in Ueno. He had thought they were beautiful pots. Years later, when he noticed them, he realized how derivative and poor they were; for now he had seen finer ones and knew that these first possessions were not really beautiful at all. This was an example, he thought, of how one changes and grows. We found this man's serenity and simplicity very moving.

In the afternoon I went with Betty Lifton to see the show of his pottery and a large collection of Hamada's work at the Mitsukoshi department store. It is the custom for leading department stores to have such exhibitions; and this one had fine exhibition rooms, well arranged with glass showcases and open display shelves, with spotlights and indirect lighting. Leach's work, in a small room, was gray and subdued, simple and solid. There was not much of it because apparently it sells so fast that he has trouble keeping anything to show. In a large room on the same floor was Hamada's retrospective show, which was breathtaking. Here was a prolific and imaginative artist at work, who in his large bowls and plates was painting in ceramics in a free and abstract way, using the rich, indigenous colors of Japan, the colors of rock and clay and earth, ocher and brown, olive green, gray and red. The bowls and large platters were spectacular and bold. The designs on them varied: there were wide jagged stripes, crossed bands, vague swirls of thick color. On other shelves along other walls and on tables and showcases in the middle of the room were smaller pieces, some with geometrical designs, some with delicate calligraphy. There were vases and jars and pots and plates and rectangular bottles of varied shapes.

There were many people at this vernissage. Bernard Leach was there admiring his friend's work, and Hamada was there, a remarkable contrast to Leach, a short stocky man of great vigor, not at all the long-haired Japanese artist type. He was an earthy peasant type, except for his heavy horn-rimmed glasses and British tweed suit.

To my delight, I saw Mrs. Matsumoto there. She knows a great deal about the arts, and we looked at some of the exhibits together. It was very lucky that we met there, for Betty Lifton had had to leave early and I would never have gotten home in time for our evening engagement. I did not realize until she and I were well on the way home how impossible it would have been for me to get back on my own at this hour of the day. I had planned to pick up a cab. But when we got out onto the street, at the rush hour, jammed with traffic and no cabs in sight, I could see that I might have waited for hours. The subway, though very crowded, was very fast.

DR

Since we got here we have been reading the English-language newspapers, which are a partial translation of the leading Japanese papers, with additional articles of interest to Westerners. The press is full of news of struggles within the Japan-Soviet Society and the atom-bomb protest organization, Gensuikyo, concerning the weakness of the protest against the Russian tests; various splits have taken place in these organizations as a result of the Russian resumption of tests. Yesterday a group of students from International Christian University, accompanied by some of the professors, paraded to the Soviet Embassy in protest and also apparently left milder words of protest at the American Embassy. Ambassador Reischauer had given a speech the day before in which he said that the United States had had to resume testing because it carried the security burden of the free world—remarks that seemed not a little insensitive to the particular Japanese feeling about the atom bomb. I've gotten a very keen sense of how the Ambassador has to tread a wary course between the country to which he is accredited and the country whose policies he must loyally try to sell, for default of which he could, of course, be severely criticized at home. Actually, however, from the whole tone of the speech, I sensed that Reischauer believed what he said, while not convincing the Japanese. To liberal and "progressive" forces in Japan, Reischauer remains something of a hero—the more so because of the opposition to his appointment on the part of the Japanese Right. But the Embassy is a huge operation where, though the Ambassador can do much to change the tone of the place, he has some of the problems of President Kennedy himself in inheriting a large structure which goes its own way.

Evey and I went for our usual morning walk—I can't say enough for the variety and visual delight of the Tokyo streets. A large, wide street with shops will suddenly become a narrow residential street, though one through which traffic may still pour, leaving us to climb up the walls to get out of the way. Little alleys run helter-skelter in every direction. Tiny children walk along the streets with their book bags strapped to their backs and when it is raining—as it has been every day—carrying umbrellas. We still have a hard time crossing streets because we aren't used to autos driving on the left-hand side of the road, and our reflexes are often wrong and dangerous.

In the afternoon, I went to the Liftons' house to meet with Professor Nagano, an absolutely charming and brilliant man who has a flexibility and lack of defensiveness that are rare among intellectuals anywhere and perhaps especially rare here.

Like other leading Japanese intellectuals, Nagano is a celebrity who has tremendous pressures on him, including the pressure of meeting virtually all American scholars who come to Japan. Nagano said he had been piloting an American visitor around Tokyo at the time of the demonstrations and thought that the American had gotten a misleading impression: on one occasion the police were very polite and told the students to disperse over loud-speakers, which gave the visitor the sense that, contrary to Zengakuren claims, there was no police brutality and the fault was all on the students' side. But Nagano said that he knew many students and intellectuals who were exceedingly gentle who had been badly beaten on the head and clubbed in all sorts of ways by the police, but that on this particular occasion the police had been polite in part because of the power situation of the moment and in part in order to build up a good record when they then started arresting the students and bringing them into court.

In fact, I gather from this conversation and from others as well that a kind of polarization occurs among Americans who come to Japan: many of course become completely starry-eyed about Japan, much to the annoyance of Japanese intellectuals who are critical of their country; others, who refuse to make an effort to understand, become more and more hostile as time goes on, taking what the Japanese regard as rightist attitudes, and thus becoming still more sharply polarized, bitter, and angry.

Nagano told me that political scientists were more interested in my work than sociologists, who were critical of my "lack of methodology"; it was the political scientists who were interested in my ideas, my theories of power, and my attitudes toward individuality, etc.

We talked a little about the cult of sport in Japan, and Bob spoke of one of the people he interviewed who was a fan of *karate*, a kind of fighting in which one uses the edge of the hand; while this can be a deadly weapon, the sport is cultivated for its spiritual meaning and discipline. This student was troubled by the fact that *karate* was associated with rightist connotations and he wanted to purify it and make it respectable, for it symbolized the past for him. Yet even among the young concerned with the cult of the body, of sex, and of sport, there seems to be lacking the kind of mindless anti-intellectualism more common among athletes in the United States; for in Japan such people would still remain interested in politics and in cultural matters, would read *Asahi* and the serious weeklies and monthlies. One of the leading monthlies, *Chuo Koron*, has a circulation of 100,000; another, *Sekai*, to the Left, has 70,000 to 80,000; and there are a great many others.

Nagano, in talking of Japanese women, said that they were realistic and practical, while the men often maintained a code of honor more suitable to samurai days—reminding me of Everett Hughes's similar comment on German men and women during and after World War II, when the women had managed on the black market somehow to keep the family going while the men, unconscious of this, had preserved their ideology and their honor.

Margaret Mead and other anthropologists have said that when they visit a new culture they find people just like Uncle Ben or Aunt Mary or Cousin Jim; and it has been our experience also that we soon lose any feeling of strangeness in the appearance of people, and, with those we meet, put them into categories—I'm sure too quickly and superficially—reminiscent of people we know in the States. We know that underneath apparent similarities lie cultural differences, and we also know that some of the people we have talked to were, during the last war, upholders of *kokutai* (Japanese national spirit or honor) although, given our awareness of American present-day chauvinism and our absence of insistence that other people be heroes, we can accept Japanese moral plasticity probably more readily than like qualities among ourselves.

In the evening, we were taken out to dinner by the Matsumotos along with Professor Kawasaki and Mrs. Kako to Shiobara, a beautiful restaurant on a hill, sitting like a villa in its own garden. After removing our shoes at the door, we were shown into a private *tatami* room facing the garden. There was no menu. The Matsumotos simply asked for dinner—they said this was the thing to do if one wasn't worrying about the bill. Three girls in traditional dress took care of us, bringing first the hot wet towel which is such a pleasant aspect of Japanese dining, and then hors d'oeuvres and plum wine while we sat away from the table looking out into the garden. Finally, after considerable time, the six of us were seated at table by Mrs. Matsumoto.

There followed then for over two hours a wonderfully aesthetic series of dishes which would first be brought in and placed like a vase of flowers in the center of the table, then taken aside by the leading girl for rearranging onto individual plates, while another girl would pass the dishes about and still another would sit on her knees at my end of the table to pour *sake* for me, to clean away any crumb of rice with a towel, and often simply to be inactive and quiet. The enormous labor that went on behind the scenes was even greater than what went on in our presence; for instance, one dish was decorated with white radish strung out in the shape of a fish net—most delicately cut into gossamerlike threads to decorate and cover a large and handsome fish. Actually the food was so delicate and came in such relatively small amounts—Mr. Matsumoto said that he had persuaded the restaurant to give half portions—that it was not overwhelming. Unlike a Chinese dinner, rice came late in the meal, preceded by various sorts of raw fish, a delicate bit of filet of beef wrapped in a taro leaf, chicken and sweet potato, several kinds of soups in tiny cups, and ending with a variety of raw fruits.

The food provided a series of conversation pieces: what the items were, what the sequences were, and when our waitresses were out of the room, where they came from. (Two were born in Tokyo and one was from the country.) The proprietress, whom we never saw, was said to be a very poetic person. She had sent her cook to Paris to Cordon Bleu to learn Western-style cooking, but this person had discovered that he could use a knife to cut meats or vegetables much more finely than anybody in Paris. There is room for only two parties in one evening at this restaurant and we were lucky to get a reservation only a day or two ahead. For our Japanese hosts to come to Shiobara is a rare treat, too expensive to do on their own. We had begun with a very bitter green tea made of powder which the Japanese drink while also eating sweets and again at the very end after the fruit when we had little sugar candies—in each case, the sweets were put on branches of little twigs, indeed nothing is served just by itself but always in some kind of decorative arrangement.

Tokyo, October 6

Today we met with Matsumoto and Mrs. Kako to discuss our November schedule. Invitations have come in from different universities, research institutes, newspaper and broadcasting groups; Matsumoto has been admirable in defending me from obligations which would be excessively burdensome while also tactful in suggesting those issues on which I could make the greatest contribution here. This I think runs in two directions: to indicate that not all Americans are "militarists" while also not being pro-Communist, and also to indicate that one need not be helpless in the face of the threat of war, but can do something—Japanese liberals and some (but by no means all) socialists sit uneasily between the United States and China, feeling that Japan is caught between them. (In this morning's paper is a story, which may or may not have been in the American press, of a Japanese Socialist and Diet member concluding that the United States must be a "guided democracy" because, although he had talked to intellectuals at Columbia and Harvard, he didn't find a single one who took an "un-American" view of the Two-China problem and who was willing to see Taiwan "restored" to China.) I realize at the same time that I tread on terribly touchy ground, with the Japanese Left eager to seize on any criticism of America, even if I say no more than what I have already said in my translated writings; on the other hand, candor is in many ways so characteristically American and "un-Japanese" that I have tried very hard not to temper my views to the susceptibilities of people here.

During the discussion, I asked Matsumoto if it could be easily arranged for us to meet some business and labor leaders. He has extraordinarily wide contacts—one day he plays golf with a conservative businessman, an official of the Bank of Japan; while on another day, he will play golf with a Socialist leader. After this conference, Evey and I went over maps and schedules and decided it was a great mistake in our short time here to spend so much time and energy seeing the sights; careful arrangements had been made for us to visit temples, folk-art museums, the Inland Sea, and various cities in southern and western Japan. (When next day we told Mrs. Kako and Matsumoto that we should perhaps cut out some of this and concentrate on city life and city people, they were more than willing.)

This evening there was to be a discussion of power structure with three younger Japanese political scientists, two from the University of Tokyo and one from the University of Hokkaido, and Matsumoto with characteristic tact said that he would absent himself in order that the younger intellectuals need not be inhibited by his presence. The three men who were to talk with me had supper together to discuss the strategy and course of action for the meeting. When Evey and I came in, there was the usual flurry about who should sit where, and then Professor Fujimoto explained their decision on the course of the procedure: Professor Yamazaki would begin by saying how *The Lonely Crowd* had been received in Japan, and Professor Odawara would continue by discussing the reception of the work of C. Wright Mills, especially *The Power Elite*, and then I would have a chance to respond. Both men had written out statements which they read, elaborating as they went along.

Yamazaki began by discussing an article he had written in 1954 expounding my work and especially the theory of the veto groups, and he added that *The Lonely Crowd* itself had come out in translation the following year (by all accounts, a very poor translation—Professor Hidetoshi Kato of the University of Kyoto has since done what appears to be a better one). Thereafter, *The Lonely Crowd* was criticized as romantic, backward-looking, excessively optimistic, and so on. Yamazaki said that he had then defended me against this criticism in an article drawing on many American writers, including Kenneth Boulding, David Truman, Harold Lasswell, Herbert Simon. The theory of the veto groups had unfortunately been linked to Galbraith's theory of natural harmony and balance and this in turn to traditional American pluralism. I had the sense that those Japanese who had been responsive to *The Lonely Crowd* had been pushed into a corner by the more numerous and better-defended supporters of C. Wright Mills.

At this point it was Odawara's turn. He began by saying that there were three schools of thought in Japanese intellectual circles: the first were the straight Marxists who had been badly shaken by the Khrushchev speech against Stalin in 1956; the second were more "forward-looking" Marxists (among whom he apparently included himself); the third were more eclectic and never became clear to me. *The Power Elite* had been published in America in 1956 and translated into Japanese the next year in an excellent translation; in the vacuum created by the de-Stalinization campaign, Mills had swept the boards, for he had shown the Marxists that they could be forward-looking without being any the less Marxist. (Nagano had said yesterday that from the perspective of some Marxist circles, both Mills's work and mine were dismissed as "psychologizing.") Odawara said that my work was concerned with social relations, whereas Mills's work was concerned with social structure—the real thing. And I think it was he who said that, while I had tried to explain mass society, I explained less well than Mills why in a mass society there were no mass movements—contrary to the view of Kornhauser in *The Politics of Mass Society;* what this appeared to mean was that Japanese intellectuals are worried about the bourgeoisification of their working class along American lines and they see this as an effort by big business to prevent the development of mass leftist movements.

Yamazaki had made, I thought, the interesting and subtle comment that Mills was not directing his work to a specific audience whom he was trying to liberate, but was rather a voice in the wilderness; he was not addressing the power elite, who wouldn't listen, but neither was he addressing its helpless victims. In contrast, in all my writings, in which he was steeped, Yamazaki said I was talking to specific minorities, such as intellectuals or Jews or other minorities, to whom I was trying to bring understanding and succor; I was not directing my discussion to the population in general.

Odawara said that his only criticism of Mills was that his view was somewhat static and didn't analyze decision-making in dynamic terms —as usual with such words as "static" and "dynamic," I wasn't sure what he meant.

When his pungent flow of rhetoric stopped and had been translated, it was hard for me to know where to take hold. I decided to pick up what had been said about concrete decision-making and to say that I wanted to deal with two instances where the analysis in *The Power Elite* would seem inapplicable or to have left something out. I said that scientists don't appear in *The Power Elite* and yet men like Edward Teller had had enormous influence on American policy; for instance, the recent decision to resume bomb testing. Then since Odawara had spoken of monopoly capitalism, I said that it seemed to me that Japanese monopoly capitalism before World War II was not linked to the military in the way that Mills had described for the United States; otherwise, why would Japanese big businessmen have had to be assassinated to make room for right-wing activity? I added that many of the Japanese tycoons had been internationally-minded. What I was trying to get at were the differences of monopoly capitalism in Japan, Germany, and the United States; and I indicated that the question as to who was a proper Marxist was not easily answered, since Marx himself, were he alive, might well take account of technological developments such as the growth of the influence of scientists. (Odawara had used the word "radical" a number of times in referring to Mills—and I thought that the word, like the word "decisive" or other plus words, is more a matter of tone and of what people say about themselves than of actual content.)

This reference to the Japanese past turned out to be just the wrong thing to say. Odawara launched into a passionate ten- or fifteen-minute flow, not pausing for the interpreter, who made frantic notes. When the latter started to interpret, it was clear that Odawara was recounting for me the whole history of Japanese pre-war militarism from the Manchurian Incident onward. With some misgivings, I stopped the interpreter in mid-stream and said that I was relatively familiar with this history and didn't mean to raise an historical argument, but was simply using this as an illustration. Yamazaki then made an equally long run, and I could tell from some of the words that he was talking about the same thing, but I didn't feel I could stop him without being certain; I would have to wait for the interpretation. And sure enough, he too was recounting for me the pre-war history in much the same terms as Odawara had done, i.e., in terms of monopoly capitalism and its "real" stake in the war machine in spite of apparent superficial resistances. Again, I stopped the interpreter—but this time I was rather angry, feeling that I was being condescended to, as if I'd never heard of Tojo or the other actors in the pre-war drama. I said I wanted to change the subject completely and that I was afraid I was being rude, but we had so little time.

Bob Lifton interpolated at this point that the interpreter had not fully translated my statement, that my historical analogy had been misplaced as well as misunderstood, and that I apologized. (He told me later that he felt it was well to stop this discussion, for otherwise it would indeed have absorbed all of the time in a defense of the universal view among intellectuals as to the causes of the disasters of World War II; the desperate fear of the Japanese that the pre-war patterns would be restored in alliance with American militarism helps give the Communist and Marxist interpretations of pre-war history their tenacious holds over the young.)

I then tried to say something about the attitudes toward C. Wright Mills's work in the United States. I said I defended that work among conservatives in America and especially his book *The Causes of World War III*, but that there were a good many students who were attracted to *The Power Elite* by its "paratrooper" tone, and because it simplified the world for them and made it unnecessary for them to bother with troublesome details. Moreover, I noted that one article mentioned had referred to Walter Lippmann's *The Public Philosophy* and how striking it was that Lippmann, living in Washington and watching day-to-day decision-making, thought that decisions were too much guided by non-elites, by demagogic politicians and mass opinion, while Mills regarded all decisions as controlled by a small elite group.

I suggested that one reason for the appeal of Mills to the Japanese Left was the fact that it had actual power, as the demonstrations showed, and might some day be in charge; therefore it was nice to think that there was a bundle of power that other people had that one might oneself grab. I referred in this connection to Mills's first book, *The New Men of Power*, about the labor leaders who were completely disregarded in *The Power Elite*. I suggested that Mills was attracted by power and that while this might appeal to the Left in countries where the Left was strong, in America it did leave him and his disciples crying in the wilderness in just the way Yamazaki had suggested; indeed, many might refuse to take any action because without a revolution nothing could be accomplished anyway. I went back to the decision to drop the first atomic bombs on Japan and said that this was a decision which was not directly influenced by monopoly capitalism, that the scientists had had a hand in it, but that capitalism might have an indirect effect on such decisions by orienting people toward winning or in other subtle ways. During all the time I was talking, I realized that the battle against Riesman and in favor of Mills was a battle on behalf of, or against the influence and reputation of, particular Japanese scholars.

In concluding, I said something about the humanistic side of Karl Marx: it seemed to me that the claim that one was an heir to Marx should not be taken at face value; there were various traditions that called themselves Marxist; and Mills's tone and hardness that appealed to so many people were, it seemed to me, as much in the tradition of Lenin as of Marx.

I asked then if people wanted to reply to what I had said, but instead Yamazaki said he had a few questions he wanted to ask me. The first was about the population cycle, and did I think that the rise in the birth rate in the United States since the war disproved my theory. I said that I thought that the theory was probably a mistake. But as I said this I had the feeling—as I did throughout—that any criticism I made of *The Lonely Crowd* might simply undercut my Japanese followers and increase the arrogance and self-confidence of Mills's followers.

Fujimoto then asked me about the theory of the veto groups and how this was connected with the generic concern of American political science with pluralism—he put it in more conceptual and abstract form than that, and I was in the whole conversation constantly groping as to what was being referred to. As Bob Lifton said afterward, there is an even greater desire among the Japanese to categorize thinkers and schools than with us. I felt that what I had said, for instance, about the veto groups was being taken with a literalness in which hypothetical and tentative ideas were being frozen and reified.

Odawara asked how I would interpret the U.S.S.R. and Red China in terms of inner-direction and other-direction. I said that if I were studying these countries I would probably develop some other scheme relevant to their historical problems, that I didn't think the scheme of *The Lonely Crowd* was universal; but that if I were to speculate very roughly about the U.S.S.R. on the basis of limited knowledge, I would think of it as a Victorian society which, when I was there thirty years ago, was emerging from a traditional peasant culture into a more inner-directed industrial society which was now developing organization men in a way characteristic of other industrial societies; China was a different story, but I did not feel that I knew enough to comment about it.

He then asked me whether I felt that the current development of right-wing thought in America was the result of what Richard Hofstadter referred to as status anxieties or status politics rather than interest politics—and once more I was struck by the close textual analysis, and I had to remind myself what it was that Hofstadter said. Rather than reply on the theoretical level, I spoke of the fluoridation controversies and of Martin Trow's article on small businessmen and support for McCarthy, trying by these illustrations to indicate that right-wing radicalism was not necessarily connected with monopoly capitalism, nor invariably with the loss of status, and that it might in part reflect the power of traditional American political rhetoric. Odawara then asked, referring to *The New American Right*, whether it wasn't true that the power elite was tolerant of the sorts of rightist sentiment I had described because it was in the interest of the monopoly capitalists. I said that that tolerance was a very complicated matter and gave the example of the fight of Secretary of Defense McNamara against the right-wing generals, pointing out that McNamara had come from big business, namely the Ford Motor Company, but that he wanted to restore civilian control over the military and that he was opposed to right-wing extremism of the sort familiar in Japanese history which had its sources in small towns and rural areas.

Afterward, Bob Lifton joined Evey and me for a drink. He said that it was difficult for Japanese to be universalistic, even for the best intellectuals: people think in terms of groups and group pressures and interests, and it would be almost unheard of in Japan for an individual to take on himself political initiative of the sort people have taken on, for instance, in our Committee of Correspondence. Furthermore, there is little humor or irony or playfulness in such an intellectual discourse, but a heavy-handedness that Americans often sum up in the word "Germanic." For me, perhaps the most important residue of the occasion was a sense of the intellectual history and drama to which I had been exposed, in which I had been an unwitting protagonist: I felt not only that Japanese intellectuals, like those everywhere, but perhaps more so, were attracted to power; but that in the power struggle between Mills and Riesman the latter had been vanquished and, with him, his Japanese defenders.

Tokyo, October 7 **ETR**

I am beginning to see more variety and beauty in Japanese faces. I am conscious of this when we walk on the crowded streets, as well as right here in International House, among the staff and the scholars we have met with. There are the broad, high-cheek-boned faces with a masklike quality; there are the traditional doll-like, delicate, oval faces; there are the dark, long faces with bushy eyebrows and almost European features—these faces are the most expressive; there are the voluptuous faces of Indonesian beauty; there are the craggy, irregular faces, lean and bespectacled; there are the soft characterless Buddhalike faces, and so on.

Today we went with Nat Glazer by subway to the Asakusa, an entertainment district. When we emerged from the subway, we were at the entrance of a huge new department store. Otherwise, the buildings on the street were small and run-down. We walked a few blocks—all of this navigation was managed by Nat, who already knows the city—and then we were in the midst of it. Whole families were out strolling in the arcades (Sunday seems now to be a partial holiday, though almost everything is open and people seem to be working). The arcades, lined with shops of all kinds, were trimmed with lanterns and artificial autumn leaves. The people seemed to be happy and gay, as at a fair or festival, not buying, just looking. At the end of the arcades, we came out on an open park with a large ornate temple, looking quite as gaudy and profane as the arcades. Here people swarmed up the steps, threw in their coins, and swarmed down again—all as a perfunctory duty, enjoying the festivity of the crowds and the sightseeing, taking pictures, but without any pretense of religious feeling. Busloads of uniformed school children kept arriving and departing, adding to the confusion and gaiety.

We strolled across the open square beyond the temple to the streets on the other side. Here are restaurants, movie houses with lurid advertisements of horror films, strip-tease music halls (a fad imported from the United States, since nudity in Japan—with their mixed bathing, their crowded family living—is hardly salacious), pachinko parlors, and gambling houses. The people wandering about the narrow streets in this area were mostly rather beat, young boys and girls in groups or occasionally in couples, and some rather tough-looking young men.

We wandered off in another direction toward the river and watched a baseball game being played in a stony park, then came back across a wide boulevard to the subway entrance. This area was rather depressing, not at all like the elegant downtown part of the city with its modern architecture and the colorful narrow streets around the Ginza, nor like the charming area in which we live.

In the evening, Betty Lifton took the Youngs and me to a meeting of the "East-West Discussion Group" (which Betty founded in 1952). The members of the group were Japanese, many of them students who were interested in the United States, and Americans from all walks of life, a few of them students. We were late, and as we came in, the speaker for the evening, a Japanese student who had spent a year at Columbia University, had already begun. There were twenty-five or thirty people in the room, sitting on the floor. The speaker was talking about American students; he had felt quite cut off from them. He said the only ones he had had any contact with were the Jewish students, and they were a racial minority; he didn't think American students were interested in desegregation. What he said was naturally distressing to the American students present. And the discussion that followed didn't help matters; for when he said, in answer to a question, that he had been shocked by the anti-Communism in America, a rather brash American student got up and began to make a speech addressed to all the Japanese in the room, ending with, "Are you for democracy or are you for Communism, or don't you know what you are—just vegetables!" The chairman tried to answer him: "We want to develop in our own way in our industrialization. We want to keep our minds open about democracy and Communism." Others made comments. But the low, quiet voices of the Japanese were overwhelmed by the loud insistence of the American. Finally the discussion got back to a more amicable track. The episode made me wonder about the value of student exchanges, which in this instance, at any rate, had served only to strengthen prejudices and misunderstandings.

Later in the evening Betty and I joined Bob and Dave and went on from their house to visit a young Japanese weaver who lives near them, on one of the little winding streets behind a high wooden fence. Mari Susuka, a woman of an earthy type of beauty, invited us into her large studio filled with looms. On the floor were basketfuls of skeins, silks and wools of many colors; there were partly woven materials on various looms; she showed us things she was working on, rough wools, exquisite silks, touching the threads lovingly. Then she led us upstairs to a studio where her mother, who is a painter, greeted us. The mother is in her sixties but seems amazingly young and energetic. The studio walls were covered with her paintings, abstract, complex, and dense, with some resemblance to Mark Tobey, and very beautiful.

Miss Susuka brought out from cupboards on one side of the room examples of her finished work, including some fine silks used for kimono and *obi*, in which the design is woven into the material as in tapestries, sometimes a sprig of flower or a bird, reminiscent of the traditional Japanese screen painting. There were also wools similar to English or Irish homespuns, rough and of heathery, earthy colors. We then joined the mother, who showed us photographs in a family album, with the title embossed on the hard cover, "Past Days of My Life." In it were faded daguerreotypes, very Victorian, with the grandparents and the parents in family groupings, Miss Susuka and her sister as children, and so forth. The Liftons told us later that showing family albums was a Japanese way of establishing themselves with strangers, of being friendly and relating themselves to others. When we had finished looking at these, they brought out the guest book, even more a Japanese than an American custom. We noticed that guests before us had written flowery phrases, and we tried to think of something appropriate.

Then the mother and daughter brought in refreshments, Japanese cakes and tea, and to top it all an American-style apple pie. We were very touched, and though not hungry and by now quite tired, we ate and conversed, partly in Japanese and partly in English, with the Liftons valiantly translating. The mother told us something of her life. She seems to be a woman of remarkable strength and courage; her husband died rather young and she had had to make her living and bring up her two daughters. It is hard to imagine what it must have been like in Tokyo during the war years, with two-thirds of the houses destroyed and families disrupted and scattered. The mother did not say more about that period; I wondered if the photograph album was perhaps one of their few possessions to survive the war.

Tokyo, October 8

This afternoon, we went to the Kabuki theater with the Liftons. The building with its huge and ornate pagoda-shaped façade looks exotic among the modern structures of Tokyo. Since the plays begin in the afternoon and go on all evening, perhaps five plays in all, people wander in and out during the intermissions. Coming through the ornate

ETR

entrance, we were struck by the unexpected simplicity of the interior. Many of the women in the theater were dressed in kimono, and the audience was rather subdued and elderly looking. It was nowhere near full—this was surprising since everything in Japan is usually crowded to overflowing.

Kabuki was something more strange and exotic than anything we could have imagined. Stylized, ritualistic, the action like some slow-moving dance; the men impersonating women, the twangy music of the *samisen*,* the extraordinary voices of the two men seated in an alcove at the side of the stage, singing to their own accompaniment, describing and commenting on what was happening in a falsetto *recitatif*—all this seemed like some ancient and remote expression of a culture closed to us. Every so often from the top balcony there would come a guttural yell which we thought was an expression of disgust, but no, we discovered it was their way of shouting "bravo." What did it mean, for there was nothing particular happening at that moment so far as we could see? Perhaps it was something in that falsetto voice, perhaps it was the motion of the hand, or the lifting of an eyebrow, or an angry glance in that white masklike face. We were aware of great finesse and long-drawn-out dwelling on a particular emotion. Even violence seemed lost in stylized action, frozen attitudes. When the hero in disguise walked up the aisle toward the stage playing an ancient pipe, with a huge straw hat on his head covering most of the face, this was an unforgettable sight, an unforgettable sound. How great the power of the theater to evoke the extreme and strange and fearful! Nothing we could be told, nothing we could read, not even painting or sculpture could have such an effect, could tell us as this person in this costume did, playing this thin wailing line of music, how remote and incomprehensible certain aspects of this culture are to us.

DR

Kabuki is a dying art. The young do not go, nor do they apprentice themselves to the severe discipline of acting—a discipline which reminded us in some ways of the Habimah Players whom we saw years ago in New York. The highbrows of Japan prefer the Nō plays or the *bunraku* puppet shows out of which Kabuki grew as a popular culture form, which has now in turn become rather old-fashioned and middle-brow fare. There has been some attempt to write modern Kabuki drama, but one might say that the fate of Kabuki is a paradigm for the present situation of traditional Japan.

* A guitarlike instrument.

Tokyo, October 9

This morning we went out in a drizzle and were greeted by a downpour which soaked us to the skin; even my raincoat was no protection. Huge puddles formed on the street and I could see why many Japanese wear boots and why the old-style clogs which lift the wearer two inches from the ground are a great help. Yet, even in the downpour, boys were going along on bicycles balancing on one hand trays with bowls of soup and noodles piled high, mounting curbs and winding through the terrible traffic like jugglers. The streets were full of people hurrying or waiting at bus stops, and the proverbial cheerfulness was hardly dampened.

This would be a fine day to go to the movies, but we have found in Tokyo few art theaters which re-run the movies of such great Japanese directors as Kurosawa—indeed, I have talked to a number of people who have not seen his marvelous film, *Ikiru.* We were told that many Japanese intellectuals are interested only in French or Italian art movies and pay no attention even to their own best directors. It's almost impossible to find a re-run of a Japanese film—a film stays a week and then is gone for good.

This evening our hosts had arranged a dinner discussion on modernization in Japan, with a number of men of influence in the mass media and political life. They included Mr. Kimura, a leading political scientist and a member of the committee now engaged in considering revisions of the Japanese Constitution; Mr. Nagayama, an influential director of a number of publications; and Mr. Nara, an economic planner with much international experience. Matsumoto was our host and proved characteristically skillful in turning first to one and then to another of these men to evoke matters he thought would be of interest to me, while preventing the discussion from being monopolized by any one person on any particular topic.

Nara, for example, gave a figure-studded picture of Japan's present economic situation. He noted that underemployment had helped make possible Japan's spectacular economic growth in recent years, but now was an aspect in curtailing that growth; he discussed shortages of technical and engineering people; he pointed—as the papers constantly do—to the balance of payments problem and the precarious dependence on exports to the United States. And he spoke of the congestion in Tokyo as undercutting previous economies of scale.

As I had read elsewhere, Japan has a reinvestment ratio of well over 30 per cent, and I have gotten the impression that Japanese industrialists follow in their own businesses the national rate as though it were an index of reliability for their own destiny, even while they praise free enterprise. Paradoxically, socialists object to the high growth rate because they think it will lead to inflation, because it is obviously uneven, and because they fear it will improve the position of the monopoly capitalists. Indeed, the latter are able to raid small businesses for technical and key people (though on the whole they refrain from raiding each other) because they can pay much higher wages in the double-decker economy of Japan: the Japanese believe this double-decker economy to be unique, though the concept resembles our notion of the dual economy. Of course the gap in Japan is far greater than with us, although Nara indicated that the general average of the gap was but 15 or 20 per cent in the level of wages.

Matsumoto asked Kimura whether businessmen thought that the government had had any hand in the great economic growth since the war; he replied that the businessmen believed that they had done it themselves, while of course the government had played a large role—I gather through more or less Keynesian measures. He added that it was necessary to limit the growth of Tokyo, and I asked how this could be done, how could people be kept down on the farm. To which he replied that trucking and other costs in Tokyo had become so prohibitive that firms were beginning to move out to the suburbs. There had been talk of moving out some government departments such as the patent office, but he felt it was necessary to move out the Diet before any government departments would actually be moved; this, however, was considered much too drastic. Moreover, there were plans to build highways so as to make it easier to leave Tokyo for places 40 or 60 kilometers away, which then could become, as it were, new towns. I said I thought the highways might bring even more traffic into already half-strangled Tokyo, but this remark wasn't picked up. There was also talk of moving some of the universities out of town, but Bob Lifton, who had joined us after dinner, said that if the University of Tokyo remained in town, the pressure to get into it would only be increased by this.

Nara left with me several reprints of his articles in English on economic progress in Japan. One of these, from the *Japan Quarterly*, emphasizes what he said orally, namely that there are simply not enough high-paying jobs in the big industries of Japan and that the small industries are, by Western standards, low in productivity and therefore must pay low wages; plainly his model for a proper economy is a Western one, and whatever human advantages and salvages there may be in the Japanese pattern are not for him. With all the difficulties, the growth is staggering: Japanese production has doubled in the five years since 1956 and the country manages to support over twice as many people as Great Britain on the same amount of arable land. Nara has an unusual sense of the possibility of Japan as a model for other Asian countries, with as high a rate of saving and investment as the U.S.S.R. has achieved but without state coercion—though I think he would like to see more planning and especially more government action in the realm of transport and other areas where private enterprise can't manage.

Matsumoto turned to Kimura and asked him about the recent discussions on the position of the Emperor. Kimura went into a long legalistic discussion of the difference between the Emperor as sovereign and the Emperor as symbol. He regarded it as an outrage that, when the Emperor of Ethiopia sent a gift to the Emperor of Japan, it had to go first to the Foreign Office, then to the Prime Minister, who sent it back to the Foreign Office to give to the Japanese Emperor. So, too, when visiting dignitaries arrived, they couldn't be greeted by the Emperor, but had to be greeted by the Prime Minister. Some people wanted to change this to give the Emperor a legal standing comparable to that of the King of the Belgians or the British Monarch. I was puzzled why the issue mattered so very much. (Bob Lifton remarked to me later that among intellectuals in the generation that preceded the war the Emperor was still sacred and terribly important, while in the generation that grew up and had to live through the war, there was great resentment of the Emperor and a wish that the Americans had gotten rid of him; to the new post-war generation, the Emperor is rather a matter of indifference and there is no objection to him.)

Matsumoto then asked Kimura about other constitutional changes that were being considered and the latter launched into a discussion of the need to revise the constitution so as to legitimate Japan's actual development of the Army and other defense forces, contrary to the famous Article IX of the MacArthur-imposed Constitution, which required Japanese disarmament. Here, as with the Emperor, I wondered why people cared so much about bringing the formal in line with the informal structure. They seemed to care more about discrepancies between theory and practice than about the bitter and pressing problems that Nara was concerned with.

The discussion then turned to Nagayama, and I asked him about NHK, Japan's BBC, of which he is an advisor. He said that, as an example of Japanese growth, the network had expanded fourfold in the last five or six years, to the point where there are now eight million "television families" and near saturation of radios. NHK collects a monthly fee from all radio and television households, and while the state income-tax collection gets an estimated 70 per cent of taxes due, NHK collects for about 93 per cent of the estimated sets. NHK's main trouble comes less from competition of commercial stations than from conflict between local programming and national scheduling. The regional differences of Japan remain great and of course there is conflict between rural and urban cultures and between the generations. NHK doesn't run Westerns and emphasizes its educational channel. It is on the air more hours a day than any other.

I asked him about recruitment into NHK and he said that they gave entrance exams and questionnaires to applicants from the universities. When the latter were asked what they looked forward to in life, many said they looked forward to retiring at fifty-five. They saw their work as a way of earning a little competence, having a roof over their heads, and gaining access to consumer pleasures; but they had little ambition. He said this was an entirely new phenomenon for the go-ahead Japanese people.

Turning back to Kimura, Matsumoto asked him why the political parties in Japan were so inadequate, particularly so in contrast to the press and mass media. Kimura pointed out that most Conservative Party politicians came out of the bureaucracy—Ikeda was a former Finance Ministry man. Such men don't attract a personal mass following which would also permit them to develop their own individual political style in the American or British manner. Kimura then turned to ask me what could be done to make young people more interested in politics and less apathetic. In general, he was one of those older men who "doesn't understand" the young, resents them, and fears them. He said that he had been the day before to play golf at a nearby country club and that there were many businessmen and government people there, but no professors or intellectuals, and he felt the gap. He then criticized the professors, pointing out that they made a good living from writing for the press and expounding radical views rather than taking a responsible hand in the political process or planning. He thought they were distracted from this by being pampered by the press. I didn't know how to reply, but I said that I thought if Japanese Marxism became more differentiated and less provincial it might reinterpret recent Japanese history so as to make it both more interesting and more comprehensible to the young—this was in response to Kimura's complaint that the professors and their students weren't at all interested in Japanese traditions, but only in the immediately contemporary.

Matsumoto then raised for discussion the Chiang Kai-shek veto of admission of Outer Mongolia to the U.N. and said that the United States had asked Thailand, Burma, and Japan as Asian countries to intercede with Chiang to get him to relent and not to use his veto; Thailand had refused and Japan's intercession had had no effect whatever on the stubborn Chiang. Matsumoto then asked Kimura how he would vote in the U.N. if he were the Japanese representative, and he said he would follow the American lead and abstain; he said this without resentment. I asked if this was for fear of American economic reprisals and was told yes: the Japanese were terribly afraid of illogical reactions of Americans against Japan which would cut the latter's precarious hold on prosperity and plunge many millions not into underemployment, but into unemployment. Japan was therefore bound to do America's bidding.

After the discussion broke up, Bob Lifton came up to our room and we talked for a while longer. He said that the Emperor question was dynamite, since efforts to strengthen his position only increased the fear among the Left that the Conservatives were Rightists in disguise who wanted to restore the pre-war militarist regime. I was then astonished to learn that Kimura was a leader of the Democratic Socialists. He seemed to me a very strange kind of socialist, not only because of his general conservative outlook, but because of his specific interest in defense, where I felt he wanted not only to straighten out the legal situation but also to increase Japan's armed strength as against the more pacifist tendencies which seem dominant among the various brands of socialists here. Moreover, one of the questions he had asked me was how to increase national cohesion and consensus as against differences of class and generation—again hardly a typical concern for a socialist.

I commented on the rigidity of the older Japanese, their "over-socialized" quality and their abstractness of outlook. The youthful freedom of speculation and generalization, which Matsumoto shares, was absent in some of the big-shots we talked with this evening. Partly, no doubt, language barriers make the discussion less free and easy and more pedantic, but partly this lack of ease reflects a caution and fear to go out on a limb all by oneself which the Japanese themselves regard as one of their chief problems.

Bob Lifton agreed that younger people felt an enormous resentment of such people who were still in charge. Yamazaki had said to me in conversation that between the younger generation of Japanese political scientists who were oriented to Fromm, Riesman, Mills, Lasswell, etc. and the older generation who were oriented toward more abstract theory there was no communication whatever.

Tokyo, October 10

Last night a typhoon was expected to hit here and the maids brought around candles in the expectation that the electricity would go off. The wind and rain were furious during the night, and I found this quite exciting; when I came down to breakfast it was still howling, but the kitchen produced breakfast with Lord knows what struggles to get here on the part of the staff. The staff seems intensely loyal and devoted.

When Evey and I realized that Yamazaki had come down from Hokkaido for the discussion with me and was staying on in Tokyo, we arranged to see him again. During our lunch conversation, I asked him about the sources of academic mobility in Japan. He said there was no open competition for places but everything was done in terms of who one's teacher or sponsor is and in terms of friendship and connections. I asked him how it happened that, since the teachers of the present generation of scholars were conservative, they sponsored so many young radicals into leading university posts. One answer I got was that many of the older professors were liberal or personally generous; also many of the younger men tended to mute their views until they were established. Another element was the purge by the Occupation, which cleaned out some of the more rightist faculty members and opened up places for young and previously imprisoned or otherwise hounded radicals.

I asked Yamazaki who were the writers, either Japanese or foreign, who were most esteemed in Japan or most exciting for his students. He first mentioned Maruyama, the political scientist, then he said Erich Fromm, Mills, and myself. In the Left generally I was thought to be a conformist and closer to the Right, whereas Mills was a radical and against the regime. And in order to explain this, Yamazaki said that the Japanese image of the American regime was based on Japanese pre-war experience with an oppressive rightist government. People are categorized into either pro-regime or counter-regime and Mills, of course, seems counter-regime. The regime is a compound of monopoly capitalists and bureaucrats—the concept of veto groups runs head on into this way of thinking.

I asked Yamazaki whether there were any women studying political science and he said he had four in his seminar, along with twenty-five men. He seemed to think that that was quite a lot of women. He has his students doing a survey of voting behavior, in an effort to arrive at conclusions about political socialization in Japan. He said, however, that it was difficult for university students to interview in rural areas because they would be given the answers they were thought to expect or they would be given a "don't know" answer, because respondents were so afraid of the authority. Indeed, he emphasized again, as many people have, the survival of "feudal" elements in the rural areas.

We went to dinner at the Liftons' in the evening. Our fellow guests were the Yoneyamas (he is a leading economist and statistician at one of the major universities) and the Sugawaras (he is a distinguished sociologist). Both men had spent a good deal of time in the United States and they and their wives spoke English with ease and elegance. As with other young Japanese couples who have lived in America, the wives on returning to Japan miss the sort of husband-and-wife sociability to be found in the larger academic centers in the United States; and even by contemporary Japanese standards, these partly Americanized wives can appear overly forward and assertive. Indeed, the Japanese men who have been in America seem to become more assertive and even forensic—not all of them, of course, for that depends on their receptivity, the age at which they go, their temperaments, and much else.

Professor Yoneyama said that he had caused a sensation when a few years ago he got the president of his university to invite wives to an annual occasion when professors were honored. Up to that time, wives of colleagues had never met. Professor Sugawara put in a word about how embarrassed he was, after going to the United States for a year and renting his house to an American professor, to return and have many colleagues tell him that for the first time they saw the inside of his house, although he had known them for a great many years.

The dynamic and vibrant Yoneyama then told us about a talk he had just given, entitled "Returning to Japan," to an audience of several thousand in one of the many cultural events sponsored by a leading Japanese publisher. His own speech was followed by one from a man in humanities, one from a natural scientist, and several educational films—the whole running from 6 P.M. to 10 P.M. For this occasion people had started to line up before five o'clock, and at 5:30, when the doors opened, the hall nearly filled with students, who could get a bite to eat and leave their work in time for the occasion, while hundreds of professional and white-collar workers, who could not get there so early, were turned away. This event and others like it are indicative of a culture hunger that, if paralleled anywhere in the world, might have some analogies in the U.S.S.R.

Yoneyama described his talk as a criticism of elements in Japanese life which he found not genuine (a word which he used in English because there was no Japanese equivalent). Ads, fads, deceptive politicians, mixtures of Japanese and American patterns—all these he condemned as not genuine. It was my impression that the audience, which itself suspects that Japan is not genuine, ate it up. Bob Lifton compared this use of "genuine" with Paul Goodman's use of "not serious" to refer to statements or ideas in the United States which he regarded as not meeting the issue or as inauthentic. Bob raised the question as to how long a fad has to remain a fad for it to become genuine—a kind of generosity out of keeping with Yoneyama's astringent attack. Thereafter during the evening we kept referring to whether something was "genuine" or not: was it genuine for the Liftons to serve us on *tatami* but not to seat us in the Japanese style—the Liftons said that seating us in the American style with them opposite each other was authentic for them.

Yoneyama is of the breed of brilliant Japanese professors who are constantly called on for lectures and rapidly become celebrities. This occurs not only because they are underpaid and need the money but also because of a wide audience for intellectual matters, even for rather specialized ones; the gap between the specialist and the mass audience is narrow. I realize that I have been meeting the more distinguished and relatively unspecialized men, but it also would seem that such men are not devalued by their more specialized colleagues. In a sense the intellectual pattern here resembles that of England: for one thing, there is but a single metropolis, so that when I asked the guests whom they saw socially, they indicated that their circle included journalists, government people, professional people, in addition to their academic colleagues.

I asked if the Socialists had any plan for the economy and was told that they had slogans but no real plan. They want the underside of the double-decker economy to be raised so that one no longer has privileged workmen and miserable ones, but they have not shown how this can be done, given the very low productivity of the poorly paid workers. (This productivity is about one-third that of the American worker, but of course wages are so low as to make competition possible; much of the low productivity is due to the lifelong tenure of the worker, who is kept on no matter how incompetent he is.)

When we went upstairs again after dinner, Yoneyama began talking about his university. He said that because he wasn't an alumnus he would never be appointed today; there was an iron-clad home-guard (my term) pattern which prevented the appointment of excellent people and saw to it that the billion yen recently raised from big business was largely spread among alumni who were teaching there. Bob then asked Yoneyama whether this handicapped him in getting money for research, and he said no, he could get it from the government. I asked why the university remained distinguished in spite of this in-group selection, and Bob Lifton suggested that its excellent business connections plus the intellectual level of the Department of Economics attracted brilliant students, a few of whom could then of course be persuaded to stay on as faculty. Yoneyama, however, thought the place would eventually decline. He feared in his own institute that the alumni would be given some say in its management, and since he is much to the left of this group, he is deeply troubled.

Paradoxically, the university has the most democratic procedure for picking its president, instituted among the American reforms after the war: the president is elected, and clerks and other employees have a vote, as do the students, who also have a veto. Yet it was said that the place is the most autocratic university imaginable.

I asked whether the president of a Japanese university was ever an entrepreneur in the American style, building the place up, but I gathered that this didn't happen. I asked how Todai (University of Tokyo) kept its high standards and was told that, when one or another department declined, tension would arise with the other eminent departments and something would eventually be done about it, although how something was done never became clear. Economics at Todai is weak now because before and during the war all the liberal professors were arrested—it is still a matter of pride to have been arrested—and those who took their places were purged after the war while the former liberals and left-wingers returned. But the latter had been out of affairs for many years, and though fine people, they were no longer in the swim of economics. Efforts are being made now to rectify matters, but it takes a while. Bob Lifton said that the tremendous pressure of good students to get into Todai kept the place going, and that in spite of the low salaries paid junior faculty, as against the high salaries in business, there was no difficulty in recruitment. Bob

Lifton said that one source for university professors at Todai is Zengakuren leaders, who if they hold top positions in the student movement are blacklisted by business, though they are acceptable if they hold less than top positions. There are not enough wealthy Todai students to fill professorial chairs with those who can afford the low pay, however.

Yoneyama explained a form of home-guardism that applied not so much to the university as such as to the seminar of the professor who (German-style) looked after his own students: he helped arrange marriages for them, advised them about jobs, and indeed sponsored them through life; while they spoke of themselves as members of so-and-so's seminar. Indeed, various leading universities have lesser universities within their network, so that Todai would appoint the professors at Hokkaido or Yokohama, while Hitotsubashi would have other institutions within its orbit.

I asked how students chose which university to apply for. Yoneyama said their high-school teachers guide them in this, depending partly on their teachers' connections and partly on their judgment as to the ability of the student. There are perhaps four universities of the first class, including Todai, Kyoto, Hitotsubashi (all government), and a good many of the second class, such as Yokohama or Kyushu or Hokkaido. A student can apply to one in each of these lists since they have their examinations on different days; and he can also, if he has the money, apply to private universities such as Waseda, which have their examinations on still different days. At Hitotsubashi, students when they enter must declare a field of concentration: economics or sociology or whatever. They must have integral calculus and mathematics of a pretty high order to get in—a unique requirement among Japanese liberal-arts universities. Bob Lifton said that Japanese high-school students reach a proficiency in math and physics attained by only the top American students.

I stole a glance at my watch and saw it was already 11:30—we had not finished the long Japanese dinner until ten, and I hoped we had not kept these busy professors a captive audience. A few seconds later, Yoneyama looked at his watch and moved to go; and so we all started to leave. Sugawara offered to take us home if we didn't mind riding in their tiny car; he told me that his wife was the driver but that she was a very good driver—as if I might doubt that a woman could drive a car. Their "tiny" car turned out to be a Volkswagen, and we had by far the most pleasant and unanxious ride we have had in Tokyo to date. On the way Sugawara remarked that Japanese law professors were far more interested in social science than seemed to be true in the

United States, except at Yale Law School. This was due to the fact that the law faculty was part of the general university and that many people attended it who were not going on into practice. He himself felt that books like *The Lonely Crowd* were relevant to understanding the legal order, and he didn't see how lawyers could be anything but interdisciplinary.

I am reminded by this that I had been asked what Americans meant by the term "behavioral science." The question had arisen because when Prime Minister Ikeda came back from his meeting with President Kennedy one of the things he said was that there would be more cooperation between Japanese and American scientists, and a report had then been prepared in America suggesting cooperation between both natural and behavioral scientists. Yoneyama thought some Japanese would take offense at the term "behavioral," but mainly for political reasons—because they objected to the initiative coming from Ikeda, because they felt there was already ample cooperation between Japanese and American scholars, and because they wanted to see more cooperation with the Communist countries, of which there was very little. An argument over the word "behavioral" might provide leverage for this kind of political point at the next meeting of the Japan Science Council.

Tokyo, October 11

The morning began with our frequent good luck of breakfast with Richard Storry. He told us of just seeing a wealthy businessman, another former student, who was proud of having been the go-between for fifty-two marriages. The tie of a professor with his students or of a boss with his employees is much closer and more "feudal" than similar patterns of benevolent paternalism elsewhere. We talked about Kimura and what sort of socialist such a man was. Storry compared him first to Gaitskell, but I said I couldn't imagine Gaitskell greatly concerned with the monarchy or worried because young academicians don't play golf; and he said no, perhaps Kimura was more like Gladstone, which made sense to me. I said I realized how really conservative the Conservative Party must be if such a man feels that he must take the socialist side.

On our walk this morning we passed small children coming out of school neatly dressed in their uniforms with their briefcases, holding hands, the best-mannered children I've even seen. They don't seem to fight or scream but at the same time they don't seem oversocialized, but are friendly and cheerful. I've seen them playing amicably on swings or inventing their own games. Indeed, so far we've not seen mean or vindictive faces here, although we have seen stern and dignified ones.

We had lunch with Nat Glazer and his assistant, a graduate student at Todai, and talked about the highbrow Japanese weeklies which are a recent phenomenon and have gained wide circulation. Some contain a coverage of the foreign press that one could hardly find anywhere in the United States. Nat pointed out that in small local bookstores he'd seen three architectural magazines on display, whereas in the United States he knew only about three places where one could buy *Architectural Forum* on a stand. And he spoke of the extraordinary cheapness of Japanese books—a good scholarly book of 300 or 400 pages will sell for 56 cents in hard cover. I said it seemed to me that Japanese professors nonetheless spend a large part of their income on books. Nat's assistant was translating E. P. Thompson's *Out of Apathy*, and I asked him about interest here in the *New Left Review*—he said it had many readers in Japan; and he in turn asked me about *The Monthly Review*, which he said had many more readers in Japan than in the United States. (I am asked about *The Monthly Review* again and again.) The assistant, however, didn't know *New University Thought* or *Studies on the Left*—though I'm sure that now that they've been mentioned he'll go and look them up.

This evening we had an interesting session with a group of newspapermen. It began a little after five, sitting around a table with tea in the private dining room at International House, and then at seven we moved over to dinner, adjourning a little after nine. Matsumoto began by saying that I was interested in the Japanese mass press, and at first it was hard going, with only Mr. Nagao, an editor of a leading daily, the oldest man there, taking the burden of discussion. He responded to my comment on the relatively high level of the Japanese press by saying that the Japanese buy papers but do not read all of them. The papers support cultural events both in their columns and otherwise: they are always sponsoring concerts and lectures. I pointed out that the editors, being neither Canadians in London nor Californians in New York, were part of a cosmopolitan, metropolitan world in which they wanted to stand well, and Nagao agreed. But he also thought that there was some tendency to glamorize news, though less so than in the United States. He pointed out that sports coverage in *Asahi* began with two columns and was now a whole page and sometimes two, and that there was full and increasing coverage of the entertainment world. Many women read this and not the international news or editorials. Still, he agreed with me that people paid deference to culture.

Nagao asked me which three magazines or papers I would take in Japan if I could take no others from America. I found this a hard question and said I would take *The New York Times*, and probably *Time*, and perhaps *The New Republic*. I commented that American newspaper writers and readers were cynical and he agreed that this was less true in Japan. Mr. Ishizaka, an editorial columnist, then pointed out that in the pre-war militarist period Japanese liberals and Leftists had to learn to read between the lines to understand what was going on—as the discussion later developed, it became clear that he was extremely liberal.

One man mentioned a study of television in Hokkaido, and I raised the possibility that women might begin to know more news than men "working in the fields." But one study of readership of the press pointed out that about half as many women as men read editorials and political news. However, many letters to the editor are written by women and often deal with serious political matters; and women are in general getting more critical, even though they remain more conservative than men.

Nagao pointed out and others seemed to agree that, because the Japanese press is a popular press, there is no paper like *The New York Times* or the *Manchester Guardian* to cover events as seriously or as fully as these—they don't have room to be papers of record as the *Times* is, and a speech by Khrushchev or something like that would be reported in a weekly with a circulation of about 50,000, read only by specialists or particularly interested people. These weeklies don't make a profit, but are run for prestige and public service by the three giant newspaper chains.

We then got into a discussion of the provincial press. During the war, when newsprint was rationed, the provincial papers, many of which had been small and losing money, were forced to combine; thus in Hokkaido, for example, one very strong provincial paper was created out of three or four small struggling ones. Since there was only one, it tended to be politically neutral, and the national papers, then competing for circulation in each prefecture, also tended to be neutral to attract people away from the local press. One of the participants attacked this neutrality and said a partisan press would be better; I realized a little later that this man was a strong Rightist, the only one at the table, who like so many Rightists looks to the United States for a model and no doubt would like to see such papers in Japan as the

Chicago Tribune, which have guts and really stand for something. I pointed out the dangers of a partisan press, as for instance in France, in that people read only the paper that confirms their beliefs and presents no facts that contradict these beliefs and that in the United States broadcasting, which is less partisan than the press, is more trusted. I said, moreover, that I didn't see that partisanship had suffered in Japan for the lack of a partisan press, since there are political parties, political professors, and partisan weeklies. One of the men then commented that Americans don't think of the Japanese press as neutral but in fact blame the press for stirring up the demonstrations. We kept referring to the demonstrations (and American reaction to them) again and again—the issue comes up in virtually all serious conversations here and obviously had a traumatic impact on people.

Nagao said then that another reason for neutrality was that Japanese editors are not inner-directed, that feudalism was only got rid of ninety years ago and was replaced by a bureaucratic government which also gave no real freedom to Japan (moving from tradition-direction directly to other-direction), so that editors are not rugged individualists. I raised the question how this apparent lack of partisanship could be reconciled with the often fanatical right-wing extremism in Japan and with the alleged power of "monopoly capitalists." Nagao answered that these more ideological people were not inner-directed but even in the extreme Right Wing remained part of their group. They were advocates of authoritarianism but not of individualism. Matsumoto said that the press was not neutral, but non-partisan, which was different.

I remarked that if one had to live with rugged individualists one would see that their absence was not an unmixed evil. I spoke of the other tradition of American newspaper editors such as Hearst who cared more for what they themselves thought than anything else and sought power through the press.

Bob Lifton then asked: might a sensational paper in Japan be a success? Nagao first turned the question away by saying he hoped Hearst or Beaverbrook wouldn't come to Japan and try it; he seemed to think it might possibly work. Bob responded that the Big Three are part of popular culture but they haven't been dragged down to the lowest level of that culture. Another editorial columnist remarked that popular culture is compartmentalized in the sports column. Mr. Tagasaki, an editor of another large daily, added that there are also sports papers which are new, have greatly grown since the war, and now have half a million circulation. He then spoke of the indecent newspapers that concentrate on sex and scandal—they have circulations under 200,000.

Matsumoto gave the example of the *Manchester Guardian* during the Suez crisis which criticized the government (and increased its circulation); but Mr. Sasaki, formerly a correspondent in Rome, pointed out that during the Boer War it had lost half its circulation for criticizing the war, so that attacks on the government didn't always pay. (I was struck on this occasion, as on many others, with what intensity these cosmopolitan Japanese follow the world press and world history.) C. P. Scott was against the Boer War and was plainly a hero—men such as Matsumoto especially admire this kind of independent conscience; and I think what Nagao had in mind in speaking of the other-direction of the Japanese is their self-proclaimed pliability, their "low posture" and willingness to bend with the winds.

Returning to the riots and demonstrations of June, 1960, Nagao said that because *Asahi* was critical of the government, it lost some advertising from leading businessmen. Bob Lifton asked if its circulation had risen, but apparently not—circulation already saturates the country. However, the public supported *Asahi*'s position. I said I had heard that the businessmen had cracked down on *Asahi*, and it was agreed that *Asahi* had become more sober—this was the word frequently used. I got the sense that there had indeed been such a crackdown. Ishizaka said that a change in mood came about when Kishi resigned, for then the people had gotten what they wanted. Tagasaki said that *Asahi* was wrong to play up the demonstrations, since they were the work only of a small minority. Most of the students were interested in baseball, and in the rural areas people weren't sympathetic with the demonstrations. They feel differently from people in the metropolis, and television and the newspapers had little influence there. Moreover, since the demonstrations failed to achieve their objective (by which he apparently meant not only unseating Kishi but overturning the government), they were a failure and the press presumably shouldn't have reported them or given them any prominence. Tagasaki seemed to be putting the others on the defensive for playing up demonstrations that after all were not representative of the majority.

Bob Lifton pointed out that the American press all reported the demonstrators as Communist, and Tagasaki said that the organizers were in fact Communists and that they had done the work. By this time it was quite clear to me where he stood, and I pointed out that it is always taken for granted that Communists exploit other people and they are always accused of being behind demonstrations by conservatives, as in our own South. But I said that it could be possible that Communists themselves might be exploited, that they could be made use of by larger forces for their organizing ability without those larger forces necessarily falling captive to the Communists but in a sense vice versa—that we had a mythical view of the Communists as always winning in any such relationship. I think it was Nagao who said that socialists in Japan were getting more careful not to be used by the Communists.

Nagao said that a number of American newspaper publishers and editors had recently been in Japan and were uniformly critical of the Japanese newspapers for their role in the demonstrations. It was impossible to get them to understand that the papers were not against the Security Treaty but only against Kishi and the way he had rammed this through. They didn't realize that Kishi had been a member of the Tojo war cabinet or that the Japanese felt him to be someone who had been forced on them against their will. Returning to my former comment about businessmen cracking down, he said that there had indeed been a change in attitude in the press.

Tagasaki, recurring to the theme that the demonstrations were played up as popular sentiment whereas in fact they represented a small minority, also attacked the demonstrations as too violent. I responded that by American standards they seemed to be remarkably peaceful. One girl was killed and rightist students were in some cases violent, but on the whole the Zengakuren demonstrators seemed to be relatively unviolent. Tagasaki said that this was only because the police did not attack the demonstrators. In America, he said, the police would shoot and a great many would be killed; he admired this and thought it should have been done in Japan. I commented that, contrary to the impression the group had, there were some Americans who were sympathetic to the demonstrations, and that I knew students who were envious of the power of young people, whether in Korea or Japan or Turkey, to become politically aroused and to upset conservative or reactionary governments. This view obviously came as a great shock and surprise to the group, whatever its political position.

Bob Lifton pointed out that there were some Japanese students who did hope for revolution, and since this didn't occur, for them the demonstrations might be regarded as a "failure." He said it was hard today to recollect the hysteria and emotional feelings at the time of the demonstrations which in the American colony were exaggerated; even Americans who had lived for a long time in Japan and felt very much at home had suddenly felt unwanted and frightened—and I had the sense that many Japanese themselves were frightened by the mass emotions that were aroused. Still, it was striking to me that the liberal newspapermen around the table had taken so very seriously the criticism of their press's treatment of the demonstrations, especially in *Time* and on the part of American publishers. Perhaps this reflects again, in part, Japanese modesty and feelings of inferiority. It also seems possible to me that Japan is so dependent on the United States that even liberals and people of the Left are hesitant to reveal to Americans the strength of Japanese neutralist sentiment for fear of arousing in the United States further restrictions on Japanese exports—exports on which the very life of the country depends.

Bob Lifton asked whether a neutralist politics would succeed in Japan, and Ishizaka said that he himself would like to see this; he was beginning to speak more freely now, perhaps because I had shown my hand. He said it was extremely important for Japan to be neutral—a policy, I gathered, favored by the Democratic Socialists. Sasaki pointed out that the Japanese have no faith in Soviet promises and that for this reason the Japanese would never go over to Russian Communism. I asked whether the attitude toward China is different. Bob Lifton responded that young people are interested in China. Tagasaki said that the Japanese people cannot read Chinese or speak it, and that people are extremely critical if there is an article on China—it arouses too strong reactions either of the Left or of the Right (his implication seemed to be that such reactions should be avoided).

I changed the subject and asked about the career of newspapermen. Nagao said that they were largely graduates of law and economics in the major universities, although, like many others, he denied that there was any favoritism vis-à-vis Todai or any other particular university. Unlike the situation in the United States, people do not start working for small papers and hope to move to the metropolitan press, but rather want to start in the major papers. Hundreds apply to *Asahi* and if they pass an examination will spend their whole life there. A young reporter may be assigned at first to a local town where he will be trained by the chief correspondent of the paper, and after a few years he may be moved to Tokyo. I asked about the pay of newspapermen, pointing out that except for weeklies like *Time* this is very poor, relatively, in the United States. I was told that in Japan business now does pay better, so that journalism is less attractive, and yet the number of applicants tends to go up and up. I got the sense that journalism, like broadcasting or architecture, is a glamorous profession. I asked whether there were columnists and was told that there were no Walter Lippmanns in Japan. I have noticed that there are no by-lines on domestic news stories, although reviewers have by-lines.

The Big Three saturate Japan, competing with each other but not subduing each other; the victims are the local newspapers, which are forced to consolidate.

Nagao thought that Japan was now in her Weimar period and that a right-wing return to power was quite possible. I said I was glad that people were alert to this danger but that it seemed to me, on the basis of all of two weeks in the country, not a terribly serious one, since militarism seemed thoroughly dead in Japan and since conservative businessmen and party politicians were reactionaries only in the sense of wanting to go back to nineteenth-century free enterprise and not in the sense of having samurai ethics and outlook. I agreed that these conservatives wanted a more authoritarian system and a strengthened position for the Emperor, but it didn't seem to me that they were militaristic or fanatical—in fact, the very lack of inner-direction about which Nagao had complained earlier seemed to me to militate against fanaticism. Nagao didn't wholly agree: he felt that in a heightened cold-war climate or in a recession the Rightists could again come to power and the Japanese would bend with the prevailing winds, just as at first they had been for the demonstrations and now had cooled on them. Democracy in the American sense had weak roots in Japan.

Chatting in the bar afterward, Bob Lifton commented on the article of the newspaperman who had been so very critical of Japan, insisting on the lack of inner-direction and individualism. He felt that what I had said about the lack of demagoguery and rampant cowboy individualism was certainly true, and yet that there was something oppressive in the Japanese atmosphere to which these people were responding, even if they didn't give it the right label. Hence, praise from a foreigner, even qualified and largely justified praise, would only lead Japanese intellectuals to think that the foreigner—like all foreigners, really—couldn't understand their country and was naïve; thus, they wouldn't take seriously anything he said, even if it were sensible, but would assume his entire lack of grasp. In general, they are made uneasy by praise. At the same time, any criticism of America is likely to be misunderstood, he thought, even by the most discriminating, unless it is put in perspective at the same time by criticism of the Communist countries. For everyone has to belong to a group, and if one doesn't belong to the American group—which in Japan is assumed to be monolithic—then, of course, one must belong to the enemy camp.

This is especially true since humor and paradox, hard enough to understand in the United States, seem hardly to exist here. Thus, Bob felt that, even with such an exceptionally sensitive, intelligent, and cosmopolitan group as these newspaper editors, it was quite possible that I would be misunderstood, though he thought that much of what I had said and my candor would nevertheless get across.

I suppose that the Japanese sense of inferiority leads to the assumption that any praise cannot be really meant or must be from a stupid and incomprehending person, while at the same time the assumption by the Japanese that they are unique and cannot be understood by the outsider is, of course, enhanced by the presence of a naïvely admiring foreigner. Perhaps one need not criticize the Soviet Union in the same breath as one criticizes the United States, but it is important to stress the many-sidedness and complexity of American life, although even then, in the skewed perception of one's hearers, not at all unique to Japan of course, it is the criticisms that conform to their prejudices which may stick in their minds.

Tokyo, October 12

This morning Matsumoto arranged for us to see Mr. Hirokoshi, president of one of the large automobile companies. We were driven, not to one of the plants, but to the downtown headquarters in Tokyo—a building in the very best modern taste, with the best modern gadgetry (the elevator doors open automatically, but in this still low-wage society, they are not automatically run). On every floor there are attendants sitting—often in pairs—to bow and lead the visitor on to the office, where he is again met by two or three hostesses. We were ten minutes early and were shown into a stunning reception room with handsome easy chairs around a low table; there was a balcony from which one could look across at the Diet building a few blocks away—it looks a little like the Boston Customs House. A secretary brought us green tea and we were then ushered into the executive's enormous office, also stunningly modern.

Judging by too few examples, the Japanese business class is stouter than the population at large, and Hirokoshi is no exception. He is in his sixties but looks much younger. Everyone here retires at fifty-five—a grave problem—except the boss, who doesn't have to retire until he cares to. Hirokoshi had just returned from the United States, where he had met with General Motors officials, talked to a Chamber of Commerce meeting, and ended up with a few days' vacation in Hawaii. Shortly he was to play host to a group of American businessmen who were visiting Tokyo. From the whole conversation it seemed clear that he was a "business statesman" of the American type, spending at least as much time on affairs outside his company as on those within. He is an officer of the Japanese equivalent of the National Association of Manufacturers and is active also in in-service training programs and in the Conservative Party. Waiting to be screened after the war, like a good many others, Hirokoshi had worked on a farm cultivating rice, and he had entered the company from banking when it barely existed, its plants largely destroyed by bombing, and no money in the till. Starting almost from scratch, he had managed to put the company together.

Feeling my way cautiously, I asked him about politics, and here again he struck me as very "American"; in general I have gotten the impression that Japanese businessmen who finance the Conservative Party politicians regard them as a low order of life, inferior in ability and integrity, trying to please the voters.

I asked him where he recruited entrants into management, and he denied that he favored any particular university. They give an examination, for which there are a tremendous number of applicants, and then, as is customary in Japan, when someone is taken on, he is really taken on for life. Hirokoshi did the unusual thing, when he came into the company, of firing a number of people—very "un-Japanese" of him.

We got onto the subject of unions, and here as in other ways our host, in spite of all his modernity, impressed me as being much more of a tycoon than a comparable metropolitan American manager would be. He felt hamstrung by the union, forced to pay what actually amount to large social-security benefits, subject to twenty-four-hour flash strikes, and to the check-off, which he says allows the union to make political progress through moneys that he has to collect.

To limit the unions, the pattern here has been to avoid taking on permanent employees, and all the life-long responsibilities this entails, by hiring so-called temporary workers who may work for as long as three or four years. But, Hirokoshi said, these too were being unionized and he was worried about this development, which would limit his flexibility. He pointed to the bonuses, which are something like 30 per cent of a year's salary or more—these are group incentives.

He had the same misgivings about today's youth and its lack of ambition. And he was troubled about the lack of responsible politicians. He referred again to the failings of the Conservative Party and to the restrictions placed on the imports he would like to make in order to be able to export in the future. He said that the Bank of Japan had a tight-money policy; one of his sons works for the Finance Ministry, but he and his son don't agree. I said I guessed that was a sign of the times.

I at one point asked him about trading with Red China, and he paused for a minute and said he didn't think it was likely or possible because the goods they delivered were not of good quality—perhaps there were ideological reasons in the background, but he didn't mention these.

Our next appointment was with Mr. Koremitsu, an official of the Finance Ministry. Outside the ornate, Victorian-style building were parked many Cadillacs with chauffeurs polishing the spotless cars. They carry little pails in the trunk for this and little brushes for specks of dust. We went in a carpeted side entrance and found our way down vast corridors to Koremitsu's office. We were greeted by the interpreter, who, it turned out, had gone to one of the better denominational colleges in the United States, through a Methodist or Presbyterian connection in Tokyo; actually, he wasn't used much, since Koremitsu spoke excellent English.

The office where we met was Victorian too: overstuffed chairs with antimacassars, a painting of a Dutch canal on the wall—décor such as I imagine one might find in the mansion of a very high British official in Singapore or perhaps of a Dutchman in Djakarta.

In talking with Koremitsu I got a better or less inadequate picture of the precarious situation of the Japanese economy. On the one side, small protectionist American manufacturers put pressure on the United States government to reduce imports from Japan. Japan itself tries to deal with this by a voluntary restraint on exports of textiles and other goods, only to have Hong Kong increase its exports—and make the Japanese exporters furious. At the same time, imports from the United States are growing enormously as the result of the "leisure boom"—a common phrase—which has created pressure for importing consumer goods (such as the citrus fruits or Brazilian coffee on display everywhere) and beyond that for the steel and machinery to manufacture their own products. The big industrialists, perhaps not totally averse to what I like to call conspicuous production, want to expand, and this often requires importing American machine tools; for although Japan has of course its own machine-tool industry, it needs American ones to start certain new lines. Thus, the big industrialists are constantly chafing at restraints on imports.

Koremitsu illustrated the sense of concern over what sober Japanese economists and financiers consider the reckless overbuying of the producers, repeating what had been said to us already, that Japan has no natural resources whatsoever and has to depend on skill and hard work. He felt that these human resources were being undermined by the consumer orientation of present-day Japan.

Koremitsu brought up the problem of retirement at fifty-five. He said that much of his time and effort went into finding jobs, often part-time, for older employees who were being retired on a pension which would hardly pay the rent in high-rent Tokyo; while he in turn is besieged by people looking for consultant jobs and other part-time work who have been retired elsewhere. I get the sense that, throughout Japanese economic life, there are many supernumerary personnel who are given honorary titles in order to keep them afloat (even though they may sink the company or the economy). There is a feeling that the retirement age of fifty-five must give way. The contradiction of paternalism and impersonality, of nepotism and meritocracy, is very sharp here.

We got onto the subject of the Conservative Party politicians, and Koremitsu said that they were a poor lot, of low ability and little integrity. He complained that the young don't go into politics, and I suggested half humorously that business paid too well. At one point he tried in a general way to get my judgment as to economic prospects in the United States and said that he hoped—and this seemed to be general—that American prosperity would lower the power of the lobbies against imports from Japan and would therefore permit the Japanese economy to improve.

As I reflect on our discussion with both these men, I realize even more fully than before we came what it means to depend entirely on international trade, where every gallon of oil, every bit of steel, must be paid for by exports. Indeed, as standards of consumption rise, highways begin to eat up the 12 per cent or so of Japanese land that is arable; and the move away from rice and noodles and fish to a more "Western" diet of bread and dairy products and beef also means either imports or uneconomic use of land. I begin to see why the spectacular growth rate of the Japanese economy and the promise of the Prime Minister to double the national income within the next few years are not regarded as unmixed blessings by the Conservatives, let alone by the Left.

As we were shown out through long corridors and down an Otis elevator to our car waiting at the side entrance, the interpreter asked if I could tell him briefly what was at stake in the Berlin crisis. Among

DR

intelligent people of all shades of opinion there is great fear of the unquiet Americans, whether in the international arena—and the whole struggle over Berlin seems at once distant and mysterious even to highly educated Japanese—or in terms of such immediately relevant matters as tariff policy. We are getting the impression that, in spite of all the evidences of boom—of construction going up everywhere you look, of new cars crowding the streets, of television antennas high over the poorest thatched roofs—there is disquiet.

ETR

This evening we went to dinner with the Sekiharas, who live in a distant part of town. Before we left International House, the taxi driver was given five minutes or so of detailed instruction by one of the young men at the desk. We were to go to the Liftons' first, pick them up, and go on from there. We realized, as we listened to the young assistant explaining, and the long discussions he got into with the driver, and the many questions and further explanations, that this was no simple matter. In fact, we discovered that in Japan no house has an exact address, it has only a vague and approximate location, for there are no street names or numbers. (We had already learned that we must always carry with us our map of the city showing the location of International House so that we could show a taxi driver where to take us.) We thought this driver looked rather like a country bumpkin from Hokkaido, and indeed we had been told that this was so, that many taxi drivers did not know their way around the city; at last we got into the cab, with some doubts. We had been to the Liftons' once before, and the driver seemed to be going in the right direction and things looked vaguely familiar. It is a long way, and the man did well, stopping only twice to ask the way. We recognized at last the very narrow street with high wooden and bamboo fences on either side where the Liftons live, and we recognized their gate. This area is like a quiet country village, the roofs of the houses nestling behind garden fences in the branches of squat trees, the gates as various as the fences. We thought, as we waited for the Liftons to come out, that the fences are not barricades, as in Europe or in Mexico, but rather they are partitions for privacy, for the small world within. The Liftons assured us, as they got into the taxi, that the Sekiharas lived nearby.

The streets in this area are very narrow. Sometimes our taxi had to stop behind the inevitable telegraph pole to let another car pass; we drove much too fast, as usual, for all the hazards, including pedestrians and bicycles. After a while we realized that we were going around in a maze and not getting any nearer to our destination. The Liftons thought we must be very near, but finally the driver stopped at the police box, a sort of cement pillbox where a policeman or two always can be found (the police are familiar with their "villages" and know where everyone lives). The driver came back quite confident, and soon we were driving through all the same streets again. The Liftons realized we had missed the street by one—it is necessary to count very carefully. Through all this I was reminded of watching, on our walk a few days ago, two fire engines clanging down the street, then branching off in different directions. By going in concentric circles they might find the place of the fire, or by looking for smoke. It seems extraordinary that this sort of village arrangement can exist in such a great city—perhaps it is only possible in a society that values aesthetics more than rationality. When after the war, with most of the city destroyed, they had to rebuild it, they kept the jumble of winding streets as they were.

We finally arrived at the Sekiharas, and while we waited to be let in, we noticed the beauty of the overhanging roof, the pebbles and bamboo clumps on one side of the doorway, and the polished wood of the walls and door. We were greeted by our hosts—he a grave, sensitive, and frail-looking man and she robust and vigorous. Leaving our shoes on the stone step, we entered a modern room, one whole side of which opened onto the garden, lit up now in the night, so that it seemed a deep, soft, and green extension of this white room. A pool just outside, with darting goldfish, seemed to be a part of the room, and the water running into the pool, splashing over the stones, filled the room with sound. The whole effect of the room, with its modern furniture, its white fireplace, was a blending of the cosmopolitan and the Japanese, like the meal, which began with cocktails and hors d'oeuvres, then went on to raw fish and delicacies such as fresh ginger root, soybean soup, meat and vegetables, rice and pickle, then on top of all this, apple pie and green tea. It was served buffet style.

We sat in comfortable chairs eating from our knees or from small individual tables. Mr. Sekihara talked about architecture in Japan. Architecture is not a field that the elite goes into as sometimes with us. The names of architects in Japan are hardly known, because architecture was not an individual's creation until very recently. All traditional Japanese houses are alike in form and specifications; they differ only in size and number of rooms. In this sense, all Japanese houses are "prefabricated"; lumber can be bought already cut to size for replacement of any part. And so there were only builders, not architects. But with the coming of architects from the West and with the new tech-

ETR

nology and new materials, Japanese architects have recently come into existence. They are self-taught, as is Sekihara himself. He spoke of the tremendous influence of Frank Lloyd Wright in Japan—yet we thought the influence had been all the other way! Sekihara mentioned the corner window and the garden as an extension of the house, as examples of his influence. Sekihara at last got onto the subject of his own work; we had seen the stunning hotel he designed in the Hakone Mountains when we drove up from Ninomiya.

Sekihara told us that he had worked under Raymond until he began on his own. Raymond was one of the first Western or modern architects to work in Japan; but Sekihara is very Japanese and loves the details of the traditional Japanese house, as is evident in all his work. He told us that in designing the hotel we had seen he had built scaffolding on the site at various heights to see what the view would be from the different levels; he had wanted the view from the dining room, with glass windows all around, to look on one side into the trees and on another side up into a mountain pass and on the third side down into the valley.

DR

I found Sekihara a really extraordinary man, vigorous and sensitive: like some of the best architects, he combines sensibility with a businesslike understanding.

He said that when he was studying architecture, before the war, all the models by which he was taught were European: classical Greek, Gothic, Baroque, and so on. Frank Lloyd Wright had been in Japan but had apparently not had any influence until "Japanese" architecture began to spread to the United States and in that way back to Japan. Sekihara was very depressed and left school. During the war years he was given but one building to design, a sanitarium for soldiers and others. He wasn't drafted at the outset because he was married, and then his draft-board building was bombed and the records were destroyed, so that he, so to speak, didn't exist.

I asked him how in fact he existed during the war years, and he said that it was in a way a very good time. People lived with hardly any money and a great sense of community. A friend of his who had nothing to do, because many businesses came to an end during the war in the near-total mobilization of Japan—greater than in any other belligerent except possibly the U.S.S.R.—anyway, this friend would go fishing every day and would bring back quantities of fish for Sekihara, who would in turn give some of it to his friends. Nobody bought new clothes or new anything. There wasn't the status rivalry in consumption that there is at present. He said that when he read of air raids elsewhere he was sorry for the people, but he himself found the air raids quite endurable after a while. Being an architect, he had had a shelter dug underground for his family, but often he wouldn't sleep in it because he assumed from the pattern of bombing that bombs would fall somewhere else—as he put it, he took chances on the rationality of the American Air Force. He realized that it sounded strange to say all this and that at first the bombings were terrible but that one gradually grew accustomed to them.

Bob Lifton and I both remarked at this that Herman Kahn and others, in talking about nuclear warfare, appear not to take account of this slow acculturation to disaster, but assume that if the same number of people are killed or buildings destroyed, it doesn't matter whether it is done in one hour or in three years, whereas it was clear from what Sekihara had said that his family learned to live with danger and adapt to it over the course of time. He spoke of the air raids rather in the way that I've heard a number of Englishmen do—not with bravado but with acceptance and even a certain amount of excitement in the experience and in the beauty of the bombs and fires amid the terror. Also, there was rationing, which made it possible to get whatever there was cheaply, and one could live with hardly any money.

Later he spoke of the organization of his office. He has about twelve draftsmen, engineers, and others working with him, and he has recently found a building in downtown Tokyo into which he can move and expand. But he doesn't want to become big—not like the firms with 300 architects or the architects who work for the big contractors. Many young architects begin with him and then go out on their own, although some prefer the security of staying with him. Sekihara teaches at the Institute of Fine Arts and finds assistants among the students there; but his work is also known outside Japan and people write to him from the United States, Yugoslavia, Mexico, and many other places, asking to work with him. I asked him whom he admired. He spoke of Le Corbusier, Mies van der Rohe, and others. He had recently been in Mexico and much admired the Mexican architects. They had, in fact, urged him to come. I gathered from what he had said that he had been first entirely "modern" in the Bauhaus style and had then, in a pattern that is characteristic of present-day Japan, tried to synthesize the past with the present and future, going back to the

DR

traditional cities of Japan, Kyoto, and Nara for illumination and refreshment of spirit.

The lack of city planning and zoning in Tokyo means that he must abandon the beautiful house where we had dinner, because a number of industries have moved into the area: there is no in-migration, as with us, of ethnic groups, but rather of shops and small factories, so that what was once a peaceful suburb is now crowded and noisy. His wife has been looking everywhere for a place to move to, not finding any. Real estate in Tokyo is incredibly expensive; it is the one big city, as Nat Glazer noted, where, as in the London of a generation ago, people still insist on having their own plot of ground and where building has not gone up in the air.

Kyoto, October 13

We got up early to take the train for Kyoto. Matsumoto is accompanying us—we could not persuade him not to. Mrs. Matsumoto came with us in their car to see us off. The courtesies of the Matsumotos are fabulous.

The trains here are like the best planes in the United States: there is very tasteful decoration, trays by one's seat where one can be served if one doesn't care to go into the dining car; enough room between the rows of chairs (even if one is not in the Japanese equivalent of the Pullman) so that one can lean back or get in and out without disturbing one's neighbor; as a train fan it's a delight to me to see railroads that are really used and where passenger service is taken seriously. Leaving Tokyo, we passed dozens and dozens of commuter trains, and even after an hour's fast ride out, there were still commuter trains and the station platforms were often as crowded as a New York subway platform. The line from Tokyo to Kyoto and Osaka is one of the main lines of Japan, and where one is not going through villages, rice paddies, or mountains, one is going through larger and smaller industrial constellations and modern plants—a little like the ride from Boston to Baltimore or Washington.

ETR

The train passed through the outskirts of Tokyo and Yokohama, into hilly country and small enclosed valleys—flat land, every bit of which is cultivated. Then we came out to the sea and for miles followed this spectacular coast, reminding me of southern Italy, with cliffs and great rocks jutting into the sea, stretches of beach with fishing villages here and there, then again mountainous peninsulas. The train plunged through a series of tunnels and after a while we were inland. We crossed huge plains of rice fields, with mountains barely visible in the haze of the distance. Where the harvest was finished, the straw was hung up to dry on long poles looking like thatched fences dividing the fields.

Whole families seemed to be working together in the fields, men, women, and children, their bicycles or motorcycles lying near the paths, and a straw hut put up for shelter. Some were wearing large pointed straw hats, the women wore blue and white kerchiefs and smocks over pantaloons. The work looked hard: small, slow motions with sickles in boggy ground—these immense spaces and plains slowly, patiently covered, little by little, by laborious movements of human feet and hands. As our train sped by, I could not help but feel the contrast between the silent static people seen from moment to moment through glass, their endless task stretching out to the horizon, and the modern world of the railroad, new factories, high-tension towers like robots carrying wires, and highways in the process of being built by yellow bulldozers at work on mounds of earth—all this an incongruous invasion of the ancient landscape.

When we arrived in Kyoto, the first things we saw were the modern buildings around the railroad station, one of them being the new post office which Matsumoto told us is the most up to date in the world, all automatized with pneumatic sorting, etc. The city struck us, as we drove from the station to the hotel, as open and flat, with its gridiron plan and wide streets. It seemed dusty and hot and our impression was not at all of the beautiful old city we expected. It was less interesting and charming than Tokyo with its irregularities and its hills, winding streets, and little villages. Here was an imperial city, grandly planned after the Chinese model in the eighth century, noisy and crowded and somehow disappointing. As we drove past the Imperial Palace (hidden behind walls and trees), there were crowds of people and police, because, we were told by our driver, the Crown Prince and Princess were coming. However, when we got to the Miyako Hotel on the edge of the city that abruptly ends because of the mountains rising up steeply behind, we had other impressions. Here, from our windows was a broad panorama: we could see purple-black tile roofs, temples, walls, distant pagodas sticking up against misty hills, not far away a red Shinto gate, and beyond all this a great irregular semicircle of mountains.

Kyoto, October 14

Matsumoto, who loves the art and the temples, gardens, and palaces of Japan and who worries that we have too little time to see these things, took us this morning to visit the Shugakuin Imperial Villa. It is a large estate in the foothills, at one time the summer palace of the Emperor. While the Japanese house is standard, so to speak, varying only in size and beauty of workmanship, the Japanese garden is a thing of infinite variety depending on the terrain and the imagination of the maker. The main villa, just inside the gate where one enters the estate, was surrounded with huge trees so that it seemed almost hidden by the forest, yet beautifully cared for, a wooded garden.

When the tour began, we proceeded through the woods, crossing a small pool on stepping stones, then climbing rustic stone steps between trees and rocks. There were occasional stone lanterns by the path and one magnificent large Korean stone lantern. Finally, as the path led uphill, we came to a gate leading through a bamboo fence into the next garden, whose character was quite different, with dwarf trees and shrubs. There was an exquisite pavilion here, into which we could glance through the open *shoji*, all polished and empty with some fine scrolls on the walls. The highest pavilion, quite small and simple, was in a meadow bordered in back by the forest and in front quite a distance below by a large pond. This pavilion we could go into, for it was bare and plain, clearly a place for meditation, for writing haiku poems perhaps. As I stayed there and felt its quality, I thought I understood better what Bernard Leach meant by the value attached to contemplation in Japan.

This afternoon we were taken over to the University of Kyoto, where Dave was to give a lecture as part of the program of the Sociology Meetings which are being held there this week. This famous university is quite a jumble of buildings in many styles, some Victorian brick, some Spanish stucco. When the university was built, the Japanese had no architecture suitable for large institutional purposes—the magnificent Tokugawa fortresses I suppose were hardly appropriate—and so they borrowed the Western architecture of the time, but in its least attractive forms. We entered one of the brick buildings and were shown into the office of the chairman of the department, where a number of professors were gathered, all rather elderly, portly men. There were overstuffed armchairs arranged around a table, and after the introductions everyone sat down and was offered a cup of tea. We have learned now to expect this and find it a lovely custom. However, given the few minutes that we had and the difficulty in understanding one another, the exchanges between us and our hosts were meager indeed.

When the tea was over, everyone filed into the lecture hall nearby. It was not large, holding perhaps three hundred people or so, but it was packed. I had the impression from their youthful faces and dark uniforms that most of the audience were students—Dave tells me there are only about a hundred sociologists in Japan, and so this would explain the preponderance of students. It was an attentive audience and a fascinating one. For Dave this lecture, his first confrontation with Japanese students, was an anxious occasion. He did not anticipate having to lecture without an interpreter; but there was none—it was not clear why, perhaps because sociologists supposedly knew English—and this was unfortunate, for watching their faces from where I sat on the stage, it did not seem to me that what he was saying was getting across. He was lecturing on "*The Lonely Crowd* Reconsidered," being quite critical of it; he had been assured of their familiarity with the book; but when he said something startling or witty, there was almost no reaction. He himself wondered whether the audience, assuming that many could follow the English, would be able to assimilate so quickly an author's detachment from "his own" work, his making criticisms and expressing changes of view rather than defending the book. It might even have seemed to them, in their compartmentalized way of looking at things, that he was not being "serious," that he was not speaking for any sociological school. Yet at the end, to my surprise, there was great applause. Then there followed a question period, with several questions well expressed—one from a girl, though I couldn't see more than two or three young women in the whole audience. After the questions there was more applause and then the chairman introduced the other speaker of the day, Georges Balandier, the distinguished French anthropologist. A perfectly charming man, his English sounded so French that it was barely understandable to us and certainly less so to the audience. It seemed to me wasteful and unimaginative of our hosts to make such poor use of their foreign visitors, for it was hardly more than a ceremonial occasion. At the end the chairman gave a speech of thanks and presented the speakers with gifts and me with flowers. There was bowing and applause—all a wonderful example of the Japanese "guest culture."

Kyoto, October 15 *DR*

At breakfast Matsumoto joined us to discuss the big lecture I am to give at the end of this week in Osaka. He has both high hopes for the occasion and considerable anxieties—hopes that I can speak to the Japanese condition and anxieties that I may be misunderstood, inadequately interpreted, or say something that will affect the precarious balance of Japanese-American relations. Matsumoto has had long experience of those relations and in the course of talking with him many interesting things have come out. We discovered, for instance, that when General MacArthur was here he saw in all perhaps a dozen Japanese. His twice daily trip from his home to the GHQ was heralded by soldiers with guns at the ready and was an impressive sight for many Japanese. But MacArthur appears to have offended many more Japanese by having his picture taken with the Emperor in a way that emphasized his height and the Emperor's smallness; and when the Emperor was in formal attire, MacArthur was dressed in casual style with open-necked shirt, smoking a corn-cob pipe. This apparent effort to show his superiority created very ambivalent reactions in the Japanese, the more so as the Emperor had never before permitted a picture to be taken of himself with anyone except the Empress.

After breakfast we visited the Imperial Palace, and as we waited for our turn to take the guided tour, we watched groups of school children in uniform, brought by dozens of buses, being shepherded through the huge grounds. When the children saw us they would shout in a friendly way, "Hello-goodbye"—and wave eagerly. Evey and I would wave and call back, but then they would go on and the next wave would come and repeat the process until we grew weary. Many of these children had ridden all night in buses to come here, but we did not see a quarrelsome or unruly or even discontented child.

ETR

The Imperial Palace has walls within walls. The grassy area inside the first wall was once a moat, and here people were strolling and picnicking. As we entered the inner gate into the courtyard in front of the Coronation Hall, I had an almost kinesthetic sense of horizontal space: it was empty and white with the sun shining on the evenly raked pebbles; it seemed huge, suggesting a room rather than a courtyard, with the gates, walls, and the long, low pavilion under the ceiling of the

ETR

sky, small trees on either side of the entrance looking like potted plants. The coronation pavilion itself is magnificent yet simple, delicate yet savage: these huge, deep roofs of layer upon layer of bark (resembling thatch) have something primitive about them—yet the lattices and sliding screens beneath these roofs create a contrast of great sophistication and delicacy, not to speak of the intricacy and richness of the detail, the brass studding in the great doors, the polished wood, the workmanship of the décor. There were other equally beautiful pavilions in other courtyards. And beyond the walls was a large garden with a pond, pebbled shores, and arched bridge.

DR

We had lunch at a nearby restaurant with Professor Suzuki of Kyoto University, Professor Murata, and Matsumoto. We were shown into a second-floor *tatami* room looking out onto a very small garden with one carefully stunted tree. In the center of the room was a table with a little gas stove, such as we are familiar with from Japanese restaurants at home—but the first such we've seen here—for cooking sukiyaki. By now Evey and I know how to arrange ourselves in a Japanese room, with my back to the ornamental recess and Evey at my side, as the guests of honor. Evey, however, was served first—a sign of Westernization.

We learned that Suzuki, though he teaches astronomy, is actually a kind of ecologist. He has advanced a theory of the development of feudalism in Japan and Western Europe as being based on small river valleys, which permitted local lords to retain independence; in contrast, he points to the centralized despotisms of China and Russia, where the huge river valleys encouraged an imperial and bureaucratic pattern to emerge. He has been an explorer in Thailand and elsewhere. He often writes and speaks for the mass media and also appears to be close to the Institute of Humanistic Studies at Kyoto, whose members include many of the distinguished men with whom we shall talk in the next several days.

Suzuki apologized for his poor English and said he hoped we wouldn't mind if Murata acted as interpreter. We run into this apology constantly: nobody expects Americans to know Japanese, but many Japanese apologize not only for their poor English but for that of their countrymen. (Indeed, Matsumoto told us at breakfast that efforts to introduce the new Michigan methods of language training into the teaching of English in the high schools and colleges here had been foiled by the textbook publishers, who felt that their investment would be jeopardized, and by the high-school teachers themselves, who felt that they would be made obsolete by the new methods. He had tried to cope with this by running annual summer seminars in the new methods of language training in English. But after years of effort he still felt he had made almost no headway. He was told, for instance, that a new dictionary would be necessary. The old dictionaries would be put out of business. Matsumoto also feels that the lack of fluency in English greatly hampers Japanese foreign policy, making it difficult for instance to have good men at the U.N., hampers economic policy by limiting export possibilities to the United States, and hampers cultural possibilities also by limiting contact with people such as myself. Of course, a great many people can read English who cannot handle it conversationally.)

After a while we got into a discussion of political matters and I asked Suzuki how he voted. He said he didn't vote—there was no party that really pleased him. In general, many intellectuals feel as he does. He spoke of the veto groups in Japanese politics and how similar they were to the American, except that there didn't seem to be any Adlai Stevensons or Senator Fulbrights. I asked Suzuki whether his "rightist" views made it difficult for him to write for the popular press, and he said that if he only said a sentence or two he would be misunderstood to be plainly a Rightist and would have no audience; but if he could explain his views at length about the dialectic between tradition and modernity, he could be understood and listened to.

I wanted to know more about Japanese academic life and how university groups like that of Kyoto functioned under a gerontocracy. (I was thinking of some of the older men at my lecture yesterday, formalistic and grave, looking a bit like war lords, heavy-set and solid, though without the energy of the industrialists we had met.) It was explained that before the war the government universities, such as Kyoto, were under the Ministry of Education; but the Foreign Office had set up the Institute of Humanistic Studies at Kyoto in order to make people familiar with foreign cultures and especially with China—relations with China being both important and complicated. The Foreign Ministry gave a great deal of freedom to the Institute. After the war, however, it seemed logical to transfer the Institute back under the Ministry of Education, and the result had been a lessening of fluidity and freedom. Suzuki himself, although a man of distinction and renown, is still an associate professor, and since the holder of the chair of full professor in his university is only three years older than he, he expects to remain in that status. Murata is an assistant—not even an

DR

assistant professor. He has been here eight or ten years, has published a great deal, and is well known.

To be sure, as I discovered from him later, his being well known without being a full professor is held against him; although he has done a great deal of serious and scholarly work, he is criticized as a mere "journalist," though perhaps to a slightly lesser degree than he would be in the United States. His promotion and that of men such as Suzuki will be slower because they have outside reputations—"outside" in terms both of field and of public. Murata has been offered jobs paying much better (what he earns at the university will not even pay his rent) at private universities in Tokyo where he says his name would attract parents and be part of the promotional literature. But naturally he doesn't want this; for one thing, he wouldn't have the students he has at Kyoto. Since the end of the war, with the growth both of industry and of social science, faculty members are in demand as consultants, and he, for instance, has been asked about consumer habits and is an advisor to NHK, the broadcasting company. I am more and more impressed with the penetration and originality of his understanding of Japan and with his seriousness as a scholar and thinker; like a few other Japanese we have met who have been in America, he is candid and open and less formal than is the Japanese academic norm.

ETR

Kyoto, October 16

Strolling through a park with Professor Murata and Professor Osabe after lunch, we got onto the subject of movies. Osabe said that in *Ikiru* and *Rashomon* the presentation of different points of view is a typically traditional Japanese form, but not knowing this it had struck me as a very interesting psychological innovation. In *Ikiru* the different points of view are finally glossed over in a consensus of the group of acquaintances and friends about the man after his death. In *Rashomon* there are not only the three main characters, but three is a pattern throughout in terms of characters and setting: there are visually the three bands, for example, the earth, the wall, and the sky, recurring in the shots of many of the scenes. Three is a meaningful number for the Japanese, he said, and this theme of three exists throughout their culture: there is the go-between, there are many games with three alternatives. Three also expresses ambivalence, as well as non-competitiveness and an attempt to avoid conflict. There is, for example, a balancing toy, *yagirobe*, that is popular.

On a street with a narrow sidewalk we walked in two's again. Osabe

ETR

and I, speaking French, got onto the subject of aesthetics. He said that in Japanese high culture, the moral and the aesthetic are one, that is, the aesthetic takes the place of the moral; but in folk culture the aesthetic gives way to the moral. As we discussed this I thought of similarities in our own high culture: Ezra Pound's winning the Bollingen Prize; and I thought of our popular culture, our comic strips where the good guys have to win and the bad guys must be punished. And yet I had the feeling that the Japanese carry these things further than we do. I was reminded of the discussion with Miss Yamamoto about the students who felt that murder was moral if it was sincere—sincerity being for them both an aesthetic value and a moral one.

DR

Professor Osabe, who is an expert on Stendhal, teaches French literature but is really interested in Japanese popular culture and contemporary life. He is an exceptionally lively man, perhaps thirty years old, who started a long argument by saying that Japan was becoming a feminine nation under the control of women. He spoke of the protests of women against violence on television and in street processions. He felt that the traditional maleness of Japanese men was being undermined. Like Suzuki, he shares certain cultural values with the Right Wing, but not their political values. If he had to vote, he says, he would vote Socialist—an indication, I think, of the lack of a true conservative party here, for he would vote conservative if there were a party that wanted to conserve what was best in Japanese culture rather than simply what was old or reactionary.

I argued with him, saying that I came from a culture which made a cult of masculinity and that I felt that the sensitivity of which Japanese men were capable was something admirable. I pointed to the small *sake* cups out of which we were drinking, and in general the tiny portions served on an endless array of beautiful dishes in a Japanese meal, as against the huge plates or huge coffee cups of the Harvard Club. He said that there was no connection between smallness and femininity, and as the discussion went on, it became clear that he used the word "feminine" for almost everything he didn't like in modern Japan.

We had a very exciting talk, during our walk after lunch, about the work of the director Kurosawa, who made *Rashomon* and *Ikiru.* (I've asked a number of Japanese intellectuals whether they have seen the latter film and hardly any of them have; they say they don't go to movies—or that movies are for children. There is a small student documentary-film group, I am told, at the University of Kyoto, but nothing like the interest in films among equivalent American students.)

Later in the afternoon there was a reception for us given by the Matsumotos and the Kyoto Committee at the International House Liaison Headquarters, with perhaps fifty guests. In the receiving line, when people bow we are tempted to bow to them, but they expect to shake hands with us; and so we often end up both bowing and shaking hands. They never seem to expect that Americans should learn their language—or their customs. (They learn in school to use Western cutlery and often to cook Western food, and I have seen advertisements for lessons in Western table manners.) There was tea and coffee, but no alcohol was served. Most of the people were faculty members from Kyoto University, but there were some from Doshisha, as well as a man from the British Consulate, a sociologist from the Municipal University of Osaka, several press people, and Mrs. John Reinhardt, the wife of the attaché of the American Cultural Center here. People only stopped for a minute or two as they went through the line, and when the line broke up, it was hard to know what to do or how to move about. I took my place in a corner where I saw a young man whom I had met at the Sociology Meetings and who teaches in the Education Department at Kyoto. He remarked that most of the students there don't go into teaching, any more than the law students go into law. A member of the law faculty asked me what I thought of Justice Brandeis, and when I said that I respected his ideas but didn't especially like him personally, one of the older sociologists said, with astonishment, how candid I was—the older people, at least here, seem to gulp if there's anything in the least critical or impolite.

In making small talk, people are very polite (as in many cross-cultural encounters). They assume that this isn't one's first visit to Japan, but when it turns out that it is, they ask where one has been and how long and so on. Some people seem to have memorized a few sentences of politeness and if one tries to go beyond this, assuming that they understand English, one gets into an impasse and a deathly silence.

One man with whom Evey and I talked looked very "American" and turned out to have been at Bowdoin; his father had wanted him to be a Buddhist priest but he had broken away—his father is a priest and is always putting pressure on him. The longest conversation I had was with a professor of classical Chinese poetry who had just come back from talking with scholars in Hong Kong. I asked him about the interest of students in modern China. He himself has about five students in his seminar, and another man who teaches historical Buddhism has three or four. But a magazine published in Japanese in Peking, containing many articles on modern China as well as on traditional China, has a circulation in Japan of 100,000, and many students follow it. These men, however, appear to regard the interest in contemporary mainland China as sentimental, i.e., as leftward leaning—though I should add that I still have to meet anyone in Japan, including conservatives, who doesn't criticize American non-recognition of China and indeed fail to comprehend it or see how it can be in America's interest.

People came to the party promptly and left promptly at six. But Evey and I found that after an hour and a half of standing and making small talk we wanted very much to sit down; and with the Liftons and Kato and the Matsumotos we finally did, and had a little after-party party, very relaxed and quiet, before we piled into three cabs to go out to the Katos' for dinner.

Professor Kato has had a young architect build him a house. A student of a student of Tange's, the most famous modern architect in Japan, this architect regards Tange as too "Westernized." The Katos live in a suburb about twenty minutes out on the west side of Kyoto—the west side is better because one gets the morning sun and it is less misty and damp. (The Katos had tried to get into a new housing development where modern architects put up buildings as single competitive demonstrations of their work, but there were about 600 bidders on each house and in the lottery the Katos didn't win.)

The living room is Japanese in the sense that one takes off one's shoes and faces onto a garden, but it is Western in its furniture, its prominent television and hi-fi, its children's bunnies, toys, and Popeye—a combination living room and child's playroom. We had met Mrs. Kato with her husband in the United States in 1955. She stayed in the background in Japanese fashion throughout our evening, joined some of the time by Mrs. Kako, with whom she sat in the living room in a kind of second row. Our friend from lunch, Professor Osabe, was there and we got into further discussions of what was masculine and what was feminine. He talked, as many others have, about the lack of individualism in Japanese culture, the subservience to the group, the lack of vigorous expression of personality. Bob Lifton and I repeatedly raised the question how, if nobody takes responsibility and everybody passes the buck, does as much get done in Japan as is obviously done, namely, the building of an advanced modern industrial society. Bob Lifton described from one of his interviews the process of approval of a minor decision in a big company, where there must be twenty stamps of endorsement so as to spread responsibility if anything goes wrong. Bob himself suggested that such a system allows great power to the subordinates who know their own minds, for they can get things approved by people on top who really pay little attention—he said this was part of the power of the young right-wing extremists before the war, who could push decisions in their direction, although they stood fairly alone. We found no satisfactory answer to our questions—not that intellectuals or anyone else in any society really understands how it hangs together.

In the Japanese fashion, dinner was ordered from outside: three charcoal stoves were brought in with hot dishes of soup and other items such as noodles and macaroni. We sat on the floor Japanese style and dipped our chopsticks into the common pots, made sanitary by the boiling juices. (The Japanese are great hypochondriacs and enthusiasts for sanitation. One can see policemen and bus drivers as well as motorcyclists with masks over mouth and nostrils, such as doctors wear, to prevent breathing germs or dust. Taking off one's shoes is another sanitary precaution. Spotlessness, however, is not uniform—as in Europe, men will urinate in the street, sometimes against a wall and sometimes not. Garbage will sometimes be dumped outside—though since the DDT of the Occupation there are very few flies.)

After supper we looked at Japanese television, and some of it seemed put on to justify Osabe's views as to the feminization of Japanese culture. One program was a traditional Kabuki-type play, the women rushing in to protect the men from each other. Another was an Osaka situation comedy which would have been incomprehensible to us without our interpreters and was nearly incomprehensible to them because of the Osaka dialect and the rapid-fire exchange of talk. There was a weak father who was being pushed around by the mother, who favored a particular suitor for her daughter's hand and had as an ally the father's "fighting friend"—a man with whom the father was constantly quarreling, the two enjoyed quarreling and made a kind of game of it. This was a serial drama—a kind of combination of soap opera and Lucille Ball. Then there was a newscast that was impressive. Newscasters here are not celebrities and subordinate themselves to the news. There was a discussion of the coal miners' strike, with elaborate figures on the decline of coal mining, the coal miners' wages, and so on, intermingled with shots of the mines and the miners. The whole thing was of a high order—indeed, all the programs we watched were technically excellent, including the last one, which was an American-style song-and-dance act—with chorus men dancing to an American song and a girl jazz singer who, like the other Japanese singers we've heard, had many of the vices and few of the virtues of the American model.

Bob Lifton commented on the close ties between mother and son, in connection with the discussion of femininity. Osabe said at one point—I would never have dared ask him—that he was married and had a five-year-old daughter. His wife did not accompany him. It is virtually impossible to get baby-sitters in Japan and Mrs. Kato was able to be with us at dinner only because one of her husband's students had been impressed into service as a baby-sitter for their four-year-old daughter, who came shyly to say good night to us. When Kato took us upstairs to his study, lined with steel bookshelves and filing cabinets and containing a large number of American social-science works, he apologized for his daughter's toys on the floor, saying that he liked to have her playing about on the floor while he was working there. He has another television set in his study—courtesy of one of the broadcasting companies, since he is a television critic for the papers and an expert on Japanese popular culture. Kato said that one reason why he regretted not living in the housing project is that all his present neighbors are of an older generation whose children are at the university and there are no children with whom his daughter can play, whereas, of course, there would be many couples of the Katos' age in the housing project—this seems a very "American" concern.

Three taxis were ordered to take the Liftons, Mrs. Kako, and us back to our several destinations in Kyoto—when we tried to pay the cab at the hotel, the driver got someone who could speak English to explain to us that Kato had already paid him.

In this hotel we have seen several traditional wedding parties, in which the bride is dressed in that antique way and supported by two bridesmaids, since her headgear comes down over her eyes, which must, in any case, look downward; her hair is carefully lacquered, while the back of her neck—the most seductive spot for the traditional Japanese—is left open. The women are all in kimono, some of them extremely expensive, the *obi* alone costing perhaps several hundred dollars, while the men are in cutaways; photographers with old-fashioned tripod cameras and lights are on hand in the corridors.

The Japanese interest in photography seems to be in one aspect part of an aesthetic and artistic heritage which includes ideographic writing; but it is also related to the contemporary interest in gadgetry and to the diary-keeping which is apparently so common here that several manufacturers can make a living by selling notebooks for diaries. It also occurs to me that taking pictures may be a way of mitigating the awkwardness and embarrassment of many social occasions. It provides something to do, and of course the pictures of family groups bespeak the family consciousness of Japan and the need to celebrate and commemorate the ties of kinship and other groupings.

Kyoto lives at a much slower pace than Tokyo: residents of the Kansai area (Kyoto, Kobe, Osaka, etc.) say of Tokyo that it's a nice place to visit but not to stay. Kyoto is a city of a million, living off tourists and the luxury trades: beautiful ceramics, silk weaving, palaces, temples, and Shinto shrines; and processions are endemic. Nevertheless, the University of Kyoto (Kyodai) is in some ways more progressive than Todai or any other university in Japan. Being outside the capital, it escaped close supervision in the pre-war and war years. There are many men of the Left on the faculty. Kyoto has a Socialist mayor (who now runs as an Independent), and, I gather, there is more interest in city planning than elsewhere.

Kyoto, October 17

We left our hotel this morning in what I've come to call our tank, the *Asahi*'s Impala, which looks in contrast to the smaller Japanese cars almost as if it were a Cadillac. Kato and Mrs. Kako were accompanying us on a visit to the Otoyama Company, a little over an hour's drive toward Osaka. We were on a road crowded as always with traffic, one of the main highways of Japan, passing hundreds of buses pouring into Kyoto with tourists and children, while alongside it a new road was being built. As we were passing some of the construction of this new road in which bulldozers were working along with men wielding rakes and shovels, Kato commented that preparing Japan for the Olympic Games in 1964 was one of the ways used by responsible leaders to get things done, just as "in the name of the Emperor" had been used in the Meiji period. Japan had to be cleaned up "for the Olympics." The roads had to be built, the railroads repaired, and so on, and all this was done quite consciously because it avoided individual responsibility for taking the initiative.

We learned about the man we were to see, one of the success stories of contemporary Japanese industrialism: a man who had begun in a small shop and after the war built a huge machine-tool and telephone combine. We stopped first at a modern plant, very much like new suburban American plants, let us say, on Route 128 outside Boston, save that workers' dormitories were part of the complex. Both in layout and in individual design, these plants are handsome, and much additional construction is underway. The last important visitor to the factory, we were told, had been Mikoyan, who had commented on the youthfulness of the workers as compared with the middle-aged Russian workers; this reflects not only the casualties of the war generation but also the fact that nearby farmers have often sent their sons and daughters into the plant. Indeed, until recently, farmers would sell their land to these expanding industrial complexes on condition that jobs in perpetuity be available for their children, an arrangement hard to imagine in more mobile America; and even in Japan the growth of modern, somewhat more impersonal industry has made this difficult and farmers must now accept lump-sum settlements for their property.

We were ushered into the office of Mr. Otoyama, a man in late middle age who has retired from the active, day-to-day direction of the enterprise he has built up. As always, we were bowed in by several hostesses at every point, and we were again the beneficiaries of Japan's pleasant custom of always serving something, no matter how brief or businesslike the visit—coffee this time rather than tea. After introductions to some of the executives, we went off with a man, fluent in English, who was to show us around the plant.

This tour was memorable. I have worked at Sperry Gyroscope, and visited other plants, but this was an experience of a new sort. The plant was beautifully designed and spotless, spacious, and airy (where not air-conditioned, as it was in the sections doing high-precision work, which needed to be dust-free), and with not an item of sloppiness to be found anywhere. As our party went around, nobody seemed to pay the slightest attention to us, in spite of the fact that we were haunted by two photographers from the company taking hundreds of pictures from all conceivable angles for the company's house organ. Indeed, in one part of the plant a movie was being made for the company with klieg lights, a director, and so on, but still people went about their business. The factory rooms and many aisles are decorated with the chrysanthemums and flower arrangements which are so omnipresent here that we have almost come not to see them.

I've never seen such a pace of work: the young girls putting assemblies together, working with pincers or magnets under microscopes—it seemed to me that we were seeing the heart of Japanese productivity. Workers are trained in school for three months to do this work. Girls work on the most detailed operations, while men do the slightly heavier work. There are balconies from which one can observe the plants, and the quiet is extraordinary. Workers don't talk to each other.

There is occasionally music of the Muzak sort, but it is quiet rather than noisy. We watched the way in which the making of neon lights has been mechanized in the highest degree, the carefulness of inspection, the apparently easy and rational flow of work. Kato told us that in white-collar offices in Tokyo there is consistent sabotage. People take two-hour "coffee breaks" without notice, disrupting work, but there is nothing like that here.

In addition to touring a number of plants, we saw the welfare facilities, including a huge hall for games and dances, rooms for various hobbies including flower arrangement, photography, and so on, and quarters for the union—a left-wing union, which nevertheless the management houses. We saw the extremely cheap menu in the cafeteria subsidized by the company, where people could have either pork chops or noodles for 15 or 20 yen (386 yen to a dollar).

Many people come to visit the plant from the underdeveloped countries, for whom it is a model, but very few come from the United States, presumably because Americans assume that we have plants just like this, or disapprove of the paternalism.

In the course of our tour, I inquired about the career line of the managerial group. While some of the top executives are not college men or even high-school graduates, most now come from the universities, from engineering, law, and economics. I asked whether leading industrialists sought to marry their children into the nobility, and I got the impression that although this occurs it is not always clear in such cases which partner is marrying upwards. Titles have been outlawed since the Occupation, although people are still referred to as the former Prince this or the former Baron that. But Kato says that these titles mean far more to the Americans than to most Japanese. On the whole, the self-made Japanese, in contrast to the "low posture" of most of their countrymen, are confident tycoons, polite but not deferential.

At any rate, when we returned from our tour to meet with Mr. Otoyama and his associates, I had begun to wonder what I could ask him—as in all these situations I felt that I was being interviewed no less than he. With little small talk, we got immediately on to serious questions. I said, while Kato translated, that I had visited Corning Glass and Western Electric in the United States but that the pace of work seemed even more intense in his company and that in spite of the strong union I didn't get any impression of slowdown on the part of the workers. (What I had in mind was that in this intensity of work, and in what Osabe calls the "active patience" of the Japanese, lies part of the explanation for the astonishing leaps in productivity.) Otoyama said that it didn't matter how good the work was technically if the heart—putting his hand on his heart—wasn't in the right place and he feared that there was lack of heart among the workers and in Japan generally; he kept recurring to this theme, and indeed the sense of lack of heart or feeling comes up again and again in discussions. Among other things, he seemed to mean by this the difficulty of establishing relations of reciprocity with one's work force: if one "gave" people things, one was always in the position of patronizing them.

I asked about trade with mainland China, and in order to make clear that I wasn't trying to trap him into comments which an American would regard as "subversive," I said that I had long believed that the United States should give food to China in the present shortage. He pounced on this and said that there is a Buddhist proverb: "Before speaking [giving] to someone, one must know who that person is and how it will be received." He felt that an American gift would be regarded by the Chinese as humiliating and would not be well received unless it was given in the right spirit. He went on to generalize and to say this was true of many American efforts to help other peoples and that the good will of Americans should take account of the Buddhist proverb. In this connection I told him a little about the Peace Corps, and the sense I had that many of the students in the Peace Corps had a pretty good sense that they had to receive as well as to give, for instance, in learning about the culture of the country to which they were going. I think he felt that trade with China was a necessary development but a difficult one. Again, I realize that neither on the Right nor on the Left is there *any* fear of China here—there is much more fear of America.

It was perhaps at this point that Otoyama stated his philosophy, namely, that 90 per cent of what one achieves is decided the day one is born and only 10 per cent is one's own personal doing. Indeed, he said that 90 per cent of the fact that we were meeting in this room at this time had been decided when we were born. He said that this was not necessarily a Japanese attitude but his own personal one and he stated it with humility—though he denied that the idea itself was a humble one, but rather an accurate, factual description of how things are. He said that if one has this philosophy, one can relax, because matters are largely out of one's hands. I thought it was astonishing that a self-made man who had had little education and was one of the richest men in the country should talk like this and seem really to believe it, with a combination of self-confidence and unpretentiousness.

We moved for lunch into a large room with a long table and white napery and were seated with Otoyama's quick sense of protocol. I was offered beer or orange juice and said I'd prefer the latter, whereupon everyone was given orange juice, even though beer was available. I said I didn't want to veto anybody's having beer, but all denied that they wanted beer. Otoyama asked if I wanted to take off my coat since it was warm, and when I did, others did. In these "state dinners" there is at least one waiter for every two persons. He hovers about, refilling glasses and taking away used plates. Again, Otoyama and I carried on the sole conversation, with the "retainers" sitting quietly. They were not yes-men, because they never said yes or boo or smiled but seemed impassive.

I said that American self-made men didn't take the attitude that 90 per cent was given in the situation (although in fact I thought this was the proper attitude to take toward one's culture) but assumed that they had done it all themselves without any help from the society. However, I said American philanthropy sought to give back some of the "take" from industrial achievement and that I thought this a good tradition. (This is not the custom in Japan and there is very little concern for the public welfare.) Otoyama talked, as everyone does, about the gap between the young and the old and the lack of heart among the young people. I asked what he thought would happen when all his young workers got older; I explained how older women workers, for example at the Hawthorne Plant of Western Electric, were difficult to move. But he seemed to think that the paternalistic and authoritarian pattern of Japanese industry and the willingness to go along with the group would avoid difficulties of this sort.

I asked about the attitude of the union toward all the benefits and welfare services that he'd provided, and he said that the union and the workers took these for granted. I do think he feels somewhat hurt at being unappreciated in this way; the gap between what he does for his workers and what is done in a small plant is huge. For example, he is intensely preoccupied with safety, whereas from reading the papers it is clear that Japanese mines and many other small businesses which run on a narrower margin are not careful at all.

As Evey and I got up to go, we were presented with two beautifully wrapped gifts. Everything in Japan is wrapped with as much care as if it were a flower arrangement, and these packages were no exception. Everyone then accompanied us down to the entrance. And even after we had gotten into the car, everyone stayed to bow as we drove off. It seemed to me that, apart from other considerations, the bowing and saying of farewells, the gift-giving and studied politeness were efforts to retain in the new impersonal and metropolitan Japan the human relations of an earlier Japan (a theme developed in Jim Abegglen's book on the Japanese factory). Of course, many Japanese resent the strains and pressures that result from having to live at once according to traditional and according to contemporary codes of conduct.

Our two cars set off for the Kori-Danchi, a new housing project near Osaka which is considered one of the best examples of a planned community—a Japanese Park Forest—including five-story apartment houses without elevators (the mailmen struck and refused to deliver to the fifth floor); two-story row houses with small gardens; and independent houses, each of which was designed by a different architect in a competition. As Professor Kato told us earlier, the pressure to get into Kori-Danchi is very great, with six hundred applicants for every vacancy, and distribution by lot. We were received in a small apartment with all modern appliances, save central heating, which barely exists in Japan. "Japanese" elements were the deep bath, the removal of shoes at the door, and the use of *tatami* mats. According to Kato, the *danchi* is the dream of the white-collar class and the model of up-to-date consumer habits—so much so that companies wanting to market new devices begin at this or other housing projects, and there is a great deal of direct-mail advertising sent to them. Interestingly enough, the elementary school in this district is Catholic.

In the central office the manager showed us a relief map of the project, which presently has three thousand families; additional buildings are going up all over. It is carefully planned, with each sub-area containing its own elementary school, meeting hall, supermarket, and other facilities—including in one area a Japanese garden, beginning to be laid out on the still bare and bulldozed earth. The manager rattled off the figures of size and population while I watched people come in to pay rents and make inquiries of the clerks. Many Japanese don't like the concrete of these apartments, for they feel that wood is the traditional and warm building material; the *danchi* are at least as controversial here as similar developments in the United States.

The main shopping center differed from the typical American counterpart in one important respect: the large bookstores in which, besides popular magazines, children's books, and so on, one can find volumes in English as well as many translations from English, German or French, and of course highbrow Japanese books as well.

Outside the pale of the shopping center, in an unoccupied lot, were some makeshift sheds where farm products are sold "illegally"; our host defended this, saying it kept prices competitive in the supermarket and was a cooperative effort of local tenants and farmers. It is of course objected that these informal markets destroy the orderly appearance of the *danchi*, and so a struggle apparently goes on between those who value orderliness and neatness and those with Jane Jacobs' attitude toward urban development.

In the private-homes section were many small houses with gardens and villalike walls (in one, high metal fencing); Japanese architects had competed to build, and there were some very attractive dwellings, but all on a much smaller scale than one might find in a community done by comparable American architects.

As we walked about, I got to chatting with Mr. Kashiwagi, the reporter from *Asahi* who was accompanying us. As it was terribly hot climbing up hills and steps, I asked him if it would be all right as far as the photographer was concerned if I took off my coat; he said it would be better, since the Japanese liked informal poses. (In fact, the picture of Evey and me printed in the next morning's paper had me coatless against the background of the *danchi*.) He spoke excellent English, having majored in English literature at Kyodai (University of Kyoto). He had debated whether to go into academic life or journalism—he turned down a Fulbright to the United States to enter *Asahi*, where he has been for seven years. First, as is the custom, he worked in one of the prefectural outposts and is now on the "social" desk in Osaka, which doesn't mean society news but rather what we would call the city desk: covering everything from murders to foreign visitors. I asked him what he was hoping for in terms of career, and he said that he had the idea that the big bosses were planning a career for him as a foreign correspondent and that he thought he would be moved to the foreign desk in Tokyo. But he felt he had no real control over his fate; the trouble with his life was having to work about a twenty-hour day—*Asahi* has something like thirteen editions. Of course, here he was driving with us, arranging photographs, and wandering around the housing project for several hours, and then he was coming over to Kyoto to interview me later that evening in a more formal way, so that the hours on the job are not always strenuous, but there are too many of them. To get a job on *Asahi*, one takes a stiff examination on the news or editorial side. The photographers come in by a different route: they are mostly amateur photographers who send in their pictures, and if these are liked, they are asked to come on the staff.

Kashiwagi doesn't work with any particular photographer but with whoever is assigned.

He had his formal interview with me in a quiet corner of the hotel lobby after we got back. He was interested in my impressions of Japan and curious as to why, unlike other tourists, we weren't planning to see the various sights, such as nearby Nara. I explained that since our time was short here we had decided to concentrate on the purpose of my visit, that is, modern Japan—seeing people and seeing such things as *danchi*. Knowing that both Japanese and foreigners are supposed to prefer beautiful and quiet Kyoto to ugly and noisy Tokyo, I deliberately launched into praise of Tokyo and the attractions of some of the very metropolitan qualities that offend many "Japan fans." But I added that it was hard for me to see how, as many Japanese believe, they can solve their traffic problem in Tokyo and elsewhere simply by building more roads: the American experience should show that this is no answer. Actually I love both cities, and I didn't want to denounce old Japan in favor of modern Japan. Japan is not an either-or but a both-and culture; still, it is hard for the Japanese to locate foreigners, and they tend to slot people ideologically and politically.

As in my experience with reporters and interviewers in the United States, things I thought important seemed to slide by without Kashiwagi's taking a note down, but he was busily writing when things of no importance were said; I wondered what heresies I had uttered and what misunderstandings I would cause my hosts. I was aware that *Asahi* was anxious for a good story because it would be a way of publicizing my public lecture in Osaka on Saturday afternoon, where, in competition with the opening of the Japanese World Series, they feared a poor turnout. I had debated whether or not to stay away from politics, with which I would deal in the lecture, but in fact I touched on the subject without exciting the reporter's interest. He seemed to be an intelligent and pleasant man, and I enjoyed the opportunity to talk with him. He was especially intrigued by my comments on Japanese children and their apparent gaiety and contentment. Both in my initial press conference and in this interview, I gave an impression of my attitudes which was useful in later encounters with people; for example, my comments on the *danchi*, whether right or wrong in themselves, were more sympathetic than most people expected and perhaps suggested that I was open to unconventional views and was not eager to hear traditional pieties.

After the interview, Kato, Evey, and I had dinner together. He told us about a study that had been done in the Tohoku region of the

DR

actual number of words spoken in a family from dawn to dusk: the wife would say hardly a word, and the husband might get up from the table with the plow over his shoulder as a sign that people were to go out into the fields, and he also would say little. Kato, referring to Ned Hall's book, spoke of the "silent language" of the Japanese—not that we've seen very much of this, since to make the simplest decision seems to require endless conferences and talk, and I have never seen so much back-seat driving in my life. Moreover, when I'm being translated, what has taken me five minutes to say often takes twice as long to be interpreted—partly of course to make things clear but partly because there seems to be a good deal of padding, and people always fear that they don't understand and are saying, "Did I make myself clear?" "Do you get me?" "Am I getting across?" in many different ways. (We were told that when American and Japanese businessmen meet, the Japanese businessman will say repeatedly, "I'm getting you," or "You're coming in clear." The American businessman will take this for acceptance of his views or offers, when it doesn't mean that at all; and then he will feel that he's been double-crossed.)

ETR

Kyoto, October 18

This was a beautiful sunny day. Professor Murata came with his friend Professor Takeuchi, a poetic-looking young man with longish hair, in open shirt and sandals, to take us to see the pottery kilns in a village, Kiyomizu, in the hills above the city. Takeuchi is a scientist by profession, but the folk arts are his hobbies. To many of this group of young scholars, the hobbies seem to be as important as the profession.

The four of us were driven in our *Asahi* limousine on a road that became very narrow and winding as it ascended. It was impossible to pass a car at one point, and we had to back down into another road in order to let it pass. Some of the hairpin curves could be taken only after several backings and turnings. When our friends decided we were near enough, we got out of the car and walked. We were in a community of small, poorish-looking houses; scattered here and there were the tin roofs and tall chimneys of the kilns. We went into one of these dark little houses and found ourselves in a potter shop where a few men—and one or two women—were working with pinkish clay at wheels. At tables others were painting on the pottery to be baked in the kiln. Although these people worked with great skill, their products were not the finest of the folk pottery but simple objects for everyday use, Takeuchi explained. The finished pieces we saw were tasteful in their

ETR

shapes, subdued colors, and suggestion of design, often a sprig of branch or flower.

We went outside to the kilns, which seemed rather makeshift, with corrugated tin sheds and huge piles of wood constantly being stoked by two or three men into the ovens. The whole area of several blocks consisted of such shops and kilns, and wood smoke filled the air.

DR

Takeuchi makes a hobby of studying the various craft industries around Kyoto—industries that originally grew up because this was the court center and one where, after the cutting off of contact with the outside world, there was still wealth for the employment of local artisans. We saw Communist posters on the wall protesting the so-called anti-violence bill which would curb demonstrations, and Takeuchi said that these workers and even employers were radical in part because their "upper-middle-class" wares suffered heavily in any depression since they weren't essentials but luxuries; and thus men were often unemployed and businesses went bankrupt. As at Mr. Otoyama's company, the workers paid no special attention to us even in places where visitors must be uncommon—partly no doubt out of politeness and partly out of the "instinct of workmanship."

The pottery workers have extraordinary deftness and grace, and in fact we find this characteristic of Japanese generally. Some of the ceramic workers make good money, as much as three or four thousand yen a day ($9 or $12), and live in modest homes around the area where we walked. Their pay is based partly on seniority and partly on skill—but such highly paid workers would often vote Communist, in keeping with the radical pattern of the district. Murata has suggested that the radicalism in Kyoto—including technical pioneering such as the first streetcar or city planning—is a kind of countercyclical response to the court pressures and other hierarchical and feudal patterns of the city. Furthermore, since the capital is now in Tokyo, the students at Kyoto, and the faculty also, seemed to have been less monitored in the bad years before and during the war. They, and the ever active teachers' unions, thus take a large share in the demonstrations and protests that keep radicalism alive in the city.

ETR

We drove back into the city to the Nishijin area, where the silk factories are located. These are large, dreary brick structures, typical nineteenth-century factory buildings, facing one of the wide main

ETR

streets. Here we were greeted by an official and taken to his office, where we were seated on silk upholstered chairs and given tea and a short speech about silk manufacture. On the wall hung portraits of substantial-looking gentlemen, the owners and directors of previous years. After this ceremony, a young man was called in to show us around.

This factory produces some of the finest silks made in Japan, and the work is taxing. In rather dark, noisy, crowded quarters men and women sit over looms, quickly throwing a shuttle back and forth, often following some intricate and complicated pattern. It is noisy because of the machinery that keeps the belts running. The work is so fine that it is apparently terrible for the eyesight, and the workers work so fast that it must be terrible for the nerves too. We saw some exquisite *obi* brocades being made, as well as the magnificent purple silk for robes worn by the *sumo* wrestlers.

Silk weaving, like pottery making, is one of the old industries in Japan, and the conditions of manufacture have not changed very much even in recent years. The workers are highly skilled, and many of them artists in a sense, but their working conditions and often their pay are not nearly so good as in the new industries.

DR

We had lunch with Professor Noguchi, a young and most attractive ecologist, whose paper comparing patterns of modernization in rural villages Evey and I have been reading at odd moments. As often happens, his English was too good to require an interpreter and too poor for easy communication. Except at International Christian University and one or two other places, there seem to be no chairs of cultural anthropology in Japan, presumably because Japan copied its pattern of academic organization from Europe (with much the same role given the law faculty that one finds in Germany). Thus, anthropology is practiced by people on the side, so to speak—but Noguchi is in effect an anthropologist, as are some archaeologists we've met.

We went on in the afternoon to the Institute of Humanistic Studies at Kyoto University for a meeting on modernization, later continued on *tatami* at the Hamasaku Restaurant. The occasion began rather stiffly and ended up with extraordinary gaiety and freedom. Murata and Noguchi and Osabe were there. But what gave the evening its special flavor was the leadership of Professor Mori, the head of the Institute, a man of remarkable personal and intellectual qualities. While his "field" is French literature and he also knows a great deal about

Enlightenment philosophy and the French Revolution, one of his principal interests is Japanese popular culture. He had given us his article "The Seven Beauties Test," in which he used photographs of girls ranging from an old geisha type to a modern Hollywood-style Japanese girl to test the preferences of respondents in different age groups and areas. Mori is a leader without being a boss—a man with a wide intellectual following but apparently without influence at the University of Kyoto itself, except in the Institute, which is his "private" enterprise. Another senior participant was Oshita, professor of history, whose field is Western history.

I began the discussion by saying that Japan seemed to me unique in being the only country in the Orient to modernize. Was any other country at all like it, I was asked. (I was reminded by this question of the intense interest of many Japanese I've met—including those not always or not ordinarily exposed to foreigners—in how they compare, how they stack up, what other peoples think of them. This is very much the attitude Tocqueville and other foreign visitors encountered in America; but it would, I think, be rarer in America today. It is also the attitude I encountered in the U.S.S.R. in 1931.)

I was asked how I would characterize modernization, how I would define it. I said that perhaps the first requirement, according to Kenneth Boulding's view, was the "invention" of the full-time organizer, and that this was more important than any technological elements, for the organizer was the introducer of impersonality and rationality and of the techniques that facilitated these. And I said that I was interested in finding other models of industrialization besides the United States and the Communist countries (meaning the U.S.S.R. and China), for instance, Japan and Yugoslavia. I pointed out that in Japan the close family and kin ties persisted, that there was very little philanthropy on the Anglo-American model but at the same time very little graft and no bargaining: in other words, a unique combination of universalism and particularism. I said that only Great Britain seemed to be as honest a country as Japan, and how did this come about?

Mori replied that this was the result of national unity, that Japan, like Britain or even more so, was a homogeneous country. It had gone through a series of national crises which had made a deep impression on the unconscious—a unity formerly reflected in the Emperor and which made Japanese treat other Japanese as members of that unity even if not as members of the family. I asked if this unity could bridge the gap between workers and employers which appeared so wide ideologically. Would unions not want to sabotage or cheat management? I added that I was struck by the intensity with which workers produced at the Otoyama Company even when by Japanese tradition it was very difficult if not impossible to fire them. Mori replied that Otoyama is a controlled company, that is, a very carefully managed one and not a good example. In other plants there would be free coffee breaks at any time or a great deal at least of white-collar sabotage and taking time off.

Oshita also spoke in answer to the question, referring to Kawashima's article "Familistic Structure of Japanese Society," which points to the "soft" relation between employers and employees. Even in feudal times there were good relations between lords and farmers. There were peasant revolts, but they were only based on brief periods of starvation, and after the revolt was over, the peasants would rebuild the lord's manor. A familistic attitude is transferred to the company, and it is felt that the interest of the individual coincides with that of the company so that good production will be helpful all around. But he added that the patriarchal and despotic aspect of feudal patterns also exists—and Mori commented that there was jealousy among the "brothers" in a family and in a company.

Noguchi—the man we met at lunch, who half apologized for his ecological approach, as too technological or deterministic—pointed out the difference in patterns between European and Japanese agriculture. Only rice is grown in the East, whereas mixed farming in the West leads to the enclosure movement and the destruction of the feudal community. In Japan, where enclosure was not feasible—indeed, as we've observed here one small rice paddy leads into another, bounded by a small row of trees and an irrigation ditch—the original communal form was kept. (These men are familiar with Karl Wittfogel's theory of the hydraulic and despotic society; they feel that the separation of Japanese land by mountain ranges and small river valleys created a different pattern of irrigation and of rulership than that made possible by the great rivers of China and Egypt.)

I spoke of peasant and other struggles in Europe as partly based on differences of religious belief or ethnic group, citing Everett Hughes's account of the Protestant Rhineland industrialists who tried to suppress the many festival days of the Catholic workers and thereby provoked the first strikes. I advanced the notion that industrialization usually proceeded by means of internal colonization, whereas in Japan, with some small exceptions, this appears not to have been the case.

Noguchi pointed out that in the sixteenth century Japan had a unified national market, highly organized and based on sea transport, including the Inland Sea. It had cities comparable to and larger than European cities. Already at that time Edo (later Tokyo) was the largest city in the world. During the Tokugawa period (1603–1868) there were many cities with populations over 10,000, while in Europe comparable towns had 2,000 or 3,000 people. However, when urbanization began, a dualism was created in Japan between the urban and the rural; that is, when modernization, building on the Tokugawa base, moved into high gear during the Meiji period, farming was not commercialized as it was in Europe, and the rural community remained relatively unchanged while in the urban setting modernization took advantage of the conditions already provided for it. The government took a strong hand in importing machinery and advanced technology—Noguchi's implication was that, if matters were kept centralized, commercialization would be geographically confined, and its spread to rural areas avoided. (Even today farmers are not supposed to sell their land without getting special permission from an agricultural commission. However, since their land brings ever so much more for dwellings or industrial use than for raising even the most intensive crops, they are under great pressure to sell and often manage to. *Chuo Koron*, the leading monthly in Japan, has an article pointing out that land prices in the last ten years have increased 1,200 per cent in the Tokyo area, as against salary increases of 250 per cent—a farmer with less than an acre can get $100,000 for it.)

At this point Mori raised the question, a very productive one, that occupied much of our later discussion: the difference between Japan and the rest of Asia, he said, could not be explained in these economic and ecological terms alone, without reference to the enormous curiosity of the Japanese, which he regards as the most powerful of any nation. And how is this curiosity to be explained? As an amusing example, he referred to Japanese curiosity about food: Japan has welcomed and assimilated Chinese, Mongolian, Western, Indian cooking (indeed, one can find restaurants of every conceivable variety in the big cities). No town seems too remote for its coffee shop—a silent socializer in Western ways, as Murata has pointed out. I responded that the Russians seemed to have a somewhat similar curiosity, at least among the urban and educated groups, and I asked whether curiosity extended to the rural groups in Japan. Mori said that in Russia only the intellectuals are curious, while in Japan the peasants are too.

Feeling both free and stimulated in the atmosphere created by Mori and his group, I said I'd like to try off the cuff to suggest some possible reasons for the exceptional Japanese curiosity. I noted that the children's curiosity didn't seem to be repressed and that, in Freud's theory, this would have consequences for adult life: children were not shut out of the adult world, either in sex or in other areas, though they were not forced into it either. Moreover, in a crowded society where people live very closely together it is possible to make a great deal of use of the "silent language" where people become responsive to minute cues and no one has to shout to get attention. Furthermore, the very exclusion of foreign things during the Tokugawa period created an intense curiosity when the ghetto was opened—I added that today, in the Soviet Union and other totalitarian societies, the forbidden things excited enormous curiosity. And I concluded that receptivity, a "feminine" characteristic in Western society, was possible in Japan because this society was the opposite of a "male vanity" culture where *machismo* was highly valued. I noted that friends of mine who had taught in Latin America said it was difficult to teach the men anything because they had to appear to already know everything; but this was not true of the Japanese men, whose manliness expressed itself in other ways.

Osabe said that "active patience" might be a better term to describe the Japanese attitude. He thought this quality reflected the density of population in urban centers in the Tokugawa period. Craftsmen at that time ran rather large organizations such as the building trades and their skill was highly valued. However, after the Meiji Restoration many things were imported and many people valued these things more than the native products. (Osabe, like Murata, belongs to the younger group of "new nationalists," whose attitude is a little like that of some liberal Americans of the post-war period who began to find virtue in our own society as against European imports and European standards of judgment. Osabe doesn't reject the modern but he considers it as much contemporary Japanese as "Western.")

I asked whether the attitude of the samurai would be closer to *machismo* than to active patience. Noguchi replied that after the eighteenth century the samurai were curiosity-minded. Often the samurai were intellectuals and small bureaucrats rather than warriors, and they supported the arts, the tea ceremony, and music. When Kyoto became a cultural center after the shift of power to Edo, a samurai might get promoted by means of such things as musicianship or poetic skill. The Shogunate, however, was against the "corruption," the luxurious tastes of samurai, and sought to re-establish simple living.

Osabe noted that the samurai of the western regions who had a hand in the Meiji Restoration had been influenced by commercial ties and were not typical. They were more open-minded than their Chinese counterparts, although less open than more urbanized Japanese. The willingness to use things imported from outside goes far back in Japanese history, including the use of iron from Korea and China. There was no resistance to materials from the outside, including technology, whereas the Chinese never tried to adopt Western military science until the Opium War—the implication was that China was a land empire, self-contained and proud, whereas Japan, even in the closed Tokugawa period, was different. However, Osabe added, openness in Japan is for technological but not metaphysical things; as I would put it, no "nonsense" is imported and "Japanese" attitudes remain intact. Mori remarked that China introduced Marxism but not a Western way of thinking. One Chinese philosopher explained Marxism by reference to ancient Chinese philosophy. China, as Osabe said, was half the world.

Someone said that if the gap between the receiving culture and the outside cultures is too great, then it is impossible to accept the outside culture and its technology; but the gap between Tokugawa Japan and the West was not so great as to make the task of catching up seem overwhelming.

Suggesting that Japan had followed the route of Athens rather than Sparta, I asked whether the submissiveness of the women made it possible for the men to be receptive without feeling that they were being unmanly. Mori replied that women are also curious and exercise active patience in their own small spheres. And Oshita added that foreigners in the Meiji period were struck by the high social status of women and their relatively high intellectual level.

Noguchi agreed with me that there was a chauvinistic tendency among the samurai and the Right Wing and that one must look at the social origins of this. There was no chauvinism toward science and technology, but only ideological chauvinism or *kokutai* (nationalistic spirit). People in the Meiji period admired German technology. When democracy came to be discussed after World War I, certain reinterpretations of the term were introduced. "Democracy" meant that the rulers understand the people's will, that is, they guess at it, and government is for the people and not by the people. This attitude in turn is closely connected with the familistic structure of Japan, which can be seen as a series of small boxes, one inside the other, ending in national control of all groups in the society. Enclosing everything is the Emperor. Consequently, nationalism in Japan has meant nationalism in terms of the state rather than of the people (unlike, in other words, what might be the case in France or in Nazi Germany).

Osabe continued by saying that people were ready to be unified because of the familistic folkways. The community puts limits to curiosity and flexibility, but these very mores could be used as grounds or justification for revolution in the name of the Emperor; that is, the enlightened, open-minded people could change things by making use of the name of the Emperor.

Mori went on to say that the Japanese accepted neither Christianity nor Mohammedanism. There are of course Christians and they are quite influential, but they appear to have been converted more on cultural and moral than on theological grounds. There is no monotheism in Japan but rather an enlightened pantheism. There is little metaphysical interest and a realistic attitude is taken toward the world. Openness, lightness, frivolity, and gaiety are characteristic of Japan (as against the more serious Chinese). Because there is no God, the Japanese do not know shame (what I think he must have meant is that they don't have a sense of sin) and anything is permitted. Correspondingly, Hegel, Kant, and Marx are all regarded as phenomena, that is, as real objects which can be accepted simultaneously.

The fact that the Emperor was the high priest of Shintoism added to the dynamism of Japanese modernization. The Japanese are not tradition-directed, but other-directed. (This same observation has come up quite a few times from different people. I have sometimes pointed out that other-direction involves psychic closeness rather than mere behavioral receptivity and that it is the latter which is often meant when it is taken for granted that the Japanese are other-directed.)

I responded to these comments by referring to Fromm and Bachofen and asking about the patriarchal and abstract as against the particularistic and concrete elements in Japanese life. I said that people were suggesting that the Japanese were "feminine" in their concreteness and realism. Shinto and Buddhist priests are not celibate (although many Zen monks are) and the kind of double standard between the this-worldly and the other-worldly to which Max Weber referred and which took out of European life in every generation some of the most intellectual men and turned them into celibate priests seemed to be unknown in Japan. Moreover, the opposite tendency of romantic love has rarely been known either, and marriages have been based on practical considerations. Consequently, I suggested, the men in Japan are more realistic—at least outside the more militant samurai tradition—and hence more "feminine." I wondered whether this might be related to the lack of cattle farming in Japan or horse breeding, observing that stock breeders were often aristocrats also interested in human breeding; the country gentry in England and elsewhere have not been scholars, unlike the landed gentry in some rice-farming areas.

Oshita replied that one must not overestimate the intelligence of the samurai as a whole; the upper-class samurai were not all able to read and write, although there were lesser samurai, important in the Meiji Restoration, who were intellectuals. Noguchi added that the ruling class in Japan had similarities to the European ruling class in its preference for military over civilian virtues but that, at the same time, Japan had the civilian model of China. For lesser samurai, moreover, literature was a means of social mobility, and after the Tokugawa period all samurai aspired to literacy.

In the same connection, Osabe pointed out that there was high literacy in Japan (except at the top) before the Meiji Restoration. Popular fiction in the period might sell as many as 30,000 copies—certainly large by any Western standard at the same time. There were schools in each community, some for commoners and some for the samurai. Figures show that at the beginning of Meiji there was 50 per cent literacy for the men and 10 per cent for the women. Here again technological factors were important: paper had for a long time been produced cheaply in Japan and ink and brush were available for anyone.

I raised a question about the abstractness and lack of concreteness of the left-wing thinkers, suggesting that their doctrinaire outlook must be "un-Japanese." And I also asked why Zen, with its cutting through of metaphysical abstractions, was necessary if Japan was already so realistic and concrete—or was Zen one of the sources of Japanese realism, e.g., in the saying that when hungry one should eat, when tired, sleep. Mori replied that Japanese "realism" is not always rational. (His comment is characteristic of those within his group who refuse to dichotomize in the Western logical style and who see irrationality blended with rationality.) He spoke of being in Indonesia and wondering whether such a country could "progress" in the European way—"reality" is too difficult for such underdeveloped countries and they resort to phrases such as "individualism in totalitarianism" and "totalitarianism in individualism." (However, such phrases are not un-Japanese, although "totalitarianism" is too strong a word for the groupism of Japan.)

We moved on then to dinner at a restaurant and as the evening wore on things became informal and extremely gay; the men took off their coats and rolled up their sleeves. Oshita drank glass after glass of *sake* in his beer glass rather than in the tiny cups the rest of us used, on each occasion saying *dozo*, meaning "please," and pouring somebody else's cup also.

I asked about attitudes toward China. How much did the left-wing students who were sympathetic to China know or try to know about the country? I gathered that there was strong sentimental attachment but little concrete following of such matters as the 1957–58 Hundred Flowers episode or the problems of the communes.

Oshita and others recurred to the similarities between present-day Japan and Weimar Germany. I suggested that one difference was the existence today of a strong peace movement in Japan, far more than existed in Weimar Germany. I said, however, that I was surprised to find that the Japanese seem not to have heard of the Committee for a Sane Nuclear Policy or any peace activities on American campuses. The group seemed to be astonished and pleased at my own interest in peace and this led them to become freer in their discussion of the United States. At first they had been guarded, and critical only of Russia and Germany in line with what they assumed I could accept.

When I pointed out that even Japanese businessmen wanted peace, contrary to the leftist stereotype of warlike monopoly-capitalists and imperialists, I think it was Oshita who said that while Matsushita (a leading electronics tycoon) wants peace for the sake of good business, nevertheless he would back war if the government went to war. I said it was true that Japanese businessmen didn't want to fight either with their own government or with other countries, implying that the Japanese might well be glad that they didn't have heroic businessmen or martial ones. Some of the group seemed amused at this idea. Mori brought up the case of a conservative businessman he knew who voted Communist because he thought there should be at least one Communist delegate in the Diet, otherwise the United States would not worry about Japan and would not give aid.

Mori thought that the underdeveloped countries would have to become Communist in order to develop. I said I hoped they would become socialist in many different versions of socialism, but not Communist—but this distinction between Communism and socialism, though nominally reflected in the organization of Japanese left-wing political parties, does not appear to be at all a strong one in Japanese intellectual life.

I had mentioned the Peace Corps and Oshita felt free to say that the Peace Corps seemed to him a form of "peaceful imperialism." He said that at the time of Japan's Manchurian adventure some left-wing idealists had become associated with the Manchurian affair and with Prince Konoye. But these men were simply duped by the militarists and he felt the same would happen to the Peace Corps. He also said that he wasn't going to take part in the conference that was planned as the result of the Ikeda-Kennedy talks between Japanese and American scientists, for he felt that this cooperation would only be a disguise for American imperialism.

(It should be clear that the Japanese Communists and Left Wingers I have met who talk in this way have little similarity to their American counterparts: they do not seem fanatical or bitter or alienated in the special way in which our American Communists are alienated. In personal quality, they are more like European socialists and left-wing social democrats; such Communists can also be found in Europe, though hardly at all in the United States.)

I replied that many students in the Peace Corps, or concerned with it, also shared fears that it could become contaminated by the cold war; their wariness might differentiate them from the Japanese youth who had been naïvely idealistic about Manchuria. But I also added that preconceived attitudes like those of Oshita might have a somewhat self-confirming quality: if people avoided involving themselves in such activities as scientific cooperation or the Peace Corps, they would also avoid the opportunity of influencing these activities away from imperialism and exploitation by the cold war. Oshita accepted this comment with characteristic grace.

Indeed, to continue the theme of fanaticism, I'm struck by how much easier I find discussions, even rather stiff and tendentious ones, with Japanese intellectuals than with many Americans. While it is true that Japanese elders tend to awe the younger men, who are often self-inhibited rather than realistically stopped by the gerontocracy, I myself have hardly ever felt crowded or claustrophobic in a discussion here. Rivalry certainly exists, but it is subdued and not aggressively supported. Being myself conciliatory, I find this atmosphere very agreeable. Nor do I find myself getting at all impatient as a result of the delays caused by translation. To be sure, I'd give anything to be able to speak the language, but while translation is progressing, I have time to think about the next question or the most recent observations, or can observe the faces of people, or simply rest. Japanese who know English are themselves patient about hearing the translations; some appear to like to reflect on the matter once again in another tongue.

By this time I felt free to ask people how they voted. Oshita said he voted Communist; Osabe, to my astonishment, said that he sometimes voted Communist and sometimes socialist—I was astonished because he had expressed such "nationalistic" and pro-samurai views, hostile to the "feminine" aspect of Japanese culture, and thus I expected him to be conservative politically; he said he was radical politically and conservative culturally. Murata, whose outlook is somewhat similar, said he voted socialist. Mori, I think, voted right-wing socialist. I was struck by the spectacle of men of rather diverse views being extremely intimate and colleaguial. I remarked later to Bob Lifton and Murata how rare such a scene would be in the United States, how much more sharp and polemical such a discussion would be; Murata said that it would be extremely difficult to have such a discussion in Tokyo, but the quieter atmosphere of Kyoto and the gentle generosity of Mori made things possible here which were not possible in the capital.

On such occasions it is always hard to know when to adjourn the evening, and we are the ones to do it since everyone must remain until the guests of honor are gone. The food itself, coming in an endless array of extraordinarily beautiful dishes which are then whisked away again and replaced by others, took at least two hours, and as usual our Japanese hosts were happy to find that we liked raw fish, seaweed, and other delicacies that Westerners are supposed to find unappetizing. Then we were told that our "tank" was waiting for us in the street. Indeed, we could hear the honking of cars that could not possibly pass ours, which filled the whole street. As we went downstairs amid much bowing on all sides and put on our shoes awkwardly while trying to stand on one foot and use a shoehorn, we asked if any of our hosts wanted a lift anywhere but were told that they would stay on to have a beer and continue the discussion. Again much bowing, and we looked back to find our hosts, as well as the girls of the restaurant, in the street still bowing as we drove off.

Kyoto, October 19

By good luck there was visiting Kyoto, at the same time we were, Mr. Tamaki, a leading Buddhist theologian, and we went to visit him at a temple compound, where, to our surprise, we were ushered into a modern room in a modern building with the usual overstuffed chairs. Tamaki speaks excellent English, and after greetings and inquiries about Paul Tillich, whom he greatly admires, he launched into a discussion about the need for pastoral counseling.

He put this in terms of *The Lonely Crowd*, saying that many rural people were tradition-directed, that the leaders and priests of his own Buddhist sect were inner-directed men who wanted to drive their followers away from tradition-direction toward inner-direction, but that in fact the young of Japan were increasingly other-directed, so that the leadership could not talk to them. He appeared to view other-direction benignly and inner-direction critically, as a kind of formalistic and moralistic stiffness inconsistent with the psychological temper of the new age and with what the ministry needed. He gave the example of the inner-directed priest who thinks he is modern and progressive because he tells a troubled parishioner who comes with a problem, "It's your problem," rather than as in the old days giving a traditional answer. In Tamaki's view it is insufficient to say, "It's your problem," for it is also the problem of the social group and the priest cannot simply throw the responsibility on to the individual but must help the individual as a member of a group.

We talked about the YBA, the Young Buddhist Association, and I asked if there would be any overlap between this and the Zengakuren movement. Tamaki said that the YBA on the whole was conservative but that there were some radical students in it and many who were concerned with peace—there had apparently been a Buddhist meeting the previous year in which many YBA students had paraded and protested on behalf of peace.

We also talked about the problem of recruiting younger people into the sect. Priests inherit their jobs—indeed, we've met several faculty members who are the sons of priests and who are still fighting the internal battle against their fathers. And the young priest who later showed us about is the son of a priest in one of the northern prefectures. As long as his father is alive—and his father is still young—he can stay at the Temple, which is also a kind of Buddhist university, to study and to help in the administration of the huge enterprise, but when his father dies he must return to take over what we would call the parish.

There is not so much hostility now to religion as there was immediately after the war when all supposed "feudal remnants" were suspect, but neither does there seem to be any great "return to religion" among educated Japanese young people. (One of our friends in Kyoto is a Buddhist whose children have been converted to Catholicism in school, and he and others have told us that there is no anti-religious feeling even among left-wing faculty members; here and elsewhere in Japanese life the effort is to reconcile conflicting beliefs.)

Tamaki arranged for us to be guided about the Temple, which is a large compound with some 500 employees, a number of them presently learning to use computing machines, as our young novice guide explained. We were conducted through a series of temples, dormitories, classrooms, and offices. We went into one temple, very ornate, where incense was burning and priests were chanting and a small number of old people were in prayer. Evey and I, having removed our shoes, tiptoed in, not wanting to disturb people, but our guide talked loudly as if we were in a European cathedral and paid no attention to the worshippers. We were taken to see the new girls' dormitory, with a handsome auditorium, *tatami* rooms where the girls could learn flower arrangement and tea ceremony—the standard preparation for marriage of a nice girl—as well as various lecture rooms. All this was quite modern; indeed, we found the combination of modern business methods and buildings with traditional temples and ceremonies very striking, and there appeared to be at least as much pride in the one as in the other.

We had lunch at the Liftons' attractive Japanese house. They had rented this for several months so that Bob could finish his work of interviewing students at the universities here for his study of youth in Japan. They had invited several American friends of theirs, and we talked among other things about problems of intercultural exchange. Japanese professors who go to the United States often lose their Japanese connections and suffer if they speak English "too well," being turned into interpreters on their return—this danger is diminishing, but it is still unwise for a Japanese to leave for America unless he already has very solid connections at home. We also talked about American professors who might profit from coming into the American Studies Program at Kyoto, and I mentioned a number of men in different fields. In such invitations there are of course political problems on both the American and the Japanese sides. There is also the requirement that guests be famous; that the people I mentioned are all cited in Japanese scholarly works does not by itself make them sufficient celebrities.

In the late afternoon we went to one of the big downtown hotels for a discussion on international relations with a group of fifteen or twenty political scientists from various universities. In charge of this occasion was a remarkable man, Professor Matsuyama, but despite his qualities it was a very difficult evening. The younger people were completely or almost completely silent and the older men had the characteristic gravity of the Japanese gerontocracy. Professor Matsuyama, a historian, speaks German and French but very little English, and another academician, Professor Tamatsukuri, acted as interpreter but also began the discussion. He said it was not helpful to United States-Japanese relations when American statesmen and military figures referred to Japan as a United States "rampart in the Pacific," for this brought up remnants of former anti-American attitudes among the Japanese, feelings from which most Japanese were now fortunately free. He indicated that to refer to Japan as a rampart or base in this way treated the country without respect for its problems and people (in other words, as expendable). The Japanese have an inferiority complex (his term and not an uncommon one here) and this should be taken account of in American dealings with Japan. Japanese people are always very polite in dealing with Americans, with the result that Americans don't always know Japanese attitudes: for instance, the English-language newspapers here published by the three big chains temper their comments and do not translate from their Japanese-language editions things that would offend American sensibilities.

Then, however, he went on to talk about beginning to fear that Americans were soft. He gave the example of the Harvard Glee Club, which had recently toured Japan, many of whose members had stayed in Japanese homes. These students were too polite. The Japanese students wanted to hear criticisms from the Glee Club students but heard only praise and polite remarks.

At one point, as I recall, I tried gently to interrupt and to say that I was not here as a representative of the American government or the U. S. Information Agency, and that in talking to me in this way he was not talking to someone who could carry back his complaints. I said I, too, agreed with his remarks about Japan as a rampart or base in the Pacific, but I had no influence with the military, diplomatic, or mass-media groups that use such language. However, I could not stop him. He had written out what he was going to say and he was going to say it. When he finally got through, I picked up his remark about the Harvard Glee Club and noted that I knew some of these students, that I did not think they were being hypocritical in praising Japan or the homes in which they had been put up; on the contrary, being musical they would tend to admire Japan and its artistic quality and hence their praise should not be taken as obsequious flattery. I said I granted that such praise might not be the most helpful thing but that I had no doubt it was honestly meant. As far as hurt feelings went, including even comments of American military leaders, these seemed to me not the really serious problems of Japan.

I tried to change the subject to the actual topic of international relations by saying that a number of Japanese intellectuals had spoken of Japan as being presently in its Weimar period and that they feared the return of Nazi-like right-wing groups, remarking that the defeat in World War II was like the Versailles Treaty for Germany and that the post-war Japanese governments were the first really democratic ones. I questioned this parallel, saying that it seemed to me that militarism in France, Germany, and the United States today was a considerably greater danger than in Japan and pointing out the alliance between Rhineland industrialists and militarists which had little parallel in Japan even in the pre-war period, and even less today when the Japanese economy rests largely on international trade. (I mentioned the South Manchurian Railway to show that I was aware that there were some business connections with the adventure in Manchuria in the 1930's, but I argued that such connections were not central to the Japanese business outlook.) I said that if the Japanese economy doesn't crash, the return of right-wing militarism seemed to me almost as unlikely in Japan as in Great Britain.

Matsuyama commented that for the younger group of professors everything about Nazi Germany is ludicrous but that Japan had been much influenced by Germany, both at the time of the Meiji Restoration and in the pre-war period.

It is hard to give a sense of the dead-panness of the group. I was having to carry most of the burden of keeping the discussion going, with assistance from Matsuyama. Seniority then swung the spotlight to a man who said that America was trying to exclude China from the public scene and that this was leading China to be stiffer to the world outside—the implication was that Japan and other countries would suffer because American intransigence heightened Chinese intransigence, a point which Bob Lifton, who accompanied us, said was a very important one and also emphasized. What could be done about United States recognition in the near future? I replied that if the Kennedy Administration had come into power with more freedom, with a larger majority, it might possibly have done something at once which would have been a *fait accompli;* there would have been a great howl, but it would have been over and done with, since the China lobby is not something of enormous interest to Americans.

I pointed out what I've continued to stress in discussions with intellectuals here, namely, that ordinary Americans are strongly anti-Communist and want Communism to disappear from the world, that they are if anything more opposed than big businessmen and intellectuals, who are more open and cosmopolitan. I commented that the very existence of democracy in America made it difficult to get away from

Victorian morality in the public domain that led to such doctrines as non-recognition being applied to countries of whose government we don't approve. Lifton and I both mentioned the strength of moral feeling against Chinese Communism resting in part on disappointed missionary efforts, especially in the Middle West. And I added that it may be too late when American policy vis-à-vis China does change, because of Chinese resentment and pride. I said that while I had myself encouraged recognition as something that was needed, and also the sending of food, I was not at all sure that China would be so delighted. Presently the Chinese were apparently more provincial and doctrinaire than the Russians, though not necessarily so for all time.

Tamatsukuri asked whether through the mass media the attitude of the common people could be changed on the China issue. I said that I knew many intellectuals in and outside the United States who felt that the mass media created public opinion, that they did indeed do so in some particulars but that they also reflected it. I said many Americans have a cowboy attitude of toughness that preceded the media and an "agin the government" spirit that could always be called upon and that too preceded the media. I concluded that the Republicans would feel that they could defeat Kennedy for reelection if he came out for the recognition of China.

I then spoke of the fear and ambivalent admiration that many people in the Soviet Union have for the Chinese people, while the latter think the Russians are soft and corrupt. I said that in talking to Japanese people I did not get this feeling of fear about China. Matsuyama responded, "When we think about China, we think about restaurants and about Chinese culture. When we think about Russia, we think about 1945 and the war and 1946 and Japanese prisoners." I asked if there wasn't also a certain guilt in Japan for the treatment of China, treatment that had helped bring on the Pacific war and indeed Chinese Communism. Matsuyama responded that Japan killed the Chinese army, whereas Americans were killed (in Korea) by the Chinese army. His implication was that there *was* a certain guilt while on the other hand, having beaten the Chinese, several times in fact, Japan didn't fear China. (Evey believes there is another factor here, namely, that China is another Asiatic country, that Japanese in China are not snubbed racially, and that this leads to a certain unspoken harmony—a harmony, I would add, felt even by liberals and conservatives who are anti-Communist but who feel profoundly uneasy about American hostility to China.)

An assistant professor then asked me about McCarthyism and

whether it still affects American scholars. I said that McCarthyism in its worst ravages was over and that even at its height some professors at leading universities had been free to speak out even if they were attacked. But I said I thought McCarthyism had helped intensify the drive for specialization among younger scholars, which took them out of any controversial area—this had not been so much a conscious process as a secular tendency within scholarship itself that McCarthyism had facilitated. I also said that students and young scholars felt they could have an impact in the field of race relations but not in foreign relations. But McCarthyism had been part of a climate which had created that attitude.

How had professors resisted McCarthyism, someone asked. I referred to Lazarsfeld's study done for the Fund for the Republic on which I had worked, and spoke of the great variations among different institutions, differences, for instance, between Wisconsin and Ohio State—I was hoping as I do generally here to give a sense of the variety and complexity of American life as against the simplifications that prevail: different simplifications among different political groups, but simplifications just the same. Matsuyama brought up the John Birch Society and said that the Republicans will accuse Kennedy of losing Laos, Cuba, and so on. I was struck again with his unusual quality and wide knowledge of Europe and America.

Another assistant professor, who had been at the University of Michigan, said that Americans mostly read only the local papers such as the *Detroit Free Press*, which gives sensational news, rather than reading *The New York Times*. Were the mass media responsible for American attitudes? He had studied international law. It seemed to him that statesmen and responsible journalists should make policies but that in the United States a small group, including a handful of demagogic senators, could block good policies of the government. I replied that if it were only a few people, one might conceivably change them, but that in my judgment fundamental attitudes toward foreign policy were more decentralized than that. I said that while the local papers didn't carry much foreign news they did stress who wins in games, they emphasized violence in what they selected—he had himself referred to news of crashes on the front page—and that there was much addiction to violence in the comics and elsewhere. I said ours was a business press, run as a business, and in general responsive to what editors thought people wanted. I pointed out in this connection that *The New York Times* has comparatively few readers, at least by Japanese standards. I also said that there were sources of violent opposition to Communism outside the press, such as large elements of the Catholic Church, and that many immigrants wanted to be 200 per cent Americans. One couldn't judge America on the basis of Japan, since there was nothing like Tokyo as a centralized capital from which all the major media spread out.

An economist entered the conversation to ask about the place in the United States of Marxist and quasi-Marxist books that sell extremely well in Japan, such as those of C. Wright Mills and Paul Sweezy and Leo Huberman. (Mills, indeed, comes up in ever so many conversations.) I said I had learned that *The Monthly Review* (the Marxist journal edited by Sweezy and Huberman) has a greater circulation in Japan than in the United States. I said I didn't think Sweezy had much of an American audience either among academic people or among students. Mills, however, I said, was quite widely read. In the academic world both Mills and his critics, such as Daniel Bell, are considered outsiders. The larger questions they deal with are not considered susceptible to research. I said, however, that some sociology students appeared to be reading Mills for less genuine reasons, namely, in order to be told that other scholars were not important: these students were glad to learn that they didn't have to read difficult works. In fact, the problem always was how were decisions concretely made, and here it was necessary to go into detail and not stop at the generalizations whether of Mills or of his critics. The economist replied that these large questions about what influences the United States are of most concern to Japanese scholars.

I might add that the foregoing is one important and striking difference that seems to exist between Japanese and American intellectual life—the Japanese seem more like the Poles or the Yugoslavs in this respect. Compared to the relatively small number of American intellectuals who both do serious academic work and concern themselves with large, often speculative questions, the Japanese academic community supports a great many journals, broadcasts, and newspaper columns devoted to such large questions.

Kyoto, October 20

This morning, accompanied by Kato and the Liftons, we visited the Toei movie studio, an enormous operation with a dozen huge indoor stages, street scenes for "typical" Japanese films including a bridge that seemed to extend over a river but that ended in nowhere—right beyond the bridge were vegetable and rice patches—and a tremendous outdoor stage for battles and ceremonies. Toei concentrates on what Kato calls

"Easterns," movies representing traditional Japan, which are extremely popular—far more so than the more artistic, contemporary movies. Like every other "sight," the studio was thronged with busloads of school children, shepherded by their teachers, and as we got there a famous male movie star was being driven out through a sea of admiring young faces and we drove in through the same faces. We were first taken to see the filming of a drama of merchant life in the Tokugawa period; the actors all wore wigs and elaborate costumes—it seemed to be a kind of ante-bellum soap opera with exquisite chalk-faced women and proud and handsome men. The scene was shot over and over again, but with much greater speed than I'd seen in Hollywood. I got the impression that sets are built up and torn down with lightning rapidity in the tremendous construction operation of Toei, to which whole factories appear to be devoted. We went then to the shooting of a pre-Tokugawa samurai drama. A special sword expert was showing two principal male figures how to handle the huge long spears. Kato told us that all types of Japanese, even modern intellectuals and students, like the ancient costume dramas, just as many of them like cowboy Westerns, which are often dubbed on television as well as shown in the movies. This is an aspect of the pluralism that Kato thinks is characteristic of Japan which allows somebody to be a Communist and yet to like samurai dramas.

We had dinner with a group of Orientologists at one of the famous restaurants here. There were eleven of us grouped around two tables, with Bob Lifton acting as interpreter at my table and Matsumoto at the other. Our host on this occasion was Nambara, professor of Oriental history at Kyoto, and one of the world's leading Chinese scholars. Professor Kanesaka, whose theories of nomadism and horse culture had been so fascinating for us, also teaches Oriental history and was there, as were Professor Seki, the expert on classical Chinese poetry, Tanaka, professor of Buddhism at Kyoto, and Matsuda, professor of Japanese history at Ritsumeikan University, who was asked by Nambara to begin the discussion by telling us about the early Japanese receptivity to Chinese thought. Tanaka spoke about Buddhism and we got into a discussion of the Buddhist belief that man was basically good: Buddha is in every man—this view is shared by Zen and by the majority of (Mahayana) Buddhist sects. But there is a large branch of Buddhism that has an idea of original sin somewhat similar to that of much of Christianity; this is the Pure Land sect. Here the belief is that man can be basically good and still be so sinful that only faith will save him. Seki seemed attracted by the idea of original sin and rather missed it in much of Buddhism. I pointed out that there were more or less heretical versions of Christianity in which man also was thought to be basically good, such as the Arminian heresy or the Dutch Family of Love or, in some respects, the Quakers. I said I was puzzled about the impact of Christianity in Japan: where there was great poverty, as in China, there were "rice Christians," but what about Japan? Nambara answered that in the sixteenth century, when Portuguese Jesuits had converted many Japanese, there had been similar inducements, but some leading *daimyo* (feudal landholders) had also been converted—it was suggested that this partly reflected Japanese curiosity and openness. And in the nineteenth century, members of the elite were converted to Christianity on cultural grounds, for in the Meiji period Christianity was associated with the cultural superiority of the West. (I learned later from Kato that a group of Christians in Kyushu, the southernmost territory, who date back to the early-sixteenth-century conversions and who kept the faith secretly alive despite repression, recently converted to the new Omoto religion, a kind of revivalism with a strong interest in peace and, unlike Buddhist sects, politically progressive.)

We then got into a discussion of developments in modern China, for I had earlier explained that, while we were not uninterested in early Chinese history, we were especially eager to know about modern China and about Japanese attitudes toward it. Several men, including Kawashima, assistant professor of Chinese thought, pointed out that the Japanese love the Chinese, from whom they feel they inherited so much of their culture and to whom they feel culturally close. There is no fear of them, as there is of the Russians. I asked about the Hundred Flowers movement (a lifting of restrictions which in 1958 encouraged outspoken criticism but then very soon, out of fear it would get out of hand, clamped down on the critics). I was told of new groups in China that this year have gained a somewhat similar freedom to speak out. These are small groups, mostly in the universities, who talk quietly.

Of course, the American attitude toward the recognition of mainland China came in for criticism. It is terribly difficult for the Japanese to understand this attitude, the more so as they want to be friends with everybody; and since they lack the kind of moralism that lies behind the non-recognition policy, they must attribute it to sinister "imperialistic interests."

We talked about Chinese seriousness as against Japanese "frivolity" and were told that there is no art presently in China except perhaps music. The Chinese write only history—indeed, they have written history for many centuries—and believe that history is "the mirror of man." The Japanese are more apt to write novels, and they are more imaginative, childlike, and playful.

I got the sense that many of the younger men were left wing in their own sympathies and associated this readily enough with their Chinese scholarship; moreover, their interest in the Chinese classics or in Buddhism did not make them at all hostile to contemporary China, which they felt was to some extent built on Confucian themes. The seriousness of the Chinese seemed to strike them as sincere rather than as deadly, especially since they have no fear of Chinese militarism or adventurism—perhaps in part because they assume the realism of the Chinese and their logicality and good sense. It was pointed out that we were being served in Mongolian style, eating from a common dish, and that this was a characteristic Japanese import. (Whether the hostess, who sat waving a fan at each table and ready to chat if we were not otherwise amusing ourselves, was such an import, I didn't ask.)

Osaka, October 21

Early Saturday morning we packed my best suit and a clean white shirt, put my lecture notes in a briefcase, and in the tow of Matsumoto, Kato, and Mrs. Kako, set off in our tank for Osaka, where I was to give my first public lecture. I had written a full outline of the lecture in Tokyo, and copies had been made for Kato as interpreter and for one of the reporters. This turned out to be very fortunate indeed, for when we arrived in Osaka and opened the trunk of the car we were dismayed not to see our bags. There was much embarrassment, much telephoning, much apology each way. Evey and I said we could get along without the luggage or in fact could go back to Kyoto easily enough after my lecture (it's only forty minutes by train and three different railways make the trip, although it's nearly two hours by car in heavy traffic). Fortunately, Kato's copy of my lecture notes was available, or I would really have been sunk.

On the way over in the car, in fact, Matsumoto and Kato had discussed at length the Japanese interpretation of various phrases in my notes and I had been periodically asked what these meant. We continued this process at lunch in our Osaka hotel. This long discussion was valuable in reminding me of what was problematical for a Japanese audience—for example, the Japanese know (from movies) the existence of Texas, and also California and New York, but Vermont or Iowa or New Jersey are almost unknown. The Peace Corps is unknown. Though we would have two hours, I felt I must go slow and explain things, despite the grandiose demands of my title: "The World Position of American Civilization."

Osaka has a completely different atmosphere from Kyoto: it is often compared with Chicago. The second city of Japan, with a population of around three million, it was entirely destroyed during the war and now handsome new modernistic buildings line its main streets and its rivers and canals. The new Osaka Hotel, where we stayed, is actually an old-fashioned commercial hotel, with many Japanese guests and with what appeared to be American salesmen. Our room, big and high-ceilinged, had a television covered with the usual lace runner that hangs over the front when it is not in use. The dining room was simple and the food unpretentious. Our room overlooked a Dutch-style canal along which barges and a few small motorboats moved; opposite us were restaurants, factories, and nondescript buildings.

The audience at the lecture, about 500 people, seemed to be largely composed of students, mostly male. Kato told me that some of his students had come over from Kyoto. While he was translating, I had a chance to look at the audience, though half blinded by the lights. I noticed several people asleep in the first row, who woke up periodically—I doubted if I was putting them to sleep but thought rather of the pressures under which Japanese students worked. It was, judging by my American experience, a very dead-pan audience. I said things I thought were humorous or ironic, but without effect—I've had the same experience in smaller groups, too; people who are so ready to laugh on other occasions may find it difficult to imagine laughing at a lecture by a famous *sensei*—and in any case I was mostly extremely serious, well aware that every word I was saying not only was being tape recorded but was being taken down by a number of reporters.

At lunch Kato had suggested that I conclude my talk by saying what Japan should do. I had hesitated about this, feeling that I knew too little, and, in any case, who was I to tell the Japanese what to do. But I did accede to his suggestion and said at the end that I hoped the Japanese would develop something like the Peace Corps, for they also had a mission for the underdeveloped countries, for whom they might be a more relevant model in some respects than the United States. I added that I hoped that Japan's own hope to become a bridge between the United States and China could become a reality—and I said that, of course, I meant mainland China and not Chiang Kai-shek (knowing while I said this that I treaded on dangerous ground as far as the United States is concerned, and indeed my remark was picked up by the English-language *Mainichi* the next morning). I said I hoped that the Japanese effort on behalf of peace could be intensified and that they should not be afraid to criticize militarism, whether in the U.S.S.R. and Red China or in the United States, even while recognizing the precarious position of Japan in international waters. I got a mild round of applause when I finished and another when Kato finished his interpretation in Japanese.

Out in the hall I was greeted by a young woman from the Kyoto liaison office of International House who happily presented me with a briefcase which she assumed was the one we had left behind. I was dismayed when I realized it was the "other" briefcase, filled with papers of Social Science 136 (the course I teach at Harvard). At this point there was more embarrassment, more apology, more telephoning—in a way it was awful but it was also illuminating, for I felt that the very effort to have everything go smoothly and to make amends for what was after all our own oversight had led to haste and further misunderstanding. I should add that when we got back late in the evening from a concert and a walk around Osaka we found a bellboy from the Miyako waiting patiently with our lost luggage.

After waiting a few minutes to let the audience vanish, our party was taken next door to the new Asahi building, where we toured the studios of ABC (the Asahi Broadcasting Company), which seemed to occupy the top several floors of the modernistic skyscraper. We were proudly shown an enormous record library and an equally enormous library of tapes. We were also shown a number of broadcasting studios, both for television and radio, and a sound-effects room full of ingenious devices. Everywhere there was new gleaming equipment. We went through a large news room, less tense and cluttered than the *Asahi* newspaper itself, where, as usual, people didn't seem to pay much attention to the visiting firemen but kept to their work.

That evening in a large theater housed in the same Asahi complex of buildings, Kato, Evey, and I had first-row balcony seats for the modern jazz concert of the Osaka "Roon," the initials for the Association of Music for Workers. The concert ran from six to nine and we arrived during an intermission at seven to find the hall packed with young people, including a few small children—next to us was a mother with a girl of perhaps two who sat on the balcony rail held by her mother and clapped her hands in time with the music until toward the end of the evening she began to cry and was taken out, leaving behind her a toy pistol and a bag of candy which were later reclaimed. It was hard for us to think of this alert and well-dressed audience as "workers," until we realized that this term includes many white-collar workers who are unionized in Japan. The Roon organization began in Osaka with a group of workers who wanted to play music but then decided that they should also listen to good music. About 400 got together and invited artists not only to perform but to help educate them in their musical tastes; this original group had grown to an organization of 100,000; and while this is by far the largest Roon, the movement has spread to other cities, to Tokyo and Kyoto and elsewhere, and is now a national movement—endangered, Kato believes, by its success, incipient bureaucratization and non-participation by people who come to concerts rather than taking part in a democratic, self-educative enterprise. Moreover, the Osaka Roon is the only one, apparently, that sponsors modern jazz or any kind of experimental program, and it comes under heavy criticism from its sister Roon in Tokyo and Kyoto which play only classical music and whose intellectual and academic advisors consider the Osaka programs lowbrow and vulgar. Kato is himself one of the organizers and advisors of the Osaka Roon.

The curtain went up on a jazz quintet playing very hot jazz in the most exciting and vigorous way. There was a marvelous drummer—we were later told his drums were given to him as a present by Art Blakey, the great American drummer, in admiration—a saxophonist who could also sing and play the flute, a trumpeter who also played the flute, a double bass, and a pianist-composer. The group played with a combination of enthusiasm, rhythm, and precision that we've rarely heard. After the first number a man came out who in the United States would simply be an Emcee but who in this setting was also an educator trying to explain to the workers what they had heard, what to look for in the music, as well as playing the comic in his descriptions of the qualifications and interests of the individual performers. The next number was to be a composition on traditional Japanese themes by the pianist-composer; Kato said that he and other members of the audience were familiar with the folk tunes on which it was based. Then the combination Emcee and adult educator introduced a young woman vocalist in a very sexy and slinky evening gown, cut low in front and slit in the back. She was witty, pretty, energetic, and bouncy in belting out songs, mostly American. She is not a great singer, nor is the saxophonist, who also sang both American and Japanese songs, but there was a warmth and spirited connection between audience and performers that manifested itself not in wild applause or in the stylized shouts of approval requisite in Kabuki plays but rather in generous laughter and animated interest and unraucous applause.

According to Kato, these singers usually don't know English but learn the pronunciation of American songs from records and from phonetic arrangements by the band's arranger. On each occasion the Emcee-educator would explain matters, tell the derivation of the song or theme, and try to give the audience a sense that they were learning something as well as enjoying themselves. The average age of Osaka Roon audiences is twenty-two. Many workers leave school after junior high, that is, around fifteen or sixteen, and enter the labor force, and there were many such teenagers in the audience, all in good clothes and on their good behavior. Most of the audience, according to Kato, have dreadfully poor language instruction in school and cannot understand the English words, yet they much enjoy hearing songs sung in a foreign language.

After a few numbers and much patter, the modern jazz quintet sank out of sight on one stage while a Latin American band rose behind them on another enormous one, bandstands and scaffolding arranged to make attractive shadows and silhouettes with the artistic use of lighting. Kato told us that some of the young designers and painters of Osaka cooperate with the Roon by designing such sets in an effort to bring art to the masses. I don't ordinarily like Latin American music, but I did like this next band, called the Fresh Men, and indeed have never heard a Latin American band quite so good. There was a virtuoso bongo drummer more like an orchestral kettle-drummer, and the regular trap drummer, who was almost as good. Again, the Emcee explained what it was about, and the vocalist reappeared in a different dress to sing Latin American songs.

Then another stage rose and the quintet was playing alongside the Fresh Men in a Radio City Music Hall display: without apparent leadership, three drummers worked together, the saxophonists of the one and of the other, the two pianos, and so on, in a rendition of "When the Saints Come Marching In." Curtain and orchestras sank down at once while the audience was still applauding and then rose again with different lighting to bring the audience in on the clapping in a grand finale—Kato says that sometimes the audience joins in the singing. Evey and I enjoyed ourselves hugely.

Afterward, Kato introduced us to two very young officials of the organization, with whom we tried to share our enthusiasm. But, as Kato later confirmed, it was inconceivable to them that sophisticated American jazz lovers would find these Japanese versions really acceptable, let alone superior; they thought we must be flattering and polite. This puzzled us because it would be hard to find on records better examples of either genre, and Roon has sponsored a great many concerts and imported American and European artists. For, given their large membership, they can pay large fees, and they listen carefully to recordings, read reviews, and try to maintain a high artistic level. This seems to us one more example of the way in which many Japanese, perhaps most, have not caught up with their own achievements and still look defensively to America and Europe.

Osaka Roon divides its concerts into three series, A, B, and C, the first being classical music, the second popular, and the third experimental—ours had been a popular concert. Patrons can attend two series out of three, but most only go to one. The experimental group had earlier put on a musical comedy written for the group by Osaka intellectuals. Kato at his home recently played us a tape of this: we thought it a most creative work in a vein reminiscent of Bertholt Brecht, combining in its score modern jazz, popular Japanese folk songs, traditional *samisen* music, and Broadway-type musical-comedy scores, along with a Brecht-type libretto in which a criminal, a student, and a pawnbroker or loan shark engage in a kind of three-handed game of steal the money and get the girl—the girl being in effect everybody's dream girl. I thought the musical far too sophisticated for most people and certainly for most workers, and our host said that it hadn't gone over well. It had also been very critically handled by the newspaper reviewers, who feel that the Osaka Roon is too lowbrow or popular as compared with the highbrow fare in Tokyo or Kyoto. Indeed, Kato is one of the few more or less certified intellectuals and academics who are interested in the Roon movement or at least in the Osaka version of it. From the point of view of the older generation, it combines two heresies: it is politically "progressive" and culturally and musically unconventional. In the experimental series they have played electronic music, Japanese compositions of an atonal sort (there is much interest in Arnold Schoenberg), and progressive jazz.

We were so stimulated by the concert and excited by Osaka that we went out for a walk in the rainy streets, still jammed with people at ten at night. We saw our first full array of pachinko parlors, with the players, mostly but not entirely men, standing solipsistically before their machines while listening both to the "music" of the endless steel balls and the jazz blaring from loud speakers. Most of these new enterprises are owned by Chinese and Koreans; hence Kato, despite his sympathies for popular culture, has misgivings about patronizing them, since he says he's become something of a "nationalist" and like most Japanese tends to look down on the Koreans, who, a bit like the Negroes or Puerto Ricans in the United States, are relegated to the lowest and often the underworld jobs. The bright neon lights of the advertising signs, which so annoy the traditionalists or highbrow Japanese, seemed delightful to us; there is artistry and color here and in some of the signs in which electric lights make for a kind of comic-strip movement there is whimsicality; and the Japanese letters always seem to us beautiful, even though to a Japanese they only say, "Buy Matsushita Toasters" or "Peace Cigarettes."

I returned to my room to work on my article about the Berlin crisis for *The American Scholar*, terribly aware of how hard it is here to keep up with what is happening in the world, in spite of reading the four English-language dailies published here, for the American papers come five weeks late and only to a few places. Meanwhile, Kato was working with an *Asahi* journalist and for a time with Matsumoto going over the story of my talk that was to appear in the paper the next day, aided by a tape recording and by shorthand notes. The highly educated newspapermen here, competitive as they are with each other, show at their best a rare conscientiousness, and of course Kato and Matsumoto were eager that I not be misinterpreted or misunderstood or misrepresented. (Although the occasion was sponsored by *Asahi*, *Mainichi* had a reporter there who spoke English and who had quite a good and careful story in the English-language *Mainichi* the next day. A still fuller version, taken from the transcript, appeared in Monday's *Asahi*.)

Kyoto, October 22

Strolling around Osaka this morning, we wandered into a bookstore where people were standing and browsing and reading books—many students read books and magazines only in this way, as libraries are terrible and there are few public ones. The bookstores don't mind, and neither do the buyers, who regard a well-fingered book as a good buy—though there do not seem to be many buyers, in comparison with the browsers. As Kato said, in commenting on the willingness of coffee houses to allow people to stay for a whole day nursing a single cup, "feeling Western": "The Japanese are generous." In one very tiny bookstore were books by Frank Lloyd Wright, and any sizable bookstore has paperback classics in English and German as well as in Japanese. The books often have beautiful covers and are arranged with style and taste.

DR

On the drive back to Kyoto, Kato pointed out that every factory has its shrine somewhere in the corner of its lot or compound. One would find a similar shrine somewhere in every big office building. Kato thought this not incompatible with the modern scientific world, since in that very world there was always some element of chance beyond our control or prediction. And, of course, there is no place so hygienic or functional as to be without flowers—in the Otoyama assembly room there were flowers, as there are in every landing of a hotel or office building. As we left Osaka, we had a glimpse of the superlatively handsome Dentsu building by Tange, perhaps Japan's most famous architect, of which we'd seen pictures in *Horizon* accompanying an article by John Burchard; Dentsu is a big advertising agency and the building combines modern and traditional Japanese themes.

ETR

In our conversation with Kato driving back to Kyoto, we got on to the subject of language and the difficulty in translating English, and particularly Dave's English, into Japanese. There are words Dave uses frequently that do not exist in Japanese, such as irony and cynicism; the idea of something slightly less than, or more than, cannot be literally translated because in the feudal Japanese language things are hierarchical, either above or below; in other words, shadings or horizontal comparisons cannot be made. It is a language of the concrete; symbols can suggest abstract ideas but there are no words with abstract meanings. And so there is often misunderstanding; for example, when the Emperor went on the air to tell the people that Japan was surrendering, at the end of World War II, he was misunderstood, and some people thought he was saying the opposite. (Perhaps this is not a good example, as purposeful misunderstanding can happen anywhere.)

Kato went on to talk of the written language. The old language of Chinese characters is beautiful and poetic. The addition of *kana*—a system of phonetic symbols for syllables—was made almost universal in the Meiji period, but it was considered cut-and-dried and unpoetic, and thus the language became a mixture of the two. The spoken words are exactly the same, but in writing, the calligraphic beauty of the Chinese characters adds associations and overtones which are lacking in the same words in *kana*. This struck me as a fascinating idea—as if for us a poem written in a beautiful hand were therefore more poetic than if typewritten. This is not entirely correctly put, because the associations of certain Chinese characters would be their use in ancient, familiar and beautiful writings. This discourse on the aesthetic beauty of written characters only emphasized for me the importance of the visual, that is, the concrete over the abstract, for the Japanese: the character as a thing in itself.

Late in the afternoon we drove up a narrow winding road to the top of Mt. Hiei, a strangely shaped mountain with steep wooded slopes. In the new hotel on top we gathered for our meeting in a room looking out over ridges of this mountain down to Lake Biwa on the left and on the other side into the valley where Kyoto from this height seems to nestle. We sat, ten or twelve of us, at a long table, sipped tea, and as we talked, the evening descended. It was the same group that we had met with at the Institute for Humanistic Studies. As I looked around the table, it seemed a varied group. Murata has an expressive face that wrinkles up when he laughs; he seems to have a lighthearted youthfulness and warmth. Osabe is slight and pale, with broad face and delicate features. He talks with his lips almost closed, inaudibly. He rarely smiles and there is something sardonic about him. Suzuki is perhaps the most distinctly Japanese in appearance. His face has an impassive quality, his hair straight and longish with a lock falling across his forehead much of the time. This lock of hair seems to take the place of facial expression, as it invariably falls over his eyes when he becomes intense and involved in what he is saying. Professor Mori is clearly the *sensei*, the master to whom the younger men defer. While they are in their thirties, he is in his late fifties, or thereabouts. He is gray-haired, wears steel-rimmed glasses, and has a worn, kindly face. We felt familiar and at ease with them. They were as usual smoking constantly, Peace or Hi-Life cigarettes, and Mori was also smoking a pipe from time to time.

Osabe had passed around a two-page article on nature symbolism which was to be the theme of the discussion. He began by speaking of the symbolism that is necessary for communication in Japan even in the most intimate relations between husband and wife. A man and a woman can communicate their feelings through watching their child fly a kite better than they can through words. Until there was a child, the wife could only address her husband in a formal way; once they have a child, she can address him cheerfully as *otochan* (papa) without any embarrassment. *Ikebana* (flower arrangement) is an art of communication between husband and wife that survives from feudal times. The wife by delicately bending the branch of a plum tree is telling her husband that her affection is delicately bent. The husband does not look at her but at this branch and knows what she feels. The meaning is expressed in this form, which is a form of art. "While this is hardly a modern form of communication," Osabe said, "it is a unique art developed under special (feudalistic) conditions and something worth keeping in our Japanese heritage. Because our society is still so status-conscious, communication remains difficult. That is why a child, who is outside the status categories, close to nature, and uncorrupted by society, has a great meaning for us; the child expresses nature in the form of human life. In our art and our literature and now also in our movies, nature has an important place and is used symbolically to express certain feelings."

Riesman: In flower arrangement the woman knows the language well, but does the man?

Mori: The man can't understand the technique of flower arrangement, but he understands its form and meaning.

Murata: It has a more elaborate meaning than nature symbolism because it is "shaped."

Mori: Man can always understand something made by man, the work of art.

Osabe: I think for us verbal communication is often a disturbance of communication.

Mori: Among peasants in a rural community there is understanding without words. In the city it is different.

Murata: Our language is ritualistic. There is silence in a family because there is no need to speak. Everyone knows what is going on, what is meant.

Lifton: But is there misunderstanding because sometimes people *think* they understand what is meant?

Mori: Yes, in a new situation, in a situation of crisis. But this happens even in verbal communication. Our language is an approximation of things, a talking around things, and we cannot be precise because our ideas are expressed in concrete objects which are symbolic of feelings and can be easily misinterpreted. In a situation of crisis the "national unity" is broken and there is misunderstanding.

Murata: But the emotional pattern remains the same. Young people seek friendships where words are not necessary. They feel intimate if they look at the same thing together, if they look at the mountains together, or the moon.

Osabe: We do not talk much, we are quiet, but we have a great deal of symbolic expression which is borrowed from nature. We are a part of nature and have no higher value than nature. You in the West have Christian symbolism and morality, which is higher than nature. Your modern novels are concerned with people and psychology. Japanese novels are more concerned with settings in nature.

Riesman: But how can you tell what the modern girl is thinking—can her feelings be expressed by bending the flower one way or the other as in the old days?

Osabe: For new surroundings we need new symbolic meanings, and we will then discover that this is not unlike arranging flowers.

Lifton: Students attempt to do away with this. They go to the other extreme, that of logic, although the other is still there underlying in their feeling. Isn't this the spiritual conflict in Japan?

(People seemed to agree, but did not pursue the point. It was beginning to grow dark—the sky and the lake still light, but the mountains black, with lights blinking here and there far below in the valleys. We were being served a second round of tea.)

Riesman: Japan is a print-oriented society. How does this affect the non-verbal communication you were speaking of?

Osabe: The written words (characters) are symbolic forms of natural objects.

Mori: To go back to your earlier question: watching television or listening to the radio has replaced flower arrangement. By watching together, two people are communicating. You will notice that couples in coffee shops don't talk.

Sasahara: Flower arrangement has no meaning in itself, but it is a way for a woman to express her femininity. Perhaps I can't understand the flower arrangements of my wife, but I can understand the fact that she is expressing herself.

Lifton: Does a beautiful meal or kimono express the same thing in your wife as flower arrangement?

Sasahara: Flower arrangement is more formal and elevated.

Murata: Hunger gets involved in the question of the beauty of food.

Suzuki: Flower arrangement since the war has been taken over by mass culture.

Mori: In post-war Japan these things have been commercialized.

Riesman: Do the intellectuals here pursue obscurity to avoid massness?

Mori: No. This does not exist in Japan. The highbrow doesn't fear mass culture. I know in the United States professors don't go to movies. But in Japan they go to movies and watch television.

Osabe: In the thirteenth century the peasants drank water of the shrine together; drinking from the same source was an expression of deep ties of friendship. And this was the religious and artistic origin of the tea ceremony, an expression of harmoniousness. Though it continues today, it has lost much of its original vitality and meaning. It is not easy to find new forms for this feeling.

Murata: Sharing of food in *sukiyaki.*

Riesman: Perhaps the closeness of living in Japan enforces a communal sharing. It is quite different from the open spaces of the United States. This closeness in Japan affects the feeling and the gestures.

Osabe: Yes, our small finger gestures.

Suzuki: The density of population is not due to the smallness of Japan but to concentration because of irrigation in certain parts. One finds these same small gestures in all rice-growing countries, in India and China, for example. Very different from dry-farming countries. But also our architecture until now has all been of wood. Our buildings are small; one cannot build large buildings of wood. Earthquakes also have affected the size of buildings. All these things affect the feeling of density.

(It was now completely dark. We remarked on the changing beauty of the view. This brought the discussion around again to the subject of nature.)

Suzuki: In the West the distinction between a human being and an animal is clear. But in the East the concept of nature (as scenery) does not exist; it is *there.* Nature is all one, and we are part of nature. But there is an hierarchical order in the world, in the animal world.

Mori: And the human being is the highest. This is why the study of apes and primates has prestige. But there is continuity of the whole animal kingdom; this is a country of coexistence, of balance.

Osabe: We have still something of the old religious feeling of animism. In Buddhism there is the belief in the sacredness of animals and plants.

Riesman: But this differs from Indian Buddhism, doesn't it?

Osabe: In India some sects were angry with the British for DDT'ing.

In Japan this would be incomprehensible. Because here there is love for humanity, too.

Riesman: In America we have anti-vivisectionists who do not love humanity. But also our affection for cats and dogs has a childlike quality.

Mori: I knew a German professor who was devoted to his dog. When he had to leave the country and could not take his dog with him, he shot it. This is inconceivable to us. Our dogs do not come in the house. They are not companions in that way.

Riesman: The Japanese oneness with nature seems to create a different attitude toward nudity than ours. But are the Japanese taking over our Western unnatural views of it?

Murata: For the common people to share baths is natural in Japan. But other forms of nudity are avoided as immoral.

Sasahara: These are the open attitudes of Japan, like the attitudes of Polynesia; it's the nature of our culture.

Riesman: Is there an oversensitivity about this openness?

Suzuki: The oversensitivity of the Japanese implies our identification with foreigners. Also the people who are the hosts and guides of the foreigners try to please them, that is their business. This is our "guest culture." And this guest culture is strong even in rural areas.

Mori: But also, since the Meiji Restoration, Japan has been imitating Western culture and does not want to appear backward.

At this point the discussion was interrupted for dinner. We went downstairs to the main floor and into the huge glass dining room, where a long banquet table was reserved for us. There we resumed the conversation in twos and threes, because at this table and in the noise of this large room it was not possible to keep the conversation general.

Professor Mori, who was sitting opposite me, spoke of Rousseau and the impact that his writing had on the Japanese, who were ready for a "return to nature" after the Meiji Restoration. Rousseau's ideas have had a very important influence on the education of children, as in the freedom to express themselves in painting.

Osabe talked about the favorite indoor Japanese game, pachinko (similar to our pinball). Pachinko perfectly symbolizes the post-war period: it is made of the same materials that machines are made of, glass and steel, and also it is a sort of machine. This is in contrast to the favorite pre-war game, mah-jongg, still popular with many; mah-jongg sets are made of indigenous Japanese materials, wood and ivory.

Pachinko is a game played mostly by men in crowded pachinko parlors in the amusement areas after working hours. A man plays alone, standing up, as in the factory he may just have left. Isn't it the fascination with the machine and playing with the very kind of thing the people work with that is the main attraction, more than the luck and small prizes? The Japanese are in love with machines, try to make them beautiful. The dashboards of their cars are beautiful; they polish and clean their cars all the time. You never see a dirty car in Japan, he said.

A conversation on the other side of the table was on quite a different subject. Sasahara spoke of the completeness in the Japanese way of seeing things. (Sasahara is an anthropologist who uses the Rorschach test in a method he has developed along with the study of ecology.) He said that Americans break the Rorschach plate up into parts and analyze it. The Japanese aesthetic is one of wholeness, as in the arrangement of flowers and scroll in the ornamental recess. I was thinking as he talked that for us it looks like incompleteness and asymmetry. We would be more likely to have, on a mantelpiece, a balance of two vases or two candlesticks, one at either end. But the Japanese see the asymmetry of one vase as something to be filled in imaginatively and therefore quite complete.

Our Japanese hosts were playful and gay, and after dinner we wandered around the hotel; there was a potter who made souvenirs of plates, on which we all wrote our signatures, Dave's and mine looking very dull beside the beautiful calligraphy of the Japanese; there were the usual showcases, for tourists, of Japanese silks, china, lacquer ware, etc.; there was a game room with pinball and tenpins on a small bowling table. Our Japanese friends suggested we play. The men took off their coats, rolled up their sleeves, and threw themselves into the game with gaiety and energy.

On our drive down the narrow mountain road with hairpin curves, Murata talked about the way the Japanese present baseball on television. It is done from both a psychological and an aesthetic point of view, he said. There are the intense close-ups of the pitcher's face, there are shots which show the beauty and grace of the action, there is the overall view of the scene, and these are constantly cut in on each other.

Kyoto, October 23

The Miyako Hotel is in an ideal location for us. We can start out walking in any direction (except the back of the hotel, which is a steep mountainside) and find ourselves on some narrow street with little shops, or houses with small gardens. These streets are quiet, with almost no traffic, only a few walkers, sometimes in clogs, making a nice clopping sound on the stone pavement. Children too young for school play in the yards behind houses and in temple courtyards. They play with small things, dolls, pebbles, balls. Their voices are strikingly high and chirping, like birds. We pass an elementary school and hear children singing. This school is the only ugly building in sight, yellow brick like American schools of the nineteen-twenties. Our street winds down then into a market street, part of which is an arcade roofed in with rippled blue plastic glass. The grocery shops spread their wares into the arcade on counters, or display them in boxes and barrels. Everything is shining and wet, washed and scrubbed, so that the vegetables look very bright and the fish glisten. Alongside the stalls of fresh food are candy shops, dry-goods shops, toy shops. What one feels in all this is great abundance and color and variety. We come out then onto one of the many small streams that lace through the city, fed from the mountains. We find our way back to the hotel by the main thoroughfare, which is teaming with trucks, buses, motorcycles, trolley cars—another world from that of the quiet alleys we have just explored.

The *Asahi Journal*, a weekly highbrow magazine published by the *Asahi Shimbun*, arranged to have a tape-recorded discussion between Dave and Suzuki on the subject of "The Present Day and Present Generation." The discussion will then be edited and published as an article. This is a common method of getting articles for magazines.

The discussion was held in an old and charming restaurant which was once a private house. We were introduced to the editor of the *Asahi Journal*, some assistant editors, and the man in charge of the tape recording; Suzuki was already there and also Murata. We then sat on silk pillows at the long table, and after tea and brief conversation the discussion began.

Owikawa, the editor, began by asking Dave about his impressions of the youth of Japan. Dave replied that he was struck by how happy the Japanese children seemed in comparison with American children; that Japanese children do not seem to be bitter or envious; that American children, by contrast, appeared to be noisy, precocious, and discontented.

Suzuki said that this difference might be due not so much to the stage of development (that is, their precocity or lack of precocity) as to the way in which children develop in Japan: children have their own culture with their own special festivals and celebrations; shrine festivals have shrines for children to carry, so that children can participate in the adult world, but on children's terms; there are children's magazines and television programs; perhaps all this keeps them from being frustrated.

Dave said that in the United States children want to grow up as quickly as possible, drive cars, make love, and in these ways anticipate maturity. But here in Japan, the children's world may be happier than the adult world: perhaps the children have the benefits without the burdens of adult life.

Suzuki noted that the Japanese made a clear distinction between adult and child, a dichotomy like that between animal and man. But the child moves and develops in age-graded stages from infancy to adulthood.

Dave went on to observe that in America the question of who is winning occupies much of our emotional life; but that here in Japan, while there is a great deal of competition, it is somehow managed and contained; life seems less competitive, the premium is less on winning and more on consensus; there is a boss, but his authority is not a matter of continual contest; and the child is not made to feel inferior because he is "weaker than" somebody else, but has his place.

Suzuki agreed and said that in much of the mass media, particularly on television, there is the basic theme of "let's be friendly," coexistence. It was strange, he observed, that Americans and Japanese are so friendly with each other. The Occupation might be seen as two opposing forces, coexisting in a phase of transition.

Dave said that Japan was modernizing in its own way, quite different from that of the United States. In another setting, modernization has other meanings, and there is opportunity for cultural invention. Suzuki thought that the mass media had a strong effect on industrial societies in making them alike, and that if there had been television in the Meiji period, Japan would have become like the United States at that time. The main difference, he thought, in the ways of modernization in the two countries had to do with space: in the United States there was still room to move around, and in Japan, since there is no room, progress has had to be even more rapid and to go further.

Dave wondered if the lack of elbowroom in Japan forced Japanese children to be content with little, and so limited their ambition; they must be content with small rooms; they must put on uniforms in school, which may also be like spiritual uniforms for them; they feel crowded and pressured in trying to get into the universities. But in the United States, too, there is getting to be less and less room.

Suzuki mentioned the game of the Chinese Box, where only one square can be moved at a time. He went on to say that in the Meiji period there was more room and the young men could compete for success, and so the young had great ambitions; that today the ideology of success continues, though the society has been frozen, and so the young become frustrated. Television stories of success are mythology today. All this has an effect on Japan's view of international affairs: in the Meiji period, Japan believed in free competition among nations; later, when Japan felt frustrated, it invented the idea of the Co-prosperity Sphere in Asia.

Dave observed that the big bosses have huge offices in crowded Tokyo, and perhaps these take care of frustration and the need for foreign adventure! Japan's peaceableness today should become a model for the world.

Suzuki said that neither greed nor great ambition was possible in Japan and people had to be satisfied with slow movement on the escalator. There is a contradiction in this with individualism: the old individualism does not work for the Japanese, but they are not yet aware that they should have a new value system.

Dave observed that there seemed to be room for some individual expression in the handling of aesthetic detail, such as flowers, and that there seemed to be small enclaves of autonomy and ingenuity which have not been institutionalized by the society.

The editor remarked that the conflict between individualism and a formalized social structure could not be solved so easily once one had reached the stage of being a university student. Dave agreed that the escalator was not suitable to university life, that he had noticed a stiffness in students, that they could not ask questions after a lecture, that there seemed to be little give and take.

Suzuki said that here in the Kansai area people have developed a talkative culture, they enjoy conversation; in fact, there is coexistence between organized hierarchical society and the intimate society of small groups where individuality can be expressed.

The editor wanted then to get back to the subject of non-intervention and the model Japan might be for other countries. Dave said that American foreign policy tends to be dominated by Adenauer and Chiang and that the mild British and Japanese do not get through to us; he wished these two countries could be stronger in their convictions. The United States is impressed by people with convictions because we have not got enough ourselves. If Japan could send men of conviction into the foreign forum, they might make a difference:

Japan has taken some leadership in peace and the abolition of nuclear weapons, but should take more.

Suzuki wondered if they could project the balance they have achieved between the individual and society onto the international scene. Could there be intimacies between countries which would support the formal, organizational, and economic ties between them? The Japanese frontier is a technological one. American youth has a new frontier in terms of the Peace Corps. But what could the frontier for Japanese youth be? The Japanese youth have a real desire to go abroad; there is an accumulation of energy which could be used on the international scene, but they are uncertain about the appropriate way to go about it.

Dave replied that there was a real problem for youth in a gerontocracy like Japan. Also perhaps the Japanese overestimated the Peace Corps. It was late in coming, very small, full of problems and complexities. In Japan, there seems to be a contradiction between the global aspirations of the Left, with their large and abstract slogans, and the concrete and specific things they might do. The Roon group is an example of a concrete and specific accomplishment in Japan. Might it not become an internal Peace Corps? Why was there so little integration of the large Zengakuren ideas and practical accomplishments?

Suzuki thought the situation now was like that of an overcharged battery. The Zengakuren were discharging, but without any real creativity: their activity is a movement to discharge rather than to give. The Roon is another form of discharge. Because the battery is overcharged, the Roon is not enough for the needed discharge; a channel abroad is needed, too. Moreover, the Roon has the problem of being too large for any kind of action; it has become a mass. The editor added that there is the idea of coexistence within Japanese society; moves are slight and not drastic; this is the "wisdom of Japan." The result of this is also a kind of incompleteness: the Japanese do not think things through to the end. The Meiji Restoration, which was in fact a revolution, kept the Emperor, for example.

Suzuki said that the incompleteness was what supported and held together Japanese society; it minimized human sacrifice; very few were killed in the Meiji Restoration. "Uro ga kuru" is the expression for mild mental confusion caused by sudden outside change: on the whole, the Japanese can keep their spiritual peace and recover quickly—they did so after World War II. On American television, the mob easily goes insane, for example; but on Japanese television, an insane hero does not arouse an insane crowd; the people remain quiet observers.

Dave remarked that the Japanese do not seem to have great resentment against the Americans for the bombing of Hiroshima. Suzuki said that the Japanese suffer, but transcend their suffering.

During this discussion, we had been served tea. We now had a break, wandered around to look at the exquisite screens and scrolls in this room and the adjoining room, and to look at the garden. Then we sat down to lunch, and the discussion continued informally.

Dave had been asked by Otis Cary to speak in the afternoon to the students who live at Amherst House, which is part of Doshisha University. This sort of residential house is unusual in Japan, and there is a good deal of competition among the students to get into it.

The house itself looks very much as if it were a building from Amherst, transported brick by brick to Japan. But the flowering bushes and ginkgo trees and bamboo surrounding it remind one that this is, after all, Japan. Otis Cary led us into a dark paneled library where the students were already assembled in a semicircle. They stood up and bowed, then sat down as we took our seats. There was no talking among them, which gave the gathering a classroom atmosphere. As I looked at these students, regarding us so blankly, my heart sank, and I wondered how Dave would begin. I knew that he didn't want to give a lecture, but wanted to have a discussion. He began by asking about student life in the university, including the student movement with its radicalism and idealism; and then he went on to inquire what happens when they go on after graduation into business; how do they feel about this; where could they park their ideals? Otis Cary translated these questions fluently into Japanese.

At first it did not seem that anyone would answer. Finally an undergraduate in economics said that the students think about this question very much; it is difficult to take their idealism with them out into society. Another student spoke up, saying that there is little time to consider these problems; he is a graduate student, he works long hours; he falls into bed at night exhausted; when a *demo* (demonstration) goes by, he hardly gives it a thought, he merely says to himself, "Oh, another *demo*." Another student, very informally dressed in open shirt and sneakers, who said he was an undergraduate in engineering, explained that he was active in the student movement; he thought it wasn't just a matter of taking one's ideals, as is, right out into society; it is not just a one-way street; you have to match your ideals with what you do, live your ideals now and keep this posture later—this is a possible attitude. He spoke earnestly.

Another boy, who Otis Cary explained was their top judo athlete, said that he got his values from Zen; he doesn't expect to have to change them when he goes out into the world; and so long as Japan remains self-reliant and pro-capitalist he could see no trouble ahead. He mentioned two books he was reading in economics, both of which were about how to manage—"squeeze," Otis Cary added—labor both politically and economically. (Otis Cary explained later that this student comes from a rightist family in the weaving center.)

Another student said he had been reading *The Organization Man* and wondered how one could live in the "organization." He thought perhaps he should have aimed at a non-business career, but he had majored in economics, is a fourth-year student, and has already been picked up by a company. Dave remarked that in some of the better American universities, students try to select careers where this problem is not so pressing, such as medicine or teaching or city planning; in the United States students can sometimes change their field or their university, which is not possible in Japan; this rigidity must be a great problem for the Japanese students.

A student whose field is fine arts and aesthetics said that he was active in religion, especially in the Y.M.C.A.; while the Y.M.C.A. members are not politically active, they approach political problems indirectly; for example, they take specific cases such as certain laws, typhoon damage, etc., and try to see how to face them.

A graduate student said that he felt oppressed by obligations on all sides; he is working his way by teaching and tutoring and also must study very hard; he feels useless unless he can do his share in the place he is in, only then could he begin to worry about student demonstrations. I was struck that the graduate students who spoke up were all hard-pressed and harried, while the undergraduates seemed to be taking life easy.

Dave decided at this point to bring up a new question for discussion. He wanted to know if they felt that work in itself was an ideal; does the engineer enjoy making things, or is what they do just a way of making money so that they can enjoy life outside their work?

The first one to speak on this was skeptical, did not think there was much chance of enjoying one's work, although it might be possible for some, perhaps for engineers in terms of cooperating and running their own concern; but most are pushed into the third alternative of simply making money and having to get enjoyment outside, and there isn't much to do about it.

A quiet, serious-looking boy who had not spoken yet said that when he writes to his father about discontent—his father is a sea captain who is rarely at home—his father writes him long letters saying life is a happy place, work can be a happy place; perhaps all their talk is meaningless, like conceptual games; people must go out and feel life, feel the real thing—this desire is what directs him.

The young man who works in his spare time at the Y.M.C.A. said that when he can't find real meaning for existence, then he is being used by an organization or by society. When he doesn't feel this way, he feels creative, wanted, loved by someone; but in an organization, he feels caught.

When Dave asked if it was possible for students to enjoy their studies, a boy who had not yet spoken said that this was a difficult question to answer; most students find that going to the university is not what they expected. They are disappointed by the programs of study and the way they are carried out. He wanted to make a comment about the first topic, about the student movement: most students don't get involved in the student movement and don't know anything about politics; students have to work very hard to get into a university, and once in, they have to decide right away what they will specialize in; this is disappointing; then they worry about the job they must get for life; some want to be journalists or tradesmen; but—to answer the second question—they won't find anything worth living for in any of those jobs.

A young instructor who is affiliated with Amherst House explained that there are two groups of students at Doshisha: there are those who chose to come to this university, and those for whom it was a second choice, who failed elsewhere; the first group tend to enjoy the university life, but the second group are frustrated, and the abler of them tend to keep aloof from the other students; he himself belonged to the second group, studied Marxism, and joined the peace movement; he didn't become a Communist, since, in the weavers' area where his father was a priest, people don't care about Marx; and he also studied a great deal of history; but after he came back from his studies in the United States, the problems of relating his ideals to reality were very troubling.

Another instructor said that only 10 to 20 per cent of the students really enjoyed the curriculum; the rest just do the work as they are ordered to do, or they are athletes, or are interested in other things; and the teachers have very little concern about bringing greater awareness to the students through the subjects they teach; there is very little reflection going on about what education should be.

A student remarked that it wasn't until his junior year that he became interested in economics; and then it was not the courses that interested him, but the subject. He said he wanted to try everything while at the university because everything will be good to have later on in life; he reads all the titles and tables of contents of books in the library; in this way, he will know where to go for information when he needs it.

Another instructor remarked that there was one big difference between students now and ten years ago when he was an undergraduate; there was a lot of turbulence then, they had the idea that they could change things, that they could break the old traditions; there was a lot of optimism and hope; they were earnest about their involvement; they had a hero complex, but today the students haven't got this, they are more realistic; they don't feel that things are going to change; there is darkness ahead rather than light over the horizon; this is why students today can't get deeply involved in the *demo.*

Dave wondered why, with their spectacular activities and accomplishments of last year, the students now so belittled them. Perhaps this sense of failure is a self-confirming prophecy?

Another student who had not yet spoken said he felt as if he were in the doldrums, with no motivation; the *demo* made him wonder if this was the thing to do, especially in Kyoto, where they had so little effect; the more he thinks about ideals, the less he is sure; and he hasn't the energy to pursue the search for meaning; at the evening service he attended last night, the discussion was about whether or not there is a God, and he kept wondering: "What difference does it make?"

A third-year student from a coal-mining region who was involved in the *demo* of last year thought that perhaps what they accomplished looked better from the outside. But, he said, the Zengakuren were completely shattered after last year; too much heroics was involved and there was a lack of realism.

One of the overworked graduate students said that what mattered most to him was having friends in whom he could confide and be confided in; classes weren't important; he got his best mark in a course he never attended and his worst in the one he did attend. He recounted a popular story about how student papers are marked: the professor turns on the electric fan and allows the papers to blow around the room; those papers that are blown the farthest receive the highest marks.

Dave wanted to know if the best part of their education was outside the curriculum, and several students agreed that it was; but there were too few places where they could meet and have discussions, drinking, and bull sessions; their activities, their clubs, their mountain climbing, and also their reading, television, and public lectures—all this was more interesting than their curriculum. The student who teaches at the Y.M.C.A. said he got a lot of pleasure "in showing those who do not understand, to understand"; another found a common bond in a small religious discussion group; in classes there is no possibility for discussion, but in this group there is a common bond which makes discussion meaningful.

At this point the discussion was brought to a close, and after applause and ceremonious bows, most of the students filed out. The instructors, however, stayed, and one or two students, to continue the conversation informally. One of the instructors explained that the students in this gathering were not representative of the university as a whole, that most of the students were "organization man" types and spent their time playing mah-jongg. Another of the instructors remarked that the educated and sensitive Japanese try to move away from mass-produced things, such as *danchi* (apartments), but he understands that Mr. Riesman in a newspaper interview seemed to say that the Japanese must find themselves within these new developments.

Dave answered that it is a traditionalist view to believe that one can only find autonomy in a free-standing house; this is not realistic in a crowded society; aristocratic values may not be possible in the *danchi*, but some of the population would have to be dead if people could be housed only in the traditional way; Japanese society, however, is very inventive in finding ways of using small space for large effects; this requires ingenuity.

One of the students said that, even taking a positive attitude toward *danchi*, this housing should be criticized for bad design: there is no common meeting ground; it is all up and down; perhaps the buildings are well designed for privacy, but not for creating a neighborhood. Dave agreed with this. As I listened, I was struck by this concern for community and neighborhood, because one doesn't have a sense of communities existing in the cities we have seen. While the cities, to be sure, are made up of villages, one does not feel that these villages are communities, for whatever life there is, goes on behind fences and behind *shoji*. The people in the streets are always busy going somewhere, they are not standing around gossiping or loafing, as people do in Italy; there are no squares or fountains where people gather. In this sense, the Japanese cities are more like American cities. Community must mean the family or clan—and, of course, a family can comfortably gather in a Japanese house, but not in a small apartment. Another student wanted to know which people were the lonelier crowd, the Americans or the Japanese. Dave thought that on the whole there was greater social ease in the United States, an easy boy-girl intimacy, for example, while the game of pachinko may be symbolic of Japanese loneliness; but, he added, the differences must be judged in terms of aspirations: the Japanese ask less of life, and therefore are content with less. Many young people in the United States are in psychotherapy; in Japan, psychotherapy hardly exists, and so people must fend for themselves, sink or swim; there may seem to be, deceptively, more psychological health in Japan; but aspiration is greater in America. The student continued the discussion by saying that the quality of friendship in the United States is different from what it is in Japan; for example, if he had a date, but could not get a blind date for his roommate, then he would not go out with his girl friend; instead, he would go out for a drink with his roommate; people get bound to each other and there is a kind of stickiness in Japanese friendships.

Another student said he liked to lose himself in a crowd or in nature, become one with nature, that is the way he finds himself best, or in a Buddhist temple. He recalled that Mr. Riesman was quoted somewhere as saying that tradition changes, and when it no longer changes, then it is no longer worthwhile; he was also quoted as saying he preferred Tokyo to Kyoto—why? Dave explained that while on the whole the Japanese are not ashamed of watching television or playing pachinko or enjoying other aspects of the modern industrial world, there were some intellectuals in Japan—and even more in the United States—who would deprive others by setting themselves up as merely snobbish judges of what is beautiful and what is "authentic." But this only closes off appreciation of new human creations: how many Japanese are aware of their great modern architects, Tange or Yoshimura, for example; of their great filmmakers, Kurosawa or Ozu? Isn't there room for appreciation of both the old and the new, and isn't this typical really of Japanese adaptability and eclecticism?

It seemed at this point time to stop. After the students and the instructors had politely thanked Dave and left, we stayed and had dinner with the Carys, going over the discussion. Apparently it is most unusual for students to talk in a large group as they did this evening with professors and strangers present. Because it provides this kind of experience, Amherst House is much sought after. Yet this experiment of a residential house, which has been going on for many years, has not inspired other such experiments.

Osaka, October 24

Matsumoto had arranged for us to make a return visit to Osaka because he wanted us to meet an Osaka merchant, a friend of his, to give us an idea of what such a man is like and thus a clue to the essential spirit of one of the great commercial cities of Japan. We entered a dark Victorian-style brick building with the name of the company painted in English and in Japanese on the glass above the door. We took an elevator up to Mr. Inaba's office. This was quite unlike the huge and lavish offices of the president of the automobile company we had visited in Tokyo. It was simple and small, paneled in dark wood, with an old-fashioned desk and filing cabinets. Inaba greeted us warmly after he and Matsumoto had bowed to each other in greeting. We sat around a table in large easy chairs, and after we had talked for a few minutes, the secretary brought us tea.

Inaba was lean and elderly, perhaps a little old-fashioned, not at all the tycoon-war-lord type such as the large men with impassive faces we have seen coming to the Rotary Club meetings at International House. This man was expressive and sincere and spoke English easily. He began by saying he had read *The Lonely Crowd* and had given a talk on it to one of his businessmen groups. He and Matsumoto joked a little, Inaba saying he was not an intellectual but Matsumoto was a brilliant man—and so in his presence he shouldn't open his mouth; they had been classmates and Matsumoto was always the brighter, he confided to us with a twinkle in his eye.

Then the discussion got onto the subject of Japanese trade. Inaba said that Japan is virtually cut off from the rest of the world because the Japanese do not know foreign languages and in general are not good salesmen. They are cut off not only linguistically, but psychologically as well. He said it was vital for Japan's survival to overcome this. We asked about his own remarkable facility in English, and he said he had gone to school in the United States, that it was quite common for the sons of merchants to go abroad to school to learn English. He had gone to Mt. Hermon School. We said we had seen the school and had driven by it many times on our way to Vermont in the summer. He said that the headmaster had been very kind to him, but that a Japanese can't go abroad to school without getting an inferiority complex. He said in fact no Asian could study abroad without having this experience, and he understood very well the feelings of Africans and Indians who go to Europe and America to study. He said his sons had also gone to school in the United States to learn English. But his sons were not going to carry on his business—and this was not unusual in Japan; business is not always carried on from father to son.

He talked on, stimulated by Dave's questions. He said that Osaka businessmen have no influence with the government. He spoke of the aristocracy as being effete, and there being no landed gentry any more. He said that making money wasn't the most important thing to him, he was not romantic about it—like people in Texas! He liked to make money and have enough to be comfortable, but for most Japanese merchants it was the most important thing. He then returned to the subject of his sons. One was a lawyer, another was studying medicine. When the oldest son came back from his studies in California, he was disgusted with Japan: he looked at their house—a good Japanese house—and looked at the street lined with good Japanese houses and said it was like the Congo. Inaba laughed genially. He then showed us photographs of his sons. We asked if they were married. They were, and he went on to say that the marriage of the first son is of course important to the family, the parents must agree to it. But the marriage of the third son doesn't matter so much, he is pretty free to choose whom he wants. He then asked us what we had enjoyed so far in Japan. We mentioned a number of things, including the new apartment housing, *danchi*. Inaba said that *danchi* are not Japanese; but he had noticed that the women there look different from other women, better dressed, happier. Dave remarked that in *danchi* the women had gotten away from their mothers-in-law. Inaba agreed that this was very important. The women probably read the *Ladies' Home Journal*, he added with gaiety.

We suddenly realized that we had already been an hour with this busy man, and moved to leave. He seemed pleased with this visit and wanted to continue the conversation; he asked if we would have dinner with him this same evening. We hesitated, since we had planned to spend the evening with Murata and Osabe seeing the night life of Osaka. However, we were very taken with him and said that we might have dinner with him if he wouldn't mind our leaving early for another appointment.

After accompanying us back to the hotel, Matsumoto departed for Kyoto. Later that afternoon we met with three young men, a year or two out of the university, who had been students of Murata and now had white-collar jobs in large companies in Osaka. We all sat around the table in our hotel room and had tea sent up. After the introductions and explanations of our interests by Murata and some chatting among themselves, since they had not seen each other for some time, Murata asked Dave if he would like to begin the discussion with some statement or question. Dave spoke of his interest, as a sociologist, in Japanese society and particularly in the younger generation's place in it. He wanted to know how each of them felt about the transition from the university to the jobs they had now entered, which he understood the Japanese called "getting on the escalator."

Mr. Matsuda, the first to speak up, said that he was working for an insurance company in the training of personnel; while there were no longer the privileges of being a university student, still he enjoyed the freedom of being out of the university. His work is interesting enough, and is a continuation of his study of psychology and human relations in the university; he isn't so alienated as he might be in some other sort of work; but if he could do what he really wanted and money were not an issue, he would like, together with his wife, to run a kindergarten.

Mr. Watanabe, who works as a researcher for the Mainichi Broadcasting Company, said that when he was a student he thought life was full of possibilities; but now these possibilities are narrowed down; he knows he will probably have to work for the company the rest of his life. His work is quite interesting and permits him to go on with his studies; he wrote an article on the development of the Japanese newspaper; he is interested in comics and cartoons and collects them; but he would like a more "human" job, such as teaching or journalism.

Mr. Kubota, who works for the ABC, one of the large broadcasting companies, does newscasting, goes along with the cameraman and edits the film; he had to learn how to do this on the job; anyone could do it; the university doesn't help in this kind of training—one has to learn oneself. He does the direction, not the camera work, and it is interesting because he gets around; he goes places and meets people; the colors and shapes of the settings of each murder or party are different; but even so the work gets monotonous after a while; some broadcasting companies, like NHK (the government broadcasting company), would be more interesting; they do documentaries and they go deeper. Since the national news comes from Tokyo by microwave, the reporters in Osaka have only the local news to cover; ABC has a minimum number of broadcasters, and this makes the coverage superficial; it's very different from newspaper work. He had made his own work more interesting by helping organize the union in the company.

Matsuda said that it is important to be an expert in his job, but this is not the only important thing; he wants to do something outside his work to make him more of a human being. He often feels lonely, but he can overcome this feeling in a small group.

Kubota thought there must be some field in which he could be more human, but he wondered if he really could be human, even in the best job. Dave said that the dialectic between work and life is inescapable; it is a profound and unsolved question in industrialized countries; but he thought that these young men, while influenced by nihilistic existentialism, were not cynical; they seemed to have rather the active nihilism of Malraux as a young man. Matsuda said that all three of them work for big companies, and it is partly the bigness that gives them this nihilism. In smaller industries they might, as intellectuals, have more freedom of action—but, he added with a smile, to be slightly nihilistic has a lot of sex appeal.

Dave wanted to know if the girls working as clerks in the insurance company had these feelings, were they discontented? Matsuda thought that on entering the company they were excited, found it interesting, enjoyed the social life and making money. But after a few years, when they are nineteen or twenty, their parents want them to leave their jobs and get ready for marriage, take classes in flower arrangement and tea ceremony. Those who are not going to get married are very different types. Between the ages of twenty-four and thirty they go on mountain-climbing trips and try to conceal their frustration, though they may still be hoping to marry. By the age of thirty they give up this hope (these are the unattractive girls) and form small, tight groups and go on tours, visiting temples and shrines. Very few girls work in companies because they have to support themselves, but do it to fill in those years when they have nothing else to do. Murata explained that the men cannot marry until they are twenty-five or older, and so the girls want to work for a few years; they work hard up to about the age of twenty-three, and after that pretend to work hard but don't; and again after thirty they begin to work hard.

Dave asked about marriage and how they chose or would choose a wife. Watanabe, who is not married, said that in college he liked girls who were politically involved; but now his ideal is a girl who could understand his life and tastes and could share them. In college he had plenty of time to meet girls, but now he has no time. When he marries he wants a house with a garden—that is the minimum.

Matsuda, who is married, lives in *danchi*, but he would like to have a house and garden. Now that he is married he takes better care of himself—he used to drink a lot and spend all the money he earned. Now he saves as much as he can.

Kubota said that he has no chance to meet girls, but even if he did he wouldn't be able to marry because he has to support his parents and sisters. He works from ten in the morning to nine at night—a housewife would have too much leisure with his long hours. If he had a wife, he would like her to work also; then the budget would not be so tight. He would live in *danchi*, and if they had children he would put them in a *danchi* nursery. He is not so romantic about having a house and garden. He would be satisfied to live near a park where he could walk. He thought that in marriage the man and woman should take the responsibility and not have a marriage arranged for them. Even so, the husband often develops intellectually more than the wife, or vice versa, and in this case continuing the marriage might not be good; quick divorce and remarriage should be allowed.

Dave asked if they kept up their political interests in their jobs. Watanabe said that in his first year at the university he read Marx and Lenin because he wanted a point of view on the world. He joined the Zengakuren, but he was backward and really didn't know enough, and the Zengakuren were too political for him; he was more interested in cultural movements. He worked for U.N.E.S.C.O. and hoped to go abroad. In his company he is the chief of the information bureau of the union; he enjoys this because he can meet people in other departments in this way. Matsuda felt about the Zengakuren as Watanabe did. Kubota said they must make a society where there is no poverty—this has been his belief since childhood. He turned against his teachers in school because they were very militaristic; he was against the Occupation because it censored newspapers; he had become familiar with Marx and Lenin in middle school, but in the university he was not interested in formalistic Marxism or making footnotes. After graduation, in ABC, where he works, he organized the labor union; while he appreciates the function of the labor union, he thinks the real problems must be solved on the level of politics. He hated teachers, he repeated, and he was against the entrance exams to the university; now he rebels against the government and resists the money of ABC.

Dave then asked how each one felt about his own future. Kubota didn't think he had a chance in management, though he would like more salary. (I was surprised that he could say this immediately after saying he resisted the money of ABC, but this sort of compartmentalization seems to be typical of Japanese thinking.) But if he were in management, then he would not be so related to the world as he is in reporting; and so he doesn't really mind. Matsuda said he probably had a good chance to get into management and this would satisfy him. Watanabe said that he was interested in the functioning of the organization, and also he thought it was worthwhile to work with the labor movement.

We thought at this point we should stop. We thanked them for giving us their time, realizing how precious this was for them, when they must work such long hours and have so little leisure—no time even to meet girls. I have the impression, though, that it is not that there is so much work to do—they probably spend half their time doing nothing, waiting—but that they must put in long hours to show they are loyal workers and eager to get ahead. There was something very appealing about these wiry, overworked, and ardent young men. What seemed to me remarkable about them was that, while disillusioned, they were still idealistic in a way, and while resigned to their fates, they were still ambitious.

At the appointed hour Inaba called for us in his Cadillac at the hotel. I was disappointed that his wife was not along, for I had hoped on this occasion that the Japanese custom might be broken. In intellectual circles the wives sometimes do go out with their husbands if it is a sociable occasion, especially with Americans, but businessmen seem to be conservative about such things. Also, his wife probably doesn't speak English. Even before we arrived at the restaurant, Inaba was in a very good mood; and as the meal went on, course after course, with *sake* served by three or four young women in beautiful kimono, he became even more expressive and jovial than in the afternoon. The conversation was both serious and light. For a while he was asking Dave about civil defense, upset about it and thinking there was a sort of craziness sweeping America. He said that the Japanese knew only too well there was no defense against atomic bombs, and if there were, there was no room or money in Japan for bomb shelters—there were not even enough houses.

Somehow we got on the subject of arranged marriages; Inaba said that when one saw the photograph of a prospective bride she looked very attractive, but then on meeting her for the first time she was often disappointing; this was a difficult situation because one didn't want to hurt her feelings. Clearly, for the Japanese, appearance is very important, even more important than for us. I am reminded that Inaba, when he picked us up at the hotel, met Murata very briefly at the door, and he told us as we drove over to the restaurant that he liked him immediately and liked his looks. And also I am reminded that when Tamaki spoke of Paul Tillich he brought up first of all his distinguished appearance, his head with its shock of white hair.

Inaba went on to say that when visitors came to Japan he showed them two things, his Zen monastery and the Minami area of Osaka—two extremes of Japanese life. We said that we were going to see the Minami area this evening. But what about his Zen monastery? We were curious, could he mean that he owned a monastery? Apparently so. He wished there was time to take us there. It was somewhere outside Kyoto, with a beautiful garden which was partly his creation. We had to hurry through the last part of the meal unceremoniously, not at all correct, when one should spend the whole evening eating fruits and sipping tea or *sake*. But our friends were waiting at the hotel by now, we explained. And so Inaba graciously ended the meal and took us back to the hotel.

Murata and Osabe took us on the subway, new and shining, to the other end of the city, and we came out at the Minami. The streets were brightly lit and filled with strollers. I was struck once again by the beauty of the vertical signs with Japanese calligraphy and the intensely brilliant colors of the neon lights. We passed many pachinko parlors, where men in their workclothes were intently playing this solitary game.

We left this area and walked through some arcades with attractive shops and windows filled with cameras, umbrellas, toys, clothing, candy. We walked on through more streets, past a large bathhouse building. We saw all kinds of people going in, even some very poor peasant types. Murata explained that the Japanese don't come to these baths to get clean: even for the most simple people, the bath is a sort of ceremony, a sensuous, aesthetic experience. He spoke about it in such a way as to indicate that we Westerners could not understand its truly spiritual meaning—how Japanese of him! We wanted to go in the building but found we could be admitted only if we were going to take baths. We walked on past theaters, movie houses, girlie shows. The area seemed to be laced with canals, and the neon signs reflected in them were quite beautiful. We were soon in another, quieter area of old Japanese houses overlooking the canals. Murata said that these were inns where wealthy businessmen kept their mistresses, and some were restaurants (geisha houses) which had their regular customers who came three or four times a week. Beyond, on the next street, were what had been houses of prostitution (before the passage of the law making prostitution illegal). On these badly lit narrow streets there were very few people, only here and there a few dubious-looking characters loitering. We turned back into the brightly lit square and took the subway again across the city to the other amusement area, near the railway station. It was now about ten o'clock, and crowds were pouring into the station from all directions, rather like Grand Central at five o'clock, and the traffic was a solid mass. We asked why this rush hour at ten o'clock, and Murata said that all the young bachelors were going home from their evening on the town—and some young women, too, but we saw very few couples.

Murata and Osabe wanted us to see one of their favorite coffee houses. We were exhausted and thirsty and glad to sit down. This coffee house was no ordinary place, in fact it was fantastic. It was rather like a Swiss chalet several stories high. Inside, it was ornate and dark, there were rooms leading into more rooms, with nooks and crannies dimly lit, tables and booths with Japanese lanterns. Then we came on a sort of high glass-ceilinged place, like an ornate conservatory, with waterfalls, pools, plants, vines, and grottoes. Jazz music was softly playing. The place was neither Oriental nor Western, but gave the impression of mystery and fantasy. At the different tables were boys together or girls together, occasionally a boy with a girl. We sat at a table near the waterfall and had the usual orange-flavored soda. Osabe said these coffee houses were places where young people could come and absorb Western things, coffee and jazz especially. They could come here and see what Western culture was like, even better than getting it through books. As a student he used to do this, sit alone for hours in a coffee house listening to jazz. Murata thought that coffee houses provided a place for young people to go with their friends, have some privacy, and get away from their parents. Osabe and I talked for a while in French, while Murata and Dave talked in English. Osabe talked about his love for Sherwood Anderson and for some of Faulkner. He said Mori liked more masculine writing, Hemingway and Steinbeck. When I asked him whether he liked Kawabata's writing, Osabe replied that he was an old-fashioned and rather feudal writer. This surprised me, for Kawabata had seemed to me very modern in his subtlety of style and psychological understanding. But I realized that Osabe was thinking of the subject matter—and perhaps this style is less new than it seems, simply Japanese.

We finished our drinks and walked back through the little alcoves and rooms, which were nearly empty now. The Japanese do not stay up late, and when we got outside, the streets were almost deserted.

Kyoto, October 25

We left Osaka this morning with Murata. This trip to Kyoto was faster and more restful by train than by car, but because the train was an ordinary commuter train without elegance, it was not the way our Japanese hosts would have wished us to travel. We talked during the trip about the relation of boys and girls in Japan, continuing our conversation of the coffee house last night. Murata said that boys and girls do many things together, but they have a brotherly-sisterly relationship with each other, partly due to the fact that the parents will make their marriage arrangements for them. Also, they often enjoy even more doing things with their own sex. Though they like the American "boy meets girl" movies, this is romantic for them and is something they almost never experience.

Murata went on to tell of one of the tragedies that occurs when a boy picks up or meets a girl with a sexual relationship in mind, while the girl looks on him as a "big brother." Her marriage to some other man is arranged by her parents, and then after the marriage she discovers she was in love with the first boy without realizing it. He spoke also of the non-sexual relationships of the young men and women workers in the factories: they are allowed to be sociable together, even to have dances and parties, but they are supposed to have a brotherly-sisterly relationship, and marriage between them would be frowned upon; indeed, they would be likely to lose their jobs.

When we got back to the Miyako Hotel, where Murata left us, we had an hour to spare before our lunch with Professor Sasahara, and we decided to take a walk. Our walks are a joy and a constant surprise to us. We have explored the area around this hotel in every direction. On this walk we crossed a small footbridge toward what seemed to be a temple enclosure. We passed through the gate of the enclosure and in the grove in front of us was a huge dark wood structure, its pillars made of great cedar posts, holding up the heavy scalloped roof; just under the roof were the jagged toothlike designs of the beam ends painted white. Later we discovered that it was an ancient gate of the Tokaido Road, and that there was another like it at the opposite end of the city, where scenes of the movie *Gate of Hell* were shot.

We had lunch with Sasahara in the sukiyaki bar of the hotel, by an open window, with the sun pouring in. Sasahara is one of the group of scholars in the Institute for Humanistic Studies. He is the anthropologist who uses Rorschach tests in studying cultures. He has given Rorschach tests in Nepal, Afghanistan, and Tonga, and makes comparisons of these with the Japanese. The people he tested in Nepal and

Afghanistan saw only minute detail in the plates, while the Japanese saw the plates as a whole. The Tonga island people in the South Pacific never saw the edge or frame of the picture, while the Japanese always did. He thought this difference was due in part to the kinds of farming done in each country. The people of Tonga do dry farming, burn out patches of jungle to plant taro gardens, but these are all mixed with weeds and there is no clear line where the jungle begins and the planting ends. The Japanese, on the other hand, have irrigated rice fields which are clearly outlined and defined. The Japanese garden is framed by a fence. As he put it quite poetically, the Japanese see things as complete but live in an incomplete world.

Sasahara spoke also of the contrast between the indistinct coastline of Tonga, with its coral reefs, and the clear-cut coastline of Japan. He showed us photographs, some of them aerial, to bear out his ideas. He believes the various environments even within a country also have a great deal to do with the different ways people—for instance, rural and city people in Japan—perceive things. He said that of course other factors were involved: rural people are more limited in their perception because of their lack of education, and also they are more religious than the city people.

Later in the afternoon Kato called for us in his Renault and drove us out to his house for a discussion with three of his students: an attractive young woman, a rather frail young man with glasses, and a sturdier youth in student uniform who turned out to be an athlete. While the conversation proceeded, Mrs. Kato served tea. She did this deftly, with Misao, their little girl, sitting in her lap, climbing up and sliding down, and sometimes running to her father and crawling over his knees as he talked or listened. Misao did not seem to bother her parents with all her activity. There was in general a wonderfully easy-going atmosphere; also, there seemed to be an equalitarian and friendly relationship between Kato and his students that was probably unusual in Japan. The students were seniors who had recently taken their exams for positions in various companies, Kato explained. Dave began the conversation by asking what these examinations were like.

Miss Yamashita said that she was an editor of the university newspaper and that she had wanted to go into broadcasting or advertising, but the only positions open to women are those of announcers or actresses. She said the way for a woman to break into reporting either in newspapers or in television is from the top, so to speak; if one writes a novel and becomes famous, then one is made and can get any position. She said jokingly that perhaps she would take a year out and write a novel. As the only job she could get was in business, she had taken a position in a furniture company. I have noticed, in talking about the problem of women and careers, that most educated Japanese are outraged by these injustices and cannot imagine any such restrictions on opportunities for women in the free and democratic countries of the West; they think it is only the backwardness and feudalism of Japan which is holding them back. This may be true, but they idealize the forwardness of the rest of the world. In her interview for the job she was asked whether she had to support a family and if she were planning to get married. Answered in the affirmative, these would be counts against her.

Mr. Sakamoto, the frail young man, told us that he had taken exams at several different broadcasting companies, and had not heard from them yet. He said the exams were absurd, with such ridiculous questions as the names of movie stars. What he really wanted to do was get into movie production. At the university he belongs to a cinema group that makes movies, shows films, and criticizes them. He is especially interested in documentary films. But no motion-picture company wanted candidates this year. And so the accident of an unlucky year may rule him out. He went on to explain that his older brother is in commercial movie directing and he wouldn't want to compete with him. He thought he would end up doing newscasting.

Mr. Miyoshi explained that he had been accepted by the Matsushita Electric Company. All the exams for the big companies have pretty much the same form: there is a physical exam, a test of one's command of a foreign language and Japanese, an exam in one's major field, a section that consists of a composition on some given subject, a general information test, and an interview; a recommendation is necessary as well. Miyoshi was not very happy about working for Matsushita. He looked forward to a rather gray life in his work, especially in the first years. He would like to be in the division of human relations or in publicity, but he thought it would be many years before he would do any interesting work.

Miss Yamashita said she didn't think her life or work would be gray. She thought life in school was rootless; it would be good to get out and have a job and earn her own money, have an apartment, perhaps share it with a girl friend.

Miyoshi said he was interested in philosophy but did not think that this would lead to anything practical and so did not major in it but in sociology. Two of his friends who majored in philosophy had committed suicide. He seemed to imply that not majoring in philosophy had saved him from suicide, although he added that politics also had been a factor in their suicides.

Sakamoto said that he had been a *ronin* (a student who failed the entrance exams to the university and spends a year or more cramming to get in) for a year before getting into the University of Kyoto, and during that year had done a lot of reading. He had read a book by Michio Nagai in which Professor Kato, our host, was mentioned, and when he came to the university he decided he would study with him. He wasn't very interested in politics, though he had taken part in a few *demo*, mainly because his friends did. But this was physically exhausting. He would prefer to express his political attitudes through documentary films.

Miyoshi observed that since he has become a Boy Scout leader (the Boy Scouts are Buddhist) he could no longer take part in *demo*.

Sakamoto said that the leaders of the student government were Communist. He is good friends with them, their offices are next to his, and he makes movies to help collect money for them. He is not a Communist, but this doesn't bother him.

Miss Yamashita explained that in her first two years at the university she participated in every *demo* because she thought this was a student's privilege. But now she feels that this should not be a privilege only for students: one should be able to continue to take part in *demo* later on too, and there should be continuity in one's activities. She does not want to participate now if she is not going to continue to do so; and so she has given it up. She went on to say that it is unfortunate that the student movement has split: the Communist Party was too moderate for some. Nevertheless, she thinks they should stay united.

Sakamoto thought the *demo* weren't a success because Ikeda is not much better than Kishi. Miyoshi objected to this. He said that Kishi had been taking Japan too far to the Right; the students overemphasize the shortcomings of the *demo*; the *demo* were an overall success.

Dave agreed and thought that the students' hope to start a revolution was excessive; to overthrow a prime minister was still quite an achievement. He said that students in the United States would be happy to accomplish half as much; American students are only just beginning to be active; and so far only the Negro students have taken part in sit-ins.

Kato said that management complains that youth today is not creative. He wondered if the examination system didn't have the effect of screening out many of the creative youth.

Sakamoto confirmed this by saying that the editors of student newspapers were considered dangerous by management.

Miss Yamashita thought that the generation ahead of them had had more reliance and independence in running the student newspaper. Also they were more involved, more serious, and less optimistic than this generation.

Kato said that the older generation had lived through the shift of policy in which their teachers, before and during the war, bowed to the rightist dictatorship, and since the war reversed themselves. The students were disillusioned and didn't think them reliable.

Sakamoto observed that in their own generation students were becoming "good boys and girls." But a few years ago things were different. When Italian neo-realism was introduced into Japan, the students went wild about it, got terribly involved, had no time left to study, and even failed their exams. But today students aren't that excited about anything. They study hard so that they won't fail their exams.

We had finished tea by now and it was beginning to get dark. Dave asked if they would like to ask him any questions. They seemed pleased and a little hesitant, and then Miss Yamashita asked about racial discrimination in the United States and in the universities. Dave replied that even in the universities, where there is greater tolerance than in other areas of the society, there is some embarrassment in the social relations between Negro and white students. The white students who are likely to be friendly with Negroes are the radical ones. The Negroes who go to college are for the most part middle class and conservative. They are not politically radical and they are not interested in the peace movement. They are only radical in the area of race relations.

I think Miss Yamashita was rather baffled by this complicated reply and so did not pursue the subject. They all seemed to be searching for questions to ask. Miyoshi wanted to know about the role of Christianity in American civilization; he didn't think Buddhism had much influence on Japanese life, at least in terms of change. Dave thought that Christianity and the religious spirit generally were decreasing in the United States, even though there was greater church attendance than ever. He said that in certain intellectual circles there is an interest in theological questions, influenced by Tillich and Niebuhr. And among other groups as well as students there is a strong Christian spirit of service to mankind.

There was again a silence in which they were searching for questions. Miss Yamashita, who is obviously a "queen" (a leader, that is, who is both brilliant and beautiful), said that she had seen in American movies that boys and girls are very eager to date, in order to catch someone. She wanted to know if that was the way it really was. She has a date once a week with two or three boys, but we gathered that this was unusual. Sakamoto said that students often formed clubs, such as the cinema club he belongs to, and that they have a coffee house where they go regularly. They don't have dates, but girls who work there act as hostesses. They also have hiking clubs, and hiking is something they do jointly with girls' colleges. Miyoshi explained that the cultural meaning of dating in Japan is different from what it is in the United States. In Japan if you date a girl it either looks as if you are engaged or, if you are not careful, it may look as if you are immoral. And so there is a feeling of tension and anxiety about it.

They then got onto the subject of comparing themselves with the preceding generation of students. They felt that they had less access to the professors, that the great professors seemed far away. Miyoshi thought that the pre-war students had a better time because they lived in dormitories and could have intimate friends. (There are so many students now that this is impossible, and most students must live at home and commute.) Miyoshi feels very isolated; that is why he joined the Boy Scout movement—to find friendships and closer relationships.

In discussing their reading and hobbies, the subject of China came up. They said there was a good deal of news on China in the papers. They were very interested in China and would rather go there than anywhere in the world.

During all this talk Misao was cozily cuddled in her mother's lap, or ran to her father, or climbed on Miyoshi's knee—he seems to be a frequent visitor and baby-sitter for them. Finally the students got up, thanked everyone, and bowing politely, produced copies of *The Lonely Crowd* for Dave to autograph. Misao then ran and got one of her picture books for him to autograph.

Later, as I thought about the discussion with these students, I was struck by how innocent they seemed, how untouched by Freudian thought. They seemed content with their simple relationships and friendships uncontaminated by anxieties about sex or homosexuality. Yet no doubt such anxieties exist among some young Japanese, as one realizes in reading, for example, Mishima's *Confessions of a Mask*. One hears also of cliques of avant-garde students in Tokyo who are quite sophisticated, where girls are as emancipated or even more so than in the United States. But these students we talked with were probably the norm. Sexual relationships develop late in Japan, partly because of a kind of Puritanism, and partly because the young cannot afford luxuries such as prostitutes and mistresses.

Kyoto, October 26

We have just come back from an all-day visit to a farming community with Kato. It was a spectacular train trip of an hour or so from Kyoto through mountainous country. We got off the train at Kameoka, which is a market town with a few small industries. At the new municipal building, we were taken through a large office with clerks at desks working on papers—but with no sound of typewriters. (We do not realize how blessed we are with our alphabet until we see what the Japanese are up against: a Japanese typewriter would have to have at least 2,000 characters.) The superintendent of schools and the county agent greeted us. Even in this crowded and cluttered office, room was provided behind a screen for conversation and tea. Kato had been able to arrange this visit for us because of a friend of his in the town who is the patriarch of the Omoto sect, a sect working for peace; in 1958 Kameoka declared itself a "peace village."

It had been planned that we should see one of the farms in the area; and after finishing tea, we were driven out to the country, followed by a press car and photographer. The farmhouses are clustered together in villages of perhaps six or eight houses at the foot of the mountains, so that every bit of the flat land of the valley may be cultivated. We stopped in front of a high, thatched-roof farmhouse surrounded by smaller buildings and a few large overhanging trees. We were greeted at the gate by a youngish-looking farmer, quite "American," hearty and vigorous, in wool shirt and khakis. He showed us around his newly built barns and sheds, where he kept chickens and pigs. The photographer with his flashbulbs kept taking pictures as we admired the place. When we finished the tour, the farmer invited us into his house. We left our shoes outside and entered the large dark kitchen, where his wife, a stocky peasant type, was busy at a huge black stove. After introducing her, the farmer led us into the next room, where we sat on *tatami* around a table. There was a lot of "junk" in the room, mostly piled up in the alcove: magazines, toys, and a fancy and hideous lamp; he had brought this back from Pakistan, he proudly explained. The farmer's elderly parents then came in. It was clear that they were very proud of him. He had taken over the management of the farm about ten years ago. The old man sat down with us, and the two women served tea. As it was chilly, the wife brought a pot of glowing charcoal and set it down near us. The farmer told us that he had gone to Pakistan, sent by the government, to teach the newest Japanese methods of rice farming. He reminded me, as he talked, of agriculture-school types or prosperous and independent Vermont farmers I know.

We returned to the municipal building a little later to meet with two young farm hands, sons of local farmers. In their early twenties and unmarried, they were rough and country-bumpkinish. Another man also joined us, clearly more educated, who turned out to be in charge of the youth organizations of the community. He explained that he comes from a farming family, but now that he is a community official he will probably not go back into farming. The other two will probably remain farmers, they told us, though one of them makes furniture on the side.

Kato made a little speech explaining our interest in talking with them. They then invited Dave to ask questions. In answer to these, one of the young men was quite talkative. He said that farm hours are too long. He has taken on making furniture as well, because farming alone cannot support a family—even though there are only two children in the family. The other young farmer said that his family could make a living from farming because they have half a dozen dairy cows besides their rice crop. Both boys went to agricultural high school but learned most of what they know about farming from their parents. The majority of their friends have left their family farms and gone to the city. They get jobs in the city, and some even commute from here to Kyoto. The boys complained that finding a wife isn't easy for farmers because the girls prefer to marry men who work in the cities.

They went on to describe a play that the dramatic club of the youth organization had put on. It was thought out by the group, that is, they all contributed ideas, with the help of some of the schoolteachers. One of these boys then wrote the synopsis and it was produced as a sort of improvisation. Its message was that farmers should do things cooperatively: they all want farm machinery but their farms are too small to pay for it, and so they should own the machinery on a cooperative basis; and chickens should be fed on a cooperative basis; then the young men would be able to make up the expenses for their marriage, which now are usually paid for by the parents. They performed this play twelve times, to different audiences—a great success. They did this play in the evenings in their spare time. In answer to our questions, they said they watch television and listen to the radio in the evenings—they enjoy this as much as putting on plays. They read the local newspaper, especially for the sports news. And they have read a book that is very popular, *The Young Man's Way of Life: How to Live.* There are agricultural magazines distributed through the Department of Agriculture which they also read. But one of them went on to say that reading didn't influence him very much, that he was more influenced by his whole environment. (There is no public library in the town.) Dave then asked him about politics. He answered that he learned about politics through the mass media, but it was too confusing. He hopes for a more stable system of politics in the town. The other young man said that he wasn't interested in politics at all. He hears about the Zengakuren and wonders if "this disease" is prevalent everywhere. (The disorder of *demo* and defiance of authority seemed to be what troubled him, not the politics of the Zengakuren.) Both boys vote for the progressive parties and don't discuss politics or anything else with their parents. (It was clear to us that these two were not typical of the rural population—that is, in their voting and in their involvement in cooperatives and in their work in the youth organization. Most of the rural population here, as in America, is more conservative.)

Then Dave asked if they would like to ask him any questions. There was a moment of embarrassment and finally the more talkative one asked what the position of agriculture is in the United States, is it more stable than in Japan. Dave said that our big farmers are like big industrialists and have their lobbies, but that there are millions of small farmers who are poor, and they have to take outside jobs or leave the farms for the cities, as here in Japan. The other young farmer remarked that the outlook for the future of farmers is gloomy, but he thinks he will spend the rest of his life as a farmer. The first one said that Japanese agriculture relies too much on rice and wheat; the situation is changing radically, as wheat is being imported more cheaply than they can raise it. Japanese diet is also changing from rice to bread and beef and pork, so the traditional production only of rice is a mistake. Diversity would be better. Cooperatives on a big scale are the only hope for the future, because they allow farmers to economize on both labor and equipment.

On the train back to Kyoto, Kato spoke of the changes in social class that had taken place in Japan. He said that in medieval Japan the peasants imitated the warrior-landowners; and in the cities the merchants and craftsmen imitated each other and became much alike. In the Tokugawa period, when the samurai moved to the cities they became scholars. It was the samurai who were the most active and intent on modernizing Japan. They were the ones who brought about the Meiji Restoration. He went on to say that the position of the samurai in Tokyo and in Kyoto is somewhat different. In Tokyo the samurai tradition is still strong and the samurai class has a great deal of influence on the government and on business. But in Kyoto and Osaka the businessmen have had the most influence, because they were already well established in the cities, with their fortunes made, when the samurai began to arrive. These samurai were usually poor, and so the merchants and bankers helped finance them; the samurai therefore became obligated to them and dependent on them.

DR

Kyoto, October 27

Another rainy day: the heavens are pouring. We have seen the sun only about three times since we have been here. The rain is now especially feared here, as there is such a terrible preoccupation with fall-out, and it is thought that the rain makes this worse and endangers the vegetable crops, or rather makes them unfit for human consumption. While the English-language papers are full of claims that the Japanese are less critical of Russian testing than of American, the Soviet threat to explode the 50-megaton bomb seems really to have aroused people here in a kind of cumulative sequence, and yesterday the students of Kyoto University for the first time held a demonstration against atomic testing, both Russian and American—previously they'd been sympathetic to the Soviet Union and had not done this. Since this is *not* the rainy season here, we wonder what it's like when it really rains. The rain brings out the colorful Japanese umbrellas as well as the "Western" somber and black ones that came into use as a sign of culture in the Meiji period—the latter are actually too big for the small bodies of the Japanese, much like the American cars that are imported by big-shots.

It is the greatest good fortune for us that Kato took a seminar on mass communications that Reuel Denney and I gave at Chicago in 1955. Kato has a remarkably wide acquaintance and through him we have met all sorts of people to whom otherwise we would have had no access. Dr. Ushida is a non-academic friend who shares an interest in Japanese popular culture and is one of the founders of a group that makes it a point to see *Japanese* movies rather than only foreign imports and to treat these seriously as aspects of popular culture. Dr. Ushida is also the pediatrician for the Katos' little girl, Misao, and for the children of Osabe and other colleagues. He makes enough money from the practice of medicine in the morning to have his afternoons free for study and writing, and to these harried university professors this seems an admirable course. He is known for his knowledge of Russian literature and recently visited the Soviet Union. As a student he was a Communist but became disillusioned and left the Party. Now in his sixties, he is still interested in politics but relatively apolitical and even cynical.

All this Kato told us while en route to his office, which fronts on a main street. The office is quite unpretentious, by American standards very old-fashioned: it is the kind of office one would find in the residence of a country doctor of the old school. American journals and some textbooks line the walls, along with a few German journals, as well as Japanese ones. Children's crayon drawings also are stuck on the bookcases—gay but not at all artistic. We later learned from Kato that while most Japanese children fear doctors, who are always giving injections, which most Japanese adults, as we learned, demand when they go to the doctor, Dr. Ushida is loved as a friend by his child patients and is not at all feared. We sat in comfortable chairs such as one would find in an American summer cottage—indeed, the sense of being in a summer cottage is heightened on a somewhat cold, rainy day like today when the wind comes howling in through the cracks of the sliding paper walls and one becomes aware that Japan is no country for Westerners or even perhaps for Japanese in the wintertime.

Dr. Ushida, with Kato acting as interpreter, suggested as a topic for discussion differences between American and Japanese methods of child-rearing, and Kato added that Dr. Ushida was a kind of Japanese Dr. Spock bringing the news of permissiveness to the parents of the children whom he treated. Evey and I raised questions about how Japanese children are indulged without becoming spoiled. Dr. Ushida said that children didn't behave as well as they used to, that they used to be quite quiet in his office and not disturb other patients, but now this was no longer the case—of course, to us, judging by American standards, the children seem angelic, hardly ever unruly or quarrelsome. Dr. Ushida explained their relative good behavior by saying that in the Japanese home there are no rooms in which children can be isolated; they are always with adults, so they don't suffer from loneliness or hunger for love, while at the same time they must learn not to get in the way of the adults, especially since in the paper-thin Japanese houses or apartments if they cried they would disturb not only their own parents but people in other apartments or houses. (Of course Japanese children do cry but they are promptly hushed by their mothers, and their mothers seem to us to spend endless time with their children, hardly leaving them out of their sight.) Kato added that in the cities children couldn't be allowed out on the street because of the dangers of traffic. (Sidewalks are a rarity and so are parks or any protected places to play.) Since children don't have playrooms in the small houses, they are always underfoot. Evey asked at what age they become independent, and Dr. Ushida said that only when they fall in love with somebody of the opposite sex—especially when the boy "deserts" his mother for a girl, and this is apt to happen in senior high school between the ages of fifteen and nineteen.

I recalled Dr. Milton Senn's articles on Soviet child-rearing and said it seemed to me that Soviet children were somewhat similar. Did he agree after his visit to the U.S.S.R.? He replied that in the Soviet Union parents, teachers, and children all had a common aim, whereas in Japan, with the loss of authority of the Emperor and of the father, this common aim had collapsed. (I thought he meant by "common aim" some Marxist or ideological goal, but it later turned out that he meant simply the industrialization and technological progress of the U.S.S.R.) Kato added that parents in the age group around forty had had their whole world collapse on August 14, 1945, at the time of the surrender, when they were suddenly told that they must be democratic; and children became other-directed by being turned over to the authority of their peers while the authority of the adults was destroyed. Younger parents, such as Osabe or himself, had grown up in a more or less democratic milieu and were not so confused; they could bring up children in the new permissiveness without feeling utterly lost.

Evey asked Dr. Ushida about mental illness, in which actually, so far as our limited experience runs, there seems to be rather little interest in Japan. He replied that only children who were overprotected sometimes had trouble, though some of this, he thought, was constitutional; and he added that children who were fatigued sometimes had spells of vomiting. He again referred to the hesitancy of mothers to let go of their sons. He also said that there was sometimes conflict in bringing up a child between the grandmother and the mother: the former was at once more strict and more sweet.

Dr. Ushida asked if we had seen Kurosawa's film *The Seven Samurai* (we hadn't); apparently he had written an article comparing the Japanese and American versions, showing that in the Japanese version there had been class conflict between samurai and peasant, whereas in the American version there had been racial conflict between Texas cowboys and Mexicans—there were other differences too, of which Kato and Bob Lifton had spoken earlier, in comparing the American version with the Japanese.

We then got onto the subject of politics, with Dr. Ushida saying that he thought that the duty of intellectuals in all countries was to combine against atomic war, and he wondered in this respect if the American intellectuals were not freer than the Soviet ones. When he had been in the Soviet Union, the ten or so intellectuals and physicians he had talked to seemed cut off from news of the outside world and seemed to have dogmatic views. Was there any way of reaching them? I talked about the recent London conference to which Erich Fromm and Homer Jack had gone, and about the various Pugwash meetings. He asked then, as many others have, about McCarthyism, and about the danger of its revival. I said, unfortunately yes, that McCarthyism was over as a national crusade, but its roots in provincialism and ethnic resentments remained, so that feelings of frustration in foreign policy could be channeled in this direction. I added that while American intellectuals were much freer than their Soviet counterparts to speak and write their views and to obtain information, they faced a population that was more jingoistic than the Russian masses. Dr. Ushida said that at least 90 per cent of Japanese intellectuals were socialist or left wing. I pointed to the phenomenon of the strongly anti-Communist ex-Communist as a peculiarly American one, without which McCarthyism would have been far less effective. I asked Dr. Ushida about Japanese Communists.

He said that they could be divided into the old bureaucrats and the young fanatics. Many sympathizers had left the Party after the revelations concerning Stalin, but they didn't find a home in either of the socialist parties because these were bureaucratic also. In himself and in many of his friends there were anarchistic tendencies—and Kato added that his friend Osabe had such tendencies. I asked how people of anarchistic tendencies could be sympathetic with Red China, which was even more fanatical than the Soviet Union. Dr. Ushida didn't know anything about China but he thought the Chinese did admire the industrial progress of the Soviet Union. I suggested that such progress could be bought at the price of bureaucratization and freedom; and I asked whether he had any sympathy with the humanist socialism of some Yugoslavs. He said he did.

Dr. Ushida explained that he was interested in Russia because Russia, like Japan, had been a backward nation in the nineteenth century, and the Russian intelligentsia, like the Japanese, had made an effort to catch up. He pointed out that Witte and other leaders under the Czar had had this goal even before Communism.

He then made a remarkable comment. He said that Russia as a backward country had imported Marxism and made it more pure, just as

Japan had imported democracy and made it more pure—this was in line with his general comparison of the two countries as "backward" and making efforts to catch up with the West. And in both cases the remarks seemed to me equally wrongheaded: the Russian Marxists are often Leninists in spirit, and this is anything but a purification of that humanistic side of Marx that Erich Fromm emphasizes. And "democracy" in Japan also has elements of caricature. Kato has spoken of the disgust of his generation, who were in school at the time of the Occupation's reforms and who watched their teachers slavishly turn from authoritarian patriarchal attitudes to no less authoritarian, though supposedly democratic, ones. "Democracy" is a plus word here, where the Leftists want to preserve the constitution against the radical Right and where everyone espouses democracy.

I said that the Japanese always spoke of themselves as a backward nation in pre-Meiji times, but since in 1868 they were far more literate than Russia at that time, were they not using Western industrial standards in calling themselves "backward"? Evey added that a country like Mexico could be industrialized and urbanized while still being in many ways backward—why should industrialization be taken as the sole criterion? I'm not sure our question got across. I tried again, asking whether highly literate and civilized Jews in the European ghettos could be thought of as backward, a view held no doubt by those Israelis who judge a society by its power plants, atom bombs, and other signs of progress. But again I don't think the point got across. Anyway, there was no answer; in fact, the various efforts I have made to get at Japanese self-hate—too strong a word—have misfired, even among people of unusual self-consciousness, or at any rate I've not found the way to get the point made. I tried once again by saying that Khrushchev wanted to match America in just those objects of national prowess, such as rockets and steel plants, that were assumed by the big powers to be the relevant criteria.

Dr. Ushida felt that the Russians he had talked to were so much better off materially than they had been before that they were quite satisfied with the regime and quite uncritical. At the same time, achievement of this material progress was the communal aim and this gave it a different spirit—or so I understood him to say—than achievement of material prosperity in Japan or in the United States. (It was not that he was against such prosperity. There is no touch of the ascetic in him or in Kato, who had written an article criticizing the asceticism of many Japanese Leftists who wanted to deprive "the masses" of their baseball games and television on the ground that these leisure sports

DR

made them apathetic, whereas in fact protection of their right to these, Kato thought, made them politically active.) From what Dr. Ushida said, I gained the impression that he had been disillusioned by his trip to Russia, and when Evey asked him this explicitly, it was so. We asked him which Russian writers he liked, and he said Chekhov, also a doctor, whom he read over and over again. We could share our enthusiasm here, and indeed I could picture Dr. Ushida as a kind of Chekhov: a man of gaiety and vivacity, and yet with a sense for the tragic in life such as I imagined Chekhov to have had. Evey spoke of William Carlos Williams, of whom he had not heard, as a similar doctor-writer in the United States, and we asked him if there were any American writers he liked—he said he read few American things but had liked *Arrowsmith*.

We talked a moment more about anarchism. I asked how this comported with the feeling for the group that was so strong among the Japanese. I gained the impression that there was no group of anarchists as such in Japan, but rather that there were anarchistic tendencies among people on the Left; Dr. Ushida said that it was impossible for a university professor in Japan to be lonely in *The Lonely Crowd* sense; only he with his medical practice was free to be on his own; and he, too, for reasons of companionship and solidarity wanted to belong to a group. What was meant by anarchic seemed to be an anti-bureaucratic feeling—a feeling of oppression, but not an explicit ideology.

When we broke up, he brought me a new copy of the Japanese edition of *The Lonely Crowd* to autograph for him. We said goodbye with the feeling that we had met a remarkable person, a fine doctor, and a man of charm and humanity.

ETR

Kyoto, October 28

This morning we went with the Liftons to see some Zen monasteries and gardens, a trip we have long anticipated. When we approached the Ryoanji Temple, the low, steep-roofed buildings seemed to be almost hidden in the mist and overshadowed by huge twisted trees and by the cedar forests of the mountain slopes behind. It was drizzly as we walked through the gate, water dripping from the roofs. We left our shoes outside the first small pavilion, along with those of other sightseers, and walked slippered on polished floors, glancing through *shoji* into gardens. As we came to the next pavilion and out onto the veranda, we saw before us the stone garden—the rocks and perfectly raked pebbles, so familiar, yet so unlike what I had imagined. It was small, a little disappointing, and there were too many sightseers.

(Bernard Leach had told us he got up at dawn one day to see the garden when no one was there.) It was surprising also to find that the garden was not something one steps into or can walk in, but rather looks at: like a scene or "a setting with sculpture," not really a garden at all. The Liftons explained that the rocks had a symbolic meaning; for the Japanese, everything is both symbolic and concrete. Mystified by their "true" meaning, I knew I could not experience this garden as the Japanese do. But little by little it grew on me: the raked pebbles, so perfectly grooved in straight lines and curved patterns around the rocks; the shaggy shapes of the rocks and the composition of their placement and spacing; the proportions of the whole—I could see the garden as abstract art, the creation of form in space, producing an intense feeling of stasis and peace.

We wandered into the pavilion by the garden. On one wall were richly painted screens of birds and trees, bright red and green and black. In the adjoining room were delicate monochrome ink paintings, landscapes and scenes of life.

As it was already noon, we decided to have our picnic lunch here, and went around to the farther side of the porch, overlooking another little garden, all rich green, with the forests beyond. There were no people here, it was quiet and lovely. We sat down and unpacked the lunch that Betty had brought—a Japanese picnic all in little lacquer boxes, rice wrapped in seaweed, small strips of raw fish, white radishes, and sliced carrots. To our surprise, while we were eating, a monk in a gray kimono appeared with a tray of tea for us. We did not know that anyone had even seen us here. He bowed and put the tray down beside us. We were quite overcome, and the Liftons thanked him in Japanese. We poured the tea into the tiny cups and sipped it with our meal; it was fragrant and sweet-smelling, almost like hay.

We went back to our taxi, which took us then to the monastery of Daisen-in. We drove through the narrow gate onto the cobblestones, the axle sometimes bumping the rocks in the road—the idea of driving into these lovely grounds seemed a sort of desecration, especially since the many small temples and walled gardens with large spreading trees gave one the feeling of being inside a sacred compound. The taxi stopped at the entrance to a temple, and we got out and walked through a small courtyard; a monk bowed his welcome to us. He led us through corridors past small rooms and gardens; there was a tiny raked garden with a few rocks, which, Betty said, also had a symbolic meaning—the raked (furrowed) pebbles representing the stream of life, and the stones being various stages of life in the universe. We stepped inside the small tearoom of Rikyu, the Zen Buddhist monk who was the originator of the tea ceremony, an exquisite room with paneled walls and sliding doors of tiny cupboards for the tea things, and a window looking out onto a garden. In this room Rikyu committed suicide when Hideyoshi accused him of trying to poison him.

We left this temple and walked down a path into a moss garden with a tree at each end, one a small sturdy pine representing the tree of birth, the Liftons explained, the other a leafless, contorted skeleton of a tree, strangely orange-colored, representing death.

In the evening, on a walk near our hotel, we turned a corner and saw a procession in the distance; we could hear drums and bells and gongs. As it approached, we could see that some of the men were in robes, some carrying round lanterns on poles, some carrying burning torches, and a group together carrying a large palanquin on their shoulders. I had again the feeling I had had at the Kabuki, of something strange and archaic. We followed for a while and noticed that along the route the houses had lanterns hung out similar to the lanterns in the procession. The scene was incongruous, for the sounds of the gongs and the bells were drowned out by the noisy traffic, and the dim flickering lanterns of the procession were strange in the electric glare of the cars and street lights.

Kyoto, October 29

This morning we took a crowded train with Kato to see the "chrysanthemum dolls" at the fairgrounds of a working-class suburb near Osaka. Families with children poured into the grounds and swarmed around the booths of toys and pop and candy, buying balloons and pinwheels. As we approached the gardens, we saw potted chrysanthemums arranged in all sorts of exotic shapes; behind high hedges were small formal gardens, and beyond these a large exhibition hall. We went into the hall, which was lighted by spotlights shining on numerous "scenes." On closer examination, the sets and figures turned out to be made entirely of chrysanthemums, tightly woven or bound together like thick cloth. These scenes, somewhat similar to our Nativity scenes and crèches, represented familiar myths and stories. Kato explained some of the stories to us. For example, the legend of the big jar into which a child had fallen; no one could think of any way to extricate the child, until a boy broke the jar and saved the child—the boy later became a famous philosopher. Or the story of the monkey who could multiply himself a thousand times: by pulling out one hair he could make another monkey, ad infinitum. Kato is very interested in popular culture and enjoyed showing us and telling us these things. One almost forgot after a while that everything was made of chrysanthemums. What a tour de force!

We came out onto the street and walked back through the crowds to the station. The train to Kyoto was nearly empty, perhaps because it was a "local," stopping at every little station on the way.

Kato turned one of the seats around so we could face each other and talk. He explained why so many of the arts were developed during the Tokugawa period. At that time Japan was cut off from the rest of the world, and the people were even cut off from themselves. Since the *shogun* limited the number of carts and allowed no bridges to be built, people could not go anywhere and had very little to do; and so they cultivated their gardens, practiced calligraphy and flower arrangement and the tea ceremony, and wrote haiku poetry. The people with this leisure were mostly samurai, who, under tight Tokugawa control, could no longer be warriors.

We talked with Kato also about the meaning of taking off shoes when coming into the house: is it an expression of the discontinuity of the outside and the inside world? Kato thought it did separate the public world from the private world. Dave wanted to know if men become gentler when slippered in the house than when outside in shoes or boots. The question amused Kato, perhaps because the masculinity of the men is not so easily defined—or undermined.

Kato had arranged for us to see some young workers who were attending Ritsumeikan night school. We met this afternoon in the conference room of the International House liaison office. There were two young women and three young men, neatly dressed, sitting in a semicircle when we came in. They got up, bowed, and introduced themselves. We then sat down, drawing the chairs closer together; Kato acted as interpreter and went around the circle asking each one to tell something about his or her work and background. They were all in the lower echelons of white-collar jobs, the sort available to high-school graduates; all seemed to be lonely and frustrated but had gotten a new lease on life through going to night school. It was not clear whether any of them were friends with each other, but all said that they had found friends in night school, and new interests. This school was not vocational but rather a program of general education in the humanities.

The first one who spoke was Miss Ishida, from Kyoto, whose father was a grade-school principal. She had gone to nursing school and was a visiting nurse in the Kyoto Health Center.

The other young woman, Miss Nagai, was from Kyushu; her father had died when she was a child. After middle school, she had wanted to work in industry, but her eyesight was bad, and so she could only get a job as a salesgirl in a shop or as a housemaid. She did not like either of these jobs. Since she had an aunt living in Kyoto, she came here to live with her aunt and now worked as a weaver in a Nishijin factory.

The next one was Mr. Maki, a young clerk in the post office. When he was in his first year of senior high school, his father lost his money speculating on the stock market, and so he had had to go to work. His father had worked in the post office and had got him a job there.

The second young man, Mr. Tsurumi, had lost his father as a child and had gone to work after middle school as a manual laborer in a factory. He took night courses at technical school and now is an engineer in an electrical-appliance company.

The third young man, Mr. Shiga, also lost his father as a child—these fathers were all killed in the war, though this was not explicitly stated. He graduated from high school and wanted to go on to the university, but his family situation was difficult and made it out of the question. Instead he got a job at a bank, where he is an accountant.

Dave asked about their friendships: did they keep their old friends from school, or did they make new ones on their jobs? Tsurumi said that among the workers at the night school he went to he made friends; but they were jealous of him and his technical skill and his going on to technical school to become an engineer. For them it seemed symbolic, a higher status; but he doesn't consider it a promotion, only a change.

Maki said that when he began to attend night school he found a friend, now his best friend, who loaned him a book by Engels. When he read this book, he saw that his feeling about poverty was subjective. This book gave him a more objective view, and he is grateful to his friend.

Shiga said that his friends were mostly union members—he participates actively in the bank clerks' union. Though he has moved often, he tries to make friends among his neighbors.

Miss Ishida said that she made her best friend at nursing school; now she also has good friends at night school.

Miss Nagai said that until she went to night school her only consolation was letters from her school friends at home. In the Nishijin factory, work is very hard. She gets too tired. There is only time for sleep. The factory is dark and it is like living in a cave. But after she started night school, things have changed. She has begun to read a lot and has made friends. She rooms with five girls who are also weavers. She tries to share some of her night-school work with them. But more often they just talk about working conditions.

Miss Ishida added something to what she had said: she wanted to get an education—she felt like an educated person, she said; she was very happy to go to night school, but at first she didn't like the socialistic thinking she was exposed to there, because her father had been a Communist and her whole family had suffered from his political activities; he had been fired from the railroad and later got a job as engineer at Ritsumeikan. But now, since going to school and reading so much, she is no longer prejudiced against socialism.

Dave then asked how they felt about their work and what it meant for them. Shiga said that his work was only a means of keeping himself going; the bank where he works is feudalistic; he is active in the union because he wants to improve the situation; he doesn't expect to rise himself, but he wants to improve the lot of all the fifteen hundred employees.

Maki said that he couldn't get any joy out of his work; postal insurance is said to serve the people's welfare; but the money collected from the people isn't used for their welfare but for the big capitalists; he would like to escape from the job, but he can't; and the work is monotonous—gloomy, gray. Dave asked him if there was any loafing on the job, or sabotage of any sort. Maki replied that the chief watched them all the time, so there was no chance for that; besides, he wants to get ahead, and so he has to seem diligent.

Miss Ishida said that her work was interesting and she liked it. As a visiting nurse she gives health instructions to patients, to expectant mothers about their own care and about infant care. She likes to visit families and prefers this to hospital work. But the Health Center is part of the city of Kyoto, which means there are a lot of papers to fill out and red tape, and she hates this. As a visiting nurse she has longer hours and harder work than office workers have. But she likes her work and wants to get ahead in it. Dave remarked that in the United States social workers often became Leftist because of all the poverty they see. Miss Ishida said that she is so interested in her cases that when she comes back to the office and sees how bored the people are there she gets angry. She went on to say that in nursing she finds that the family situation is more important than the disease; it is terrible when the housewife gets sick with tuberculosis, because there is no one to take over the care of the family; and so when she should be hospitalized she cannot be; it is even more complicated when the parents-in-law are living with her, because since she looks well they don't believe she is sick and don't see why she can't work; they don't want the care of the grandchildren but want rather to be taken care of themselves.

Dave then asked about the night school and what it meant to them. Shiga said that after he had started going to night school, which stimulated him to think and to read widely, he found that many people at the bank were suffering from the same boredom that he had known; and so he encouraged them to go to night school.

Tsurumi said that the factory where he works gets out at four and he wanted something to do to fill his free time; this had been a problem ever since senior high school, which tended to create stereotyped men; the night school was very different; people could do what they wanted; there were free discussions and no exams; it was all interesting.

Miss Nagai said that before going to night school her way of looking at the world was too narrow; night school broadened her view; the lectures were interesting; and her friends there were very different from the weavers she lives with. She did not know how to describe this difference, but the people at night school were wonderful people. The factory where she works is small, it is like a family, there is no union, and the morale is low.

Dave asked then whom they admired, who were their heroes. Miss Ishida said she admired her father; he was killed in an auto accident last year; though he was a grade-school principal, he had never been to a school of education; he used to tell her that he was a practitioner and knew more about education than the university big-shots; he was her hero.

Miss Nagai said her family background was unfortunate, there was no one she admired; she lived with relatives and had no affection for her mother. Dave then asked her if there were any books she liked. She replied that she reads a lot, especially novels; she liked *Gone with the Wind*, but prefers books of conflict to books of romance; and she uses the high-school library or exchanges books with friends.

Shiga said that when he was in middle school he read a story about discrimination against the *eta* (the outcast group who do the most menial work of the society) which gave him ideas about social problems; at night school he read Marxist economics and Romain Rolland; his hero is the president of Ritsumeikan.

Tsurumi said that the man who influenced him most was the English teacher he had in high school; this teacher was nice to people irrespective of family background and evaluated people through their own efforts, not birth or wealth.

When we got talking about other leisure-time activities, it turned out that several of them did mountain climbing and belonged to mountain-climbing clubs.

Dave had intended to allow time for them to ask him questions, but it was suddenly later than we thought, and so we had to stop the discussion at this point in order to get to our next appointment. Kato had suggested that I bring presents for our informants. As we said goodbye, I gave a box of candy to each, feeling awkward and wishing I had the grace of the Japanese in doing such things.

In the evening we met with four scholars from the Institute of Humanistic Studies for a discussion to be tape-recorded and made into an article by the *Asahi Journal.* Once a month this group gets together to explore some specific topic under the general title "Wisdom of Japan." Murata mentioned briefly the subjects they had discussed already: group cooking, department stores, annual viewing of cherry blossoms, preparatory schools, box lunches sold in railway stations, children's magazines, souvenirs and gift giving, *manzai* (the Osaka comic dialogue), historical movies with fencing, *janken* (games of three: paper, scissors, and stone), aesthetics of bath taking, *origami* (the art of paper folding), delivery of cooked meals, *domo* ("It is nothing, I am sorry"), balloons with ads, good-luck charms for cars, chemical seasoning (Accent), no tipping, the go-between, chrysanthemum dolls, the personal library, stones. The discussion today was to be about models such as the wax food displays in the windows of restaurants.

Riesman: We have already made good use of the wax food displays. A few days ago in Osaka we went into a restaurant and pointed to what we wanted. This is fine for tourists who can't speak Japanese.

Osabe: Do you feel there is something off-color about wax food models—too perfect an imitation is unaesthetic? Why is it? Because it is neither art nor reality?

Murata: Yes. Perhaps because there is a deception. But perfect models have their uses, the models of the human body used in medical schools, for example. These models are very real. The technique of making them was learned in France, but now Japan manufactures them and exports them.

Riesman: The model of food displays sets standards that the restaurant has to live up to, but doesn't that also freeze creativity?

Suzuki: Yes. It regulates the cook's cooking, and something can't be made smaller than the standard portion. But the models of food only came in with the introduction of Western food. There were no words for hamburg, sundae, salad, and so on. And since so much food is imported from abroad this helped housewives learn how to cook and arrange it. It is a form of adult education.

Murata: The salesman, too, does a kind of adult-education job when he sells to a customer. In order to sell, he must educate. So the Japanese have developed what in America is called public relations. Unless you teach, you cannot sell. The salesman has pamphlets for the customers to read. In the old days, when the channel of import was only one (such as Chinese food), the cooking of it could be taught in schools. But when things come from many different countries, the problem is different.

Suzuki: The model is an invention of mass society. In the old days each restaurant was known for its speciality. But the new stores with their new foods have to show their wares.

Riesman: America imported its foreign foods with its immigrants; they brought the techniques of their cooking with them.

Osabe: What about artificial flowers? In Europe they have them in the Catholic churches. But do you have them in Protestant churches? Or are artificial flowers protested by Protestants? (Laughter) Protestants feel guilty about things that are fictitious, don't they? With the Japanese, if things are well made there is no difference between the real and the fictitious. It is a Western idea, among intellectuals, to say that imitations are bad. Perhaps imitation in some cases is something to be proud of. For example, original ceramics are copied by the smaller craftsmen: if they tried to make their own originals, they would probably be ugly, because the craftsmen are not artists. It is better that they imitate the work of an artist than make something bad of their own.

Riesman: It is true that Protestants have expressed moral indignation against anything that is fiction and imitation, anything that's not truth.

Osabe: In the seventeenth century, Pascal began talking about patents, and imitation became a kind of crime.

Riesman: There is a very important difference in Protestant thinking.

The Protestants believe there is a *real* world, the world of nature, clearly defined, as opposed to the imitation, manmade world.

Osabe: The European idea—Rousseau's idea—that nature is better than manmade things is perhaps due to the fact that Europe is a great continent. Great stretches of land, forests, deserts are not present in Japan.

(The hostess poured more tea and then sat near the door, listening. Murata was translating the English into Japanese and the Japanese into English. Translating unfortunately makes it difficult for him to take part in the conversation as much as he might otherwise.)

Suzuki: To return to the problem. There is a proverb about reality being better than hearsay: "The evidence rather than argument . . . a picture is worth a thousand words."

Riesman: It is interesting that the Japanese are great photographers. Photos are a kind of model. What about diaries?

Suzuki: A diary is a symbolic model. The Japanese like models as souvenirs, records of life. But the model of food in a restaurant is for a different purpose. We feel a kind of discomfort in looking at models of food. Perhaps it is anticipation realized too early, or doubt about whether it is real or not.

Osabe: Those who feel this sort of discomfort are the aesthetic elite and not the masses. There are so many different types of cooking in the restaurants. It is only in the rural areas that cooking has stayed the same. But even those people want to give up their own cooking once they have been in the cities and tasted the strange new dishes.

Murata: Ever since the Meiji period the rural people have been coming into the cities. And you will find today that in rural areas people have curry.

Osabe: (After a pause, smiling, he puts out his cigarette and looks around.) Too bad we didn't waste any time, we didn't have any warming-up time this afternoon. It's too bad—wasting time is a wisdom of Japan.

Riesman: These separate *tatami* rooms in restaurants are also the wisdom of Japan.

Suzuki: We have a word, *mitate*, which means to regard a thing as something else, for example a nut as a face, or a Japanese garden as having meaning.

Riesman: For Freud there was *mitate* for everything: sex.

Osabe: A cultured man regards everything as having some meaning, even a stone. The stones in the Ryoanji have their meaning. For us a stone in a garden is a problem which one must answer. In the fifteenth century, there were stone hunters for the stone gardens. First the temple was built and then afterward the stone garden was made. In China, where there is plenty of land, the priests could choose the place for the temple, a site for the beauty of its stones and trees. With us they had to bring the stones sometimes from great distances, always special kinds of stones.

Shimamura: There are two themes in Japanese culture, permanence and change. The aesthetic is permanent, the technological is change. In our gardens we don't put plants that grow and change, because we want permanence.

Murata: A stone is very significant aesthetically: it is the most durable material that will not change.

Osabe: The Japanese do not hesitate to take up a machine and appreciate its efficiency. The criterion of judgment is clear about which machine is better. But to pick up a stone and bring it home, or a piece of wood, and gaze at them and contemplate—that is not so easy.

Riesman: By deciding ahead of time what is aesthetic and what is not, our ideas become frozen; then we will have no good criticism of machines.

Suzuki: The whole of Japanese culture is based on the feeling of creating beauty; the design of machines is not only concerned with efficiency, but with beauty as well. Viewed historically, there are three quite different attitudes in Japanese aesthetics: for the *shogun* and the samurai there was the fear of nothingness; they felt the need of filling up the world with something. For the Emperor it was the opposite: he feared the existence of things; everything had to be protected from the evil of the outside world: the walls and the huge empty courtyards of the Imperial Palace here are an example. Then there was the bourgeois aesthetics based purely on refinement, having nothing to do with fear or with feelings of power.

Shimamura: To return to our gardening and the permanence of stones, there are dictionaries and textbooks about the meaning of stones of different shapes.

Osabe: There is always the danger that stones will become frozen metaphors; but fortunately there are many schools of gardening in Japan which prevent this.

Shimamura: In the Shinto religion, stones have a special meaning. A stone on a high place is both a symbol of the god and the place—the medium—through which the god may descend.

Osabe: The stone has permanence, but the Japanese never thought of using it as a building material, except for thick walls around palaces for defense. We can keep technology and aesthetics separate in this way. In America, technology is more important, because getting ahead is so important, and who wins is so important. But in Japan, as in the backward countries, we love many useless objects for their traditional meanings. And so we are able to appreciate all the diversity of the world. A stone or a fragment of wood picked up out of a river has meaning for us—as it has in backward countries, too.

Murata: There is symbolic meaning in stones; stones are brought back from places where soldiers died, if the bodies were not found. Stones are brought back from the beaches where they drowned.

Osabe: I've been reading Malraux, but my opinion is the opposite from the one he expresses. He says that in Africa sculpture to him is more important than the people—how can the sculpture of a culture be more important than the living people! We regard a stone or a piece of sculpture as a projection or symbol of a person or people: but the symbol is not more important than the person or people symbolized.

Suzuki: Children collect stones as souvenirs from places they visit when sightseeing. Collecting stones is a sort of hobby.

Shimamura: There are many children's games played with stones, like hopscotch and marbles.

Osabe: I try to pick up a stone every day to bring home to my daughter.

Murata: There is a monument near the Prefecture Building made of stones brought from various parts of Japan and from all over the world, with the name of the place from which each one came carved on it. The idea behind Japanese imperialism, the slogan, was to "put a tent over the four corners of the world," to make the world a household, to cover the world as a family. Bringing these stones to this place was the same sort of symbolism.

Suzuki: There is a difference in meaning between collection and selection, the difference between anthropology and aesthetics.

Osabe: Malraux is only interested in the aesthetic. The Japanese are interested in the anthropological as well.

Suzuki: Many people confuse the meaning of a stone with mysticism: a tree thinks, a stone speaks, they say. The aesthetic beauty of a piece of sculpture is something else. Milestones are actually stones and they sometimes have Buddha sculptured on them—is this symbolic or aesthetic?

Osabe: Collecting stones is meaningless aesthetically, but meaningful anthropologically. Many things are meaningful and enjoyable that have no aesthetic quality. Suzuki and Shimamura enjoy the Osaka comic dialogues (*manzai*), which would seem vulgar to the French. (Laughter)

Suzuki: The anthropological criterion for judging things is in terms of its meaning for the culture. The aesthetic criterion is more absolute, more refined. The borderline is difficult sometimes to define. Tokyo is not beautiful, but it has meaning for its people.

Riesman: Cultural relativism can sometimes go too far when it ignores the moral, when it does not criticize the Aztecs or the Nazis.

Osabe: But the anthropological logic is important. We must be tolerant of various types of society, and we must ask, how did the Germans get that way?

Riesman: The anthropologist must be careful not to share the prejudices of the tribe he is studying; when he does so, he is going over the line.

Osabe: Suzuki can understand Tokyo without sympathizing with it. I can't do either.

Murata: I can understand and sympathize with Tokyo, but I dislike it just the same.

Suzuki: We don't like Tokyo and we don't like leaders of the Conservative Party. But Ikeda is a stone collector, and so we like him better for this. Stone collectors are patient people. There is a Buddhist legend which is like the myth of Sisyphus. After death, one must cross a river to get to the Other World. In this river one must pick up stones, one at a time, to make a tower: this stone for one's father, this stone for one's mother, and so on. But as soon as the tower is finished, a devil comes down and destroys it. And so one must begin again.

Shimamura: There is some symbolic connection between this story and the fact that the poorest people live on the stony riverbanks.

Murata: There is a popular song, "I am a faded-out plant on a bank of the river." We have many stony rivers; pebbles and gravel form their beds rather than sand when they reach the plains. Such rivers are not found in large continents.

Shimamura: The Japanese national song says the Japanese nation is a collection of small stones which make a big stone.

Riesman: In Western history there were kings who had great refinements of taste which separated them from the people and made them worse, more cruel. But in Japan one does not feel this great chasm between the classes. Ikeda's private tastes can be understood by the public.

Murata: By using stones, the upper class communicated with the lowest people. The upper-class people employed stone hunters in making their gardens.

Suzuki: We here belong to the first generation which can explore Japanese thought freely, the first generation not weighed down by tradition.

Murata: This is possible because it is Kyoto, it would be impossible in Tokyo.

Riesman: You're in an ideal position here in Kyoto; you're not as responsible for the whole country here, you can be playful; but you are not cut off from the world either—here you have the *Asahi Journal* to report all this. You have more freedom than in Tokyo. You have all Japan between you and the outside world, while Tokyo faces the world, more directly.

Osabe: Truth is in the marginality and not in the orthodoxy.

Murata: It is curious that the professors are indifferent on the whole to student movements and political activities. It's a protective indifference: they want to protect their own academic interests and research.

Riesman (turning to the *Asahi* reporter): Newspapermen don't seem to become cynical here, as they do in the United States.

Reporter: Many newspapermen see their jobs as a means to a better one, such as becoming attached to a political figure, or perhaps writing novels. But also the work itself is interesting. It isn't just news-gathering, it is also seasoning, putting an accent on the news. A newspaperman is a balancer, a regulator. Except for those working for *Asahi* or *Mainichi*, though, most newspapermen are cynical, especially those working for small, poorer papers.

Riesman: Isn't your relationship to this group unusual? You seem to be more sauce than seasoning. A newspaperman in the United States would either look up too much to the professors, or he would be cynical about them in their ivory towers.

Suzuki: Toshiba is a graduate of Kyoto University. He shares a common culture with us. This is simply a division of labor.

Riesman: The title of these discussions, "Wisdom of Japan," is only possible to use in a neutral country like Japan. The cold war would make such a title impossible in the United States, for example; it would sound like "Free World Propaganda."

Suzuki: If this were pre-war Japan, we couldn't do this. But being defeated, we can.

Kyoto, October 30

Kato arranged for us to meet this afternoon with some of the student leaders of the University of Kyoto. This part of the campus of the University is made up of rather dreary buildings and shabby prefabricated barrackslike buildings. The grounds are dusty and stony, with no grass anywhere. We went into one of the prefabricated buildings and came to an empty room littered with newspapers, which were scattered and crumpled in layers all over the floor. Kato thought this was the room where we were to meet, but as there was no one there, he asked some students next door. It was apparently the right place, and so we went in. It looked as if vandals had been at work. The walls were scribbled over, the plaster was crumbling, the windows broken. It was difficult walking into the room, as the newspapers on the floor were so deep! We sat on some broken-down benches and chairs. After a few minutes, four students appeared. They made their way through the newspapers, and Kato introduced them to us. They looked interesting and appealing, two of them in tweed coats, one in a sport shirt and sweater, and one in student uniform. They sat down on chairs, tables, whatever they could find, and Kato explained to them who we were, why we wanted to talk with them, and then acted as interpreter, as none of them spoke English. After we had been talking for a few minutes, others wandered in; a few came through the windows—as all the windows were open wide, they could step over the windowsills, which were not too high. Two more sat down in our group, others stood on the outskirts listening for a while, then wandered away. The students who were sitting with us had all been involved in the demonstrations of last year and appeared willing to answer questions on the subject. A philosophy student, who seemed to be the most involved and to be the spokesman for the others, said that all his thoughts and activities had been caught up in these demonstrations. He said that the demonstrations made students realize the reality of Japanese society, made them feel they were participating in Japanese history. "There is political misunderstanding and cultural conflict between the East and the West," he said. When asked about his personal involvement, he said that he had been interested in political movements since his senior year in high school, and since he had come to the University, his interest had grown stronger, and that this was typical of Kyoto students. As the students took turns talking, we began to see differences in their attitudes, ranging from the very thoughtful who did not think there were easy solutions and were concerned about diversity and individuality, to the doctrinaire who talked of unity and the need to link the peace movement with the class struggle; "the atomic bombing of Japan was a national experience, and so the peace movement should be a national movement"; much as they disliked the Russian nuclear testing, they could understand it: "the Russians need to test because of the dangers of capitalist imperialism"; "peace isn't enough, bourgeois peace may turn into a form of fascism."

When Dave asked about the attitude of their parents toward their political activities, they seemed to agree that their parents did not worry about their politics, but did worry that perhaps they were not doing their studies or that they might be injured in the demonstrations. As far as ideas went, their parents let them think whatever they liked.

Dave asked them who were their models, who offered them inspiration, and there was embarrassed laughter. There was no figure they wanted to follow. Karl Marx seemed their only source of inspiration.

While this discussion was going on, the students were constantly smoking or picking up scraps of string or wire or other junk lying around, twisting and playing with it. I have never seen so much nervous energy. During our discussion, numerous students were going in and out and then began gathering in a crowd at the other end of the room. All at once they were climbing in streams through the windows. Kato said that they were gathering for another demonstration and that these students feel less influential than those in Tokyo; here their influence is indirect; in Tokyo they can demonstrate in front of the Diet buildings. However, many of them went to Tokyo last year for the big demonstrations.

It was hard for us to hear one another talk as this mob of students—a number of girls among them—grew larger and noisier. They seemed to be getting their placards ready and hardly noticed us, though now and then a few cast curious glances our way. All of a sudden they were off; they streamed out and the room was quiet again. We went on with our discussion for a while. Dave asked if any of the students would like to ask him questions. After a pause, the leader asked if there was an anti-power movement in the United States and what forms it took; another asked if the labor movement was interested in politics or only in wages; another asked if there was a chauvinistic and nationalistic movement in our country after the war. Dave took pains to answer these questions at length.

Afterward we went into a coffee shop nearby. Kato told us, as we ordered coffee and watched students going in and out, that the students we had talked with were very anti-American but that they had been polite to us as guests. He said they came from middle- and lower-middle-class backgrounds; for example, one was the son of a pharmacist, another the son of a high-school teacher, a third the son of a prosperous farmer. Kato remarked that the students talked in nouns and adverbs, without verbs, which made it hard to translate into English—that is, they were talking in large abstractions, which was usual when they wanted to be impressive.

In the evening we had dinner with Professor Mori in a restaurant on the far side of town, famous for its turtle soup and other delicacies. It was a charming old Japanese restaurant with small separate rooms. We sat on *tatami*. Mori smoked and coughed and the cold wind blew through the cracks between the *shoji*. In spite of the discomforts and the broken English and bad French, we got along famously. He is a rather rough-hewn and direct man, tweedy, professorial, with great intelligence and warmth. He wanted Dave's advice about how to get the work of some of the younger scholars in his Institute published in the United States—a nice concern for his protégés that is not unusual in Japan.

Our discussion during dinner ranged over all sorts of topics. We talked about the students we had seen in the afternoon and how surprising it was that their parents didn't resent their radicalism. Mori said that during the Occupation, which had insisted on freedom of thought, parents were conditioned more or less not to interfere. Also, the parents knew that when the students got through the University and took jobs they would settle down and lose these radical ideas. Dave wondered why the students didn't see their Security Treaty *demo* as a great victory—they unseated Kishi, what more could they want? Mori thought that the students were very idealistic and completely unrealistic; they wanted to create a revolution, not just a change of stooges. Also he thought that the students are in general dissatisfied, they feel oppressed by the hierarchy and rigidity of the society; therefore they are dissatisfied with their *demo*, too. We asked about the girl student who had been killed in the *demo* in Tokyo. He said that she was a "queen," a leader, and a daughter of one of the professors; her death was very tragic. He went on to say that he thought the competitive system in the universities which let in so few girls was not a good thing; the girls who do get in are either queens or outcasts; the queens are both brilliant and beautiful and are too much looked up to by the boys; the unattractive ones are ignored; it would be better if the universities let in a certain proportion of girls rather than having them compete with the men.

We went on then to discuss matters of politics. Mori was fed up with some professors who didn't favor the proposed scientific cooperation plan between Japan and the United States; the Leftists treat it as a cold-war gambit—"American imperialism"; but it was set up by Kennedy and Ikeda as pure science, and it might be a very fine thing.

Somehow we got onto the subject of the Japanese soldiers in Nanking—how could the gentle Japanese have behaved in this atrocious way? Mori answered that the troops were indoctrinated by ignorant and militaristic right-wing officers, for one thing, and the troops themselves were uneducated country boys; also (and this is Suzuki's theory), in the hierarchy from the Emperor down, people who are not Japanese are seen as the lowest (furthest from the Emperor), and so are not quite human; but there is an ambivalence here because the Japanese also have an inferiority complex toward the Chinese.

We had finished our great caldron of turtle soup with turtle meat and rice dumplings, and Mori was relaxing with a cigarette. A noisy party was going on in an adjoining room. Dave spoke of how strange the Japanese inferiority complex was: how was this possible, when Japan was the only country in the East to become industrialized, and was already overtaking most of the Western industrialized countries. They admire foreign things more than their own, indeed overadmire them, perhaps because they are modest about their own achievements. Mori did not think this was just modesty; after all, the industrial revolution originated in the West. Dave went on to ask Mori if he thought Japan could survive economically without becoming more socialistic. Mori thought that eventually Japan would have to become at least as socialistic as England.

In the taxi going back to the hotel, Mori talked about his family: he has six children—these pre-war families were large, nowadays families are smaller; his eldest daughter is going to be married soon. He said she met her fiancé in her classes at the university. We remarked that she was modern, with no *miai* (arranged marriage). He seemed pleased about this. He went on talking about his children, saying that the older ones are more modern than the younger ones because they grew up under the liberalization of the Occupation. The older ones have no respect for the Tenno (Emperor) or for their parents or for old customs. But, he said, his youngest son, who is thirteen, speaks of the Tenno with respect, even reverence. He brought up the subject of mental illness; it is frequent but is kept hidden; a friend of his, a professor, has a daughter who has had a breakdown but he never mentions it. We were very moved by the way Mori opened up to us.

We had been driving miles, it seemed, through the dark rainy streets, but now we recognized our wide boulevard and the approach to our hotel. As we bade good night, I thought how completely one forgets the differences and sees the person, feels the common humanity, when there is mutual understanding and sympathy. The most important thing was not that Mori was Japanese and we Americans, but that we had so many of the same concerns, about our children, about students, about the state of the world. The difference in our origins merely added a dimension that made these discussions unusually exciting.

Kyoto, October 31

This afternoon another magazine arranged to tape-record a discussion between Dave and Murata on the effects of the mass media, especially television, in the United States and Japan. We walked across the busy boulevard in front of the hotel into the section we are familiar with now, where there are lovely old houses with the typical Kyoto latticed windows and interior gardens. We met Murata at the same tea house where the discussion of "The Wisdom of Japan" had been held a few days ago. With Murata was a young man who was on the editorial staff of the magazine that was to publish the exchange.

Murata opened the discussion and I took notes as best I could. It moved very fast, since again it was all in English, without the extra time that translation allows.

Murata: I am interested in comparative studies of the mass media in Japan and the United States. What is the background of the prejudice among intellectuals in the United States against television?

Riesman: Among some intellectuals there is a prejudice against anything to do with modern society, based on an uneasiness about mass society. Television, since it is not a necessity like a telephone or a car, has become symbolic of the vulgarity of mass society, and the television set itself is ugly and does not fit into the attractive, simple, Japanese-influenced décor of highbrow living in the United

States, while a homemade hi-fi set can look very nice. Intellectual parents see other peoples' children becoming vulgarized and illiterate from watching television; and they also worry that television is a distraction from studying, and that their children might not get into college if they owned a set; and so forth. There are many reasons.

Murata: Many of your points are just the contrary in Japan. We have more self-controlled children, and they study very hard. It is true, their bedtime gets later, but television is considered educational. The ugliness of the set is not a problem, it is considered decorative in a Japanese house.

Riesman: The educated American parent thinks only reading is hard, and that watching television is soft and sloppy. The Japanese can leave to society and to the schools the inculcating of habits of work. But in the United States this is not possible. Television viewing is not done with any intensity or any critical sense with us.

Murata: At the end of the eighteenth century, Japan developed a visual appreciation: for example, the frame of the window in a temple makes the landscape outside into a sort of picture; we developed the shadow art, the lantern slides; we enjoy viewing; and it is part of our folk culture to appreciate moving pictures. Television is a part of this art of viewing.

Riesman: In Japan there is a fear of one's child falling in social rank. But in the United States, with our frontier traditions and semi-literacy, where boys are expected above all to be tough and rough and ride motorcycles, this fear among intellectuals is even greater.

Murata: Topics of television are often discussed in school in Japan. If the parents haven't got television, the children are frustrated and feel deprived. But also the parents enjoy television. The Japanese, including the intellectuals, like anything new. They are delighted and assimilate new things very quickly.

Riesman: Has NHK (the government-sponsored station) helped legitimate television for the intellectuals?

Murata: Yes, intellectuals watch the news on television regularly. Also, the Japanese prefer seeing the real object to hearing words: the picture, we think, is nearer to reality than words.

Riesman: In the United States we have a national market for goods and ideas which are the lowest common denominator; also, we are sealed off from most of the world by the cold war. There is much bias and inaccuracy as well as much vulgar speech on television which intellectuals want to keep away from their children.

Murata: We are a homogeneous population and we share common values. Perhaps Japan is the optimal size for a national network. But also we are not talkative or speech-conscious.

Riesman: With us, many intellectuals keep up a campaign against mass media, such as music in elevators or buses, and we poke fun at television and big cars, public display and public noise. The intellectual in America insists on privacy, print, and understatement. Television is the medium of overstatement.

Murata: I once proposed in an article that primary- and middle-school should have classes in photography. It would teach children the function of the lens, etc.; and in science classes they could take pictures of insects or whatever. And also this could provide a medium for the teaching of aesthetics: the beauty and significance in a picture, how to cut, and so forth.

Riesman: I agree. In our culture, only certain things have been defined as aesthetic, with the result that until very recently the rest has been left uncriticized—such as our film, television, photography, highways, machinery, public space. But where the aesthetic and highbrow are concerned, it is different. There appear to be more *critics* of novels and painting than there are writers and painters. To return to the content of television, the intellectual parent wants to preserve childhood for the child. But television brings in irrelevant and precocious stuff for the child.

Murata: That could be a problem. Also a world television network could become an invasion. Already many say in Japan it is too bad we buy United States television films, because Japan should make its own: 30 per cent are American-made. But American television drama may be less harmful to us than to you, because it is more remote and less real; and so the crimes are less shocking.

Riesman: A study might well show that children are more frightened by a native crime. In the United States, television helps create the feeling of being surrounded by crime, of living in a jungle, and may even make people more resigned to violence and to war.

Murata: Another reason for the importance of television in Japanese life is that people go out less than in the United States. There is less to do in Japan; in our leisure time, people here either do nothing—that is, take a nap—or watch television, or do other things inside the house. There are fewer places to go, because of the population density. In the United States, people go to the beach or the movies. In the summer, American television viewing declines sharply, but there are no such seasonal variations in Japan.

Riesman: In the smaller Japanese house, the woman would always be near the television.

Murata: Yes. In fact, television has done a lot for the housewife, and it has changed the family routine. Husbands and children come back earlier to the house. The house-confined wife for the first time in history could continue to get an education. A housewife is always supposed to be doing something. Even if she has cleaned the whole house and has nothing more to do, she must begin cleaning it over again. But television gives her an excuse to sit on the floor and rest and watch television. The mother-in-law also enjoys watching television and wants someone to enjoy it with, and so encourages the daughter-in-law to sit down with her. In the age of the newspaper, only adults could read. But with television now everyone can watch together, a whole family can enjoy it—like viewing the moon or the cherry blossoms, the television screen is a kind of communication between people who may not have much to say to each other; it is a reflector of communication.

Riesman: There was a study done at Washington State University of farm women in the area; in contrast to earlier days when the men brought home the news, today when the men come in, it is the women who give them the news they have seen on television.

Murata: We have made a prediction that women will be the top intellectuals in the family—what with television and washing machines—especially in the urban areas, within the next twenty years.

(The discussion stopped for a few minutes while the tape was changed and we had more tea.)

Murata: You said earlier that American television carried the values of the Frontier. What is the effect of this on children, are they frustrated?

Riesman: Boys are frustrated because they aren't cowboys, and girls are frustrated because they aren't boys. I think some of the resentment coming out in our political life today may have its roots in this.

Murata: Most of television is male-oriented. But in the past, novels were for women.

Riesman: Yes, women have also been the audience for American fiction and for movies. There are no girls' stories comparable to *Catcher in the Rye*. Yet girls can adapt themselves and identify with such a book, while a boy can't so easily identify with a girl.

Murata: In the children's programs the heroes are always boys, and even in domestic scenes—a boy with a dog. Women have protested the masculine dominance of television programs. But the highbrow criticism has come from men.

Riesman: Women's efforts have been usually to elevate and clean up. But this is difficult on television. Violent action is more visual.

Tokyo, November 1

On our train trip returning to Tokyo, Kato accompanied us. It was a beautiful sunny day and a delight to be able to see the countryside once more. The mountains were still green, rising in exotic shapes out of the flat valleys of rice fields. The rice, which on our trip down three weeks ago, was being harvested and hung up to dry, now was being threshed. Men and women worked together in groups of three's and four's, wearing straw hats or kerchiefs, pantaloons and smocks. They were heaping the rice straw in piles that looked like haystacks. Later on in another valley we passed truck gardens of vegetables, then tea plantations, the dark green tea bushes resembling azaleas.

Kato pointed out a Zen monastery nestled in the hills and told us that the baseball coach whose team lost last year retired to this monastery to meditate for three months before returning to work. After a while Kato was talking about the war and said that his childhood—and that of his entire generation—had been destroyed: "We envy children growing up today, they have a childhood to remember . . . Now as adults we have had to put our energies into building up what was destroyed." But, he said, there was for a brief time after the war a period of unusual opportunity and freedom of movement for him and his generation. There was such a demand for talent that young people took important positions they would never get now until they were middle-aged. This will not happen again, the old rigidity has set in all too rapidly.

When the train stopped at a station, we noticed the announcements seemed to be chanted—Kato said this was in the manner of the Buddhist chants. A young hostess in uniform came by to take our lunch orders and to find out what sitting we would like to have. Kato read us the menu and helped us order. An hour or so later we were called into the dining car and were served a delicious lunch. A man in a gray silk kimono came in and sat across the aisle from us. We wondered if he was a Zen monk. Kato explained that he was not, he was probably a retired merchant. He said these kimono were very expensive and only the wealthy wore them; often such people turn to gardening and writing poetry in their old age and enjoy the contemplative

ETR

life. I thought of Inaba, who had told us about the Zen monastery he owned—perhaps for retiring to in old age. Kato went on to say that for the Japanese, tradition is not something of the past, but rather of the present—the past in the present; it is very natural for people who can afford it to do these traditional things.

DR

Kato is a wonderful observer not only of people but of places. He said he'd written an article on observations from a train window, based largely on the ride from Kyoto to Tokyo. He showed how the rice paddies changed in type and the houses changed in type and what this meant ecologically and psychologically. He seems to know every temple and building on the route. In addition to his concern with urban popular culture, he has done at least one study on a village. For him, Japan seems to be manageable enough in scale, at least in its main islands south of Hokkaido.

We noticed on this train, as on many other occasions, that people are wired for sound: the trains have attachments for transistor radios, and half the car seemed to be sitting entranced, listening to a world-series baseball game. Kato explained that baseball is played here the year round and has swept the boards in terms of favorite sports. It seemed to me that this is not only because it is an American import but because it combines individual play with teamwork and is aggressive without being as rough as football; the deft quickness of the Japanese and the lack of bulk in the average Japanese—though not in the enormous *sumo* wrestlers, who seem to belong to another race—also make baseball highly suitable. Universities have their teams and so do cities and industries, and hardly anyone seems immune from interest in the game.

Kato told us that three competing railway lines ran between Kyoto and Osaka—and all three are tremendously crowded. Still, they compete by offering services, and one of them now has television at each end of the car. There is nothing here like *The New Yorker* campaign against sound in public places, and Muzak is piped through the hotels and other public places.

ETR

Tokyo, November 2

Coming back to Tokyo gives us the feeling of having been here a long time; we enjoy recognitions and the illusion of familiarity. We walked today down the steep hills into the little "villages"—reminding us of

ETR

Kyoto now, but so much busier and noisier. In Kyoto, the trucks and motorcycles stay on the main thoroughfares, but here they tear through the small streets too. The policemen directing traffic are polite to the point of passivity and ineffectuality. Also there is much more building going on here than in Kyoto, for so much of Tokyo was destroyed. I have been reading Dore's *City Life in Japan* and now can recognize the *Shitamachi*, these busy little streets, with their shops and workshops, where the poor people live at the bottom of the hills, and the *Yamanote*, the fine residences on the tops of the hills, built on the sites of what were once great feudal estates. In spite of all the rebuilding, the pattern of the city remains the same, which is its charm as well as its hopeless impracticality. A narrow road becomes an alley wide enough for pedestrians and bicycles, and this ends at a flight of steps, descending between houses and gardens into a market street. As we walked, we passed a bean-curd seller on his bicycle blowing his plaintive horn.

DR

We had been told that Tokyo is a rough and tough city, fundamentally frightening. Some sections, of course, are disturbing and perhaps dangerous, but Tokyo strikes us as far less frightening than most cities we know. Undercurrents of violence between the classes seem to be absent here. The Liftons say that at the time of the demonstrations one did have a little of this feeling, but it was related to ideology not to class, and it was surprisingly little in view of the intense passions.

One of the things that has struck me here is the combination of a modern Western industrial society, containing even more than the usual hustle and bustle, with the retention of the level of services that only the extravagantly rich may still be able to buy in the United States and a few people may still have in the South from "their" Negroes. Since the war, at any rate, Japan has become rich enough to provide a high degree of Western comfort in building and transportation, while not yet rich enough to lose the cheap and willing services of women that make many posts abroad generally so attractive to American housewives—and even more perhaps to American men—who are upgraded by this "full treatment" and hate to come home again to a world where services are terribly expensive, poor, and often resentfully provided. The Tokyo taxi drivers, on the other hand, are urbanized to the extent of not getting out or helping you with your bags or opening their trunk or anything; but this, I am told, is a new dispensation, and, in general, service would at least seem to be done cheerfully.

This afternoon we had a tape-recorded discussion for the *Science of Thought* journal, on "Modernization and Mass Society" in Japan. Professor Hitomi is a distinguished political scientist whom we met here for the first time, while Mr. Otani works in the Foreign Office; Yoshida and, of course, Murata seem already old friends. We sat in comfortable chairs in the new Conference Room at International House. The Japanese scholars were all fluent in English, having studied in the United States. This made translation unnecessary and the discussion too fast for easy note-taking for Evey.

Otani: *The Lonely Crowd* has been a puzzle to Japanese readers and has often been misread. Does it speak of the mass society of the future or does it refer to the present in Japan? Does it suggest that society is overorganized or that it is underorganized?

Riesman: I would contend that modern mass society is at once overorganized and underorganized. Social criticism tends to emphasize the overorganized aspect by using "bureaucracy" as a pejorative word or talking about the "power elite" or the "organization man." Many faculty members like to pretend that the university is overorganized and that this can be blamed on presidents and deans and other administrators. In fact, what is thought of as "bureaucratic" behavior often comes about because too few administrators are trying to do too much and as a result lack time to proceed on a case-by-case and individualized basis; they must rely on rules because they are so hard-pressed, and in that sense, our universities and many other institutions are underorganized. If we take our society as a whole, our large corporations which set the model may be overorganized. But all around are areas in our large cities, with us as with you, where our public sector is underorganized, where problems of resource utilization and transport, of water, of beauty and scale cannot be attended to.

Otani: Is this a matter of ambivalence? Are people drawn at once to organization and disorganization?

Riesman: There is certainly ambivalence toward organization, but the contrast between the neat and the chaotic is not only a psychological matter but an institutional one. Take, for example, an Army or Air Force base surrounded by snarled traffic and slums: inside, all may be efficient, but outside there is prostitution, black market and other "free enterprise" unmediated by organizations. Some institutions bulldoze their way through American life, spreading chaos on all sides, but are "efficient" and organized within.

Yoshida: Japan is underdeveloped and underorganized in the area of small business, but overorganized in the government and large corporations.

Hitomi: Even the government and the big companies are underorganized. It sometimes can take several years to get an answer to an inquiry of a government agency. There may be large corporations which are overorganized, but on the whole we live under a very inefficient government and in a badly organized society.

Riesman: The movie *Ikiru* certainly suggests inefficiency in a government agency. But the Japanese may have a myth of American efficiency. Some government agencies in the United States suffer from a shortage of personnel, whereas Japan suffers at every level from an overabundance of personnel. This very overstaffing, however, by providing for peak loads may make for greater efficiency.

Murata: This may be so, but only if interpersonal relations don't absorb all the energy of the excess individuals.

Yoshida: What is meant by "overorganization" should be spelled out. Rational organization in Japan is combined with or laid on top of a familistic structure. For example, when a man wants to deal with a bank, he doesn't just go in cold. As soon as there has been a personal introduction, then everything goes smoothly, and this may come through family ties or a school clique.

Riesman: Here again one can overestimate differences with the United States. Americans tend to be unaware of the extent to which we employ channels of kin, school, club, and so on.

Yoshida: You attribute the other-directed type in the United States to factors of industrialization; does this mean that the same type of character is likely to appear in any society? Has industrialization brought other-direction to Great Britain or Japan?

Riesman: The Lonely Crowd tried to look at specific American changes from the age of production to the age of consumption. But if we had looked at another society we would have perhaps been interested in different questions; and to take a concept or scaffolding built for one problem and transfer it to another in another setting is not a good idea. Certainly there is more than one road to industrialization, and to see another road was one of my chief interests in coming to Japan. For example, in the United States everybody is an immigrant or the descendant of immigrants; there is no feudal heritage and there is a very small aristocracy.

The difference from Great Britain with its aristocratic traditions is marked. For example, in Britain only a very small proportion of each generation pursues university studies. Japan would seem more like the United States in being more democratic, in spite of the complaints that there are still feudal elements (such as the importance of the old men). In Japan, with its high literacy, there would seem to be a greater fluidity of symbols, ideas, and devices than in Great Britain. Possibly Japan provides a better case for the application of the inner-other typology than Great Britain, but all three countries possess a different combination of the criteria of modernity, such as literacy, industrialization, democracy, and social mobility.

Yoshida: When I was in the United States, I was asked if the Japanese liked America. When I was in Great Britain, I was never asked this. Is this related to the fact that the United States has never been defeated and is climbing to the top, whereas Great Britain is losing its empire? Would the British have asked the same question in the Victorian age?

Riesman: The British would have asked the question in a different way. An Englishman's judgment of his country would not change because of what anyone outside thought of it; and if he asked, it would be for reasons of trade or naval contest, but not for reasons of personal psychology. In contrast, an American asking such a question may have at stake such questions as: Am I living in the best country? Am I understood? Am I responded to? And even, who am I?

Hitomi: The American people easily confuse themselves with their government and their national purpose. They have a question of identity. They are not sure what it is to be an American.

Murata: This may be related to the fact that Americans have a drive to be regarded as Americans, for they are immigrants; whereas in Japan, to be a Japanese is taken for granted.

Hitomi: Japan has been other-directed since the turn of the century. The "peers" are the outside world, and the other-directed take their cue from this world. The tradition-directed people are repudiated. Japanese intellectuals are other-directed too, taking cues from outside, from the West, and not necessarily guided by an inner light or what you call inner-direction. We *believe* in independence but cannot always achieve it.

Riesman: Inner-direction and autonomy are not the same. Guidance by an inner light is autonomy, but the inner-directed person only appears autonomous, being guided by past or parental "others" and insensitive to those around him. Yet you are right that many Japanese care what people think of them and act as if they were immigrants in their own country. There is no un-Japanese Activities Committee, but there is a *de facto* un-Japanese thought-and-customs committee, and the very belief that you *must* be independent and individualistic—an idea taken from the West—is a paradoxical kind of other-direction which may be a necessary step on the road to autonomy. In any large-scale society, all "geological" strata are present at once.

Hitomi: Certainly. There is a great difference, for instance in Tokyo, between the first generation of rural migrants and those born there, and it would be a vast overgeneralization to say that all are other-directed.

(At this point, tea was brought in and we had a short break.)

Otani: Much that is imported into Japan from the United States—films, songs, and so on—is regarded as Japanese; people don't realize that these things are imported, and their quality doesn't differ from what is produced within Japan. This is a change since before the war, when French songs might be liked because they were French and exotic and because many Japanese felt so desperate about their own society. Now songs from elsewhere, American or Cuban or whatever, are enjoyed in a different way.

Hitomi: The admirers of French songs in the 1930's were a small number of highbrow intellectuals, very different from present-day teenagers; teenagers of the ordinary sort in the 1930's would have been happy with homemade songs, whereas today there is a far greater speed of exposure to novelty. Yet older patterns survive and even when the new is taken over, old forms may be kept, as in the example of a couple who made their choice in marriage but still used the go-between.

Yoshida: Children are still expected to marry through go-betweens and to have Shinto ceremonies. But the families of the young people are also generous in attempting to take account of novelty. I went to a traditional wedding where people talked about the "newlyweds" and said "here they come," which were not traditional phrases. The same behavior may fit both expected roles and new ones.

Returning to the question of conformity, Japanese are more concerned with fulfilling what they are supposed to do than what they are supposed to feel; I think this is a kind of tradition-direction. The Japanese remain organization-oriented rather than individual-oriented, and thus the persistent social structure makes for conformity even while we are changing from a production to a consumption society. Superficially our behavior looks like American conformity, but the motives are different.

Riesman: You are implying that even the contemporary Japanese bears the burden of his familistic structure, but also has its protection. He is bound and oppressed but is not thrown alone onto the personality market.

Yoshida: True, but remember that social mobility here is, if anything, even higher than in the United States. Even so, individuals in each status are protected from aggression coming from outside.

Hitomi: There is not only one "escalator" but many escalators, each of which confers a certain status. Yet we have many mental breakdowns and suicides and intense competition within and among escalators.

Riesman: In a study done at Flint, Michigan, a group of college students said they felt badly if they were not aggressive. They blamed themselves for not getting ahead, rather than blaming the escalator. Am I right in thinking that if in Japan one is on a slow escalator, one may be frustrated, but one doesn't feel at every moment that one is personally at fault and should be somewhere else altogether? Isn't it perhaps a little easier in Japan to persuade oneself to make the best of it?

Hitomi: Our students, I'm sure, have at least as much mental illness. People look for psychological help everywhere, to fortunetellers, to teachers—even to psychoanalysts.

Otani: Some say that the United States is the shape of the Japanese future, but if I understand Riesman he is saying that Japan is the shape of the American future. For the United States still has room but may soon be as tight, as boxed in, as Japan. Does this mean that Americans will be looking to leisure activities such as flower arrangement in order to make use of limited space?

Riesman: I suppose it is conceivable we could turn in the Japanese direction of employing more people to do less work with less elbowroom, but it would seem more likely that we would move in the direction of creating a still larger pool of unemployed and through automation move toward a society in which only scientists, technicians, and educated people have work.

Some of the frustration mobilized by the Right Wing may come from a feeling that opportunity and room are being cut down. Rather than meeting these problems directly, the Right Wing blames the government. Perhaps the Japanese "solution" of underemployment for almost everyone would be a less unhappy one.

Hitomi: Japanese underemployment is hardly a model. Surely we could find a happier solution.

Riesman: Of course we could, in principle. There are ever so many tasks which could absorb the affluent society: rebuilding cities, providing attractive housing, developing a more effective educational system which does not turn out semiliterates alienated from culture. We need services of all kinds, public health and a great many others. We have a responsibility to the less affluent societies and to reduce misery, poverty, and hunger everywhere. All this could occupy millions of people. Defense production is convenient because it doesn't compete with private enterprise, while any move to rebuild our cities would compete.

Yoshida: Suppose all the underemployed are absorbed—would they be happier?

Riesman: Employment alone is not enough. But in the United States employment is essential, not only because the status of being employed is imperative but because work provides solidarity with others. In Japan, that solidarity may be too tight, but in the United States it is too loose, and when people speak of individuality and autonomy they often mean the lone ranger, or in Erich Fromm's sense, "freedom from" rather than "freedom to." Work can provide a non-oppressive solidarity based not on given ties of soil, kin, or sex, but on feelings of common tasks and comradeship in voluntary groups. The term "comrade" is cynically used by the Communists, but the concept should be brought back into common use and not allowed to lapse because of Communist exploitation. Consider Murata's group, all from different disciplines and sharing a common interest which unites them despite differences in academic rank.

Yoshida: Where does the energy come from to build up voluntary groups based on common tasks? If a society is totally other-directed, where do the autonomous come from?

Riesman: Private property as a protection against monopoly of jobs is one source. It allows starting a new enterprise. Another source: the few prophetic spirits who feel personally responsible for what happens in the United States—men like Lewis Mumford. They play an important part in harnessing the energies that are already there. Certain fields harbor more of these marginal prophets than others, but professionalization is taking its toll here.

Yoshida: The United States is notable for an enormous number of small colleges, small theaters, and other such enterprises, but in Japan we always want things to get big. If a play is a success, it will be asked to come to a big theater, and if a small college is a success, it tries to grow. Small organizations such as the Committee of Correspondence could not exist in Japan. Cultured men do not take part in politics; indeed, their culture is often an escape from politics.

Riesman: Small colleges and small enterprises are not valuable per se. Often they are simply bad imitations of big enterprises. Small theaters often put on Broadway plays rather than experimental ones. Many small colleges are conservative and proud of being small only in the sense that they are not for the masses. To be sure, a more human scale is desirable; I think your own universities are much too big. The idea that everything must grow seems to me part of the capitalist spirit, but in Japan I don't see much samurai resistance to it, any more than the religious fundamentalists in the United States who denounce materialism oppose material growth and success.

Yoshida: I found the boasting of Midwestern universities tiresome, but I was impressed by Earlham College, which through its interest in the question of peace had to be involved in the problems of the outside world and thus with human values. But some of the Ivy League small colleges seem interested only in restoring the spirit of tradition rather than in looking into the classics from a social-science perspective and for their relevance to the contemporary.

Riesman: To return to the example of small colleges, we must think of the question in terms of an individual's development and what scale is proper for each stage of life. Children must develop in a small group. Perhaps the huge state universities have grown beyond human scale. They need size for libraries, for equipment, but they should be broken into sub-colleges for their students. Too many small colleges are satisfied just with their smallness.

Yoshida: One source of energy in Japan comes from the double-decker economy, which reminds us of imperfections even here in Tokyo and of the many underprivileged people right in the city, and not only in farming areas away from the city. The experimental spirit may come from our many small industries, even though these have suffered in competition with the large corporations. This very competition pushes them toward the experimental spirit.

Riesman: We have a double-decker economy also, but are less aware of it. Our lower decks confine people of a different race or ethnic group or those regarded as stupid, dumb, slow, or otherwise inadequate in terms of our growing meritocracy. In Japan, there are no such sub-groups to speak of who are labeled as stupid, incapable of rising. Americans still complacently believe that if one is good, one can make it. There is not the same entrusting oneself to a single escalator for all of life where everything hangs on the first job.

Is there any possibility of changing escalators in Japan?

Hitomi: The young in business and in big corporations enter on their work very mechanically and look for creative opportunities outside of work. But for some, graduate school offers another opportunity. There it is possible to pass examinations without cramming and take the rituals in stride without too much respect for one's professors, even though the universities are thought of as feudal. A small minority has the courage to be marginal.

Yoshida: Our economy determines the nature of what is possible. It depends on exports and these in turn primarily on medium-size industries (with steel and transistors the exception). We are turning out an increasing number of college graduates who are entering tertiary industries, which are usually small. And a fifth of the graduates are going into jobs which are ordinarily occupied by high-school graduates. Such men look forward to building up their autonomy in private life. In this, they are following the example of some corporate executives who are expert in tea ceremony or Nō plays and who find making money compatible with freedom in their private lives. As jobs become more scarce for the highly educated, this search for private life becomes more important.

Riesman: I have the impression of enormous energies in Japanese life looking for "interior space"—in gardening and in all sorts of hobbies.

Murata: This is related to the high literacy of Japan. Haiku is a national art. Eighty per cent of the Japanese, including farmers and workers, write haiku. Our society is characterized by symbolic channels for the discharge of energy.

Hitomi: This certainly isn't true of most businessmen, who work very hard and have little time for these leisure occupations. We have to make distinctions here.

Yoshida: You are right that there are differences, drawing on different traditions in the Tokugawa period. Many samurai pursued all sorts of leisure activities. They had ample time and cultivation. But some *chonin* (merchants) simply discharged their energies in wine and gambling and girls. From Meiji to the present, this dichotomy exists, for unlike Great Britain we don't have a national upper-class culture which influences all strata.

Riesman: There may be little social snobbery in Japan in the society-page sense, but businessmen seem to be quite willing to throw their weight around and to accept servility. It seems to me they are irresponsible toward the fate of the mass of men, who, since they are not starving, are not reminding the big-shots of ever present misery. The acceptance of servility goes into the home: men accept servile roles from their womenfolk. These aspects of Japanese society seem to be not at all other-directed, for men care what *some people* think, but not what the subordinate thinks.

I want to return to what Murata said a minute ago. What does it mean, to find that a businessman actually writes haiku? Is he more involved with poetry than with gastronomy? What sort of compartmentalization has he worked out between work and leisure?

(At this point, the discussion switched to students and politics. No one answered my questions—something we often experienced, although in this case our Japanese friends had sufficient confidence to tackle anything and perhaps felt that they had exhausted the topic.)

Riesman: Why do the Japanese students feel so cut off from politics? They seem reasonably effective, but do they themselves feel that they are dragooned into demonstrations and just mouth Marxist slogans?

Yoshida: The really active students are a very small number indeed. And the feeling of alienation is so strong that whatever movements one engages in can never live up to the ideals people have.

Murata: All these students as freshmen have to pass the "shower room," where they hear about different student movements. Most of them don't read any books on the social sciences. They certainly don't know their own folklore but only the required condensed version of Western thought—Mills, Riesman, Marx, etc. If they know anything about Japan, it is through Western eyes.

Otani: Most Zengakuren leaders were educated after the war and are deeply suspicious of the adults' culture. Remember that changes after the war were not brought about by the Japanese people themselves, but were imposed by the Occupation—the Emperor was changed, like the weather, from outside.

Riesman: Have these experiences of the leaders given them a quasi-Leninist or quasi-Maoist view of history, in which the only change they recognize is violent discontinuity? Certainly the students don't appear to realize their power.

Hitomi: Many students simply follow their leaders, who in turn take demonstrations for granted as part of Japanese society. In that sense, they are not alienated. And the student position confers a kind of status. Demonstrations and strikes allow a student to say, "This is the way to be a proper student"—he feels exalted and enhanced.

Yoshida: It is more complicated. Both professors and students feel that they have a monopoly on certain important ideas and that the role of the school has been to introduce new ideas, especially Western ideas. In other words, to be a conformist in school is to be alienated from society.

Murata: There is a sudden release students have after passing examinations, which they may have taken over and over. Then they are ready to accept something higher, something impractical. In the fourth year they still sometimes feel lonely and so go down to the first-year shower room and make themselves leaders, giving "pink" or "red showers" (Marxist indoctrination) to the freshmen.

Hitomi: It has been the custom for those familiar with Western culture to possess authority and this is easily conferred on the student, who must be able to quote from English, German, or Russian scholars. In the past, this note has been even more important than attention to one's own discipline, but this is changing now. Ironically, the students can't read English. The teaching of it in grade school is very poor, and they prefer to read English works in Japanese translation, the more so as television and movies compete for the students' time. Hence in the university many professors assign books which the students actually cannot read.

(At this point we stopped.)

Murata and Yoshida stayed on with us for dinner, much to our pleasure. These two men, both in a way sentimental about Japanese traditions, are at the same time entirely contemporary people. We have grown fond of them, enjoying a sort of sociability with them, and the play of minds. After ordering our American meal of steak and potatoes, we began talking about Japanese society. Murata said that while Japan is democratic, it is also status-conscious; at a certain point in life there is a great deal of mobility, but once you have achieved your status, then you must play your expected role. He said that perhaps one reason the Japanese are not mean or envious is that each status has its absolute unchangeable position; it is quite accepted, for example, that a professor writing an article for a magazine will be paid more for it than a non-professor writing the same article for the same magazine, because of the status of the professor. Yoshida qualified this: there was a meanness in Japan, in the Army, for example; the sergeants came from the falling middle class, they were bitter and became very nationalistic; they took out their frustrations on upper-class boys in the Army, hazed them, took away their books, beat them up. *ETR*

Japan's relation to China, our friends said, is not like England's to Europe, which has been more of a two-way relationship involving not one monolithic country but many countries. China was one huge country, and the only country that influenced Japan; indeed, Japan received almost everything from China: the written language, religion, the arts, the planning of cities. Japan in turn had its greatest influence on Taiwan, which still persists: Japanese is its only universal language; also, Japanese architecture has persisted because that island has the same sort of climate. In Korea, the climate is too different to be influenced by Japanese architecture.

In discussing the development and modernization of various societies, Yoshida and Murata thought that in feudal societies the development from tradition-direction to inner-direction seems to be the usual pattern; perhaps this is because feudal societies are composed of many different fiefs which must deal with each other, and so they develop certain fixed and understood laws, customs, and prices; in Japan, for example, there were fixed prices for all, while in China there were different prices for each class of person; the Protestant ethic, it seems, developed out of feudalism; the United States was founded by people coming from feudal Europe; but the big, despotically ruled countries, Russia, China, India, do not develop inner-direction and so cannot develop other-direction. What will they develop—just an absolute mass culture? What will it be like? What will Africa be like?

The question came up of the ways in which the United States and Japan are similar. Yoshida said that this should be stressed in some new study; the differences were brought out by Ruth Benedict in *The Chrysanthemum and the Sword*, but the similarities are interesting; both countries feel an inferiority complex, vis-à-vis their "borrowed" cultures, both have a flourishing mass culture, both love mechanical things, and both love baseball.

Toward the end of our dinner, we were discussing different varieties of leisure in Japan; some activities are more or less a discharge of frustration, such as the Roon movement and the more conventional wine, gambling, and girls; but for people who seek *re*charge rather than *dis*charge, there are creative things like gardening, flower arranging, writing haiku. (I am reminded here that the student *demo* were discussed in terms of discharge also and am struck by this simple mechanistic term; the frustrations the Japanese have to deal with are the rigidities in their society, and these are external frustrations, which perhaps do not require more subtle explanations.) Kabuki and Nō theater are, for example, a form of recharging rather than discharging. We talked about the slow death in Kabuki, the concentration over perhaps a period of half an hour on dying itself, much as in Elizabethan drama. This is quite different from the bang-bang machine-gun deaths in American movies, where, as Murata observed, death has no meaning and people are treated as objects.

As we were finishing our coffee, Yoshida said that on the boat returning to Japan after his several years of study in the United States, there were Americans who were failures, who hoped in Japan to be more successful—with girls, with business, in every way; and Yoshida, who had overcome his inferiority complex in the United States by making friends—wonderful friends—there, was subjected again to these feelings of inferiority by the people on the boat who needed so desperately to feel superior.

Yoshida makes one forget that he is not American, his face is expressive, his language colloquial. But I have noticed when two Japanese—as now, Yoshida and Murata—stop speaking English and turn to speak to each other in Japanese, their facial expression and gestures change; their faces immediately look more masklike, more Japanese.

Tokyo, November 3

Murata said, as we sat in the warm sun on the terrace after lunch today, that there was an important difference between the American cocktail party and the Japanese tea ceremony: the Americans want to meet as many people and make as many friends as possible, while the Japanese already have their friends—they are *given,* so to speak. A tea ceremony is a way of reinforcing the friendship with those already existing friends. And this is done not by conversation, but by drinking out of the same cup that is passed around, a symbolic ritual. The Japanese have little need for social skill and social grace, because for them the social arrangements are entirely formalized.

Later in the afternoon, Bill Caudill came to see us. We went down to the bar, which is an awkward place to talk if anyone else is there, as it is so small. But fortunately it was empty. Nat Glazer joined us, and the four of us sat around the table having tea or beer, discussing life in Japan. Caudill told us about the study he is doing of mother-child behavior in Japan; he is making comparisons between Japan and the United States. He said that American babies (three-to four-months-old first infants) are more active and vocal than their Japanese counterparts, that American mothers talk to their babies more, that Japanese mothers rock their babies more. His feeling is that the emphasis of the American mother is on encouraging response and activity in her infant, while the emphasis of the Japanese mother is on having a quiet, placid, happy baby. This led to a discussion of the Japanese bath as a place for playfulness and sociability; for example, the father or grandparent often took the baby into the bath with him. Nat spoke of seeing six-year-old children going home from school or kindergarten by bus alone—how was this possible for such young children? Caudill said that the bus driver or bus girl (the conductors on buses are young women) would tell the children it was the right bus and help them on. Everyone in Japan loves children, and Japan in a way is like one big family. What about juvenile delinquents, Dave asked, and who are they? Caudill said that they come from middle-class families; perhaps they are failures of one sort or another. Caudill said that there is probably as much mental illness in Japan as in the United States, but that mental illness takes different forms in the two countries. Also the Japanese just haven't got the counseling and therapy we have, and Freud in almost unknown here. He said that on the whole the Japanese are completely honest; it is the Chinese who own the dives in the Ginza, not the Japanese. Tokyo is not so safe a city as it was, though still far safer than our cities.

ETR

Caudill described a young businessman he knew who had a good position but took no interest in his work; all he cared about was driving cars fast, having pretty girls, and playing golf; this made him seem very modern, but he wanted an arranged marriage, which sounded incongruous; but really it was not incongruous—if he chose his bride out of love, his marriage would interfere with these pleasures, which he didn't want to give up. Caudill went on to say that early retirement was not at all a problem for the Japanese as they welcome not having to work; they enjoy their leisure, their gardening, and so forth. Retirement for them is not what it is for Americans.

DR

Tokyo, November 4

I've just read the transcripts of two tape-recorded lectures which will be published here. They give me an uneasy feeling because they are loaded with opportunities for political misunderstanding. Few Japanese understand contemporary America in all its complexity. The Left in general sees America in terms of the power elite and the presumed alliance between monopoly capital in America and in Japan. The liberals often see America in terms of traditional democratic and liberal ideals—sometimes in terms of the early years of the Occupation before the turn to the Right that occurred with the Korean War. Conservatives are supposed to be "pro-American" in the political sense, but at the same time they are often opposed to the elements of modernity and progress in Japan that are also traced to American sources; and as Japanese nationalists, they also have a hard time being pro-American rather than simply anti-Communist. (In this respect, they are probably not very different from conservatives in other parts of the world.)

Moreover, I realize how special is the experience of Japanese with American visitors or residents: the American businessman is often here for a good time, while the "Japan fan" is interested in the tea ceremony or Zen or many other things which are rejected by a good many of the younger Japanese as "feudal remnants," and the Christian educators and missionaries here would hardly give anyone a sense of the ethnic-religious conflicts of American life, which in any case don't fit into the conventional Marxism of a large number of Japanese students and intellectuals. In a way, except for the Japan fans, the representatives of America here seem a generation or so out of date. And this includes some of the diplomatic representatives who haven't kept up with developments at home.

In this last connection, I am reminded of the charge we heard made in Kyoto that malicious letters written to the American Consul in Kobe can serve to prevent a visa being granted to Japanese intellectuals or students who want to come to the United States. It is said that these letters are sometimes written by Communists as part of their tortuous strategy, and the Consul may not have any idea of such complicated motivations and may take the letters of denunciation at face value. I raised this question with a friend in the Embassy here who said he didn't think it was true; the Consul would have no independent authority in a security case, but it would be referred to Washington.

At lunch, we were joined by two "regulars" of the International House group, Professor Kawasaki and Professor Hayakawa. The latter had been asked to review *Constraint and Variety*, which a few days earlier had come out in Japanese translation. He was reviewing it for *Tokyo Shimbun*, one of the leading newspapers, and had also been asked to review it by the student paper at Tokyo University. He said that the discussion of the intellectual veto groups in the book was very much in line with his own experience, both in sponsoring general education and as member of a governmental commission on higher education. But he didn't think these matters would be of interest to the general public and was puzzled what to say in the newspaper review. The Japanese believe that their post-war system of higher education is the American one, and apparently it was imposed by American devotees of the land-grant model, while Hayakawa would like to see greater influence of the alternate model of the American liberal-arts college with its more humanistic tradition. He said that when he was sponsoring general education at Tokyo University he was quite unaware of the American experience with this and thought of himself as opposed to the American innovations, only to discover later that his own innovations had "American" precursors also.

He said that at Tokyo the Law Faculty stood at the top and could get its graduates into the best jobs (only a very small proportion actually go into the practice of law), with medicine next, and humanities about at the bottom of the list. At Kyoto University, humanities stood somewhat higher. As in America, he said, only perhaps more so, the institutions were stratified in prestige terms and the departments within them also—not necessarily in any relation to what was actually taught. He suggested to a student who had worked with him that he go to Osaka to continue his studies with the best person in the country. He thought this student very courageous actually to do this rather than going to some more fashionable but less advantageous place, such as Tokyo University itself.

We have had a number of discussions with people at International House of the problem of translation, both in general and in connection with specific lectures of mine. I think it was Kato who observed that there are three levels of translation: the first, translation of the words; the second, of the ideas; and the third, of the feeling. He added that he had reached this third level only after some exposure to me in Japan. Thus, I sometimes feel that men of a different temperament have a hard time translating me even if their English is excellent. And as I have already said, there is great ambivalence toward speaking English well. Not only does a person who speaks it "too well" get pressed into service as interpreter and translator, but also he embarrasses the older men who don't speak it so well. Some people who speak it quite well pretend they can't speak it at all, because they can't speak it perfectly. Since Americans readily accept those who try to speak our language, and indeed the Japanese are equally generous to Americans who try to speak Japanese, this "French" attitude toward language is based on other elements of Japanese culture than desire for linguistic perfection.

There are times when I realize from the use of English words as boundary markers that my translator is being too literal-minded and often taking more time than can well be spared, so that I try to compress what I have to say, but fear then to lose its texture of concreteness. In dealing with the problem of translation, the courtesy and considerateness of our Japanese hosts may lead to extravagant efforts, which nobody wants.

Beneath the surface of all that is done for us we feel there lies a network of incredible delicacies and difficulties which we only rarely get a glimpse of. Just as we are not allowed to walk half a block from a lecture to our hotel or get out of the car and walk into the temple rather than be driven through the gate, just as Evey and I must sit together at a dinner even though she would have preferred to sit next to a guest to differentiate our experience, so other arrangements are beyond our control or guidance. And we often wonder whether we may not be riding roughshod over tacit expectations that have never been voiced. For instance, the night of our arrival at Tokyo station from Kyoto we were met by Mrs. Kako and the Matsumotos' chauffeur and then picked up Mrs. Matsumoto. When we arrived at International House, we were greeted by the staff and by Matsumoto, who apologized profusely for not meeting us at the station because he had had another meeting, and then he and his wife invited us to come into their own house for a brief visit. I was fighting a cold and felt miserable, and we excused ourselves to retire but had the uneasy feeling that the Matsumotos had come home on our account. I constantly feel like the character in O'Henry's story who sells his watch to buy his wife a comb for her hair, which she has cut off to buy him a watch chain—each hoping to please, and ending by frustrating, the other.

After lunch, there was a meeting at the University of Tokyo Press with a group of social psychologists. The topic was fad behavior. This proved to be a stiff, dead-pan affair. But I was struck during the discussion by the many references to other-direction in Japanese life. The impact of *The Lonely Crowd* in Japan may be seen, it seems to me, as an element of fad behavior. The term "lonely crowd" itself appeals, and some people have pointed out that Japan is other-directed among the nations in the way that its individuals are among each other. Like the Americans whom Tocqueville visited, the Japanese we see appear preoccupied by—and stimulated by—cultural comparisons and contrasts; and Murata and others have agreed with my observation that second-rate American works often take precedence here over first-rate Japanese ones—recalling the American deference to Europe before World War I. (Today the "third generation" is insisting that Japan is not being "Westernized" but "modernized" and that the electronic age is as natural to Japan as it is to any other country; having grown up in this age, these intellectuals take it for granted and feel no sense of strain or crisis of identity comparable to that of their intellectual predecessors.)

Fad behavior among Japanese young people appears to be less affect-laden than in the United States. Girls copy an Audrey Hepburn shoe or haircut, but are not concerned with sharing the emotional states presented by Audrey Hepburn. Despite the "photographic" magazines, I have the impression that romance and sex are nowhere near so omnipresent here as in the United States—the modern novelists, of course, deal with it in a very "French" way, but their preoccupations do not seem to be general. Moreover, the close group feeling in Japan that begins with the ties between the infant and his adult guardians provides a kind of "natural" environment of belonging for the Japanese. There is, however, a problem of belongingness in the sense that people feel miserable when they are not in a group and when they are isolated; but groups based on family ties, school ties, work ties, leisure ties offer a ready acceptance. I don't have the sense of people seeking inner resonance with each other in quite the same way as in the United States.

Bob Lifton tells me that a group of school friends may continue to regard each other as friends throughout life: when they see each other, that's fine, and when they don't see each other, that's fine also. In informal gatherings, the men move readily to childlike frivolity, playing games and drinking endless little cups of *sake* and perhaps chatting with geisha girls or hostesses. It may even be that the absence of women, that is, of wives, makes for somewhat lesser anxiety—so that wives are not a problem, but a convenience to the men—all this, of course, is very speculative.

It seems impossible to have a seriously frivolous—let alone flirtatious—conversation. Either there is a formal occasion where people play prepared parts—one reason why these academic gatherings are so difficult at times, since there is little spontaneity or give and take—or people are sitting on *tatami* drinking beer or *sake* and playing *go* or finding amusement in a series of anecdotes. (The dinner party, too, is as formal as a diplomatic dinner, with set speeches and applause, even if only a dozen people are present, and with a repast so heavy as to sink sociability anyway.) I suppose there's something vaguely Victorian in all this, as well as specifically Japanese.

The coffee house is a great exception. Given the relative lack of privacy in the Japanese home and the absence of cars for all but the fairly rich, the coffee house provides for the young one of the few places for a date and one of the few where for little money groups of either sex can get together (coffee or Coca-Cola costs 100 yen, 30 cents) away from home or school. There must be dozens of coffee houses within a few blocks of International House, and no locale we've seen is without them.

Tokyo, November 6

At breakfast this morning, Matsumoto asked how the occasion with the social psychologists had gone and was not surprised to hear that it was on the sticky side. He said if we had come ten years ago we would have found hardly any of the sort of free and easy interchange we had had in Kyoto. Moreover, those who at that time spoke English were apt to be more conservative types, familiar, for instance, with British constitutional history or American colonial history—often Christians. The last ten years had seen an extraordinary decline in Japanese insularity, and in this respect we had come at a fortunate time.

I have noticed, in reading the English-language press or occasional translations of Japanese papers and monthlies, that the editorials often have a vacuous quality. For example: "There should be more peaceful coexistence in the world, and the problem is how to assure people coexistence." Reports of symposia or interviews with leading academicians also present this sort of inoffensive stuff, which, so far as I can see, says nothing at all. On the other hand, there are frank statements in the press that one would hardly find outside of an American gossip column. Thus, there was a story about how one of the Japanese cabinet ministers attending the Hakone talks got drunk and said he would go up Mount Fuji with Secretary Udall; the story said he had repeated his boast over and over, although he was much too fat to carry it out. And one of the monthlies had a description of the "kitchen" ties between leading politicians and political reporters who worm their way into the confidence of the politician by bribing the maid and hanging around the kitchen and helping the wife do her shopping and so on, and then are given tidbits of information—a very frank story, naming names and giving the first inside view we've had on how the bitter competition among newspapermen is carried on; the latter are supposed to eat their way in, because they spend so much time in the kitchen, joining the wife and maid in meals. It is said that they are not given pocket money for bribes, that they must spend time instead of money.

Some of the discussions in the leftist magazines have a kind of "Stalinist" dreariness about them, with endlessly repeated phrases about American monopoly capitalism, and imperialism, and so on. It all has a dated flavor. Khrushchev doesn't talk this way. There is a curious contrast between the wordiness of this writing and the compression of haiku or the "silent language" which is supposed to be all that is necessary among lovers or intimates.

The Japanese had looked forward with pathetic eagerness to the Hakone Conference (of Japanese and American cabinet members), and what must have been small squibs in the American press had enormous headlines here, competing only with news of fall-out. (The Japanese papers are full of advice on how to wash vegetables, but then it is pointed out that the water in which the vegetables are washed is just as contaminated as the rain water which is so greatly feared.) Anyway, it had been hoped at Hakone to convince Americans to liberalize the restrictions on imports to the United States from Japan that have created such a crisis here. The Americans have replied that Japanese goods are discriminated against because of the low wages of the Japanese workers. But this is only adding insult to injury. On the one side, the papers explain that the wages are not *really* low because prices for many staples such as rice (which is bought at a high price from the farmers and sold at a low price to consumers) are also low. But then it is added: how can we raise wages unless we can increase our exports, and we can only increase our exports to the United States. On the other hand, the labor unions use the American arguments to insist that without raising prices Japanese industry can afford to pay higher wages, for although real wages have risen a great deal here in ten years, prices have also risen and productivity, too, has gone up greatly. Yet the employers answer that unless wages are kept low, exports will have even more difficulty competing in the world market.

Moreover, the relative increase in living standards has heightened the trade crisis with the United States. It has meant, for example, a declining rice consumption and a passionate fad for all sorts of food imported from the United States: a fad for instant coffee, for instance, which is terribly expensive here but which is featured sometimes in even the smallest stores, and for California raisins, for imported lobsters—and for bread as against rice. Thus, not only the rich with their imported big cars, but also many less well off people have contributed, by a shift in consumer buying habits, to the trade crisis. Of course, the American companies and agricultural producers who sell a billion dollars' worth of goods a year to Japan have little political influence on the textile mills or toymakers who force through political curbs on the imports from Japan; and the American delegation here was in the position of asking the Japanese to continue buying heavily from the United States without leaving any opening for Japanese sales to the United States—speaking indeed about America's own balance of payments crisis, which doesn't seem to be as serious as Japan's (much as a rich man will speak about *his* troubles, which a poor man can hardly understand).

Japanese business and industry must, in fact, absorb many costs which Americans would shift to the individual or to the society. When people are employed, they are taken on for life or until retirement, and when they are retired, the bonuses are often huge—a kind of private social security; an upper-middle-income man can invest his severance pay at enough return so that he can live on it the rest of his life. Furthermore, pay rises automatically with seniority, irrespective of productivity, and is also increased by family allowances. Then the effort to absorb as many workers as possible means that every subway train has not only the motorman but a man who sits beside him to be sure that the signals are green—they call out each signal to each other. Department stores have smiling girls at the top of each escalator to thank people for their patronage and to give information when asked. Although the Miyako Hotel, where we stayed in Kyoto, has automatic elevators, girl attendants would punch the buttons for the passengers going up and then step quickly out before the doors closed. In every office, there are at least two receptionists for the tasks of less than one—of course, the serving of tea makes slight periodic demands on them. Given the fact that the Japanese ask for little in the way of challenge or excitement in work itself and seek happiness in their leisure and in personal relations, this pattern supports what strikes me as the relative equanimity of the Japanese people in the face of much frustration—though, to be sure, not without its limits.

There are, of course, groups who seem terribly overworked: the journalists and broadcasters, racing around in search of stories; the young managers, who carry much of the burden of Japanese economic advance while also taking part in the expense-account culture of nighttime and weekends; the professors teaching at three different places, talking weekly on television, and writing sixteen articles for rates measured not by their fame but by their academic status. The very pace of life in Tokyo would seem hard on all but the very rich. In the rush hours, hundreds of university students have their "Arbeit" as pushers, that is, forcing people into the subway cars and closing the doors in jams that make Manhattan seem idyllic by comparison and that bring out the rather frightening aggression of a Japanese crowd. The sprawl of Tokyo, based on its one- or two-story buildings and lack of large apartments and skyscrapers, means that many people must commute long distances under such conditions or drive in traffic that becomes increasingly impassable. Yet even this harried minority of students seems to find time to read a great deal, to follow television and baseball, to go mountain climbing or skiing, to go to restaurants, coffee houses, and tea houses. Many are able to sleep on the subway—standing up. Tranquilizers and sleeping pills are widely sold—indeed, a craze for jags based on sleeping pills among young people has been much in the papers.

I want to put down something more about the Japanese Left, now that I've had some personal contact with it, as well as vicarious contact through the mass media. The plus word on which it has made the greatest headway is of course "peace"; and as I've remarked earlier and have a better sense of now, the Soviet bomb tests have created a real crisis for many people and movements. Previously it was possible to be both for the revolution and for peace and to differ with fellow

Leftists only on the question whether Japanese monopoly capitalism is the chief opponent, or American imperialism working hand in glove with Japanese monopoly capitalism. The Russian bomb tests and especially the monster 50-megaton bomb have put such people on the defensive. The first response of many Marxists and fellow travelers was to say that "we must understand Russia's position" and to give explanations and excuses for the Russian tests based on West German rearmament and the Berlin crisis—precisely the formula used by Khrushchev himself. But this could hardly explain or justify the monster bombs or cope with the mounting panic within Japan.

In this connection, Bob Lifton spoke of a student he had been interviewing who had always regarded himself as strong both for peace and for the revolution. The student admitted that he had to come out in opposition to the Russian tests, but that he really did so for tactical reasons, so as to make it possible for him and his group to attack America when it resumed testing, without being accused of applying a double standard. But he could not really surrender his more sympathetic feeling for the Soviet Union—or perhaps his less sympathetic attitude toward the United States—and as Bob Lifton pressed him, it became clear that "peace" was really a word or a formula and that he was not so devoted to it as for many years he had thought.

I had much the same experience in talking to some of the more aggressive Marxists in the student self-government group at Kyoto. These young men were not Communist Party members; they rejected the Party as too bureaucratic and corrupt and called themselves anarchists. Nevertheless, their view of the world was based on the same dated and stilted Marxism to which I've referred. They insisted that peace could be won by a victory over monopoly capitalism and American imperialism. While hostile to the Japanese Communist Party, and while regretting the Soviet tests that had made their own position more difficult, they could "understand" Soviet conduct in a way that they made no effort to do with the United States. One of the most admirable features of Japanese life is the endless curiosity of people, and there is enormous curiosity about America in many quarters; but I found incomprehension and lack of interest among these students when I sought to talk in concrete terms about the sources of the American behavior they disliked: about the role of ethnic groups and small-town Republicanism and so on. (I realized when I was talking to the students about American Catholic and Protestant fundamentalism that they couldn't grasp what I was saying at all, because religion here has no such ideological meaning except among some of the new sects that have sprung up since the war; Japanese Christianity tends to have a noble and educational mien and not a fanatical one.) The Russian tests had helped cut whatever ties they had to official Communism and had led some of the more sensitive to search for a personal vision in the spirit of Albert Camus, but it had not led them so far as to take another kind of look at the United States—or indeed at their own country.

These students asked me why President Kennedy was so much more chauvinistic than his predecessor. The question surprised me because these same students had been leaders of the *demo* of the year before —many had gone up to Tokyo for the purpose—and had been among those who forced the cancellation of President Eisenhower's visit. Yet they seemed uniformly to fear that Kennedy was a more dangerous man, more militaristic. When I reflected on this, I could see reasons for it in the sharpness and personal forcefulness of Kennedy, which is so very much in contrast with the soft phrases in which even hard sayings are wrapped among the Japanese. Japanese Leftists tend in personal style to be as remote as can be from, let us say, their French counterparts: they avoid speaking with clarity, vigor, and personal force—they remain members of a group even in dissent, and syncretistic and catholic even in sectarian movements. President Eisenhower, with his benevolence and lack of harshness, his wooly phrases and amiability, perhaps seemed more "Japanese," even though he was the leader of a party which the Japanese take for granted is more reactionary.

In other words, "peace" is important to the Japanese not only because of concrete experiences with the atomic bomb and the fears of a small crowded country lying between the United States and Red China that it would be utterly destroyed in a nuclear war, but also because peaceable relations in the family, in the group, and in society at large are basic to the Japanese way of life.

Tokyo, November 7

This noon we had lunch with Professor Miyako, an elderly, graying man of distinction and authority. Formerly an official in the Ministry of Education, Miyako is now one of the leaders of the non-church Christian group here and deeply concerned about peace. He had also been an academician, a student of British political history, and was still addressed by his academic title. I began by asking him about the peace movement in Japan. To answer this, he said, he had to go back to the immediate post-war period. Japan at that time had welcomed the Occupation-imposed ban on armaments, and virtually all strata had liked the idea of being the first country to outlaw military force; indeed, this novelty was linked to the other innovations of the Occupation, such as land reform, universal education, and the strengthening of labor unions, as signs of entering the new world of democracy and freedom with which Japan, in spite of certain aspects of modernization, had never caught up. Indeed, Miyako explained, Japan had never had a Renaissance or Reformation or the impact of Christianity or humanism, and had desperately needed these. The early post-war days had been a period of high idealism. Many primary- and secondary-school teachers, organized into a powerful union, had dedicated themselves to the task of the democratization of Japan—and to peace.

Then, however, had come the sharp turn—the "reverse course," as it is called—in American policy, made sharper still by the Korean War. The United States insisted that Japan rearm. Under the patently false guise of "self-defense forces," Japan was doing so, and this obvious duplicity led the teachers and the young people away from idealism and toward nihilism and extremism. (Professor Kawasaki, who was with us, interrupted to say that he had opposed one aspect of the Occupation-imposed reforms, namely, the outlawing of judo and fencing—these sports were creeping back now, and because they had been purged, they were associated with right-wing tendencies, whereas this would not have happened had they been kept.) A people who had prided themselves on never again having an army were now being reminded—this is my interpretation—of their pre-war history when conservative politicians and business leaders went along with the militarists.

Miyako said that the Conservative Party has its eye on Taipei and South Korea—in fact, the papers have been full of hints of American pressure for ending the hostile relations between Japan and South Korea; and the United States through various channels is planning to lend Japan about half a million dollars, more than half of which is earmarked for Korean claims. (Ikeda, the Prime Minister, is really caught here between American pressure and the Socialist Party's use of the strong anti-Korean prejudice of the Japanese people to block these claims.) I remonstrated that the Japanese businessmen seemed to me internationally minded and not in a mood for foreign adventures. Miyako replied that the Japanese people, given their history, have been very nationalistic and do not understand the meaning of freedom of speech or dissent as these are known and practiced in the United States; if the political wind changes, the businessmen will go along, and in any case, the big steel companies would profit from rearmament.

Miyako felt—again in contrast to his picture of the situation in the United States—that there were few traditions in Japan that could stand up. Since the San Francisco Peace Treaty in 1951, democratic forces in Japan have become cynical and discouraged or fatalistic. I raised the question that these students and unions had managed to get rid of Kishi; this didn't seem to me to show weakness or apathy. But Miyako said that the others were just the same—that there were three Kishis to take the place of any one who was forced out. In a real conflict between the government on the one side and the teachers and students on the other, the latter would give way. At least half the population is extremely conservative, imbued with a belief in *kokutai* (national polity); and the social structure of Japan remains rigid.

I asked whether there hadn't been considerable protest against the Russian bomb tests, and Miyako replied that he was depressed by the extent of apathy about the Russian tests; he had expected more protest than occurred. I said that it seemed many papers were carrying stories about fall-out and rain water and so on and people were very worried. Miyako admitted that there was some anxiety, but again felt that people were fatalistic.

When I said I thought some Leftists were torn between their anxiety about fall-out and their sympathy with Communism or at least their wish not to be on the same side as the United States, this led into a discussion of Marxism in Japan. Miyako felt that those in the Japanese student and labor movements who wanted to reform society found in Marxism a handy expedient, one without any tradition of humanistic European philosophy. The intellectual leaders of the teachers' union and of the Zengakuren lack religion. (He didn't mean organized religion or even Christianity, but rather what Erich Fromm would call humanistic religion.) I referred to Erich Fromm's new volume of writings on the humanistic side of Marx and said it seemed to me that what was called Marxism in Japan might better be described as Leninism. Miyako replied that Leninism was to be found in embryo in Marxism and that Japanese intellectuals devoted themselves essentially to a materialistic view of the world.

He had once hoped that something like the Oxford Movement, some sort of religious reformation, might begin among elite university students. He could see the values in Marxism, but wanted to shift the prevailing emphases. He concluded: "This might go beyond sociology, but the main problem is that of spirit or religion. It is necessary to have religion to deal with the moral aspects of the human problem today, not only on the Japanese, but on the world scene as well, including the

United States." He made clear again that he wasn't referring to organized religion. Indeed, he told the story of a friend of his, a Japanese journalist living in Washington, D.C., whose daughter had applied to attend, I assume, a private high school. On the question of her religion, she had answered "free thinker"; they had given her great trouble, thinking that perhaps this meant she was Communist. "What I mean by religion is each individual's being in touch with God"; he added that Marx's anti-theism had contributed something to the world in bringing nearer the true religion, which would not be a religion of temples or churches.

Miyako continued that he sympathized with Toynbee's view of history and shared his goals in terms of a world religion. It might be Christianity, it might be Buddhism, it might even be Confucianism, if one could call that a religion. He insisted that a spiritual revolution is needed in Japan, but that it would take a long time to develop this spiritual point of view. All religions have compromised themselves in their relations to the state and to political parties. Religion needs to regain its purity and its freedom from political parties.

I felt free at this time to ask Miyako whether he was, as I had heard, a non-church Christian, and how did he explain the influence of this small group. Did a few convinced believers have disproportionate weight in a society characterized by relatively low levels of conviction? Miyako seemed to accept this suggestion, saying that while the non-church Christians were indeed a minority, they were scattered widely over the country. (My own impression is that the spread is not so wide, but concentrated mainly in small groups of students and intellectuals.)

Kawasaki brought up the role of dissenters in Japan and in the United States. In Japan, dissent was organized into a movement which believed in radical change instead of staying on the level of reform; this movement did not care to reform the existing situation, in contrast to the more pragmatic (and I assume he meant also more individualistic) dissenters in the United States. I said that the Japanese talk more radically than they seem to act: they have a gift for compromise and syncretism. Kawasaki thought this was a weakness, and I suggested the possibility that the very radical talk might, in some degree, make up for lack of the radical behavior to which one is compelled by one's ideology.

Returning to the problem of militarism in Japan, I mentioned hearing about a Japanese general of the Self-Defense Forces who returned recently from West Germany praising West German rearmament, and pointing out that the West Germans were proud of the Wehrmacht and of its performance in World War II and did not have the pacifistic attitude toward their own military that the general criticized among the Japanese. He thought the Germans were in this respect more self-reliant and wished that the Japanese could take the same attitude toward their own war experience that the Germans had taken, that is, rejecting the Nazis but not the army itself, which had fought bravely and well. Miyako commented that he had at one time wanted Japan to make movies such as the Nuremberg trial films, and felt that the Japanese should make some sort of confession of guilt. But he now thinks that a new Japanese film which has been much praised here, *The Last World War*, is a more important kind of film because it points toward the future rather than the past. Whereas *On the Beach* was too fictitious for the Japanese people, *The Last World War* is very real. There is Japanese modesty in this film and it is technically and artistically very fine. He hoped it could be shown in the United States.

He went on to say that although he was in general very pessimistic, he was encouraged by this film and even more by another, originally a novel by Jumpei, *The Human Condition*. It tells the story of the Manchurian Incident and carries it up to the defeat of Japan. Its author is an economist, a man of the Left. Miyako compared the book to *War and Peace*, saying it was possibly even greater (a judgment Kawasaki later said he thought was excessive; that indeed, since there was no individuality in Japan, there could be no great novels). The novel, which runs to about six volumes, tells the story of a young man who works in a company in Manchuria and is then drafted into the Army, where he is persecuted by the officers and his fellow soldiers for his liberal and pacific views. Finally he manages to escape, but dies on his way back to Japan. The book has been made into a film which runs from nine in the morning until four in the afternoon and is always packed.

It was plain to me that, for these friends and admirers of America, we still appear as something of a utopia: the land where there is true dissent, true democracy and freedom, the land where people are at the same time pragmatic and able to compromise and are not bound fanatically to the Right or to the Left as in Japan. These men are the "friends of America" in a very different sense from the Japanese conservatives who proclaim themselves as friends and have been favored by American interests here, but who, for the most part, are simply opportunists using the American alliance to advance their own political and economic interests. These latter men have no moral stake in America, and if America disappoints them, they can turn to some other great power. But the true friends are in a very different and exceedingly vulnerable situation: since what they have seized upon as "American" is in fact a minority tradition, they can be greatly hurt by American conduct.

During these weeks, we have been given numerous examples of the precariousness of the position of those Japanese liberals whose American heroes are Jefferson, Emerson, Lincoln, Stevenson, and Fulbright. Although in their own communities they ran risks in countering the prevailing anti-American and quasi-Communist orientation of many students and young intellectuals, these liberals were also independent and forthright in criticizing American policy vis-à-vis Japan. As a result, under former Ambassador MacArthur, and before that, under General MacArthur, the advice of such men was often disregarded by our Embassy and the individuals often humiliated. A number of them, for example, tried in vain to warn against President Eisenhower's visit because they knew there would be trouble, but were treated by Embassy officials in an undiscriminating way as if they were merely disgruntled critics of America. The result was that the Embassy got advice often enough from opportunists and flatterers—and then when a great wave of demonstrations came, these could be blamed entirely on Communists, with the Cassandras still disregarded. Of course, there were men in the Embassy itself who did not share MacArthur's view, but for the most part they kept quiet.

The too ready compliance, of which these Japanese men of conviction accused their own countrymen, is one reason why even such tiny movements as the Committee of Correspondence or the Walk for Peace from San Francisco to Moscow, sponsored by A. J. Muste and others, are given such wide publicity and meet such response here. In addition, these minuscule affairs make it possible for those liberals who admire the nonconformist traditions of America not to feel betrayed by their own faith in the United States.

At the same time, one has to take care that one does not misinterpret what the Japanese mean by "democracy," a word they constantly use. It does not mean social equality; the consideration, for example, shown one's equals and official superiors is not extended to those below. "Democracy" does seem to mean a way of doing business that combines commitment and high principle with lack of factionalism and internecine conflict. People refer to organizations as "undemocratic" if there is no harmony or consensus. Thus, democracy and politics would seem antithetical.

Quite unlike the democratic liberals, there is another kind of "friend of America" who admires the technical achievements of America rather than the moral and social ones. I recall a Pakistani I met at one of the International Seminars at Harvard who violently resented even the mildest criticism I made of American efficiency. He had used the model of America in his own country in the fight against tradition and "backwardness," and it was unbearable to him to have an American say that this model might not be the last word; for no doubt he had been told this at home, and was regarded even as disloyal by fellow Moslems whom he could only oppose by building up America to twice life-size. Any criticism of America that could not be dismissed as based on superstition or self-interest tended to pull out the rug from under such a man, who has many counterparts among the technologically oriented Japanese.

Among the older men, there is great admiration of British political life. The Conservative politicians of Japan, many of them former bureaucrats—university graduates to be sure, but not intellectuals—are compared unfavorably with the British Tories. Before the war, conservative politicians in Japan were often of samurai descent and were philosophers of right-wing theoretical leanings; today, in contrast, although there are a few right-wing intellectuals, these have no connection with the practical bureaucratic politicians of the Conservative Party (much like the situation in the United States, where small-time, small-town Republican politicians never read *The National Review* or Ludwig von Mises). And on the Left, the unfavorable comparison is made with the British Labour Party, with which so many of the moderates here feel in close sympathy. Not only has the British Labour Party held office, which seems unlikely for the various socialist parties here, but it seems to its Japanese admirers far less ideological, inflammatory, abstract, and irresponsible than the Socialists. In somewhat the same vein, there is a tendency to assume that at least the Democratic Party in the United States is the party of the intellectuals, and such men as Reischauer, Galbraith, and Schlesinger are thought to have far more influence in it than in fact they do.

Tokyo, November 8

ETR

This morning we drove out to Tokyo Women's Christian University, where Dave was to give a lecture. Large yellow stone buildings formed a quadrangle with lawns and trees, much like any American college campus. Dave's talk was on women's education in the United States, and the girls seemed responsive and attentive: when he discussed things that were close to home, there was much giggling and whispering. Afterward, we met with eight or ten girls in a small private house on the campus, which was now used for various club rooms. At first the girls seemed constrained, but they soon warmed up, with three or four doing most of the talking. The girls were quite varied in their styles: the traditional type, masklike, with the beauty of the doll, hair done in chignon; the sturdy athletic type with bangs and short hair; the scholarly type with glasses, hair pulled back and fastened with a barrette, another with her hair in braids; a few "society" types with permanent waves. We were surprised by the frank and easy way they talked with us. They talked about marriage. Most of them wanted marriage to grow out of friendship, and preferred making their own choice of husband to an arranged marriage; but still they were glad to have the arranged marriage to fall back on; it seemed that they met boys through their brothers or through friends, or through skiing clubs or mountain-climbing clubs. They did not think marriage was all-important, however; a career was also important—this college is perhaps not the "finishing school" that many of the women's colleges are, or perhaps these girls who were doing most of the talking were the outstanding ones. But also I think that women's emancipation is still very exciting to Japanese college girls—avant-garde and "Western."

They talked about political activities and the *demo*. Some of them had taken part in the *demo*. But they complained that there was no room for individual opinion; that to express yourself in Japan you have to belong to a group with a certain ideology, and so you depend on the strength of the group. You have to choose between the Left and Right, since there is nothing in between; and you get identified with one or the other even when you don't want to. There should be a third way. Whenever you organize a group, the same thing happens: one person becomes a leader and the others can't express their individuality. Two girls particularly talked very animatedly, but the others were interested and involved, adding things from time to time. One said that when faced with difficulties the Japanese are fatalistic, escapist, and instead of being active, they become apathetic. Another girl said that many are looking for groups in which they might express themselves and their concern for the world; that this is a strong feeling in the Japanese; but often there is nothing they can join without losing their integrity; and so they begin to feel helpless and finally give up—just enjoy life from day to day. Another agreed that she lives this way from day to day, does not plan ahead or plan her career, and knows this is bad. Another added that the Japanese lack discipline in logical thinking and are too emotional.

This evening we had another tape-recorded discussion—this time for publication in the journal of a leading advertising agency, a journal quite prepared to print serious if sprightly articles. Our friend Yoshida and a leading psychiatrist, Dr. Torii, along with one of the editors, were to take part. We met at six in the evening at a modernistic restaurant owned by a former baseball star. It was a large restaurant with many floors. We went into the bar on the ground floor, very elegant with modern furniture and large plants. Several photographers hovered about and snapped flashlight pictures constantly. The bar was empty when we came in and after drinks we moved over to one end of the room separated by a screen.

The discussion started with baseball. Why were Japanese such fanatic devotees of baseball? Yoshida said it was an ideal sport for a mass society since it could be watched directly by 100,000 people and by millions on television and didn't take much skill to follow, unlike American football. Dave said it was a game which emphasized both the individual and the group. And individual performance helped the group, while everyone had his chance to shine on his own at bat and perhaps in the field. Moreover, the Japanese indulge their children and all have an opportunity to learn baseball. It is much more of a year-round sport in Japan than in the United States because football and ice hockey don't compete with it—indeed, in November we could still see games on television. Furthermore, admiration for the grace of the body can find in baseball a "modern" outlet for traditional bodily performance. And as we have been told before, since there are no anti-television highbrows in Japan, intellectuals along with everyone else can look at baseball on television. There are in Japan, as with us, many people who know all the scores.

I think it was Dr. Torii who pointed out that the Japanese don't play baseball quite so well as the Americans (they are too small), that minor-league Americans or Cubans can do very well in Japanese baseball. Dave wondered whether this might have to do with the muted aggression of the Japanese. Perhaps they don't throw beanballs or as runners try to spike the basemen? This has been true, Yoshida said, but it is changing, just as crowds sometimes become more aggressive now.

Once more the question came up whether Japan is "other-directed."

Dave suggested that while Americans worry about having the same feelings as others if they are other-directed, Japanese worry more about having the same possessions as others—like the farmer who wants to have the newest-model tractor. Sumptuary restrictions still protect the Japanese, just as girls don't have to worry about dates or even marriage because this is arranged. Conformity in the United States and in Japan thus have somewhat different roots.

Dr. Torii then brought up the question of the adjustment of the Japanese to nature and whether society itself has become man's "nature," with taboos no longer relating to the physical universe but to other people. Dave observed that in the United States the social environment is man's second "nature," that Americans do not worry about earthquakes but may feel an "earthquake" when everyone around them is smiling while they feel angry underneath.

At one point, Yoshida and Dr. Torii got into an amusing argument about the different kinds of houses they had. Yoshida observed that Dr. Torii had a completely modern and functional house, the most functional in all Japan. He has separate rooms for children and all is on a single floor. He has a telephone-answering service and everything is rationalized.

Yoshida: I built a Japanese house—with *tatami,* as traditional as possible. Dr. Torii told me I should sell it for a tea house. I would get a lot of money for it that way! But I prefer to conform to nature rather than edit it. We cannot always be challenging nature and challenging tradition. Is it unrealistic for girls to want to wear a kimono on important occasions?

Dr. Torii: The kimono expresses a nostalgia for the past. Many Japanese are interested in "Westerns," but cowboys don't exist. They belong to the past. Even in novels, we immerse ourselves in a nostalgic past. This all is an unrealistic area of life.

Riesman: But I'm not convinced of the reality of "reality."

Yoshida: The kimono is more beautiful than Western dress, just as the *shoji* in this room are more beautiful than Western windows. Doesn't this beauty facilitate work? Every culture has its own sense of beauty.

Dr. Torii: In sport, the most beautiful swing is also the most functional; in aesthetics, the most functional object is also the most beautiful. The *shoji* is beautiful because it is functional. Of course, some traditional things are functional. But the traditional Japanese house such as Yoshida's is not practical. It can be easily robbed. The kimono is a dream of the past and very unfunctional.

Riesman: I am on the side of those who are oppressed by gerontocracy in the name of tradition. It is different when the "third generation" grows up without worrying whether what they are doing is "Japanese."

Yoshida: The "third generation" can separate the beauty of a kimono from the feudal situation of women.

Riesman: I'm on Dr. Torii's side in disliking the subservience of Japanese women, but I'll grant that Japanese women look better in kimono than in their version of Western dress. And I'm sure I would like both Dr. Torii's and Yoshida's houses, each being good of its own kind.

(Yoshida recurred to his theme by insisting that there is such a thing as ceremony in life, and that the kimono is for ceremony; Dr. Torii responded by saying that a woman wearing a kimono is not really thinking of the past, but rather she wears it as an escape, it has a Freudian meaning. Yoshida, indeed, despite his talk of the kimono and of Japanese traditional houses, is very avant-garde, and so can afford this bit of traditionalism.)

Yoshida: Let's change the subject. What is the prospect of the Japanese in their leisure life, or what we call the "leisure boom"?

Dr. Torii: The Japanese don't read classics any more, only easy things and best-sellers, which are mostly how-to-do-it books. They read books about psychology, whereas earlier they read philosophy and history. Before the war they were searching for a religion, but after the war the interest in religion broke down and people searched for something more practical.

Yoshida: Before the war, a human being had to be sacrificed for something beyond himself. Now there is a greater interest in the human being for himself.

Editor: After the war, the masses became university students. Hasn't this lowered the intellectual level?

Dr. Torii: It isn't a question of that. Philosophy is intrinsically no more difficult than psychology, and young people confuse what is difficult with what is profound—and stay away from it.

Yoshida: The new religion of the Japanese is to make life rational and this leads to activity rather than passivity.

Riesman: I see that Dr. Torii is being very critical of the Japanese from the point of view of the scholarly rationalist; while Yoshida, more anthropological in his thinking, is justifying the relaxed modern behavior as against earlier, more demanding, and self-sacrificing pursuits. It would seem that architectural functionalism and anthropological functionalism point in different directions.

To return to the earlier question of conformity, people in Japan are dismayed by the clash of competing political interests, yet this clash itself can provide elbowroom for individuality. Many Japanese act as if it were possible to get rid of politics, to dispense with dialectic, and at the same time are critical of apathy. I suppose every country interprets "democracy" differently in terms of its own traditions and its image of other countries, but it seems that in Japan democracy is equated with harmony.

The conversation continued in the same vein during dinner. Both Yoshida and Dr. Torii are sparkling and ruminative men. For a while, they went on with the discussion of baseball, making the point that since the Japanese in their work are not allowed to excel or to be recognized for their excellence (and here they digressed to explain that all professors in the state universities are paid exactly the same all over the country, depending on age and rank), people's frustrations are somewhat relieved in watching this game in which certain individuals can excel so gracefully and spectacularly.

Yoshida then brought up the question of the imperial family and their "public-relations experts" who were always trying out new roles for them. The Crown Princess is in her "Audrey Hepburn" role—but where is the Prince? The experts want to know how the people feel about this glamorization—is it right, does this movie-star image please them? From here Yoshida went on to discuss the Emperor as deity. He said this didn't really mean much, the Japanese have so many thousands of gods; and gods even exist in stones. In fact, this was all badly misinterpreted by the Americans. And so there is nothing sacrilegious about glamorizing the imperial family; the question is rather, is it done well, do the people like it?

Dr. Torii, being a psychologist, invited some discussion of Freud's theories of sexual inhibition. Dave remarked that among the students there seems to be a great deal of sexual repression; boys have an almost impossible time approaching girls; but this does not seem to lead to homosexuality or fear of it. Dr. Torii said that there was homosexuality among the samurai during the Tokugawa period, but not now. Dave wondered why, with their rather Victorian customs, Japanese had not shown a greater interest in Freud. Dr. Torii explained that mental illness was still viewed in Japan as almost entirely biological.

Yoshida remarked that the place of intellectuals is too high in Japan, they are considered sages. He said this was so partly because people felt the need for the Western (modern) world to be interpreted for them, and only the intellectuals could do this.

Again, at the end, there was some kidding about Yoshida's Japanese house and Dr. Torii's functional house. Was Yoshida's house really very sensible—hadn't he just recently been robbed? But to build Dr. Torii's house would cost much more than the little cash stolen from Yoshida's house—so what was "functional" after all!

Tokyo, November 9

At lunch with Kato today we were talking about the Zengakuren. Kato thought that perhaps one reason the students felt that the *demo* of last year were not successful was because of the Japanese tendency to see the single occasion as the decisive event. This has to do with reality as they experience it: there is the single event of the entrance exam as the determinant of their careers; and there is the *miai*, the occasion of their meeting with their prospective bride. He went on to say that the students look to the Russian rather than to the Chinese Revolution as their model because the Russian Revolution came first, and influenced the pre-war Communists, and is the center of the world Communist movement. But it is China the students want to go to: they have a curiosity about China, rather than the older generation's nostalgia.

Kato told us of the use in the old days of the Emperor's picture as a substitute for appearing before the people; everyone had to bow down before the Emperor's picture and no coughing or whispering was allowed. The picture was always a front-face photograph and could only be taken by the appointed photographer. It was hung in the lecture hall of the school. He had heard of a school principal whose school had burned down with the picture in it; the principal had then committed suicide (this was in 1890); the Japanese do not differentiate between the image and the real thing. He went on to say that the Japanese felt that the "revolution" after the war was not really theirs, but was accomplished by the Occupation. This probably prevented a Communist revolution; but an imposed revolution was a frustration which the Japanese still felt.

DR In the evening, before my formal lecture at International House, there was a dinner for us given by Matsumoto, Kawasaki, and Hayakawa as members of the committee that sponsored my visit. An interesting discussion we had concerned the festivals that all schools and colleges are putting on at this season, to which enormous care is devoted by the students. Hayakawa said that, as a professor at Tokyo University during the Occupation, he had been in a very difficult position because he had been an advisor of the student groups putting on the festivals. He had been called before one of General MacArthur's officials on account of a festival exhibit which was thought to be insulting or critical; and yet the students were supposed under the Occupation to experience freedom and democracy. He described with amusement another exhibit which made a play on the word MacArthur and the Japanese word for monkey, which he felt was of such subtlety as to escape censorship: it was all very complicated, with the monkey chasing a bird but not reaching it, apparently hitting at MacArthur's pretensions and at American "militarism."

Hayakawa sits on a leading commission for the reform of the universities; it is always a surprise to think of him as a man with grown children because he seems so youthful and ebullient that he can't possibly be more than forty. He has six children—and, of course, to educate the girls in the private women's colleges requires a large capital outlay for entrance fees (by which these colleges provide themselves with capital goods), so that many men to raise the money retire from their companies, take their retirement benefits and pay them to the colleges, and then seek another job so as to pay the annual tuition for their daughters.

I had first thought that my lecture at International House would be to the staff and a few additional guests and only later realized that it was to be a large event with an invited audience from the foreign colonies here as well as Japanese educators and the many Japanese business and professional men who are "members" of International House, a membership that allows them to use the house for weddings and other functions, to attend open lectures like this, and to feel themselves (as with the Rotary Club) part of the cosmopolitan world. I had decided to talk on higher education in America rather than on the more global topics which I felt my hosts might prefer—but with some misgivings, partly because I was not at all sure how relevant and interesting this would be for Japanese, and partly because I expected, rightly as it turned out, that American members of the audience would quarrel with my necessarily brief and elliptical discussion.

Professor Kawasaki introduced me with an eloquent statement in which he quoted from the new preface to *The Lonely Crowd* about my wish to work on two levels, one reformist and the other utopian; and I felt that he was hoping for something inspirational, rather than the concrete descriptive and somewhat ironical material I had prepared. The audience was perhaps three-fifths American (or British), including many of the people who live or work at International House, a number from the Embassy, many people teaching at International Christian University or elsewhere, and a great many people whose origin I didn't know; on the Japanese side, there were men such as President Tanizaki, president of one of the women's colleges, who had joined us toward the end of our dinner—a man who, like so many university presidents, is tall, dignified, and imposing; and a few students and former students from the Tokyo area.

After my talk, several Americans asked questions. I had said that I would be glad if the Japanese in the audience spoke in Japanese and I was sure someone would interpret. But I was despairing of getting any questions from them since they tend to be shy, especially in the presence of articulate foreigners, when a very young man rose and stumbled into a question apparently based on something of mine he'd read in one of the journals, concerning the restlessness of students in the university and their great obedience when they entered on their corporate life. Because of his awkward English and roundabout expression, I wasn't sure what the student was driving at, but I responded as sympathetically as I could. I was aware that some of the older Japanese and also some of the foreigners were impatient with this student, and undoubtedly many of the former regarded it as unseemly altogether to have the *sensei*, the great professor, cross-examined by a student or indeed by anyone; such procedure was undignified.

After the lecture, we went down to the bar for drinks with friends who had come over from the Embassy and other Americans, including several who are teaching here on Fulbrights. All the latter spoke of the difficulty of getting students to raise questions in class; they tend to wait until after class—to be sure, this isn't unknown in the United States either, but the Japanese students are in general much shyer, even when language is no barrier. Indeed, some of the Americans have gotten quite impatient with the hortatory vagueness, fuzziness, and lack of forensic talent that they encounter in their Japanese contacts. At the same time, they find a rigid doctrinaire quality in much of their experience with Japanese students and academicians. I know what they mean. Certainly the discussions I have been reading in translation and in the English-language press of the debates within the Japan Socialist Party as to whether structural reform or American imperialism should achieve the first priority have a wooden flavor despite the borrowings from Togliatti and the Italians; and I suppose I might still find it deadly even if I understood all the factional and personal squabbles concealed behind the flow of clichés.

Even so, I am inclined to think that there is a certain ethnocentricism in the insistence that the Japanese should "think straight" in a logical American (or French) style and talk as aggressively, forcefully, and even overbearingly as many articulate Americans do. The Japanese have for the most part been deprived, since the indulgences of early childhood, of opportunity for the kind of individualistic self-expression which many Americans take for granted. There is a relative lack in the Japanese of the cavalier cynicism of many American people in academic life, government service, or the mass media; there is resignation, even stoicism, but not outright cynicism, and what the Japanese themselves call cynicism often seems to me rather a kind of existentialist nihilism as a philosophy rather than a day-to-day working pose. Just as the Japanese have learned to express their sense of beauty by the arrangement of a few flowers or a piece of calligraphy or a small rock garden, so they have learned to express their sense of workmanship also within tight limits, without the elbowroom an American would require. Whatever it is like for Americans stationed for a long time in Japan, it is a holiday for me to be with Japanese who, in spite of the extremism in the content of their views, are conciliatory in manner and do not crowd me or at least do so in ways which do not touch on my childhood vulnerabilities.

At the same time, I was aware that some of the argumentativeness of the evening reflected an understandable resentment among "old Japan hands" against me as a visiting fireman who, with a bare minimum of prior knowledge, commands a large audience in Japan, not only for what he says about the United States, but even for his views on Japan. And, of course, what I say is often oversimplified and needs to be qualified, or is entirely obvious to people who have been here a long time.

Nevertheless, I'm convinced that in "conversing" with a new country it is important not to hesitate to make generalizations about it that lead right into a dialectic with its more intelligent participants. Everyone we meet has read my comments on Japanese children, on the Japanese peace movement, on the *danchi* and on popular culture, and so on; these remarks, however wrongheaded, serve at once as a conversational opener, indicating both my own openness to the Japanese scene and my relative lack of what must be common American prejudices—and while I am sometimes accused of being too flattering or uncritical, this does prevent me from scaring people off or being identified, as can so easily happen, with an American foreign-policy line. I interpret my experience as support for my views concerning the limitations of supposedly non-directive (uncommitted and accepting) interviewing, at least among the articulate, where evocative and even challenging interviewing may be required. If an American visitor were a blank to his hosts, the avoidance of leading questions and comments might be useful, but there already exist in Japan so many preconceptions concerning American opinion that non-direction would be interpreted as a form of guardedness rather than openness—even as laying a trap for the unwary. By not taking my own views and position too seriously, I hope at the same time to surmount the well-known Japanese diffidence about contradicting people. Yet I realize that one approach necessarily cuts off others; and my dialectical outlook, while effective with the younger, more flexible Japanese, is perhaps no help with the older and more stuffy ones; but with the latter I have the feeling that neither dynamite nor exquisite tact could help and that their formal gravity and Victorian manners may relax on the golf course or in a geisha house, but not around a table with foreigners.

The younger ones abash me with their knowledge of American writing, including what I have written, whether it's something that appeared that morning in a Japanese paper or a passage in the new preface to *The Lonely Crowd*. Some of their questions are scholastic; others are cosmic, such as "What form of social character will succeed other-directed man?" Still others involve an effort, sometimes literal and sometimes free, to apply the concepts to Japan. I hadn't realized, of course, that the phrase "the lonely crowd" would have such a pungent impact here where people suffer greatly from loneliness and where crowds are omnipresent in the metropolitan centers.

Tokyo, November 10 ETR

This evening Nat Glazer called us to say he was meeting with some city planners in the lobby and would like us to join them. We went down and found Nat at a table with two intellectual-looking young men and a handsome young woman. I was especially impressed by the woman's cosmopolitan style, her heavy silver jewelry, her hair in a chignon, an unusual and attractive version of the emancipated Japanese woman. After the introductions, they began telling us about "Children's Land," a sort of children's park for which they had designed elaborate plans. The site was picked in an area of Yokohama, but it was not clear whether they had the land, whether there was money for the project, or whether it was in the dream stage. However, the more they talked about it, the more interesting and imaginative the idea seemed to us: children would come here to live for several months, put on their own plays, concerts, dance recitals; it would be a place for them to run and be free; and there would be international groups of children as well. These planners had put out a book about it which they showed us, and the young woman then translated parts of it for us. Later they showed us photographs of plans they had made under Kenzo Tange for the development of Tokyo. These plans were for the expansion of the city: there were designs for building out over Tokyo Bay, and for building up into the air—spirals with hanging gardens, floating islands, all imaginative and fantastic.

When it was time to break up, we walked back with them to Roppongi. The young woman walked with me and we talked on the way. She asked me what I thought of Japanese manufactured goods. She told me that an American woman had said to her that Japanese toys were badly made and broke easily, and that Americans had the impression that Japanese things were cheap and inferior. Was this so? It troubled her, and in general she was troubled about the inferiority of Japanese culture; she thought Japanese painting could not compare with Western art, there was no Michelangelo, for example; and in Japanese literature there were no great characters such as Tolstoy created.

I thought about this afterward. To be sure, the mechanical toys are usually shoddy. But the typical Japanese toys are often made of paper, they are delicate and perishable like flowers, bright and pretty, part of the transitory world. There are toy stores everywhere and the toys are wonderfully various and imaginative. The toys perish, disappear, and each new festival brings new ones. But, on the other hand, there are things that last: there are games played with black and white stones, there are mah-jongg sets of bone and ebony. As in other aspects of Japanese life and culture, there seem to be only the extremes: things pass quickly or last forever.

Tokyo, November 11

Mary Evans, an American friend who reviews films for an English-language newspaper here, offered to take us to one of the more interesting new movies. We were delighted, for we are great fans of Japanese films, but deprived of English subtitles we would understand very little without an interpreter. She picked us up in the morning, explaining that this was the only time one can be sure of getting a seat. The story of *The Autumn of the Kobayagawa Family* is taken from a section of *The Makioka Sisters* by Tanizaki, a novel of great scope and extraordinary sensitivity that Dave and I read during the summer. Mary sat between us, translating in a whisper. To see a film of the streets of Osaka and Kyoto, now familiar to us, somehow reinforced the reality of these places; but also to be taken inside the houses, to be shown what goes on in the lives of people we see on the street, satisfied a deep curiosity in us. The film was slow and serene, photographed in soft, subdued color. The use of backgrounds of *shoji* or sliding doors and the wooden frames of the cabinetwork in the interior of a Japanese house gave a sense of careful composition to each scene. A blue chrysanthemum blockprint pattern on a screen, or a dark wood paneling, suggested a cool and quiet mood and afforded an almost symbolic background for the traditional characters; while the very active youngest daughter, often dressed in Western clothes, was pictured sitting at her modern-style desk cluttered with many objects, a confusion in marked contrast with the orderly setting for the other characters. The movie camera offered glimpses through *shoji* into the gardens, or through an open door onto a street, where wooden tubs leaned against the side of a house—the wood weathered silver, the dark-tiled roof almost purple-black. Contrasting with shots of an office, a bar, and Osaka streets at night were the close-ups in which the camera concentrated on small gestures and masklike faces. There was a remarkable scene of the family around the table fanning themselves; the motion of the fans seemed to suggest the animation of the spirit; but with the news that something had happened to the old father, the fans suddenly stopped moving—a dramatic effect, suggesting not only suspense but also the apprehension of death.

We were delighted to see acted out the things we had read about: the go-between in the *miai* (arranged marriage), and the exchange of photographs; the first meeting, supposed to be casual, in a restaurant; the old father still dominating this family of adults, going off to visit his geisha mistress in Kyoto, and so on. The dialogue, according to

Mary, was often subtle, sometimes so subtle that she gave up, saying it was impossible to translate.

The use of the small screen in this film, which gave a sense of a frame to each picture and of depth, reminded me of Hidetoshi Kato's theory of the "aesthetics of something extra," where he compares the aesthetics of the small with the wide screen; many random elements get into the wide-camera lens; and this expresses the casual quality of modern life; other art forms do the same sort of thing, especially the modern novel. This film made by Ozu, in contrast, was not casual but formal, and while its subject was the struggle between the old and the new way of life, it was the traditional, though dying, way of life that won out: in this sense, the small screen framing each shot was suitable for the theme and for the intimate and concentrated style of the film.

When the movie was over, Mary took us in a cab back to her house. We asked her if the film would be shown in the United States, and she said that it had not been chosen among the films to be exported, because the Japanese thought Americans would not understand it: it was too Japanese. This seemed unfortunate, but as I thought about it I realized this was typical of the Japanese: they do not think their authentic arts are worth exporting or would be understood. With their inferiority complex (or is it superiority?) they doubt that anything really Japanese could be appreciated by Westerners. And so they manufacture special things for export which they think will be pleasing to Americans. The tasteful kimono and *yukata* (informal kimono, or bathrobe) I have seen here apparently never reach United States shops. Nor have I seen at home the colors that one finds in the native materials: the deep blues, browns, ochers. The native pottery is only beginning to come to our country, perhaps because of our own cult of pottery making. Mainly, we get a garish or a bland and neutral version of things from Japan.

Mary lives in a one-story Japanese house on a narrow street, a dead-end alley, on a hillside not far from International House. She slid open the latticed door, and we left our shoes on the stone threshold inside and stepped into the *tatami* room. Her husband, Donald Richie, was there, and we all sat around a table, Mary and I on cushions on the floor, Donald and Dave on the two chairs. The room was, as the Japanese would say, an eight-mat room with the traditional *shoji* and a scroll painting in the alcove. The Richies, however, had added a gas heater and the two folding leather chairs—making the room less Japanese, but more comfortable.

We talked and had coffee in pottery mugs with cake and fruit. At one point during the conversation the milkman came to deliver tomorrow's milk; he was bringing it today as there would be a strike tomorrow and he didn't want them to be without their milk. Donald said that this kind of thing happened all the time; the clerks in offices would strike, tying white bands around their heads and looking fierce, yet would continue to work.

We talked for a while about movies. The music used in many Japanese films is Western; Donald's explanation for this was that since movies were originally made in Hollywood the Japanese felt it was perfectly correct to use Western music as part of the convention of movie making. He said that there was a problem in Japan of finding tough-guy types for some of their movies, because these types are not prevalent; the masculinity of Japanese men is not expressed in this way.

DR

Donald described the tough underworld in Japan. He talked about the *yakuza*, the old-time gangsters, who in earlier days lived in Tokyo according to traditional customs, preying on their victims and having honor among thieves with a kind of Robin Hood code. The *gurentai* are the hoodlums of today, who have no code at all. He went on to say that there is a great fear of calling in the police in Japan, much as in southern Italy, and when violence is necessary or difficulties arise, people seem to resort to familistic-type solutions (with go-betweens) rather than legalistic ones; this may also reflect the fear and hatred of the police that developed in the police state of pre-war Japan. We said we hadn't seen any police on beats in Tokyo; they seemed to stay in their boxes. Donald agreed, adding that a pair of policemen would occasionally patrol a bad neighborhood. He thinks that in brutality and gangsterism Tokyo will soon catch up with the rest of the world. Prostitution is as strong as ever in Japan, he said, but now the police and the underworld control it, whereas the government had controlled it before; women legislators had insisted on making it illegal (though this has made it worse) because they were worried about how legalized prostitution looked to the rest of the world. He said there is plenty of sex life in Japan, but not for teenagers—though he thought this was changing.

Japan is the very end of the world, he said, the extreme: there is nothing beyond, no place to go; this gives the Japanese a feeling of isolation and loneliness. Talking about his life in Japan over the last ten years, Donald observed that the Japanese almost never accept a foreigner as a person; he felt the Japanese saw him at first as a for-

DR

eigner, then after a while as an American, and now at last a few saw him as himself.

ETR

Tokyo, November 12

This morning we went with the Liftons to see the movie *The Seven Samurai.* It was being shown in a small art theater located in a dank, cold basement, apparently the only film theater in Tokyo that plays Japanese revivals. We were early and found seats, but the place filled up quickly, with students mostly, many of them wearing sweaters, blue jeans, and clogs that clacked as they went down the aisle. By the time the movie began, many were standing. The movie is a splendid version of a Japanese "Western." We talked much about it afterward, and Bob is writing an article comparing it with the American counterpart, *The Magnificent Seven.*

We went with Bob to the Press Club to have lunch with Dr. Toyoda, a psychiatrist. There is some psychoanalysis in Japan, Dr. Toyoda said, but on the whole very little. And it is different from psychoanalysis in the West, because the problems are different: the Japanese do not have the inner struggles such as fighting against guilt and despair that we have. The Japanese are more likely to accept hopelessness as a state of being, or else go to the other extreme and commit suicide. They haven't got the same sense of individuality that we have. Their despair comes from an external situation: failure of an exam, or some other exclusion; and when something is shut off from the outside, there is no hope. Dr. Toyoda said that he thought Christianity created inner struggle; he had gone through a conversion to Catholicism during the war. He thought the despair of the Japanese, due to external situations, caused a feeling of shame; while the despair of internal struggle in Western societies caused feelings of guilt. Dave asked about privacy. The Japanese have no sense of privacy, Dr. Toyoda said. Each person feels his life is an open book (like the houses without walls), and perhaps for this reason also, the Japanese lack a feeling of inner life and of individuality. Dave wondered whether Zen Buddhism was an attempt of the Japanese to realize their own individuality, but Dr. Toyoda and Bob Lifton didn't think so; it took the turn too strongly of teaching the samurai how to fight and got stuck there; it is a discipline of control and self-negation.

Driving back, we continued this discussion with Bob. He said that the very deep-seated control of the Japanese may have something to do with the way they sometimes "discharge" their emotions through outbreaks of violence. He said there are Japanese movies which are quite terrible in their violence and horror. But, he went on to say, in mental illness the Japanese show no violence—an example of how deep the repression goes, how deep the sense of control.

Later Dave and I dropped in on the Richies, whom we found working in their *tatami* room in tweeds and sweaters. Donald went into the kitchen and made hot chocolate, which he brought to us in pottery mugs. The gas heater was on and the room was cozy. Donald talked amusingly about a friend who had come over from *Harper's Bazaar* and wanted to do a piece on Japanese society. But, he explained to him, there is no Japanese high society: the women stay at home or visit with each other, and there is no social life in our sense; the men have parties of their own, and the only women who know how to be sociable and gay are the geisha; the wives of the rich become old dowdy dowagers.

We got onto the subject of Japanese youth. Donald said that Japanese youngsters weren't at all prepared for life; they lived in complete innocence, and then when they got out of school, life hit them with a terrible shock. Their education was rigid and completely unrelated to reality.

DR

Donald's comment on Japanese education referred to the abstractness of the curriculum and the kind of theoretical vacuum in which students live. It has become clear to me that while getting into a good university is an incredibly arduous ordeal, often beginning in kindergarten (especially in the "captive" kindergartens that some of the private institutions have founded as feeders), it is not at all difficult to stay in once one has been admitted. Hence university students seem to relax into a kind of life that might in an earlier day have clustered around the Sorbonne; and one aspect of the intense political activity of some of the students is that they don't have to study or go to class. Their left-wing views would seem sharp and cynical if held by Americans; they read Sartre and Camus and think of themselves as nihilists or existentialists; even so, they retain a sense of democratic freedom in their own lives which does not prepare them either for the particular tasks they will face or for the social relations in what they term, too simply, the "feudal" institutions of Japanese society. The selective universities act as feeder stations for specific jobs, so that Todai will send students into the Foreign Office or the Bank of Japan while other institutions will have patronage elsewhere. But there seems to be little connection between, let us say, the German philosophy one might study at the university and the kind of outlook needed in the business world.

This evening we had supper with Joe Ragle and his wife. Ragle is a correspondent for *Stars and Stripes*, the Army newspaper here, which prints five editions for a total of 60,000 copies between Bangkok and Korea. He had come to my first press conference—plainly a very thoughtful, decent man, perhaps thirty years old. His wife is British, and he met her while studying in Great Britain. With some apology, they took us to the Hotel Sanno, an American enclave where Army personnel use American dollars, which go further than they do in the States. (In general, American officers in Tokyo wear civilian clothes, though we saw two men in the lobby of the hotel in uniform with an array of medals.) Ragle said how guilty he felt when he made use of the many privileges of the American serviceman out here, such as buying tax-free whisky and cheap frozen foods at the many PX stores. Yet it takes will power to refuse these benefits and to live entirely on the Japanese economy. Still, after two years in an American housing development in Yokohama, they have moved into a "native quarter" of Tokyo, where they are the only foreigners. They say that Japanese living is very attractive aesthetically until one really faces its negative aspects: the walls are so thin that one can hear one's neighbors having a bath or coughing, and is exposed to the rat smells and endless sounds of a Tokyo street, including the little fellow who comes around with a piercing horn on his bicycle at twelve midnight and another vendor who shows up promptly at 6 A.M.

Ragle said that a number of his friends had taken Japanese or Korean wives. Almost invariably these men treated their wives with more coldness and brutality than they could get away with in the States; they stay out late at endless parties and never even bother to phone and tell their wives they aren't coming home, then beat or upbraid them when they do get home. They justify all this to themselves on the ground that this is the way Japanese men treat their wives, while, of course, the women had married Americans in the hope of getting away from "feudal" husband-wife relations.

Mrs. Ragle said that the military thought Japan a backward country. They were critical of the poor roads, the inadequate plumbing, the smells in the street, and so on. The wives, she said, were worse than the men. They judged Japan simply in terms of lack of refrigerators and saw its virtues only in comparison with Korea or with Southeast Asia. Mrs. Ragle teaches English, in private conversation classes, to Japanese businessmen, including several company presidents. All entertain her in the "Western" room that every elegant Japanese home has (if it isn't completely Western), with its piano and its antimacassars and its excessively upholstered furniture—a room that she feels is dusted only for her coming; she wishes she could see the other rooms, but knows she never will. There is a tremendous demand for people to teach English. With one elegant lady, she is reading George Meredith—this lady hopes to write something about *Richard Feverel.*

It occurred to me that though this was a social occasion, Ragle might want to interview me again for *Stars and Stripes*, to get the interview he couldn't get earlier when he attended my press conference. Still, I was a bit startled to have him say that he hoped to get a story. Mrs. Ragle asked me whether I thought Berlin worth fighting for, and he asked whether I had been in favor of the Morgenthau Plan. I said that I had been as strongly as possible against the Morgenthau Plan or any vindictive treatment of Germany after World War II, and I explained how ironical I felt my present position was, where my attitudes on Berlin and on the recognition of the Oder-Neisse line might seem "anti-German," while in fact it was very different from the common British attitude of wanting to let the Germans suffer because of what the Nazis had done. I tried to explain at length my views on the background of the Berlin crisis and the problems and possibilities of disengagement along lines proposed by George Kennan. Acting as devil's advocate with his own audience in mind, Ragle asked me what I thought had been good or creative in American foreign policy since the end of the war; I named the Marshall Plan and our aid to Yugoslavia and Poland. He wondered how I would answer the contention that any aid given to a Communist country would be used against us. More generally, he asked whether I didn't think we were losing the cold war and whether I regarded the break between the Soviet Union and China as a serious one. The more we talked, the more gloomy I became as to the possibility of saying anything to his constituency that would not seem to them to be the "soft" and "appeasing" views with which I've already been charged by several writers to the English-language press, the most recent of whom asked what "taxpayers" were supporting my trip to preach doctrine contrary to American interests. What could one possibly respond that would not merely confirm and indeed harden the existing prejudices of the readers?

I was forcibly reminded in talking to Ragle of the frighteningly huge gap that separates conventional American opinion from that of much of the rest of the world. Even conservatives in Japan hold views, e.g., on the subject of China, which would be considered Communist in the United States; and the dominant voices in the Japanese intellectual world tend to regard the British Labour Party as too conservative. Ragle thinks that Japan will be socialist in ten years when the present generation gets older; and while this may be doubted, it cannot be doubted that America will be faced with a great many countries with which it can no longer communicate either in terms of their domestic management of affairs or in terms of their view of the cold war. I pointed out, as I have many times before, that the United States can defeat itself in the cold war by assuming that every non-rightist government is "Communist," until a wild defeatism spreads within America.

Ragle asked me whether we had found much resentment against the American bombing. I said no doubt it existed but there seemed to be little overt hostility toward Americans for the wartime events, even including the atomic bombs, at least among the young, who blamed the Japanese militarists for bringing all this on. I pointed out that this attitude was different from what I had understood was the attitude in West Germany, where there was much resentment of the American mass bombings (which I myself had felt at the time were wrong) and where many Germans feel that they were right to fight the Russians and that the Americans were rather slow in coming around to the same view. To be sure, the Leftists in Japan argue whether the main enemy is Japanese monopoly capitalism or American imperialism, but this argument does little to alter the attitude felt toward the pre-war management of Japan. Even on that subject, however, the Japanese seem not to be a resentful or a vindictive people who harbor long memories. Many Japanese Leftists were against the war-crimes trial of Tojo and others who, they felt, were harmless now and should be forgiven and forgotten. This attitude of conciliation infuriates a small minority of Japanese who admire what they regard as the severity and high principle of Western character structure; this is what I think attracts some of them to Christianity—and others indeed to Marxism. And it seems characteristic of Japan that the most important recent Christian movement here was the non-church movement; but now, as Bob Lifton has said, many Japanese Christians hold on to Buddhist and Shinto practices with maybe a touch of Confucianism thrown in.

Tokyo, November 13 *ETR*

Mary Evans came with us this morning to a showing of some films in the headquarters of one of the large film companies. Our mutual friend Hayashi acted as guide and host. We had met him last summer at the International Seminar at Harvard, where he had shown the Japanese movie *Snowflakes*, a sad story of patriarchal dominance and unrequited love, romantic and what the Japanese would call "wet." Hayashi is a modern type, speaks English fluently, and is handsome enough to be a movie star himself. But his ambition is to make films. He suggested two screenings: a film by Osamu Takahashi that had been banned for political reasons, and a portion of *The Human Condition*, Masaki Kobayashi's great nine-hour-long film on the Manchurian War.

The first film, *Man without Pity*, had as its hero a young hoodlum, tough and cruel, whose wanderings took us into streets where workers were striking, into flophouses, coffee bars, dance halls with strip-tease shows, rooming houses, and slums. The camera work was beautiful, especially in a scene of the two brothers glaring at each other through a beaded curtain as they argued in fury, and in shots of the city which gave a sense of how things look along the waterfront of Tokyo.

The section we saw of *The Human Condition* began with tanks coming over a hill, the lonely figure of a soldier running; then the flight of a small band of Japanese settlers through forests, where one by one they dropped by the wayside out of exhaustion and starvation; finally the group split in terrible quarrels over the division of the little remaining food. The wide screen was used here with very great effect, giving a sense of the vastness of armies, the desolation of the wilderness, and the endlessness of the forest.

Donald joined us for lunch at a *tempura* restaurant nearby. While the shrimp and small fish were being cooked in deep oil in front of us and handed out by the deft cooks one by one, deliciously hot and crisp, Donald told us about a film he was planning to make. As he talked, I thought that Hayashi, working for a film company, was not at all his own boss and might envy Donald's freedom. The Americans in Japan are living on another level that is sometimes quite visible. Does this increase the feeling of the Japanese of being entrapped?

This evening another discussion was held on the subject of the democratization of Japan. Professors Yoshida and Sugawara took part, with Dave and Bob Lifton. This form of *seeing* a country, I realize, is most unusual, and yet by now we have come to take it quite for granted. But of course an enormous effort has gone into planning these meetings for us.

Professor Sugawara began by saying that when people talk about the structure of Japanese society they are apt to say that there has been a great change from the rigid feudal pre-war society to the fluid post-war society. But it isn't like that: Japan is a mixture of the two. Social distance between aristocratic families and the common people in Japan was never so great as in Europe, because Japan is a more paternalistic society. Dave mentioned *The Seven Samurai.* To be sure, Sugawara said, the samurai in the film could not marry the farmer's daughter; and no farmer could become a samurai, for hierarchy was entirely by ascription. This continued after the Meiji reforms, even though these reforms introduced a good deal of social mobility. Yoshida remarked that paternalism helped to smooth class conflicts and perhaps still does. Since the Meiji Restoration the two areas of greatest mobility have been the armed forces and the universities. Bob Lifton remarked that while the students are quite democratic, free and open with each other, they are keenly sensitive to seniority. Sugawara said that the idea of seniority derived from Confucianism, and that it is still deeply rooted in the older generation today, but not so much in the younger generation. Dave suggested that pure democracy without either aristocracy or seniority would lead to a meritocracy which would be unbearably competitive.

Sugawara observed that the Japanese do not address each other by their names, but by their position, such as *sensei* or "president" or "section chief." In primitive societies it is in order to avoid black magic that the name is not used (he seemed to imply that the Japanese custom derived from this). Sometimes behind a professor's back one might use his name disrespectfully.

Dave asked then about the position of women, how much had it changed? Bob Lifton said that Japanese women are strong in many respects but submissive in terms of sex. It is an old theme in Japan that rape is followed by love; and in general there is a good deal of exploitation in male-female relations. Yoshida remarked that even women with strength of character allow their husbands to go out with other women. Sugawara said that Confucianism viewed woman as impure; Confucianism was a separation from Nature, a kind of Puritanism. In pre-Confucian Japan there was equality of women and there was sociability between men and women; but since then, with the exclusion of women, there has been no sociability in the Western sense. He added, however, that the situation is changing, especially among the younger generation of Tokyo intellectuals.

Yoshida observed that in the United States men feel they cannot talk politics if women are present; that women sometimes destroy serious conversation. Dave said that male and female separation in sociability still exists in the United States, but that some people rebel against it. He added that among the younger generation this separation does not exist and that their sociability is becoming so democratized and their informality so total that good sociability (in the sense in which Simmel describes it) is sometimes destroyed.

There was some discussion then about familistic sociability in Japan. Sugawara said that the man of the family eats alone, but all the rest of the family eat together. He spoke of an article he had written on the structure of residence: the European house has a room for each person, but in the Japanese house there is but one room; the partitions mean nothing; the community of the family is more important than the privacy of the individual; another significant difference between Japan and Europe is the fact that the Japanese house is surrounded by a high fence, while in Europe the houses are open or linked together and related to the outside community.

Dave then mentioned the lack of any feeling of potency in the Japanese to change things. They seem to need some model to follow, having very little confidence in themselves to create their own; yet they don't want to follow either the Russian or the American model. He said that he tells Japanese who ask him about this that there are choices other than the Russian and American models (both are big, industrial countries with little similarity to Japan); yet the Japanese don't feel they can get along without *some* external example. He added that when young Japanese discuss this with him and use the word "feudal," he realizes this means, "What's the use, I can't have any effect." Yoshida said that the young people feel that it wasn't the Japanese who made the changes that have democratized the country, but the American Occupation; and this adds to their feeling of impotence.

Dave asked about the businessmen and their big cars; their love of show reminded him of Texans in the United States. Sukawara said that wealth had a different cultural meaning in America; there the rich feel some responsibility to society, Christianity gives them a feeling of *noblesse oblige*; in Japan there is no such feeling. Dave remarked that this was true only in Britain and the United States, and that its source was Protestantism, rather than Christianity per se. He added that

ETR

in the United States many of the rich make a point of non-display of wealth, and even keep quiet about their philanthropy. Sugawara said that in the Tokugawa period and later a group of people maintained the traditional custom of dressing shabbily and giving money to charity—this Confucian school of thought played a part in the industrialization of Japan.

Yoshida said that in the West there is a difference in the style of housing between the rich and the poor, but in Japan the rich and the poor live in the same kind of house (if it is a traditional Japanese house) and the difference is only in size; quiet wealth does not show as it does in the United States. He said that he knows of some children of rich Japanese in Paris who live simply and drive small cars—many of the old families live in great simplicity. He added that in fact the wealthy Japanese don't *feel* wealthy.

DR

Tokyo, November 14

Evey takes notes during all our meetings except at meals. It seems not to inhibit anyone; on the contrary, as in an interview, it seems often to reassure people that what they are saying is important; and since there apparently has been some talk among people about our visit, many are already prepared for this and would be disappointed if Evey didn't take notes—some jokingly say that they wish they had wives who could do that. (Sometimes they assume that Evey is a sociologist who is working with me, as indeed in a sense she is.)

The imprisonment at home of the Japanese wife had originally a practical basis: the homes are paper-thin, constantly in danger of catching fire and being robbed. (All over Tokyo there are still fire towers where men patrol on a twenty-four-hour basis, looking for smoke. These are gradually being taken down as more and more buildings are made of concrete, and presumably as more and more have telephones.) Moreover, the mother was supposed to take care of her child, not to leave the child alone for a moment; and then there were the old folks, the mother-in-law and so on, who had to be cared for. Thus, a wife who left her home for any other errand than shopping would be criticized and gossiped about by all the neighborhood—and of course the nature of the houses and the life of the streets is such that people live very much in the open, without privacy either at home or away from home.

However, when young Japanese couples "go modern," they may do so even more drastically than anything one can find in the United

States: we heard today about a Fulbright applicant, a woman who wants to go to the United States while her husband remains in Japan; she was asked by the committee what her husband's attitude was, and she replied that they were already living apart since she was in Tokyo and her husband in the south of Japan. This indeed may be taken as an example of the many instances where the Japanese, believing themselves to be imitating the West, actually shoot beyond without knowing it. But also it may reveal a relationship that is less intimate than that between husband and wife with us.

The "emancipated" women of this sort, however, do not as yet form a society of their own. In fact, there doesn't seem to be in Japan a Society with a capital "S"; the respectable women, as I've said, stay home; this includes the wives of many of the most eminent people in business, government, and academic and professional life. Traditionally, in Japan, only the geisha know how to be sociable, and their sociability seems to be an easy, often witty kind of frivolous chatter to keep the men amused as they drink *sake*. Last night, in a discussion of democratization in Japan, I brought up Simmel's ideas on sociability and tried to think about their applicability to Japan. Simmel is talking about a society in which the women are the equals of men both intellectually and socially. Here the women are not equals, neither the geisha nor the wives—except in the most modern marriages; when men are by themselves on *tatami* with groups of friends whom they feel they can trust, they can be happily childish, playing games and singing collegiate-type songs—rather like an alumni reunion. But this isn't quite the mixture of the sociable with the serious about which Simmel speaks. And on other occasions there is a very formal senior host who would dampen any activity of the less senior persons, so that there seems to be either great formality on the one hand or total informality on the other.

We had become very fond of Otis Cary in Kyoto and had urged him if he ever came to Tokyo to look us up; when he unexpectedly arrived, we managed to find time for a walk and talk this morning. It was good to be out: a glorious, cold, sunny, sparkling day. Cary pointed out on our walk the little markets that one finds in every tiny area, for refrigerators are still scarce and incomes modest. Housewives deliberate as to what time of day is best to go out to buy fish and vegetables in the market: if they wait till near the end, everything may be gone; on the other hand, the vendor may be eager to sell a stock of goods that will be useless the next day, and thus lower his price.

But the coming of packaging and refrigerators will change that and eliminate some of the variety of Tokyo streets.

Indeed, everyone who has been away and returned testifies to the enormously rapid changes the economic boom has made in Tokyo. While two years ago it was possible to get a taxi in most parts of the city, today at a station one can often wait for an hour and not get one, with long lines of people waiting. Similarly, traffic jams seem to grow longer by the hour. And everyone is said to dress much better now than even a short time ago. The Japanese have always dressed carefully and fastidiously, so that a man would wear his one good suit every day. Now he can have several good suits. And the increase in the number of kimono one sees is a reflection of prosperity. There has also apparently been an immense growth of advertising in the last two or three years. And of course television has spread. So, too, there has been an increase in leisure, in travel and vacations. "Everyone" goes to hot springs, and trains and planes are crowded with people bent not only on business or family obligations but on pleasure and sightseeing.

We talked with Cary about Japanese attitudes toward Negroes. Last night there had been a championship fight between Moore, an American Negro who is featherweight champion, and Takayama, the Japanese challenger; Cary, watching this over television, had been conscious of the very strong resentment of the audience at having their hero beaten by a Negro, and later many people made excuses for the defeated man. Cary said that there was more violent shouting than he had heard before, more "American," and very different from the milder attitudes at a *sumo* wrestling match, where the audience shouts approval for technical feats and cheers its champion without a touch of sadism. (The *Japan Times* reported this morning, "It was believed Moore got some $50,000 plus expenses for last night's fight, compared to Takayama's $2,000, though no official purses were announced." This is an example of the frankness of the modern Japanese on money matters—the samurai class used to feel it was dishonorable to talk openly about money or even to handle it, so that when a samurai went shopping, he covered his face with a towel; but all that is gone and the Japanese speak frankly about money as they speak frankly about sex and other "natural" functions.)

Cary also said that Japanese who go to America, although they will hardly ever admit this, very much fear lest they be taken for Negroes. All this came up because Evey and I had noticed that Japanese never go sunbathing, despite the so-called "sun tribe" popularized by one of the novelists, which refers more to a cult of the body and of expressiveness than to a cult of the sun. Women on the beach stay under parasols. Certainly, many movie stars and jazz singers have almost "European" features, and this seems not only to be admired, but to be approximated more and more, so that one finds these features in many of the younger people. The Japanese are exceedingly conscious of status and power relations; they know that Negroes are looked down upon in America. Hence they themselves do not want to identify with Negroes, but with the white man.

I told Cary about the movie *Man without Pity* that our friend Hayashi had shown us, and my curiosity as to the relation, whether direct or oblique, the attitudes in the movie bore toward those of the audience. The movie seemed designed to appeal to young people with its picture of the roughneck would-be *yakuza*, the tough guy on the American model, who is cool to his aged and ailing father, shoves old women down, rapes young ones and is very attractive to them, and in general acts as the fearless hoodlum of the city streets. Did this represent the deepest impulses, or was it something viewed as exotic or vicarious? Cary seemed inclined to agree with the view Bob Lifton has expressed, that there is in many Japanese a buried streak of sadism, very deeply controlled, and generally released only in group and permitted situations as in war or in mob violence—Bob said it was very often a hysterical and superficial expression, something that erupted quickly and was over quickly; but it could also be a deep-lying character trait. Women help smooth the pathways of the society, and it may well be that the releases from control occur when the men are alone (without women), whether in war or in drunken groups in a bar or hysterical groups of Rightists, carrying on "government by assassination" in the pre-war days.

Whether an import from the United States or simply one of the social dislocations that goes with modernization, obsession with sex seems to be strong in Japan. *Man without Pity* is simply one of a cycle of films emphasizing night-club scenes and strip-teases; and the buildings of Tokyo are plastered with movie ads that depict fighting samurai, fighting gunmen in Western style quick on the draw, and nude or nearly nude girls. Contemporary Japanese fiction also deals continually with sex. Yet this may be exploration for a very few, and mostly in the realm of art. Japanese in real life as teenagers or in young adulthood seem not to be preoccupied with sex, and dating is still rare; most college girls go to women's colleges, where they are quite sheltered, and seem by American standards very immature and girlish. There is a kind of national other-direction here in which it is assumed that what the United States possesses must be somehow superior; of course there is romance in Japan and lovers' suicides are featured in the papers, but I sometimes feel that the romance with America is even stronger than romance per se. As Murata and Osabe have said, the coffee house is not only the place where dating is possible, or free-and-easy talk among same-sex groups, but also the place where it is possible to feel oneself into the atmosphere of jazz and Western culture, just as in the movies and novels that are eagerly imported from abroad.

The combination of cultural attraction to America with political repulsion or fear makes for strong and complex emotional reactions. The left-wing students look to America for an openness that is lacking in their own society, and they read D. H. Lawrence or the French existentialists or Hemingway, while in the political sphere they turn to Marxism-Leninism almost exclusively, occasionally reading Harold Laski or C. Wright Mills, but not any of the writers (Galbraith, for example) who have tried to deal with the contemporary combination of political and cultural problems in the affluent society.

Hosei University, now a "colony" of the University of Tokyo, where bright leftist young professors teach impoverished students, was originally founded early in this century for training in French law, since Japan had adopted the Napoleonic Civil Code; another university was originally founded for studies in Anglo-American law. Japanese universities imported the departments wholesale from the West, and great men like Fukuzawa, the founder of Keio University, whose eloquent autobiography I'm now reading, spread Western Enlightenment with missionary zeal. Even today, Japanese scholars will make their reputations by translating and interpreting a particular school of Western thought—and of course American thought, neglected before the war in favor of Western Europe, now dominates the scene along with influences from the Communist countries.

So Japan still looks abroad for how-to-do-it kits in every field, but the models seem increasingly irrelevant. Some Japanese conclude that communism may be an "answer" for poor countries, but not for them; they're not happy with America as a model either; some still look to the British Labour Party, but that hardly casts an inspiring image here. The Japanese have yet to look homeward.

Tokyo, November 15 **ETR**

We had a discussion scheduled for ten o'clock this morning with some of the Zengakuren leaders. Since Kato is away, we were accompanied by another interpreter, Mr. Mizufune, an intelligent young man just out of graduate school. We took a cab to the other side of town, near the University of Tokyo. Locating the Zengakuren office was not easy. Mizufune knew vaguely where it was, and after stopping several times to ask, we finally found it in a quiet street of two-story buildings. Mizufune knocked on the door, but there was no answer. He then tried the door and it slid open. The small room contained a bulletin board with notices on it, a blackboard, newspapers and magazines neatly stacked, some files, a table, a few broken-down chairs, a telephone, and a bicycle. As the room was even colder than the outdoors, we decided to stand in the sun rather than sit in the room. We stood and chatted with Mizufune, or walked up and down.

As we waited and sauntered in the street, we noticed that many people were out walking with their children, who were dressed in traditional kimono. Our interpreter explained that today is a festival day for children aged seven, five, and three. Groups of families passed by, the children looking like Japanese dolls in the finery of their kimono, with flowers in their hair; the three-year-olds were sometimes carried in their mothers' arms, older children walked with their fathers, or grandparents, also dressed in their best kimono.

After a while, we began to wonder what had happened to the students. At one point, the telephone rang and Mizufune went in and answered it. He talked for a while, and Dave and I began to be hopeful. He hung up and told us that the person who called was another student, not the one we were to see, but that he had made arrangements for us to meet with some other Zengakuren students tomorrow. We had the impression that the non-appearance of the students and the subsequent telephone call were some sort of delaying tactics that expressed the ambivalence of the students about seeing us dreadful "imperialist Americans."

Bob Lifton said later that the non-appearance of the Zengakuren was not surprising; they are impossible to find—even when they want to find each other, they have to go looking, asking neighbors and friends. It is part of their bohemian ethos not to be available and not to keep appointments.

DR

Everett Hughes helped teach me the advantages of an "anthropological" view, so that even moderately negative experiences in another culture are illuminating and therefore not unbearably oppressive. This is how I felt about some of the experiences surrounding my formal lecture at the University of Tokyo. It was revealing for me to be exposed to instances of self-defeating behavior which indicate, like the top of an iceberg, what the Japanese themselves experience day in and day out—or perhaps become too deadened fully to experience. Thus, we had gone down to the university half an hour or so ahead of the time specified for the reception that preceded my lecture in the hope of getting a sense of the students and the campus: I had asked to see the student newspaper offices and just to stroll around the campus. But we found the librarian waiting to take us through the library (by far the largest in Japan—we were told several times that it contained over three million volumes); and we had to see the reconstructed gate originally built in Tokugawa times, although we had already seen it. (On all such occasions in Japan, the visitor receives a present, and in our case it was a picture of the gate, which is indeed beautiful, carefully framed and wrapped.) During this tour, our hosts were understandably anxious to get us on time to the little reception and then to the lecture itself. Every delay, such as saying goodbye to the librarian, caused anxious scrutiny of watches, and I wondered whether the Japanese during the war followed politeness ceremonies before going into battle—although I should add that Japanese energy, deftness, and speed make it possible to obey the demands of both modern and traditional Japanese culture simultaneously, with perhaps only a modest price in inefficiency and ulcers.

Then at the reception itself in the office of the chairman of the Sociology Department, as regularly happens, it took so long to decide how our party should sit, with every Japanese politely resisting sitting next to me because that would be undue honor, that there was no time for the tea which then came and to which Evey and I had looked forward. Then there was further delay because the lecture had to be moved from a smaller to a larger hall, and what with the inevitable delays in translation, a talk which was supposed to begin at three o'clock was not over until 5:30.

The talk was called "*The Lonely Crowd* Reconsidered," and for many of the students, drawn from all the different faculties of the university, it must have been hard going indeed. My conscientious translator had to work without a manuscript since I was speaking from notes; he had studied these carefully and did his best to elucidate methodological points for the students. Since I had the only microphone, and he humbly declined to share it, I was not sure he could be heard in back of the huge lecture hall. And in so large a setting, even at best, attempts at irony and humor often fall flat. In fact, audiences here appear to be somewhat dead-pan—quite unlike those at baseball, who, we are told, are beginning to throw bottles at the umpire; none of the students shouted "Louder," as they might have done in the United States. (The talk was to be broadcast over NHK, the government radio station; I doubt whether even the Third Programme of the BBC, or WGBH in Boston, would carry so relatively esoteric a talk, which took for granted that all the listeners had read *The Lonely Crowd* and were interested in its background and in changes in the views of its authors since publication.)

Despite these difficulties, it was one of the most attentive audiences I've ever seen, many of them taking notes. No one stirred or whispered during the lecture, and those who had to leave went out quietly while those who had been standing at the back took their seats equally quietly—but in both cases without the stooping nearly double which we've seen in older and still more polite Japanese.

After my lecture, university officials gave a dinner for us at the guest house, a spacious Japanese house surrounded by gardens at one end of the campus. At a Japanese-style banquet such as this one on *tatami*, the guest of honor and his hosts sit opposite each other in the center of the long table, with less senior or less distinguished people distributed toward the ends. There was the usual nervousness as to whether we would like a Japanese meal, and in fact there was an innovation: when the chicken came—and often in the more elaborate banquets either chicken or a small piece of filet mignon is added to the various fish courses that are more characteristic—large knives and forks were brought for Evey and me alone. Hitherto we'd been content to struggle with chopsticks, and my first temptation was not to use the "barbarian" implements; but then I realized that this would not be polite. (Actually, the difficulty with the chicken is not that it's hard to cut meat with a chopstick, but that it's hard for us to allow food to dangle from our mouths and to chew it off the way the Japanese do, who lift a whole chicken leg with chopsticks and chew off a bit of it before putting the rest down, just as they hold the rice bowl up to their mouths; and of course it is good manners in Japan as in China to gurgle while drinking soup or tea.)

The conversation got onto the subject of the Japanese peace movement, or rather movements, in which some of those present had taken an active hand, seeking to found a non-partisan peace committee not tied (like Gensuikyo) to Communist or fellow-traveler orientations. I recalled hearing criticisms of our host, President Horiuchi, from some Americans because he had made a statement, at the height of the demonstrations last year, that he could understand why students weren't at their studies when they faced so corrupt a government as that of Prime Minister Kishi. These Americans felt that this remark showed irresponsibility toward the students' academic work or toward American interests, and that the President had not sufficiently criticized students for the violence of their agitation, although in fact he had done his best to keep the protests in non-violent channels. I found myself drawn to President Horiuchi and the rare sympathy he appeared to have for students; he seemed rather like a brave head of a Southern state university who would defend his students' picketing for civil rights. He is a Christian, possibly a non-church Christian, and it is this affiliation which may symbolize his charismatic power and a certain ability to cut through traditional forms.

Tokyo, November 16

We had a brief but lively talk this morning with Mr. Miura, an official of the Socialist Party. He speaks English quite well. He is a youngish man, an intellectual, who among other tasks does some ghost writing for Socialist Party leaders and for the party journal. The Socialist Party has a tiny membership, 40,000, although it garners about ten million votes or a third of the electorate in the national elections: this smallness of the membership parties is characteristic of Japanese politics on all sides.

Of course, it's not surprising that the Socialist Party is run like other organizations in Japan and that a young intelligent man is a ghost writer and anonymous, just as he would be on a newspaper. While among some of the young student activists there is at times an idealism, like that of our beats, which rejects all organization and certainly the gerontocratic structure of Japanese society, the party is a going concern according to the Japanese rules. The talk about "structural reform" in the newspapers sounds like mere wind but actually it reflects factional struggles within the party and an effort comparable to Togliatti's to get away from talk of violent revolution and to make some attempt to come to terms with the current state of Japanese affairs.

As previously with other people on the Left here, I tried to find

DR

out what Miura knew about Yugoslavia and Poland, but he knew little. He had a vague awareness of the New Left in Britain. He knew that the anti-Communism of European Socialism made it difficult, as the Rome Congress proved, for the Japanese Socialist Party to come to terms with it. On his way back from a visit to Moscow, he had gone through Outer Mongolia and spent several days in Peking. There he was under the care of a Chinese bureau or office which deals with visitors from countries that don't recognize China, and we got the sense that he had a chance to see very little—except for cultural sites—and the people he talked to seemed all to belong to this cultural bureau, which shepherds through China a great many visitors from Japan.

Miura told us that the Police Bill, which was intended to strengthen the powers of the police, helped to mobilize the anti-regime sentiment that made possible the demonstrations against the United States-Japan Security Treaty of a year ago. Anything that touches the police reminds Japanese of the pre-war police state; yet the Conservative Party feels uneasy with the lack of orderliness and seeks wider powers for the police. And in the present Diet there has been a new struggle to get through the Anti-violence Bill, which would increase police power to cope with demonstrations; but it has gone over to another session after great protests, although not with anything like the mobilizations of a year ago.

ETR

As there was to be a discussion this afternoon with Murata and Yamazaki for *Chuo Koron* at a restaurant at four o'clock, the Zengakuren students who failed to show up yesterday had been invited to meet us at this restaurant at two. In this way we could fit in a meeting with them, which would not have been possible if we had had to make the trip to their office and back. The restaurant, like so many here, gives the illusion, with its small garden and high fence, of being in the country though in the heart of the city. The room we were ushered into was large, with two long tables on *tatami*, and gas stoves burning on either side. Murata decided to come early to attend this meeting because of his interest in the Zengakuren; Bob Lifton and our interpreter of yesterday had also come, but the students had not arrived. As we settled ourselves and chatted, we began to have the uneasy feeling that the students might not show up this time either. However, about twenty minutes later two young men appeared. As they came in, they bowed almost to the floor in the traditional manner, which, for passionate revolutionaries, quite amazed us. One was tall and thin, with a face that suggested sensitivity and power, and an aristocratic bearing. He turned out to be the leader of the Zengakuren. The organization's secretary was short and stocky and said hardly a word during the whole discourse. Perhaps the most extraordinary thing about the leader, Iwanuma, was his ringing voice. The discussion was frustrating because he was interested only in making speeches, and there was very little give and take. It was impossible also to talk about anything factual, as he confined himself to abstractions. I started taking notes but soon realized that what I was writing down made little sense, and so gave up.

The discussion was finally cut short by the arrival of the editor of *Chuo Koron* with his secretary and tape recorders. We had a break, and it was good to move around, for sitting on *tatami*, even with our back rests, is tiring. Yamazaki arrived at this point also.

When we sat down again, tea was brought in, as it had been also during the discussion with the students. There was no particular subject given for this discussion, but since by now these three men were familiar with each other and each other's work, they would easily find subjects of mutual interest. It was decided that Dave should make an opening statement. He began by saying that Japan is a print-oriented society lacking the hypersophistication of the United States and Europe; Japan is more democratic intellectually; the large circulation of a newspaper or magazine does not make the publication lose prestige; there seem to be few anti-intellectuals who insist that the media satisfy their own limitations; there seems to be little rebellion against the authority of the word—except perhaps by the "sun tribe" and the *gurentai;* that is, the Japanese boy does not as a rule establish his manliness by rebelling against school and literacy. In fact, the Japanese seem to be endlessly curious and in a sense go to school all their lives, with the enormous amount of reading they do. He said he would like to know why there was no Beaverbrook or Hearst in Japan; there was respectability and respect among journalists and editors for their jobs, and they were not exploitative or cynical toward their audiences. The prestige activities of the newspapers also testified to their respectful attitude toward culture.

Yamazaki replied by referring to the American movie *Twelve Angry Men.* The jury in that film came from all different classes, and all expressed their personal feelings and prejudices quite freely; they only reached a consensus after great struggle. In Japan, if there had been a professor of Tokyo University on such a jury, all the others would have conformed at once to his opinion. This is an example of one of the great differences between democracy in the United States and in Japan. It is true that Japanese journals have vast numbers of subscribers, both highbrow and lowbrow; this comprehensiveness is a characteristic aspect of Japanese culture—"department-store culture." In Japan, all classes eat the same sort of food, rice and soup and pickles; in the United States there is more variety and role differentiation in food, it is more colorful and varied, like the society; but here there is a uniformity that makes Japan more authoritarian.

Dave replied that in the meeting of cultures one may idealize the other: each can be preoccupied with its own liabilities and deprecate what the other admires. Coming from the United States where anti-intellectualism is a real danger, he found it a pleasure to be in Japan, where this hardly exists; he was at ease with Japanese intellectual life, though not with the type of Tokyo University professor who parades his authority. He said he was aware of the problem of heavy-handed authority in Japan, and there were virtues in American breeziness and lack of deference. But he was puzzled that, despite uniformity and authority, there did not seem to be any universally admired Japanese heroes. He went on to say that in a sense most institutions have to be department stores; a newspaper, for example, must serve many differentiated tastes. To return to cultural exchange, he wanted to make a further point: in looking at another society one sees its beauty, variety, colorfulness; but the people living in the society may feel imprisoned in one way or another.

Murata said that, to be sure, Japan was a society of literacy, but the Japanese are content with symbols that don't relate to reality and there are great dangers in this. The intellectuals are left uncriticized; in the United States the intellectuals at least have the criticism of the anti-intellectuals. Dave then brought up Zen Buddhism, wondering if it was a form of anti-intellectualism.

Murata wasn't sure; he thought it might be a very sophisticated form of intellectualism: its symbols are intra-personal rather than interpersonal.

Yamazaki said that thought in Japan is polarized: there is an over-attachment to symbols and ideologies and as a result a loss of understanding about self and reality. Zen takes a detached-attached view of the world (to use Charles Morris' phrase); it could lead back to reality in feeling and perceiving, but today Zen leads to a hermit's life; and this could be considered a form of anti-intellectualism in its privatization and detachment from symbols.

Dave said that perhaps the trouble with intellectualism in Japan was that it had gotten on the wrong track, so that now there was a dualism between the narrow scholastic intellect and the unmediated brute world. He said, however, that both Murata and Yamazaki were exceptions to this narrow scholasticism and didn't need anti-intellectuality to keep them related to the "real world."

Yamazaki said that pragmatism was important in American education: the masses were being educated for practical work; while in Japan the educated people were being directed toward the intellectual life and toward flower arrangement.

Dave replied that what is pragmatic, or what is real, is not so easy to evaluate; education for business nowadays is often education for education's sake; Japan and the United States could exchange their systems of education and the results would very likely be the same: the systems are simply a way of sorting people out; no education prepares people for life as it will be lived.

Murata said that the younger generation everywhere has the same problem; their motivation and purpose are ambiguous; they have to do something with their energies; they become beatniks and hot-rodders.

Yamazaki then told about a study he had done in Kyushu, among the students at the university, which indicated a less rebellious outlook. The students rejected inner-direction as an anachronism; they favored the more immediate happiness of the salaried life; when he asked what they would like their life to be like in fifteen years, they said they wanted security, a house of their own, a beautiful wife, and two children. He said you would not get this sort of answer from pre-war students, and most Japanese would deplore this lack of ideals. But he thought this type of youth would be a stabilizing force in Japan and would be more effective than the moralizers.

Dave said that perhaps it was necessary for people to attain this dream in order to realize its shallowness. What will people do after attaining it? American students have similar attitudes, but they would be hostile to anything like the Zengakuren movement; the Japanese seem to have respect for the Zengakuren and don't jeer at them.

Yamazaki said that in post-war Japan people are enjoying their private life, and also they are enjoying their human rights, their right to organize; all this was related and connected with their sense of happiness; therefore, when the question of the Police Bill came up, or the Security Treaty, or nuclear fall-out, they reacted strongly because they knew these things touched on their happiness. And so when the Zengakuren agitated and had demonstrations to preserve political rights, the people supported them.

Murata said that no one devotes himself to private activities alone; everyone's life is diversified and has these two aspects of the private and the political. But the gap between the private and the global is so immense that it is hard to connect them.

Dave remarked that all over the world there are countries that might look to Japan as a model of industrialization. Yet Japan looks to the big powers for the answers when it might better discover its own answers, new answers. For example, Japan has solved the problem of unemployment by having underemployment; it has solved the problems of education by overeducation; but are these solutions good or bad? Such questions can't be answered by Marxist class analysis or talk of "structural reform," and so forth.

Yamazaki said there were antagonisms in Japan due very frequently to status: high-school students in the provinces did not dare frequent the same noodle shops as university students; and the latter feel inferior to Tokyo University students; there are antagonisms between the police and students, between professors and laborers, between laborers and police. There is a great deal of frustration and this is dangerous; the Zengakuren are an example of the way groups give vent to their frustrations. All these antagonisms are deeply rooted in the Japanese educational system; indeed, the educational system causes these antagonisms; and the examinations destroy the youth by creating competition for status rather than encouraging development of the intellect. He questioned Dave's idea that America is a competitive society and Japan a harmonious one: in Japan the struggle is of the strong against the weak, quite unlike truly free competition; American competition is more universalistic, pitting the good against the bad.

I was moved by Yamazaki's words—his voice has many guttural sounds in it that seem to express a passionate concern; I was moved also by his whole manner of expression; his appearance is attractively disheveled, his longish hair tossing about as he talks. I could see that Dave, too, was moved. Dave replied that he took advantage of being a guest *sensei* and learned from the criticism of things he had said: Yamazaki had clarified this very well for him.

Dave then went on to say that one important question is how to bring together public and private concerns; he said that he told American students to begin at home, to start in the university to try to change things so that they would not be cheated out of an education or destroyed by a bad one; he would say the same thing to Japanese students, and sometimes this might make more sense than taking on global questions; if students would apply their energies to manageable problems, then they would not feel so powerless; the Japanese worry too much about conflict—as if there could be a world without conflict; rather they should face conflict in areas where they might accomplish something.

Murata became very animated in talking about the possibility of something new emerging out of the cooperation between the second and third generations (the "second generation" being of the period of industrialization and Westernization, the "third generation" being their own post-industrial one), where people could do something about their own environment, where a new autonomy might develop, perhaps out of a new kind of socialism. Yamazaki wanted to know who would be the people who could change the system, and how it could be done. Dave said that in the United States he would hesitate to use the word "socialism" because it had been so corrupted; would it be possible in Japan to rescue "socialism" from the Communists? He would rather refer to the internationalist and pacifist spirit of socialism in the period before World War I; it is desperately urgent to have such a movement for peace today. We have to live on several levels at once. He could only suggest beginnings of a way of thinking.

Yamazaki said that in the Japanese progressive movement people regarded one single event as all-important: if you lose one battle, you have lost all. Dave thought that this all-or-none point of view was related to the unpolitical attitude toward conflict in Japan; conflict should be seen as an endless process, as a dialectic of life itself. He wondered whether the students' feeling that if they didn't get into Tokyo University they had no chance wasn't unduly despairing; was it a self-confirming prophecy? They seem to value power as a thing to be seized rather than as a process, and so do not value their own achievements; and if ideas are viewed in terms of power, there can be no freedom of trade in ideas. In the United States, if you didn't get into one university, you could get into another; it is a land of second chance; in Japan, things are more rigid because there is so little elbow-room.

Yamazaki said that Japanese students feel that they haven't even a first chance; they regard the power of the "power elite" as too great and unmanageable; their image of this power is of course exaggerated.

Dave wondered about these misjudgments: what needs do they serve, perhaps the alibi of a minority? The idea the Zengakuren had that they could overthrow the government was a dream of glory fashioned by people who feel weak. Japan is not an aristocracy any more but a gerontocracy. And young people viewing their elders don't appreciate their power over the elders or are afraid of that power and the responsibilities that it entails.

At this point the meal was served and the formal discussion ended.

Tokyo, November 17

This evening we met with some University of Tokyo graduate students of Political Science and two of their professors for a discussion in one of the conference rooms at International House. I put it this way because the professors, after introducing themselves and the students, kept very much in the background and allowed their students to do the talking. There were about twenty people seated with us around the long conference table. Two were women, one of them a student and the other the wife of a professor (not present), who was to act as interpreter. It was explained to us that one student, Mr. Takagi, would present a paper, after which there would be discussion.

Takagi was obviously brilliant, and it was interesting to listen to his paper as an example of the work of the best Japanese students. One of his criticisms of Japanese society was its exclusion of the "failed elites," as he called them, from public life. Dave asked about this: in what way were they excluded? Takagi answered that all competition is over after adulthood is reached, that is, after graduation. Another student added that in pre-war Japan there were more opportunities than today; then Manchuria provided outlets, and there was a greater variety of schools, such as military academies and teachers' colleges, for those who came from poor backgrounds; but today these schools have disappeared (with the reforms of the Occupation); and so the opportunities are less pluralistic. Dave asked then if this was a problem of meritocracy in a society that did not like competition and conflict. They agreed that it was. One student said that solidarity and harmony were the mental climate of Japan, and that there was discomfort in competition or in political struggle and conflict. Another student remarked that, except for the entrance exam, fair competition didn't exist in Japan; very often a writer is asked to write something not because he is the best writer but because he has connections with the editor.

Takagi said that there is a polarization in Japanese thinking, harmony versus competition; but harmony means conformity within the group, and it implies discrimination against the out-group; inner harmony creates outward aggression; Japanese solidarity would result in encouraging competition rather than harmony. Here one of the professors interjected that while the feeling of harmony exists in a group of students or instructors, when a vacancy in a professorial chair occurs there is great rivalry; the graduate students look on the professor as the image of their own future; there is jealousy, and the competitive spirit comes out. A student remarked that the chief object of competition after the Meiji Restoration was to attain a government position; those who failed at this gave up and went into academic work. Another added that those who fail in competition can rationalize their failure by saying it is unfair. Dave wanted to know if, when people failed, they felt inadequate or simply frustrated, and how much did this feeling enter into consciousness. A student replied that in talking about competition there are two levels to consider: first the institutional, that is, are people given an equal chance; and second, do people feel rivalrous—inside themselves. He thought that in America the public expression of competition was institutionalized. Takagi added that though one has to distinguish between the two levels, there are similarities, or rather there is a relationship between the institutional level and consciousness; in terms of consciousness, there is "incomplete competition" in Japan. He went on to say that when a student felt the entrance exam was the only chance he had, his reaction to failure was that it was destiny—beyond his control—and he would simply say, "I am unlucky."

In most of this discussion, although nearly everyone had made some contribution, two or three students were doing most of the talking, Takagi and an intense-looking young man with glasses sitting opposite me. This student now wanted to turn the discussion to the subject of autonomy, and particularly to Dave's writings on the subject. He wanted to compare Erich Fromm's and David Riesman's concepts of autonomy, and to clarify the relations of politics to social character; for Fromm the ideal political society is one in which autonomy could flourish. Dave replied that there was a somewhat tenuous difference between Fromm's thinking about autonomy and his own; he would say that autonomy is both a never attained personal ideal and something one can approximate; while Fromm emphasizes autonomy in relation to society, as primarily communal and collective. Dave stated his own belief that even in an oppressive society there will be a few who will transcend the society—in that sense, autonomy is supra-historic; in an oppressive society, autonomy could not exist for a whole group, but only in a few extraordinary types. Dave went on to say that he had been influenced by Fromm, especially in his view that man can achieve relatedness even when society no longer allows him traditional ties. But harmony with the "laws" of man's nature is not automatic;

this is where the struggle begins. The image men have today of a better society is inadequate and thin; the words "humanistic socialism" don't convey enough; to make such aspirations concrete is difficult and important. He and Fromm believe that the Western world created an unfortunate dualism between supposedly rational thought and supposedly irrational emotion, whose influence can be felt even in Japan. Also, today men have an international heritage on which to draw, and this confuses them at the same time that it gives them more models.

The student continued to question Dave. According to him, then, does autonomy depend on personality and not on politics, and can it exist at every stage of history? Do the political regime and ideology have nothing to do with the autonomous personality, in contrast to Fromm's view that political form can be equated with autonomy? If a society is filled with autonomous people, will it be a good society, will it create good politics? Dave answered that one could have autonomous people living in a society that was a prison; the complexity of human nature is such that people are not all of a piece; there are even some people who are fine human beings but have wrong political ideas. Perhaps the most relevant difference between Fromm and himself did not involve content but rather attitudes: Fromm had a messianic outlook and was convinced of his rightness, while Dave himself did not feel so sure of the answers. Japanese scholars should think about socialism in terms of their own culture and not be dazzled by leftist literature that comes out of a different background with different problems. Nor is it likely that the answers to Japan's problems will be found in Fromm or in Riesman.

One of the professors at this point said gently that no account had been taken of the women—he was clearly trying to encourage the woman student to speak. The young woman, Miss Maeda, very striking in a white hat, spoke up then to say that because there are only one or two girls in the department they tend to be assimilated into the men's culture; but in order to explore the quality of the female sex, that is, to be autonomous as a woman, should there not be more women, and is this a universal problem. Dave said that women can enter a man's world but often they adapt to the enemy rather than bring to it their own best qualities. He referred to Margaret Mead's point in *Male and Female* that while there are mild universal differences between men and women, nevertheless different cultures have various ways of institutionalizing these differences. He then asked her about her hopes. She talked quite freely about herself, saying that she would like an academic post; if she got married, she would not be sure how to continue, since each family reacts differently to women's careers; she had decided on a career because her family had suffered economically—her father was killed in the war, he was a military man—and she had a strong desire to rise socially again and help her family. She hoped, if she married, to find a man who would encourage her in her career. Dave wondered if a woman like herself was a model for other young women. He wondered also if such a person in looking for a husband would fall back on the *miai*. And in the rigid Japanese society, how would a man who wanted this kind of wife be able to find her? There were no answers to these questions, only smiles.

Dave said that the attitudes of Japanese men to each other may be related to the subordination of women; while the males face the competition of exams, the female labor force has had to learn to be satisfied with less—in the convent-type schools. This produced smiles also, and one young man said that for most Japanese women the "convent" was the main road to education, but that Miss Maeda was an exception. Dave said that in a democratic society men's culture and women's culture were often not equal, whereas in an aristocratic culture women might be on the same level as men—the inequalities would be in the hierarchies of the classes rather than of the sexes; Lady Murasaki belonged to an aristocratic society.

Takagi thought that compartmentalization was created by the need for different roles in the family; autonomy, too, could be compartmentalized into its various roles: the ethical, the aesthetic, and the pragmatic. Dave said that ethics is often practical, and aesthetic feeling may be also. The intense-looking student opposite me said that there should be a methodological analysis of autonomy and then it should be put together again in synthesis. Dave said that it is important to know what is the concrete historical problem. It was evident that the students had read Fromm and Riesman closely, citing specific passages as well as general concepts. In the effort to categorize, they tended to see distinctions between Dave and Fromm where Dave felt the similarities were more important. Of course, Dave has encountered many such students in the United States, but few here thus far so energetic, sharp, and erudite.

Tokyo, November 18

At Professor Hayakawa's invitation, we drove out to the Komaba campus of the University of Tokyo to see the student festival now going on there. It seemed miles away, on the edge of the city. Turning into the campus, we went past some playing fields and tennis courts, into the large driveway in front of the main buildings, where groups of students were gathered around huge floats and booths. In Professor Hayakawa's office, we were introduced to the student who was to show us around. While we sat a few minutes chatting about what we should see, a secretary brought in tea, which was warming and pleasant, as it was cold in the building.

Our student guide took us into one of the dormitories, dark and cold and shabby like a barracks; but even so, there was a festive air, with students and their families wandering around. The exhibits were in the corridors, onto which windows opened from the students' rooms—the windows being used as showcases. They were lit by lamps or indirect lighting, some of them having elaborate mechanical devices for lights to go on and off, or things to move, and some of them with tape-recorded sound or music. Our guide explained the various exhibits; they were satirical, sometimes bitter; most were scenes having to do with atomic war or testing.

DR

Sometimes the exhibits were quite fancy mechanically, with moving peace doves or lights representing the planets. In the exhibit that won a prize, a funeral march was mechanically played over and over again, apparently by an "orchestra" consisting of the four nuclear powers arranged as a quartet: Messrs. Kennedy, Khrushchev, Macmillan, and de Gaulle each with an instrument in the shape of a weapon; thus, de Gaulle's violin looked like a missile.

Another exhibit showed Kennedy and Khrushchev sitting opposite each other smoking Peace cigarettes, a popular brand in Japan, and knocking the ashes into an ashtray—the ashes were supposed to symbolize fall-out. In others, Khrushchev smoked a pipe out of which came a mushroom cloud, and said that he couldn't break the habit—words from a popular tune about a girl; or he spread "seeds," which sprouted mushrooms all over the ground. One exhibit showed a little girl and her mother standing on another planet, the girl looking at the earth through a telescope. "Look, Mummy," she said, "it is out of orbit"—and you could see that a nuclear explosion had gone off and catapulted the earth in the wrong direction.

Reflecting on the political perceptions of the students, I noticed that neither Mao nor Adenauer figured in a single one of the exhibits we saw, and it seemed that we saw hundreds. Prime Minister Ikeda appeared only as a subsidiary figure, once as a monkey trying to hide under President Kennedy's umbrella but not escaping the fall-out

DR

created by Soviet and American tests. (Ikeda also figured indirectly in a very small number of exhibits which dealt with some of the problems of student life, the high price of everything, the crowdedness, the inability to pay for beer—sometimes mocking Ikeda's promise of doubling incomes in ten years, by referring to runaway inflation.) It occurs to me that these students were unpolitical in their emphasis on the mere possession of nuclear power as against the more important sources of potential conflict, nuclear and otherwise, resembling in this those Americans who are preoccupied with disarmament and not at all with diplomacy. I should add here that although many Japanese student leaders complain about the apolitical nature of most of their fellow students, this is so only relative to Japanese norms. The types of students who had made these exhibits would in the United States hardly know the meaning of missiles and fall-out. They were the members of the swimming team or various student clubs and not at all the left-wing peaceniks we would expect them to be. It would be a great mistake to see these students in their personal lives as sharing the macabre outlook of many of these exhibits; if they are alienated from weaponry and from many conventional aspects of Conservative Party politics, they are so with high spirits and often high good humor about even the gravest threats.

ETR

After we had seen four floors of exhibits, our young guide asked if we would like to see one of the student rooms; he could show us his. He took us down to a room on the first floor that was dark and cold, with six unmade bunks, clothes hanging on a line near the window, crates piled on top of desks for bookshelves, papers and clothes strewn around, a light bulb hanging from the ceiling. I wondered how students could live and work in such crowded and dismal quarters, with no privacy and hardly the bare necessities. The contrast between this and the beautiful Japanese *tatami* room must be almost traumatic for some of these students. (I am reminded now that Dr. Toyoda told us that 15 per cent of the Tokyo University students get tuberculosis and 12 per cent have nervous breakdowns, and I can see why.)

Hakone, November 18

This afternoon we drove out with the Matsumotos to spend the weekend in the Hakone Mountains—a respite planned long in advance because of their busy lives and our crowded schedule. Leaving Tokyo, we drove through parts of the city we had not seen, then on to the

Tokaido Road through small towns made up of dark wooden houses with steep thatched roofs lining the road and giving directly onto it. This route must have been colorful in the old days, with its traffic of carts and people on foot; but now the Tokaido Road is inappropriately filled with cars and trucks, and the houses look as if they were closed up and barricaded against all this. We recognized Ninomiya, the town where we had spent our first weekend with the Liftons; then we were out in the country again, passing along rice fields. Suddenly through the clouds we saw Mount Fuji towering above a layer of low clouds, its snow-capped top touching a higher layer of clouds. It looked immense and unreal, alone in its grandeur. The Matsumotos were terribly pleased to have this show for us. After a while our road went along the sea. The breakers were rolling in, their whiteness clear and even against the dark water. We could see the Izu peninsula and the range of mountains beyond. Fujiyama had disappeared behind clouds again. Matsumoto pointed out the golf course, on our right, where he often plays—in this setting, it was easy to understand his love for the game. The sun was beginning to set behind the mountains and clouds, and the sky became brilliant. By the time we reached the hotel in the mountains, it was dark.

During the drive, Mrs. Matsumoto told us about an idealistic young man they knew who had gone to teach school in a small mountain town, completely isolated, where he was the only educated person. He wanted to do this to be useful, to help the people who needed it most. But because he was the only educated person there, he found the demands on him enormous; he had to be priest, doctor, counselor, lawyer, everything, to these poor villagers. Finally, exhausted and lonely, he had to give up and leave in order to keep his sanity. This was an example of the hopelessness the Japanese feel about doing anything individually, she said.

The Kowakai-en Hotel glittered in the night as we approached it up the steep mountain road. Before dinner we rested in our room, which, though Western-style, is Japanese in all its details: its straw-lined walls, its sliding doors and *shoji*, its bamboo ceiling just inside the windows and warm wood ceiling over the rest of the room. In the adjoining bathroom, the (modified) Japanese deep bath is set in below the window, so that one can, while soaking, look out at the view through the patterns of the open cement screened wall.

At dinner we sat on *tatami* with our feet in a deep warm pit. The guests in this dining room were Japanese and many of them in kimono. The men looked particularly elegant in their *yukata*. A superb string quartet played Beethoven and Mozart while we dined. The players were seated in an alcove, beyond which was the Western dining room, so that the music served both rooms. When I admired a charming little straw tray on the table, Mrs. Matsumoto said that these have to be made freshly all the time; like *tatami*, they don't last long. Then, laughing, she said there is a Japanese saying that wives must be changed freshly every so often, like *tatami*. She went on to speak of her life at school in England. She spoke of seeing the *Mikado* and *Madame Butterfly* while there; she thought the fast little mincing steps of the people on the stage were very funny; she didn't realize until she came back to Japan that this was the way the Japanese women walked.

It was late when we finished dinner. The Matsumotos' room adjoined ours but was in Japanese style. They invited us in for a moment. It was beautiful, if anything even more beautiful than our room. Dave and I had been tempted to take a Japanese room, but being such poor sleepers we decided we were safer in the familiar Western bed.

Tokyo, November 19

We have just come back from a drive with the Matsumotos in the mist and rain. The fall colors are rich orange, red, mustard green, and brown—the mountainsides looking like silk brocade, Mrs. Matsumoto remarked. We came out on a high promontory above Lake Hakone nestled in the folds of the mountains. Across the water, near the opposite shore, was the red *torii* (arch) of a shrine; one can get to the shrine only by boat. However, in this cold misty weather there were no boats, and on the road there were almost no cars. On the way back we stopped at the Hakone Hotel to have tea and to warm ourselves. This hotel is modern and striking, but not to be compared in beauty with the Kowakai-en; it is cold and severe in its bleak setting.

During this drive, the Matsumotos talked of the war. Mrs. Matsumoto said the Japanese expected the Americans to land at Kamakura, where they were living at that time; the people were told dreadful things about the Americans, and the women were being trained to fight with bamboo spears. People whose property was destroyed by bombings and fire in Tokyo got no compensation for it; of course some fortunate ones were spared this loss, just as the owners of forest lands were spared having their property taken from them, while the owners of farm land (in the land reforms during the Occupation) lost their farms, which were distributed among the farmers; though most of the fortunes disappeared with the war, the owners of forests are now among the richest people in Japan. The Matsumotos did not speak at all bitterly about their own losses; they suffered along with others.

We came back to the Kowakai-en Hotel for lunch, and left shortly after for Oiso, where the Matsumotos have a charming summer cottage on a little country lane, hidden in the woods, with a small garden, and bamboo and fences hiding it from the road. Their son Ken was there, and soon we were all sitting on the floor and having tea.

We went with the Matsumotos to have dinner with their friend and neighbor, Miss Sakamoto, a remarkable woman we had met at the reception given for us soon after our arrival in Tokyo. She is a distinguished scholar who has spent many years in the United States, a bluestocking career woman of an older generation. She lives in a handsomely designed modern house, surrounded with her books, cats, paintings, sculpture, and plants. At dinner, Miss Sakamoto told us of her experience as an emissary from the Japanese Foreign Office to the armed forces in Manchuria; she was sent there to give them the facts about the war, to explain that it was being lost, and to prepare them for the surrender. One officer asked her insolently if she would take the responsibility for what she was saying before the Japanese people and the soldiers. She replied, "It is not my responsibility; I have simply been told to give you the facts." The general in charge became more and more furious with her and wanted to kill her; she barely escaped, through the warnings of a friend. We got a sense, from what she said, of the fanaticism and arrogance of the Japanese military.

After dinner we continued on our way back to Tokyo.

Tokyo, November 20

We had lunch today with three career women: a writer, Mrs. Watanuki; an anthropologist, Mrs. Hayashiya; and a journalist, Mrs. Kawanaka. They were attractive, intelligent, and energetic women in their late thirties or early forties, I would guess. We have been eager to meet women, for they have been absent from most of our discussions. We were interested in getting their views on what was happening to the Japanese women. We met in the conference room at International House. Lunch was brought in to us on trays: sandwiches and tea. Mrs. Hayashiya remarked later that probably we were not given a lunch like this when meeting with distinguished men—simply an indication of the lower status of women.

Two of the women wore tailored suits, but Mrs. Hayashiya was in kimono. When the question of dress was brought up, she said she felt more comfortable this way. Also, since she had a good many kimono left over from before the war, she could go on wearing them for years. To buy new ones would be prohibitively expensive. Mrs. Kawanaka protested that the kimono was the garb of the traditional Japanese woman and a symbol of the subservience of women; she prefers to wear Western clothes, which besides are more suitable for the office where she works. Mrs. Hayashiya explained that she lectures at a women's college and writes at home and so can easily wear kimono, which she could not do if she worked in a downtown office every day. For appearing in public or traveling in a foreign country, they all agreed, wearing kimono would be more comfortable and attractive—besides, a Japanese woman is more graceful in kimono, Mrs. Watanuki added with a laugh. It was fascinating to watch and listen to three such contrasting women. Mrs. Hayashiya has delicate features and a retiring manner. The kimono somehow makes her look old-fashioned; yet as we talked she turned out to be the most outspoken of the three. Mrs. Kawanaka is smartly dressed and well groomed, the most stylish of the three, and gives the impression of an efficient, businesslike woman. Mrs. Watanuki is a tall, angular type who looks vigorous and solid; she wears jewelry and her tight suit is raspberry red. I was reminded that the subject of dress has come up several times before, and the opinion seems to be general that modern dress is the sign of being emancipated; a woman can be only decorative, graceful, silent in kimono, like a lovely antique. But the "third generation" women, if they are career women and have become famous, can afford to wear kimono, for they know very well they are not antiques.

The discussion soon got onto the subject of the ways in which Japan was not really democratic nor women really emancipated. Life in Japan, they said, is still familistic and paternalistic. This is true not only of family life itself, where the individual is completely suppressed, but on all levels. Japanese life is a society of groups: familial, social, political, scholastic, trade union, business. One has to belong to a group or one is out, one is nothing; and all groups, large or small, are paternalistic and "feudal."

Dave remarked that Japan seemed to be a harmonious country. Mrs. Hayashiya said the family appears to be harmonious because there is complete submission to the head of the family; but that isn't true harmony. Mrs. Watanuki said that in public life Japan is filled with controversy. From abroad it may look harmonious, but actually the Japanese are the most controversy-prone people; they are always arguing and opposing each other, but as groups, not as individuals. For in personal relations everyone is circumspect, never showing emotion. But groups can differ and become quite violent. There are no individual leaders, no heroes or heroines in Japan, only mass movements.

Mrs. Hayashiya said that in a questionnaire she took part in administering to school children, the boys were asked whom they admired most, and the reply was their parents. They had no other heroes. She went on to say that Christianity at the beginning of the Meiji Restoration was the sole principle which opposed strong family solidarity. It gave spiritual sanction to be an individual. There were many conversions then; but now people have drifted away. The Japanese are not a philosophical people; there is a lack of understanding of universalistic rule; justice is tied up with status, and there is no right or wrong, that is, no transcendental rightness, and there are no rigid attitudes in the religion. While the Christian God is an absolute, the Emperor is human, not transcendental; and this was the danger; he could be used, indeed was used by the militarists. (The possibility that a transcendental God could also be manipulated by His votaries did not occur to her.)

Dave asked why there was so little cynicism in Japan; he pointed out, for example, that there isn't in Japan the cynicism that there was in Germany after the war. Mrs. Hayashiya thought that cynicism requires a core of personality, a certain amount of inner-direction which is lacking in Japan; the Japanese are other-directed: "We have jumped directly from tradition-direction to other-direction." Mrs. Kawanaka added that the democratization of Japan took place under the Occupation, and therefore the Japanese did not take full responsibility for it, and it did not go deep. Mrs. Hayashiya continued that the younger generation experienced extreme change in the values of the adults after the war, and this made the youth lose confidence in all adults, who after shouting against the devils, the enemy, then about-faced to preach democracy.

The Japanese, Mrs. Hayashiya said, are trained not to respond to reason but to emotion (yet, paradoxically, I thought, they don't *show* feeling). The language, she said, is not logical, but is based entirely on feeling. "In translating Western literature into Japanese, we have great difficulty. We can't say 'freedom of thought,' we can only say 'freedom of feeling.' We can't say '*vous avez raison*,' we can only say, 'you have the right feeling.' We can't think in terms of the rights of individuals: in our language, 'to *earn* money' is not expressed in terms of having a right to it, but in words that mean 'to *grab* it.' Since even men in our society have not got rights or real freedom, the emancipation of women is more difficult to achieve than in a true democracy. Moreover, all our values militate against emancipation; submissiveness is a virtue, and maternal love is sentimentalized." Mrs. Kawanaka said, "This goes so deep we are hardly aware of being suppressed—even I, in my family life!" Mrs. Hayashiya said, "We speak of the 'passive fortitude of women.' The daughter-in-law in the family of her husband has a special status of subservience. I had to serve my mother-in-law for years, massage her, take care of her. One is conditioned to have a very sensitive radar system; one must notice the slightest feelings, misunderstandings, and complexities in a situation."

Dave remarked that in the United States women are still not the equals of men; at the same time, women are ashamed of being "just a housewife." And the women who are just that are envious and attack the career women. Mrs. Watanuki said the same is true in Japan. After the war, women were encouraged to get jobs and housewives felt guilty if they did not work. But now, with prosperity, the idea that women should stay at home is being encouraged by the social critics and journalists. But having jobs and having careers are different problems. Mrs. Watanuki said, "We have come to the point where we have to explore again what is the best life for men and women. We have achieved another level, and so must question the real goals for women; we are serious about these problems—more than the men."

Mrs. Kawanaka spoke of the many tragedies that have occurred with the emancipation of women; young mothers read novels, go to movies, and get the idea that they want to be free; and so they leave their husbands and children, get a divorce, and think they can make a go of it alone. There has been a sanction given them through the media and books to do this sort of thing, without giving them any sense of the training necessary or the opportunities open to them for doing anything which would be worthwhile or would make up for all they have given up. There are letters in the advice columns of newspapers all the time from forlorn women who regret their divorces and don't know what to do. It would have been better, Mrs. Hayashiya thought, to create a sound idea of a democratic marriage and family life. She went on to say that women in Japan do not get as good an education as men. The few women who go to the national universities do get the same education; but most girls go to women's colleges, "finishing schools for brides." Mrs. Hayashiya said she went to a women's college, where she studied Japanese literature and domestic science; she wanted to study English literature, but that was considered too dangerous and was not offered. "Women can get secretarial and service jobs, but they can't compete with the men to get on the 'escalator.' The competition for jobs even for the woman who is a graduate of one of the best universities is not fair, or open, or objective like the exams to get into the universities. If a girl isn't good-looking or doesn't come from a good family, she won't get the job that she may be well qualified for; the reasons are never told her. After graduating from the university, one may drop in the social scale. Among the younger generation, there is a new kind of emancipation: there is a type of girl who is rather beat, goes around with boys, uses boys' language, and calls herself *boku* (guy)."

Dave asked about the place of women in politics. Mrs. Hayashiya said that it was the women who started the peace movement and were most active in protesting the Russian nuclear tests. She said the women read the papers and are often better informed than the men. The Progressive Women's Rally is the leading political organization of the women of the country. Mrs. Watanuki said that in Kyushu a group of rural women compose poems, *waka,* about peace, and the good life, and children. But these rural areas are the most conservative districts, and these women-for-peace all vote for bad representatives in the government; the Socialists can't even get into these regions, which are absolutely dominated by the Conservatives (Liberal Democrats); the youth picket to keep any other parties out; the landlords give the young men feasts and bribes of all sorts to do this. But factory jobs are helping to liberalize some of the rural farm people, and eventually this will change.

Mrs. Hayashiya said that the danger now is the confusion of the paternalistic attitude with democracy. "Parental good will of the government" is a slogan that is regarded as democratic; the definition of the emancipation of women is chivalry. Another slogan is "The happy democratic family in contrast to the gloomy feudalistic family," but the old family system continues under a new guise. Mrs. Watanuki said that American visitors deplore any disorganization of the family system; Margaret Mead, for example, spoke of this. Mrs. Kawanaka recalled that up until prostitution was made illegal (a few years ago) many girls supported their families as prostitutes; these girls were exploited by their families, and this was considered filial piety. Mrs. Hayashiya said that until this law was passed, it was not considered wrong for men to go to prostitutes; yet the attitude of husbands and sons toward women was tainted by this. There is no Puritanism in

ETR

Japan and no sense of guilt. There is inhibition of expression, such as embracing in public, but this has nothing to do with Puritanism. Mrs. Kawanaka added that "idea and action don't go together with us."

I had recently read a novel, *The Wild Goose* by Mori Ogai, which deals with a daughter exploited by her father in just this way, but this was written in the pre-World War I days, and I did not suppose such customs continued. I was interested in the attitude of the women to this law, in contrast to what others had said on the subject: that the law had not changed anything, only driven prostitution underground to be controlled by gangsters rather than the police. Also I was interested that these women do not see their culture and their traditions in the romantic way that some of the men we have talked with do; they feel the suppression that for centuries has made their sex subservient, and they resent it. I am thinking of Osabe, who had spoken admiringly of the "passive fortitude of women" and of the woman's communication with her husband through the way she bent the stem in her flower arrangement. Is it possible that these differences of thinking may be not only a difference in point of view between men and women, but also a difference between Kyoto and Tokyo?

Dave asked whether, in this overcrowded country which is so competitive, the submissive wife and the comforts she provides do not give the necessary relief to the men for the great tension in their lives? Would the emancipation of women make the men more aggressive? Mrs. Watanuki said that Japanese men are aggressive in the home, but not aggressive when they should be, when they go abroad to conferences, for example. She said that, in essence, Japanese men have not changed; their aggressiveness is simply different from that of American men; in Japan "service culture" was enforced by men and still exists from top to bottom. She said that submissiveness is drummed into children so that they cannot develop their own individuality, and that this submissiveness is a hindrance to the development of democracy.

It was already long past the time allotted for this discussion. Dave and I had found it so fascinating that we did not want to bring it to a close, but at this point we felt we should.

DR

This evening Ambassador and Mrs. Reischauer gave a dinner for us to which were invited eighteen or twenty guests, including the Matsumotos, Professor Kawasaki, Professor Hayakawa with his wife and his father, and Mr. Tanaka, a former leading wire-service editor and his wife. There were also two American Embassy couples. The Reischauers were upset because their plans for this dinner had been interfered with by the coming of Princess Alexandra from Britain. There was to be a reception for her that night at the British Embassy and everybody would have to go in white tie and tails so that the dinner had been moved from seven to six and they would have to leave early, along with a number of the guests. Reischauer himself had hoped that Prime Minister Macmillan would come, but this had been canceled owing to the Berlin crisis. The Japanese guests who were going to attend this reception at the British Ambassador's would enjoy the foreign atmosphere—for these older gentlemen of Japan and their wives, a Western embassy may have much the same meaning that a coffee house does for the young Japanese.

As we sat in a large circle having drinks before dinner, Matsumoto acted, as he has so often done, as a very tactful and unofficious go-between. He got old Mr. Hayakawa onto the subject of his effort to reform the electoral law of Japan so as to prevent corruption in campaigns for the Diet; he wanted stricter laws to prevent bribery and the spending of large sums, and he also wanted people to be educated so they would not sell their votes—his model here, like that of many Japanese "old liberals," was British parliamentary government, but I felt he had no real sense of what might be called the inherent irrationalities of electoral processes or the way in which many people regard them as sporting events; he seemed to think that by a few legal changes—the law is already violated constantly in campaigns, just as it is with us—and by educational preachment, matters would be different. He has committees organized throughout Japan and they were having a convention; all this had an old-fashioned, appealing, and yet somehow pathetic quality.

At dinner, while I chatted intermittently with Mrs. Reischauer about the sociable awkwardness of Japanese wives in a Western setting (she of course is Japanese, but very much at home in both settings), I could hear Evey talking quietly but passionately to Ed Reischauer about the Japanese reaction to testing, and other quite "unsociable" matters such as the problem of Communist China and the Japanese position, caught between the United States and China. One of the left-wing journals had just published a hostile and apparently rather silly article entitled "The Real Meaning of Reischauer's Appointment," and it is possible that the Left is now beginning to harbor suspicions toward him of luring intellectuals away from their radicalism by his good qualities, his intelligence and openness. However, as I listened to Evey and thought of the handful of Embassy officials we'd met, I had a picture of the enormous intake of information in Japan that was sent in a tiny stomach tube across the Pacific in a daily cable or set of cables, only to be unraveled at the other end in its slow trickle by relatively uninterested officials who were simultaneously receiving messages from South Korea, Formosa, and a dozen other countries; it seemed to me that the Embassy's activities, and those of the ancillary agencies, including U.S.I.A., the C.I.A., and the Military Intelligence Services, all of which operate here, must at times engender a deep sense of frustration—of phoning into a dead wire. Ed Reischauer's geniality, his genuine optimism about Japan, and his knowledge of things Japanese are attractive. Plainly, he sees himself as an interpreter of the two countries to one another in terms of their best liberal traditions, restoring the "broken dialogue." His wife complained to me, as his father had earlier, that Ed has no time to read books any more. The Ambassador's mansion, an enormous pile of the 1920's like that of a Pittsburgh or Cleveland multimillionaire, with its bevy of servants, seemed hardly a place to enjoy the intellectual life. The Reischauers, however, had gotten on loan from the Museum of Modern Art some fine abstract expressionist paintings to hang on the dreary walls—one by an American, Kline, and another by a Japanese, Okada; Evey and I enjoyed the paintings much more than did our Japanese fellow guests, one of whom asked me whether I could say what it meant and confessed that he didn't like modern art.

The sort of contempt for mass culture and middle-class modernity characteristic of so many American and British intellectuals and artists has little counterpart among the Japanese. There are some sophisticated businessmen and bankers in Japan, counterparts of Americans like Walter Paepcke, but they are much rarer than with us; most Japanese businessmen appear to have an unshakable stuffiness and smugness. And among all the outpouring of intellectual, political, and literary weeklies and monthlies here, I've not found anything comparable to *The New Yorker* with its particular modishness and its witty campaign against mass culture. To be sure, "mass culture" and "mass society" are terms in common use among intellectuals and semi-intellectuals here, and the older generation and the traditionalists in the younger generation bewail the "Americanization" of Japan, much as Bernard Leach does. Yet, despite all the changes, Japanese good taste appears to run down to the lowest levels of the population if one thinks in terms of traditional courtesy, politeness, interest in nature and flowers, and so on. What appears to be missing is an *avant-garde* rejection of "good taste" as such and self-definition through rejection of the artistic and cultural products esteemed by middle brows and old-fashioned highbrows.

I keep recurring in my thinking to the tensions within educated Japanese between feelings of near total powerlessness on the world scene and feelings of grandiosity. Take, for instance, the struggle Professor Mori mentioned which has occurred over the proposed joint Japan-United States scientific cooperation which grew out of the Kennedy-Ikeda talks. A number of Japanese intellectuals and social scientists immediately jumped to the conclusion that these talks were to increase Japan's industrial war-making potential and were thus just another form of American imperialism and domination of Japan; they wanted to boycott the occasion and have the Japan Science Council refuse to participate. In contrast, the Japanese natural scientists, no less devoted to peace, seemed not to have had such misgivings; their attitude was that, if the talks turned into what the intellectuals feared, then it would be time to withdraw, but why not try it and see? No doubt also some of the left-wing intellectuals were eager to make propaganda out of the occasion and torpedo anything that involved closer ties between the Japanese Tories headed by Ikeda and the American "war-makers" headed by Kennedy.

At any rate, ten days ago matters were resolved by a compromise in which the Japan Science Council did decide to participate while making clear that it would withdraw if the conversations turned toward military objectives. The scientists themselves, as I've indicated, were not worried that they would be made the tools of American hidden purposes; and no doubt many of the social scientists who did claim to have this fear were disingenuous, perhaps not always consciously so, using the occasion to attack the Kennedy-Ikeda alliance and "American imperialism"—the latter term, relatively devoid of specific Leninist content, is often used to refer simply to American domination and overbearing power. Fear of that power among Japanese intellectuals and students sometimes seems to me displaced or extravagant, just as does their ever vigilant and certainly understandable fear of their own Right Wing, which in the very delicate balance of Japanese politics is stronger than it was last year, but whose goals remain modest in comparison with those of Barry Goldwater or the John Birch Society. But then I may miss latent dangers to which the Japanese Left is attuned.

Tokyo, November 21

Evey has a cold. I alone had breakfast this morning with two most perplexing young officials who had studied in the United States: Mr. Nagata, a counterintelligence official in the Self-Defense Forces, and Mr. Hirai, an instructor in industrial mobilization at the Japanese Defense College. The interview was of such interest that it lasted three hours rather than the planned hour. Hirai had been at the Fletcher School, while Nagata had attended a kind of national police academy run by the F.B.I. in Washington and as well had had discussions with counterintelligence officials there. Both spoke English well. Nagata looked elegant in tailored civilian clothes, while Hirai, as befitted his position, was dressed in the more standard academic garb of sweater and tweed coat. Nagata's father, a distinguished academician, had been opposed to fascist tendencies in pre-war Japan, and the son sees himself as carrying out his father's mission in opposing the present tendencies toward left-wing totalitarianism. He told me that the greatest influence on his life was reading William James in his senior-high-school philosophy course, where most of his fellows were reading, as is customary in Japan, Kant and Hegel and other German metaphysicians. The book of William James's that seemed to have impressed him most was *The Varieties of Religious Experience*, and he quoted James's discussion of his meeting with Annie Besant, which he had read many years ago.

He and Hirai had been colleagues at Kyoto University, graduating in 1953. They were in the university in 1950–51 when the Korean War led General MacArthur to order a section of the Japanese police to become a kind of internal security force. Both young men had been combatting the student Communists, who, they felt, were irresponsible and did not concern themselves with Japanese security or national interests, but wanted Japan to leave the Free World, first for a neutralist position and then in a second step to join the Communist bloc. They had gone in a rush of patriotic idealism to see if they could join these new forces, but there was no room for such volunteers; and one can imagine the surprise of the police officer, who was not accustomed to getting such recruits from the students in the major government universities, who were then, as they are now, largely "progressive."

While they were in the university, the two friends had organized a group of some forty students who were opposed both to the minority left-wing activists and to the majority of students, whom they thought apathetic, conformist, and concerned only with their own security and jobs. They pointed out what is obvious, namely, that they could have done much better financially and in every other way by entering a business concern or the Foreign Office or similar jobs to which Kyoto University graduates are "entitled." Indeed, Nagata said that they had lost most of their friends when they had taken this course, although some of them had been regained as the experience of the last ten years educated at least a few of the graduates concerning the "realities" of international existence and big-power diplomacy. Nagata thought that his father, were he still alive, would approve what he was doing. I wondered about this.

But to go back to the beginning: our discussion began with Hirai's asking me about American university students, saying that he had been disappointed in those he had met, that they seemed interested only in money and material things, and that the coeds were no better in this respect. Nagata said he had had less opportunity to meet American students, but had the same impression of them and had read surveys which indicated the prevailing desire of American students for comfort and their lack of political interest—criticisms rather like those they also made of most Japanese youth. I said that I was surprised that the students they had met were of this sort, since Nagata had seen students at Georgetown preparing for the Foreign Service and other such careers, and Hirai had met students at the Fletcher School also preparing for government careers. These men pointed out that some of the students were intending to go into oil companies and other businesses having international interests, and of course they realized there were many exceptions. It was relevant also that half the graduate students were married: this gave them an undue preoccupation with personal security. In answer to a comment of mine, they agreed that even the "apathetic" Japanese students were more political than most of the more political American students.

Both men were understandably eager to prove to me that they weren't Rightists, as indeed I had realized from the outset; they said several times that they weren't extremists. Nagata said that he was a pragmatist or empiricist in the tradition of William James, as against what he regarded as the lack of common sense, the lack of balance, characteristic of Japan as a whole—something he attributed to the Oriental lack of interest in religion as compared with the deep impact of Christianity in the West. Both men had read the article "The American Crisis" by Maccoby and me and were familiar with my views and indeed in many ways declared their sympathy for them: I kept thinking that these young Japanese who would be considered reactionaries by their friends and classmates were actually more detached in their view of the world than many Americans who consider themselves liberals. Hirai told me that he had been fortunate to have interviews, when he was in America, with many leading figures: Dean Acheson, Paul Nitze, Eleanor Roosevelt, Senators Fulbright and Mansfield, Walter Lippmann, Joseph Alsop, James Reston, Ed Murrow, and other journalists. I asked him which of these men impressed him most, and he said Ed Murrow, with whom he had had two three-hour talks of great intensity. He was very much impressed with Murrow's general knowledge of the world. He was also impressed by Eleanor Roosevelt—and again it is ironical to think of a man who, from the point of view of most Japanese intellectuals, represents the most reactionary elements in the country, declaring himself an admirer of Eleanor Roosevelt.

No, on further reflection, this is not a correct picture, but reflects the almost inevitable tendency on the part of Americans here, myself included, to try to comprehend complex political and cultural phenomena by relating them back to something recognizable from our own society. These young men, perhaps Hirai especially, feel that there were values in pre-war Japan that are worth preserving. They see their country as having completely overturned these values and at the same time as being divided in a bitter controversy that hovers near the brink of civil war. They feel an overpowering sense of duty and national spirit—a national spirit which is not that of the right-wing assassins but no doubt wants to restore some of the pre-war sense of "national purpose." (A friend told me later that Nagata's father was not only anti-war but a socialist, and she doubted that he would approve the son's present views. Mr. Jones, a very intelligent man in the British Embassy here, said that Hirai's father or family considered themselves as being in the samurai tradition and that the son was trying in his own way to live up to and perhaps in some respects to reawaken that tradition.) The sense of the past which haunts these two men, their feeling of personal responsibility for Japan, and their moral righteousness reminded me of types in the United States who are patrician nationalists and at the same time domestic civil libertarians. But Japan has largely lacked a tradition that was at once elitist and libertarian. Thus the attitudes of these two men in the Japanese setting could align them with the Right in spite of themselves, for want of other allies.

I said to Nagata that I knew the police were unpopular in Japan. He said that their unpopularity in Japan was different from that in America, because in the United States the police felt ashamed of their low incomes and resentful of those of greater income, but proud of their might and physical power; whereas in Japan, although the police are very poorly paid, this did not trouble them, but their lack of education did, as well as the low regard in which they are held. In fact, police officers are ambivalent toward the few recruits who have been educated at the major government universities; for while they are grateful that a person of high intellectual rank has joined their deprecated group, they are also afraid that such a man would ride a faster escalator than they. (The word "escalator" comes up again and again in conversation, just as does the term "organization man.") And of course, some graduates of leading universities have entered the police and Self-Defense Forces simply to make a career and without any idealism. Later, as I was walking the two men to the bus stop, Nagata said that the police and counterintelligence officers found it difficult to marry: the girls had seen too many television shows and had both a low opinion of this kind of work and a low opinion of a man's chances for survival in it; the girls didn't want to become widows too soon. In any event, his life left him no time to look for a bride. It turned out that Hirai was married and that his wife had also gone to Kyoto University and was hoping to become a physician; they have one child, and it was evidently becoming difficult to work out the two careers. Was it an arranged marriage? Hirai said no, she was a girl he had known in secondary school, and his family had been strongly opposed to the marriage—I got the sense that this may have been in part because she was a career girl.

I asked both men how they would have been spending their morning if they had not been talking with me. Nagata said he would probably have been involved in some kind of anti-Communist work—I did not press him. He did say that he felt cramped by the rules and regulations of his agency and that he was disappointed at the present stage of his career. Some day he would want to become a journalist or a social critic, but now he feared no one would listen to him. Hirai is better off in this respect: he lectures on economics and has written a good deal, and he talks to student groups on foreign policy. I asked if he was heckled and he said often, but that sometimes he had a responsive audience.

At the time of the *demo* last year, both men had sent a letter to the several thousand graduates of Kyoto University (the undergraduates had taken an active part in the demonstrations), arguing against the *demo* and saying that Japan had a responsibility to defend itself and that if it was not allied to the United States and the Free World, it would be first neutral and then become part of the Communist bloc. The writers asked the recipients for comments and response and about 1,000 people answered, the vast majority of whom—some 90 per cent, perhaps—were more or less sympathetic; the antagonists, of course, did not usually answer. I asked if most of the sympathetic responses came from older people, and the young men laughed and said they did; in 80 per cent of the cases the responses came from people forty years old or more, and only a few were young. They were not interested in the old. But they wrote again to the young men who responded and have organized a kind of discussion group which meets twice a month and has people come in and talk about international politics—most recently, speakers on Communist China. I asked whether they assigned any readings and Nagata said no, the people who attended were young business or professional people who simply had no time to read, just as he himself had very little time. Did they meet in a restaurant? The question amused them, for that would take money. They said that many business firms would be glad to pay the expenses of the group, but of course they didn't want that and subscribed their own expenses, so that they met here and there where they could, someone's office or conference room, each time in a different place. It was a real problem.

Hirai said with great forcefulness that the students who demonstrated were irresponsible in taking no thought for Japan's position in a world that was still necessarily a world of big-power politics and diplomacy. The idea of a neutral Japan was a nice idea, but a dream that could only be realized in a world that didn't exist. And the same students who were angrily protesting any measures by Japan to act as a nation among the nations would in a few years have abandoned politics and be among the "salaried men." (The "salary man" is another of the common phrases—an image of the petty bourgeois that one will become.) I asked him who is the foe against whom Japan should arm itself, and he said the continent, i.e., China, or some eventuality like the Korean War. At the time of the Korean War, he felt, had the Communists in Japan had stronger leadership they might have provoked a great deal of trouble and even a revolution. I said I thought the Japanese Communists were exceedingly weak and this seemed most unlikely to me. Nagata replied that the Japanese were a weak people, always waiting to see who was the stronger power, lacking in principles and in that sense "Oriental" and therefore readily led by a small minority, just as they had been led by a small minority into the war policy of the 1930's. I gained the impression that for him and perhaps also for Hirai the strengthening of the police and the Army was largely for internal purposes.

Though I knew that he might be reluctant to answer, I asked Hirai whether he thought Japan should have nuclear weapons. He said it was an exceedingly delicate as well as a difficult question. At the present time, he was against it. It would divide the nation even more than it was already divided; and he said over and over that Japan was a split nation, divided by a terrible chasm between Right and Left and therefore not really a nation. (I continue to find it curious how both the Right and the Left in Japan, and of course the Center, bemoan the lack of consensus and seem often to resent politics itself.) Suppose, I asked, the Chinese become a nuclear power, what should Japan's policy be then? Then, he said, Japan should also get nuclear weapons. He thought, however, that here there would be a tremendous and terrible ferment in the country: some would want to give in at once to China, while others would want nuclear weapons in self-defense against China. I said I didn't think nuclear weapons really were a defensive weapon, and Hirai was inclined to agree with that—he is obviously steeped in arms-control thinking.

He referred again to "The American Crisis" article and asked what I thought were the real chances for disengagement in Central Europe. He listened attentively while I dwelt on both the possibilities and the difficulties. He also asked what I thought about American shelter building—he seemed to regard this as both cowardly and crazy and found it difficult to understand. He said that if nuclear weapons were not really weapons, then fall-out shelters were not really shelters. Why was Kennedy backing them?

Referring to my article with Maccoby, Nagata asked why Khrushchev was acting so belligerently vis-à-vis Berlin if he was really in favor of peaceful coexistence. I went into some detail in answering and again he listened with great attentiveness—although what that means in this polite culture among these exceedingly intelligent men is hard to say. Hirai asked whether Communism was still not a religion for Khrushchev, as it was for the Chinese and for many Japanese Communists, and therefore whether "peaceful coexistence" didn't really mean that Khrushchev in a disarmed world would use his other well-known means of propaganda and subversion to take over the globe. I explained why I thought that this was not likely as long as America remained confident.

Earlier, Nagata had told me about an article he'd written at the time of the Hungarian uprising for one of the leading intellectual monthlies, entitled why he wouldn't want to be a policeman in Hungary: the article excited enormous criticism. He began by showing in the article how Japan and Hungary had been fascist countries allied with the Nazis under Admiral Horthy in one case and General Tojo in the other, and how both countries had lost the war and been occupied and how both occupations had been hard, but the Soviet one much harder, so that policemen in Budapest were having to shoot down their fellows while policemen in Japan were living in a moderately democratic society. I myself can well imagine how unpopular such a perspective was at the time among the many people here who have no real experience of Soviet despotism and who even now are romantic about the Communist countries, regarding criticisms of them as American propaganda. While the Japanese have suffered from the Russians, they have suffered neither from a strong domestic Communist Party nor from international Communism as such.

Both men are down on Japanese youth, seeing them as petty, job-centered conformists, not interested in large questions and irresponsible about the national future. They both have a strong ascetic streak, typified by Hirai's comment on all the trashy literature imported from America and the decay of values among the Japanese. Both young men, like so many students on the Left, see themselves as a potential elite whose chance may come some day. Yet in personal style they are not fanatical. At least in talking with me, they seemed eager to open rather than close channels of communication. They were grateful that I had spent so much time with them, calling their offices to explain that they would be late.

Tokyo, November 22

This evening there was a formal dinner of the Foreign Relations Society at International House at which I was the guest speaker. These Western-style formal dinners have a stiffness about them that is formidable. There was a seating plan at the door, most helpful to me in learning the names of the guests. When we were finally seated, I was on the right of Professor Kawasaki, chairman of the Committee for Intellectual Interchange that has sponsored my visit, and on my other side was Mr. Jugaku, formerly Ambassador to Great Britain; nearby was another ambassador who had an independent reputation as a political scientist. I draw on a tiny sample, but I have the impression that the Japanese who have been in the United States tend to be more talkative than those who have been in Great Britain or India or other parts of the Empire under British rule. I learned, though not from him, that Jugaku is a courageous man who had resigned as Ambassador rather than carry out the policy of the Kishi government, of which he disapproved—and resignations of this sort are perhaps even more rare in Japan than with us.

Like others at the table, Jugaku was looking forward to the visit of Princess Alexandra, hoping that she would set a good example for the Japanese imperial family. How is that? I asked. Well, she's more active than our Princess Michiko, he said. Actually, Princess Michiko is extremely active. She is in the papers every day like a movie celebrity. I guess what he may have meant is that he admired the combination of reserve and outgoingness in the British Princess—his feeling that somehow she combined the common touch with the royal air and managed her public relations admirably. Yet I felt it strange that this "old liberal," a devoted believer in parliamentary government, should be so concerned with the imperial family and with the niceties of its behavior.

At the end of the dinner I gave a talk entitled "Internal Pressures on American Foreign Policy," after which there was some lively discussion. One of the young men who attended this dinner in order to translate any questions (though my address was to be in English without translation—a compliment to all concerned) said that people enjoyed hearing English spoken on such an occasion and being at such an occasion even if they only understood half of it. This came up when I asked him why some of the young political scientists had not been at the lecture, for instance, specialists in international affairs at Tokyo University. He said they had been invited but they found the sociability of such an affair, the cocktails beforehand and the stiff dinner afterward, completely uncongenial. I can well understand that—it is another reminder of the many ways in which Japanese society fascinates Evey and me as tourists even while we are aware how oppressive and often miserable it is for the inhabitants. The very dullness of a dinner that would be infuriating and frustrating in America is "fieldwork" here.

Gamagori, November 23–24

Today is a national holiday and I've come down from Tokyo to the small town of Gamagori with Yamazaki and Yoshida for a long-planned "conference without subject matter" with Murata and Suzuki. Gamagori began as a fishing village, I was told, and is just a little too far from Nagoya for commuting, but its superb small hotel is not too far for businessmen's parties and it is a somewhat popular swimming resort in the summer. Now it is out of season and the hotel, built in pagoda-Victorian style with an antique charm, has a few Japanese families in it but is otherwise quiet.

On the way down, a trip of over four hours, I talked much of the time with Yoshida, a vibrant and interesting person with whom I've come to feel a great kinship. We talked about things small and great.

Among the small: I commented that Japanese restaurants were much more expensive than "Western" ones, and I asked why, when there were weddings, the restaurant chosen seemed almost invariably to be Western-style. He said that businessmen often have a chance to eat Western-style on their expense accounts, but their wives seldom do. A wedding is a rare occasion when the wives do go out and have a chance to see something they don't see every day; thus, they want Western food. One reason why downtown Tokyo restaurants are expensive is that land costs are so terrific, possibly the highest in the world.

Yoshida later on began to talk about his own life. He said that his years in America had made it possible for him to be interested in all sorts and conditions of life among the Japanese. Before that as the son of a distinguished professor and liberal political leader, he had confined himself to the company of intellectuals. But in America he had worked as a bricklayer, dishwasher, and roofer; he had wandered about in the ethnically mixed slums of Chicago and in the Deep South, where he would ask policemen whether he should use the white or colored toilets—the embarrassed policemen would tell him to use the white ones or to take his choice; he had found that he could talk to church ladies in small Illinois towns. After all this, he had returned to Japan with a much wider interest in his own people.

Yoshida was obviously an unusual and adventurous person even before he came to the United States. He told me an eloquent story of his first encounter with an American. He was sixteen years old or maybe a little older, and he ventured out on the street on the first day of the Occupation when other Japanese, filled with terrible tales of rape and cruelty to be expected, fled or remained indoors. He came on three American GI's who were entering a store where they wanted to buy some souvenirs and got into an altercation with the store owner. Yoshida decided to go in and interpret, explaining that the Americans didn't want to rob but to pay. One of the GI's was grateful and gave him $1.50. Yoshida refused it, saying that he had done this out of courtesy and not for money. The man insisted, however, that he take it—the first American money he'd ever earned. A month later this same GI, a Jewish boy from St. Louis, arrived at Yoshida's house with a huge load of canned goods, books, and odds and ends, which he donated, saying that he was leaving and had no further use for any of these. Yoshida asked how he had found him, and the GI said that he had had his name and then had spent a great deal of time at the university tracking him down. Years later Yoshida came to the University of Illinois and wrote that he would like to call on his first American friend. When Yoshida finally did get to St. Louis, the young man explained that he couldn't at that moment, for family reasons, put him up but Yoshida should stay with his former schoolteacher. The teacher told Yoshida that his friend actually was unemployed and had no money, but was ashamed of this, and hence had arranged for the schoolteacher to give a party for Yoshida—all of which moved Yoshida very much and gave him a picture of Americans which he couldn't forget even when he was angry with Americans on political grounds.

He also spoke of rather different experiences with the good church ladies of the Middle West to whose dinners he went to make speeches that would help raise money for missionary activities and student exchange vis-à-vis Japan. He would be asked to talk about what America can do for Japan or what Japan needs from America, and he would find this embarrassing and humiliating; he knew that the ladies did not want to be patronizing; yet he felt they were really racist at heart, not wanting to be told that Japan at this point needed very little from America and could quite well take care of itself,, thank you. He didn't have the courage to say this and spoke of the need for scholarships and material aid and so on. It was hard to be antagonistic toward these goodhearted ladies, and yet it was hard also not to resent their provincialism.

When he went South, he said, his friends at the university warned him against this and said he would be subjected to repeated incidents, but he never was. He was well treated by whites and Negroes alike. (I myself think this may partly be because he is attractive, forthright, and assertive—he doesn't look like somebody to be pushed around.) He said, as other Japanese have, that in the Deep South Negroes would stop their cars and let him pass in his car as if he were a white man—and indeed he was culturally a white man, in the South.

But he had not always been assertive. He said his character had been changed by his American experience. At first he had been miserable, clustering with Japanese and other foreign students. The latter, oriented toward the big-shots, tried to see the boss professors, who had no time for them. Yoshida decided to associate with the younger professors, who had grievances against the system just as he did—that is how he met younger faculty, with whom he formed a close association, and as a result he began to feel at home in America and at home with himself.

As I reflect on this and other conversations with some of the younger Japanese intellectuals and students, I'm struck by their frankness and lack of reserve, which contrasts so strongly with the immense reserve of many in the older generation. I've been at dinners where Japanese seated alongside and opposite each other go through a whole meal eating and staring, without saying a word, looking straight ahead. They do this in their cars as I see them being driven—I can't imagine them chatting with their chauffeurs.

Evey, who had been counted on to take notes on our Gamagori discussions, was ill and couldn't come with us. I only began to take notes in a desultory way after a while and then could do so only at intervals of translation. Even then I hesitated, because I felt it wasn't polite not to attend to people, although I didn't know what they were saying. Also, there were many times when we talked lingering over meals as well as walking outside, and of course there are no notes on that. Still, I'll do my best to reconstruct some of what was said, on the basis of the notes I do have.

The participants were Yamazaki, Yoshida, Murata, and Suzuki. Yoshida and Murata took turns translating, with the latter doing more and more of it, in part because he could do so with apparent ease: he never took notes and yet without seeming to strain himself could unreel long and complicated statements in either direction. Our first discussion started around four in the afternoon and lasted till nearly eleven, with a break for supper; the next day we met around ten and talked for nearly five hours, with three of us then continuing on the train to Tokyo.

My first notes concern the inbred nature of Japanese academic life. Ninety-eight per cent of the Tokyo University faculty are Tokyo University graduates, and the proportion at Kyoto University is almost as high. More than 90 per cent of the academics listed in *Who's Who* are graduates of these two major universities. There is probably less mobility in academic life than in any other area, although the government bureaus which recruit from the universities are almost as inbred. There is a little more mobility in industry but less than there was before the war. As a number of people have remarked to me, for about five years after World War II there was a great upheaval in academic life, since many of the older faculty members were purged. New places were created and many institutions expanded. This was facilitated by the democratization brought about through the examinations. But by now this yeasty period is over. Faculties complain about the Ministry of Education as a source of restraint on innovation, but Suzuki pointed out that even innovations often survive because of the Ministry's inertia. In the same way, the Ministry has slowed down the aim of some of the big corporations to turn university departments into institutes for training technicians. All this was an illustration of Suzuki's general sociological observation that any institution which survives must serve some purpose.

We had no assigned topics—that was just the point—although several of us had thought of various themes we wanted to discuss; my notes show that we wandered about a great deal. But one of the perennial themes concerned the sources of independence in the stifling clubbiness of Japanese organizational life. I said that I thought private property could be a resource for independence and was told that about five members of the Liberal Party (including a former Prime Minister, Yoshida) who had independent incomes were quite independent in their views—one of them, for instance, thought North Korea should take over the whole of Korea.

Another theme I kept raising was where sources of entrepreneurship were to be found in contemporary Japan, and how pressures for economic rationalization could be effective in a society marked by such powerful networks. My colleagues explained that big business in Japan is probably no more hidebound than in Great Britain. They said that when big business went into Asia before the war, it needed political and Army protection, and indeed it needed government support all during the Meiji period. Small business always depended on its immediate geographic area; its market area was, so to speak, given. Thus, little sales effort was required.

Returning to academic life, Suzuki described student culture as a zoo in which the animals were tame and were not taken seriously; being "progressive" on campus is the conservative thing to do, as well as ineffectual. Yoshida denied this, saying that the student activities have some effect and students express themselves outrageously because they realize only some of what they say will be effective. Each age grade has its permitted "excesses" as part of its culture. He added that the leaders of the Left are scared of the Ministry of Education but the latter is scared of the lions of the Left.

What he was getting at is the set of latent relationships between apparently opposed forces in Japanese political culture. He went on to describe the go-between as one of the "wisdoms of Japan" in three sensitive areas: money, sex, and politics. In the latter it is characteristic of Japanese to admire the "great guy" who, without having any ideas of his own, brings people together. "Right" and "Left" in Japan are both anxious, beneath the labels taken from the West, to assure Japanese survival in whatever is the international situation of the moment. But pressure from abroad makes the internal situation very rigid and hard. Politics is seen as dirty and is left to dirty people. Yet there is a wish for both village and national unanimity.

The press was another theme that kept coming up. It expanded rapidly in the 1920's with the growth of the working class and the literate salary man. Now it has become a cautious business and quite bureaucratic. *Mainichi*, though its management is more reactionary than that of *Asahi*, is smaller and less bureaucratized; thus, there is more room for liberal sections (e.g., the art, science, education, or women's sections).

I mentioned that I'd been struck by the emphasis on definitions in my discussions with some of the political scientists, and Yamazaki pointed out that he had noticed that when I was asked to define autonomy all the students took out their notebooks. People are still asking, "What is sociology?" Definitions have a part to play in maintaining people's academic territories and preventing trespass.

I mentioned people in lectures wearing doctors' masks over their noses and mouths and that pretty girls sometimes wore them. Did they lack vanity? Apparently the custom began in the 1920's and is part of the medical orientation of the Japanese. I was told that thirty or forty times more vitamins and injections are administered in Japan than in Great Britain. Obedience to modern science is overwhelming. At the same time, girls may think it "charming" to be as modern as all this. The masks worn out of doors are to prevent dust and smog from getting in, but those worn indoors could be either considerateness to protect others from one's cold or hypochondria to save oneself from others' colds.

I brought up the question of the great authority that print has over the Japanese and asked whether print has the authority of a foreign power and whether orientation toward print coming from a central distributing point such as Tokyo was analogous to the general Japanese orientation to power outside one's own locality. I said that it seemed to me that there was relatively little cynicism among the Japanese, and a docility to ideology and to properly global questions—in a way, a kind of innocence about print; and that, among other reasons for the docility of men as well as women to print, there seemed to be less fear of homosexuality among Japanese men, or at least no association in people's minds of being bookish with not being virile.

Murata said that in the seventeenth century among the samurai class there was a great cult of virility, and, by the same token, of homosexuality. This was allowed to the samurai. Later, when the samurai culture was softened by contact with the merchant culture, the permission for homosexuality disappeared. Suzuki, who is fond of biological explanations, said that the Mongolian races don't differentiate sexes as the Caucasian races do: the former wear similar clothes and look alike. He felt this might be connected with the custom of mixed bathing. In Southeast Asia, where men and women dress alike, it is especially hard to tell the men from the women. In contemporary Japan, he suggested, prostitutes had the function of permitting the wife to remain in her own protected culture. (Not only are his explanations often biological, but they are always functional, so that at one point I kidded him and asked if there was anything at all in Japanese life of which he was critical, since he could always find a function for it.)

From these matters we moved to a discussion of the Japanese attitude toward China. It was suggested that the relation of China and Japan was similar to that of the United States and Great Britain. Britain is ambivalent toward the United States, for we as the younger brother are now the senior, and the British, who can be cool everywhere else in the world, get hysterical vis-à-vis the United States. Now the Japanese Left is glad that the older brother, who after the Meiji Restoration became "younger," is once more catching up—but will grow hysterical and even militarist if China gets the bomb or becomes really strong and aggressive in foreign policy. The sensitivity about China in Japan is enormous and will increase when that time comes. Japan now feels like an old man vis-à-vis a young one: its pride in China's development is mixed with fear and even defeatism.

Yoshida continued to emphasize the "romantic defeatism," as he called it, of Britain and Japan, both of which he regarded as having been defeated in the war. Britain was beaten in fact by the Japanese in the Pacific and by the Germans, although later this defeat was reversed by American aid. Since the United States was not beaten, it cannot understand this romantic defeatism. While Japan waits for China to become mature, it would be well if Japan could acquire confidence on the basis of non-industrial, non-power values, because the balance of power will eventually tilt toward China. But Yoshida thought that once the Chinese got nuclear weapons Japan would seek self-confidence in rearmament, not in stress on non-power values—rearmament used for internal purposes more than for any actual usefulness vis-à-vis China. Again, the Japanese concern for survival, whatever the international climate, was emphasized, underneath the labels applied to international conflict by both the Right and the Left.

We discussed the elements of romanticism in the pre-war acceptance by some Leftists in Japan of the Greater East Asia Co-prosperity Sphere—a sort of international national socialism, I suggested. Some Leftists were taken in by the regime's invasion of China, in terms of what we ourselves would call white-man's-burden thinking; thus they became the dupes of the "realism" of the Rightists.

The next day we continued, beginning with a question which has run through many of our discussions, namely, Japanese curiosity—an aspect of the receptiveness that made the Meiji Restoration and the post-war developments possible. This is a curiosity, as Murata pointed out, about things as they are and people as they are. It takes the form of endless travel, of formal tours, of casual and continuous picture taking. It is a very different relationship toward reality than that of the Arab or the Western world. There is no veil or barrier between man and man, no feeling that a photograph is an invasion of privacy. Reality is there to be copied, and oneself is there to be copied. Murata agreed with me that the relative absence of mirrors in Japan is partly an absence of the sort of vanity which separates one from reality (though this is puzzling in the light of the elaborate get-up of women on ceremonial occasions or their fear to go out if they haven't a new kimono—but this may be status and not a feeling about the reality of how one looks).

The first ambassador of Japan to America was a samurai who kept a diary and made sketches of all that he observed; for instance, of bathrooms, or of anything else that was new. For a Christian, only eternity matters and not the moment, whereas what counts in Japan is the moment. This is why snapshots are omnipresent: it is not because of the Japanese fondness for gadgets but rather because the moment is important: the snapshot is a kind of visual haiku which itself is a poetic response to a tree or a moment of existence. Suzuki pointed out that in the Moslem and Christian worlds the stars and planets are seen as looking down on us and passing judgment, but in the East they are seen as part of us (though this is no longer true in China).

Referring again to mirrors, I suggested that in the West I am the only one who is permitted to look at myself with the penetrating scrutiny of a mirror, whereas in Japan there is no such individuation: everyone can look, and it is more collective. Yoshida added that Confucian man is instructed to reflect on himself three times a day; this is not the sort of introspection characteristic of the West, but rather to see whether one is living up to the norms—certainly not whether I myself exist, or a questioning of what I want. Yamazaki added that in America mirrors are part of our mixture of narcissism and individualism: one looks to see who *he* is; whereas in Japan society is the mirror of the individual, and he exists only in the reflection of his actions on others.

Yoshida made another comparison between America and Japan; namely, that every activity in Japan is done with a perfectionist's seriousness. If people take up social dancing, they study the theory and practice of it and become really adept, as compared with a far more casual pattern in America, where people are satisfied to perform passably. The same is true of baseball: he doubted whether there were many adult fans of baseball in the United States who are as well informed on batting averages and the temperaments of the different players as the fans in Japan. And even in hi-fi he felt there was less amateurism and more professionalism among the Japanese addicts. Yamazaki added that when Japanese did anything it wasn't simply a practical skill such as do-it-yourself to save paying a plumber or carpenter: it was a pleasure in bodily skill and a belief in continuing education. At this point there was a good deal of teasing of Suzuki for making chairs which are "too practical"; highbrows feel he is too professional and not sufficiently amateur, that he has crossed the line; the tradition had been that of the Chinese gentry and of the samurai, who were learned but "impractical" men who didn't know how to make a *real* chair, despite their great skill and gifts.

All this led into a more general discussion of the division of labor. Yoshida said that when he read Durkheim and then went to America and discovered American do-it-yourself, he thought at first that this was a kind of degeneration, that people weren't sufficiently specialized and were slopping over into other people's territory. It would be all right to grow chrysanthemums and other "impractical" things, but for a gentleman to make a chair simply to save money—that seemed a violation of Durkheimian or Chinese norms. It is in this spirit that Suzuki's violation of the division of labor by making real chairs has been criticized. Still, the division is not nearly so rigid as in the Indian caste system or in feudal estates, while it is somewhat less fluid and open than the class system of the West.

Suzuki said that in the pre-Tokugawa period the samurai were really occupied with fighting and thus only valor was valued. But in the stable, relatively peaceable Tokugawa period, they became dilettantes. Valor was still esteemed, but one could also write haiku poetry and absorb some of the softnesses of the merchant culture. He suggested that their own particular group possesses this Tokugawa samurai spirit, whereas most academicians have the earlier spirit of valor and territoriality. Before World War II, indeed, it was thought that a professor should have a territory not only in terms of his academic specialty but also in terms of his extracurricular connections: he should, for instance, write only for a single paper, whereas today this group and many others were more free-roving.

Yamazaki tried to relate this to the traditional family system of Japan, pointing out that there were in fact two family systems. One was patriarchal, typical for the upper class, for the boss, for the Tokyo University professor, or for the unanimous community obeying a distant center of power in the way that a less eminent university would bow to Todai; an eminent man at such a university would not be a specialist but would be a boss in the familistic pattern. The other family system was more equalitarian—I gathered that there were regional as well as class differences here. In the frontier community of Hokkaido, the northernmost island, this latter system would be more in evidence.

Murata, recurring to the theme of the admired dilettante, said that the *interi* (intellectuals) had been supposed to be the great fools. It was said of a distinguished professor that he didn't know that the Russo-Japanese War had taken place. At the same time, the intellectual is a kind of boss or patron who must know all and explain all. When recently a shipwreck occurred off the coast of Korea, a leading intellectual was interviewed, although it was obvious that nobody could know why this had happened. Still, he had to give a reason. The intellectual is an omnicompetent authority; in this the intellectuals follow the (Confucian) samurai tradition, for the samurai were wise men *and* governors. Today the "man of culture" is similarly looked up to.

Suzuki said half-jokingly that he was surprised to find so much disagreement among us, so many "theories." He had been in India and he thought this kind of argumentativeness typical of the Indian but not of the Japanese. (India seems "Western" to many Japanese. In some ways the Japanese seem to feel closer to England than they do to

India, and such pan-Asian feeling as there is would seem to apply only to East and Southeast Asia.)

Yoshida brought up a survey of student examination scores over a period of eight years which gave a ranking of students in the different fields. The science students are at the top, with scores twice as high as students in agriculture and education; those in technology are just below science, medicine under them, then economics, law (including political science), followed by liberal arts and preceding agriculture and education. The science students are seeking pure science and those in literature also look for purity, not for vocational training. I asked Murata why one of his very good students had gone into an insurance company rather than into research or teaching. He said that this student had started in the field of education, so that to rise as high as business was an achievement for him. He joined the insurance company because the hours were from nine to four and the pay was good, so he could lead an intellectual life outside of work. For the women, education is the frontier field comparable to science or technology for the men; this is one reason why they find the school-teacher-union meetings in which they are supposed to think of themselves as proletarians stupid and annoying. (Yoshida, who hates cant, has been a consultant to the Teachers Union and has pointed out that teachers are not really workers but salaried people; the old union members get furious with this.)

We then got into a discussion of Japanese nationalism. I said I'd seen hardly any flags, and it was pointed out that right down through the Meiji period, loyalty often remained to the Tokugawa fief, not to the Emperor. Yamazaki said that national feeling was necessary for tax and military purposes, hence the development of a *kokutai* spirit to enable people to respond to their internal obligations and in that way to their international ones (Yamazaki was clearly understating the almost spiritual meaning of *kokutai*). Yet because Japan is not nationalistic it can't be internationalist either; rather, the Japanese concern for peace is universalistic. Opposition to the Security Treaty was based on an "existential" feeling concerning a peaceable culture, rather than on concern with Japan's position as a nation among other nations. Here, as elsewhere, the attitude is fundamentally anti-political or unpolitical.

Murata pointed out that before the Meiji Restoration a single Japanese nation was already present in the sense of a single market, a single tongue, and a single culture; hence there was no need to invent the fiction of a nation, as in Europe, but rather to discover what was already there and bring it to consciousness. Suzuki added that European nationalism was the creation of the middle class, but that there was no such middle class in Japan seeking a locus for ideology. Correspondingly, the Japanese, when they decided to imitate European nationalism, first imported French textbooks. Then, realizing that these were not applicable and appropriate, they turned back to Confucian, then to Prussian, and finally to American ones. And now, only at the very end, back to Japanese. Benjamin Franklin, George Washington, and Abraham Lincoln are the heroes of Japanese ethics, with such maxims as respecting oneself and respecting others. The Imperial Rescript on Education and public education in ethics were used to try to inculcate these "Western" qualities. (There has been a move to try to restore the teaching of ethics in the schools and colleges by those who feel that under the slogans of democracy and freedom the young have become entirely too relativistic and amoral. But all such efforts are resisted by the Left, which sees them as part of a drive to restore a militaristic pre-war nationalism and to substitute national for class feeling.)

All this led into a discussion of the meaning of "public" in Japan. Prior to Meiji, towns had a sense of public spirit and there would be efforts to keep them clean or to clean them up. But later—to some degree even before the Meiji Restoration—individualism flourished, with its maxim "Do what you want," and its implication: don't bother with anything outside. As Yoshida put it, the place where one wears shoes is not to be kept clean, whether it is the street or an office building or a university campus or the mayor's office; only when one is on *tatami*, only where one removes shoes, does one act as a civic-minded Westerner would in a "public" place. This is one aspect of the discrepancy many have observed between the intransigent concern for beauty and cleanliness inside and the complete unconcern outside. And of course, as so many Japanese Christians have complained, there is not a very great sense in Japan of personal responsibility, which is also related to the lack of sense of the individual, or individuality. Public buildings which are in the Western style and where people wear shoes are just *efficient*: they are there not for beauty but for function and hence nobody worries if they get dirty. Suzuki added that the Westernizing Meiji bureaucrats, in cooperation with hicks coming to town without a sense of beauty, destroyed what there had been in Japan of "public" beauty and built Tokyo into an ugly city. (This seemed to be a rare case where Suzuki didn't think everything was functional and for the best!) Yoshida added that Kyoto and even more Kanazawa are clean cities, because they depend on a traditional merchant culture which preceded Westernization.

It occurred to me that the play *Our Town* could hardly be understood in Japan, for the feeling hardly exists, just as there is not a feeling for "our family" in the same sentimental way: family and town were there before us, we cannot change them, the boss of each is fixed. Murata added that this was rather like the feeling the citizens of New York or Los Angeles have that they can't change these cities. I suggested that the current preoccupation in the United States with "national purpose" was an effort to fill the vacuum of all the "our towns" which were no longer thought to be ours; indeed, the play is nostalgic. With the coming of heightened mobility and the loss of a feeling for one's own state, only the nation offers the possibility of being imbued with meaningful purpose.

Yamazaki added that in the United States a town is a contract; that is, it is created by a social contract: it is we who decide, we who consent, we who create our town—we can take it down again. In Japan it is given. Suzuki said that in Japan the family imitates the village community. It is a natural community, not something created, like the United Nations.

I tried to relate what had been said somehow to the political styles exhibited in the Tokyo University festival, pointing out that there was emphasis there only on the atomic powers, not on Adenauer or Mao, who might be more important, even in terms of possible nuclear war. Yamazaki said that Japanese students had a kind of apolitical politics, interested in preventing the invasion of their private lives by politics. Hence they concentrate on the atomic powers that can immediately invade them. They don't see Mao or Adenauer lurking behind the atomic powers. In private life they don't dare see conflict around them, but without conflict, one cannot have a compromise: it is this that helps give them so idealistic and global a cast. He connected this with the admiration previously referred to for the "great guys" who pour oil on potential conflict and repress it. (This puzzled me because the students appear to have contempt for politics, for compromise, for maneuver and manipulation.)

Yoshida pointed out that despite Hungary and Khrushchev's condemnation of Stalin, many Japanese remain romantic about the Soviet Union. After all, Eastern Europe still lives better than most of the Far East. And while Eastern Europe's conflicts are not understood, Sweezy's discussion of its economic progress is much admired. This occurs in part because there is no fear of the Soviet Union or grasp of what is happening in Eastern Europe or what kind of a regime Ulbricht has. And corresponding to the lack of appreciation for what Ulbricht stands for, there is also no sense of Adenauer.

This is part of a more general pattern: the Japanese think only of the big powers: they look up and not down. In all of Japan there are very few courses on Korea, and in all of Japan possibly two journalists know anything about Korea. No one feels he can make a career or even a living in studying small powers. This is partly due to the teaching of geography: Europe is seen as a single mass (much, it seems to me, the way Central and South America are seen from the United States). There is no sense of Hungary's being different from Germany.

About Germany there is a very rosy view due to admiration for its recovery after the war, which was believed until just this year to have been greater than that of Japan. In fact, there has been a general tendency to suppose that both Soviet and German growth are greater than Japanese growth. Suzuki said this kind of deference was characteristic of the school of thought of the University of Tokyo and not of the "Suzuki school."

Yoshida said that he invites Zengakuren leaders to talk to his students. I asked how he justified this. He said that this was not uncommon, but many instructors invited in these leaders as part of the latter's propaganda, whereas he did it as part of the students' "general education." He sees the Zengakuren leaders as rejecting Khrushchev, Mao, and all world leaders, with the implication that only the Zengakuren can save the world; and he sees this grandiosity as analogous to pre-war right-wing nationalism, although of course this is the last thing the Zengakuren would admit. When the student leaders get going this way, he sometimes punctures the balloon by asking them what language they will talk in the world arena—they have no answer for this and are forced to laugh. The bubble has burst.

I asked if any students in his classes—engineers, for example—objected to the Zengakuren activists coming in. He said there was no objection but there were often arguments on factual matters. Is the Soviet Union a paradise? What will Japan under Communism be like? The Zengakuren leaders respond very honestly to these questions: "We don't know what Japanese Communism will be like; it may be bad and oppressive—but for now I am a member of the Communist Party. If I found a better system, I would change." (Actually most members of the Zengakuren are not Communist and most of the leaders have split off from the Communist Party, as Yoshida had already mentioned.)

An implication of which I'm not so certain in all this was that some older Tokyo University professors (but not the very oldest conservative group) were more sympathetic or less skeptical toward the Zengakuren and saw the issue as political rather than pedagogic. This middle group, which felt oppressed if not actually persecuted during the war and pre-war periods, sees Japan as enduring a rightist dictatorship during the 1930's not fundamentally different from Nazism; it speaks of the hegemony of Japanese monopoly capitalism; it sees this entity linked today to its American counterpart, with the scarcely concealed aim of restoring right-wing hegemony. The group at Gamagori, though there are differences among them, feel more secure and less anxious about Japan both domestically and internationally. Though fond of America and oriented to American culture, high, middle, and low, they are not necessarily "pro-American" in foreign policy. Indeed, as their self-confidence is also translated into confidence concerning Japan, they could foresee their country pursuing a more independent foreign policy. And they feel secure enough to interest themselves in the smaller and less developed countries of Asia—and in India and Pakistan as well—rather than hunting for a big-power model, either in the West or in the Communist bloc.

Yoshida hoped I would meet his friend Ohashi, the free-lance writer who was described as the John Gunther of Japan but a more analytical man. In describing his recent round-the-world trip, Ohashi wrote that the Soviet Union loves circuses because these are really despotic and acrobats are not human: the Nazis liked circuses, too. Ohashi regards Japanese social scientists as weak on the theoretical side—a surprising comment in view of their often highly theoretical pronouncements; what he seems to mean is that they don't have relevant theories. During the war he was a movie producer and made lots of money while maintaining his autonomy and what was referred to as his "secret import" of forbidden ideas.

Speaking of Ohashi, Murata said that he himself would like to be a free-lance writer. But it is a precarious trade. Journals like *Asahi* hire very young professors and plow through them like a field of barley, making them famous. But then they are quickly eaten up by fame and discarded for the next celebrity. Ohashi is a rare exception who has been able to handle fame without succumbing in this way.

We got into a discussion of metropolitan Tokyo, which, with its annual growth of 300,000, will soon have a population of 14 million. I may have mentioned before the 100,000 people in Tokyo without identification cards. These people saunter into the city, live from day to day, and when they die it turns out that no one knows where they belong. Murata saw hope in regional decentralization of industry, for instance, to Hiroshima. But Yoshida said that the lag of economic levels between Tokyo and the rest of the country will continue to bring people to Tokyo, despite all hopes for decentralization. And in any case, such decentralization as occurs will operate in the realm of production but not of symbolic management or Japan's equivalent of Wall Street; all headquarters will remain in Tokyo, close to the government, the mass media, the advertising agencies, and so on.

At the very end Murata raised the question as to what we saw as a possible utopia for Japan. He himself thought that Japan's future depended on being left alone in the world. If not threatened from East or West, it could become Erich Fromm's "sane society," a model country for U.N.E.S.C.O. to popularize. He saw the shape of this sane society not in terms of a society of intellectuals (though he implied that this was what the majority of "progressive" intellectuals would themselves espouse) but as a more "natural" and sane, easygoing but active community: neither male nor female, neither democratic nor totalitarian. Intimations of such a future could be found in the Roon movement, the workers' self-educating musical and cultural activities, and in the Old Man's University, founded in Nagano Prefecture by a group of old men who wanted a chance to reeducate themselves. I mentioned the Tokyo city planners we had met who were trying to develop a children's country in an island park near Tokyo—a city of music, of peace and friendship, where children from all countries would learn to live together. What Murata feared was that too few Japanese are ready to take the initiative and develop new intellectual and cultural institutions that would aim at sanity and naturalness.

Yamazaki brought up more dangerous possibilities. He said that 80 per cent of the Tories are rural or semirural. But the Tories are pushing industrialization, which is destroying the rural base on which the party rests; they also favor free trade, which will increase the pressure on the rice-producing rural element when it can no longer count on a market subsidized and protected by the government. So he saw the party splitting between one wing which would take in the rural and big-business elements, along with the overrepresentation that the rural element has in Japan, as elsewhere, and another new Conservative Party which would capture the urban immigrants brought to the big cities as the result of the policies of the government in fostering trade and industrialization. The Socialist Party won't get these new city dwellers, for that party is weak in horizontal organization but is organized—uniquely perhaps among socialist parties—on an enterprise basis (i.e., each plant has a different union, mostly socialist). In this situation the small businessmen and small property holders in the city will be nostalgic and look toward the rural past, not toward the Socialist Party; their ideology will not be Nazi because of the failure of Nazism and fascism in pre-war Japan, but it might become so if Communist China became a heavily armed nuclear power.

Suzuki added that such a political development might divert Japan from the path of industrialization: he saw the nationalistic spirit as a brake on the further industrialization that is widely anticipated (presumably in part because the climate would not be conducive to free enterprise and in part because rearmament would remove some of the potential labor force).

He added that Korea might be the spark for an outbreak of civil strife within Japan. There are 800,000 Koreans in Japan. Mostly they are from South Korea, but now 80 per cent of them are in sympathy with North Korea. The pro-North Koreans have developed a college in Tokyo and active propaganda; many South Koreans use Japan as a kind of reverse (pre-wall) Berlin, coming to Japan as a way of fleeing to the North. He could envisage a chain reaction beginning with South Koreans trying to reunite with the far more prosperous and effective North Koreans, which would in turn unite the Koreans within Japan as the spark within Japan itself. Chiang Kai-shek would get in on it. Murata suggested that South Korea might even try to conquer a disarmed Japan as a diversion for its embittered and hopeless population. Yoshida said South Korea was too weak for this, as it would also seem to me.

Of course, the United States is backing South Korea, but the present Pak government would seem to be the last chance for America since if it fails the Koreans would feel that there was no possibility of an effective independent South Korea and in spite of America would throw in their lot with the North. There was reference to some of the brutalities and oppressions current in South Korea; a Socialist Party leader had "died" in prison and three others are under a death sentence. Takahashi, a member of the Liberal Democratic Party but an independent man, is a believer in Korean unity, for he regards the South Korean economy as unredeemable. North Korea has had the most rapid economic growth of any Communist country. The North Koreans are breaking up the village communities, which are hated because they have been despotic and ruled by strong men, and the South Koreans know this.

Returning again to utopian possibilities, Yoshida suggested a "peace belt" running from England through a Rapacki-decentralized Central Europe to India, Burma, and Japan. Suzuki said that this was not possible because, with Pakistan still building up its nationalism, it would have to depend on militarism, and India and Burma would have to follow suit. On that realistic and unhappy note, we closed.

We were sorry to have to end these two intense days of conversation, broken only by occasional walks across the footbridge to the little island with its shrine, or around the grounds of the hotel. Murata, Yoshida, and Yamazaki accompanied me back to Tokyo. While we were standing at the *sushi* buffet of the train, admiring the extraordinary dexterity, mental and physical, of the two young men who were working behind the buffet filling customers' orders and by lightning calculations keeping track of how much each customer had had, Yoshida said from his own observations made in Russia how completely different these men were from the heavy-handed and stupid people he'd encountered at the Hotel Ukraine in Moscow and elsewhere on the train to Tashkent. He said how different the unseeing, uncurious eyes of the Russians were from the darting, quick eyes noticeable in these two young men and indeed in all the young Japanese we've seen. I knew exactly what he meant, because I remembered my own sense of the tremendous stolidity outside of intellectual circles and Boy Scout cadres in the Soviet Union. Even cab drivers we've had in Tokyo who have come recently from the country and don't know their way around—and many cab drivers are imported from the country to meet the shortage—are agile in driving and agile in trying to find their way by asking; they may be quite uninformed but they are not dumb. One still sees old peasant women bent nearly double in the particular stoop of the Japanese woman who has worked too long in the rice fields. And one sees occasional road workers or railroad workers of both sexes who are on the stolid side. But just as the *sumo* wrestlers, huge mountainous men we have seen on television, are nevertheless fabulously agile and quick as well as strong, so virtually all the people we've seen have this same quality of agility and nervous energy.

The exceptions are the sage and grave men of the older generation—and even more their women.

Later with Murata we talked about the student festival that we had seen Saturday morning at the Komaba campus of Tokyo University. This campus is unusual in that the students are freshmen and sophomores in a program of general education, but the freshmen, as elsewhere, are subjected to the "pink shower"—the induction into left-wing thought by activist upperclassmen. When Murata was a student a dozen years ago at the University of Tokyo, a Communist Party member who was then a senior had come and addressed the freshmen during what would in the United States have been orientation week; many took out membership cards then and there. I asked why the older professors who were conservative made no effort to oppose this activity. Yoshida said this was a characteristically American question, since the older professors adapt themselves to the situation and smile on the radical activities of youth—he and others have referred to Ruth Benedict's term of "situational adaptation" as characteristic of the country. Murata had said in our discussion that even prior to Japan's surrender in 1945 the way was already prepared for adaptation to the new situation: the "animism" of Japanese society is such that new developments can always be sensitively and quickly responded to, for both leaders and people are prepared to adjust themselves and to reach a modus vivendi between their own limited aspirations and what is required of them in the new setting.

I inquired about the festival that had just been held at the University of Kyoto, concerning which we had talked with students when we were there. The agreed-upon central theme of "The Long Sleep," referring here to the political quietism of the students after the period of noisy demonstrations, had not been adhered to, but instead there were many divergent exhibits. Thus, the Communist Party, rejecting the concept of "The Long Sleep" as anti-political, had put up its own exhibit devoted to space exploration (which appeared to me as an ingenious science-fiction way of avoiding the issue of Soviet nuclear testing while at the same time boasting about Soviet achievements). Other exhibits were devoted to a multiplicity of student interests, including a jazz band. Outside speakers had been invited from all over Japan, novelists and journalists and social critics, to talk about the position of man in the social system. (This question had also been the theme set for the Komaba festival, although, as I have mentioned, the exhibits were largely devoted to the atomic question.) Murata thought that two-thirds of the University of Kyoto students were apathetic or non-political, believing that they could do nothing to change the system. Indeed, the "pink shower" tends to wear off after the first year or two, save for the activists; by the fourth year, students want to be well recommended and begin to attend seminars and to cultivate the favor of their professors.

Talking then about the Un-American Activities Committee, Murata pointed out that the Japanese have very little sense of the regional

DR

differences within America (or ethnic and religious differences either). He added that their sense of East Asia is not much better: he gave the example of a cartoon that had just appeared in *Asahi* dealing with Prime Minister Ikeda's visit to Burma and showing presumably Burmese maidens doing a dance to win money from Ikeda—the only trouble was that the dance was a Thai dance, and this was a first-class newspaper with a highly learned staff which doesn't know any better than that.

ETR

Tokyo, November 24

I have been reading Japanese writers most of the day: short stories in Donald Keene's anthology, a novel, and some poetry. What strikes me most strongly in the fiction is the sensitivity of the male writers, especially when they record the feelings of women. Tanizaki in *The Makioka Sisters*, a multi-dimensional novel in the conventional European tradition, depicts all kinds of people, but the central figure is a girl who is portrayed with great sympathy through her development into womanhood and her battles against traditional Japanese family restrictions. Tanizaki's *Some Prefer Nettles*, which I have just finished, is a slight novel in comparison, about a modern marriage covering a short span of time and dwelling on moods and subtle feelings rather than on the development of character. His most recent novel, *The Key*, which I had read earlier, handles material bordering on the pornographic and does so with the utmost delicacy and artistry, counterposing the diaries of husband and wife.

It is interesting that novel writing—of which there is virtually none after the eleventh century, when Lady Murasaki wrote *The Tale of Genji*, up until the end of the nineteenth century with the Meiji Restoration—seems to flourish only in periods when women are somewhat emancipated, either in an aristocratic society or in a democracy which allows for sociability. Feudalism lasted much later in Japan than in Europe; but Europe had no Lady Murasaki—and Japan lost her art completely for almost nine centuries.

DR

Tokyo, November 25

This afternoon I gave my final lecture at the Asahi Lecture Hall on "Prospects for Peace." Both Bob Lifton and Matsumoto reminded me when we discussed this lecture that the Asahi audiences would want something less complicated and detailed than what I had said to the

Foreign Relations Association and would also be looking for guidance as to what the Japanese themselves could do on behalf of peace. Kato, who was to be my translator, went over my notes when we got together for lunch beforehand, and we continued to go over the outline in the car going down to the lecture. I was greeted when we arrived by the head of the cultural section of *Asahi*, who is an entrepreneur of great scope, responsible for something like a Lincoln Center panoply of activities. (Next year *Mainichi* will get the distinguished visitor.)

We walked out on the stage as the handsome curtain rolled up in a very large and modern auditorium. Matsumoto introduced me, speaking eloquently and without notes. Throughout my talk, as often before, I felt the enormous difficulty of giving this Japanese audience any real sense of the complexities of American life. Take, for example, the role of Christianity: the Japanese tend to interpret American Christianity in terms of their own Christians or the missionaries they have met, for whom Christianity is ordinarily a living and working faith—radically different from their own secularism and from their own situational realism, again to use Ruth Benedict's term. But that Christianity doesn't have this weight for the average American, that ethnic divisions with religious overtones divide a nominally Christian society—all this is hard for them to grasp.

Nor is it easy for them to imagine the complications of strategic thinking in America, not only in the Rand Corporation but in many university centers. Most vocal Japanese intellectuals are for peace; most leading journalists are for peace; indeed most of the people we have met are for peace (but I am aware that there are a lot of middle-class conservatives, who even though they may be for peace are also for rebuilding the armed forces in Japan). The Japanese tend to oversimplify us, just as we oversimplify them—perhaps an inevitable fact of most intercultural encounters. I thought of some of my American friends at the Pugwash conference in Moscow last year who had been irritated at the Russians because they hadn't "done their homework" on disarmament, assuming it was enough to be in favor of peace; Japanese intellectuals irritate many American journalists, Embassy people, and visiting academicians in much the same way.

When I had finished, we went upstairs to the reception room where we had waited earlier. I was greeted by a Japanese who said he was a graduate of Harvard in the class of 1921 or so—he wanted to shake my hand as a fellow Harvard man. While other people were coming in, I noticed three rather shy high-school girls standing in a corner and approached them. One of them, taller and more forthright than the others, said that she and her friends were the founders of a movement to make folded-paper cranes on behalf of peace and that they would like to present me with these cranes to take back to President Kennedy. She said that they knew that as high-school girls they couldn't accomplish much. I asked them whether they were in touch with any outside groups. They said no, they had done it themselves, but the movement was spreading to other schools and a number of women had shown an interest in it. What else had they done? They had gone to the Soviet Embassy and had taken some cranes there. Indeed, they had gone about three times. But they'd gotten no reply and maybe there was no further point in it. What after all could a few girls do?

I chatted with the other two girls. All were studying English and wanted to visit America. All hoped to go to college, though they didn't have clear career aims. It is hard to convey the innocence of these Japanese school girls, so different from the poised or assertive American high-school girls or girls from many other countries whom one can see at the Herald Tribune Youth Forum every year. Finally, I let them go.

We returned to International House late in the afternoon for a second round of our discussion with the Zengakuren leader, Iwanuma. Before he appeared, I hadn't been at all sure how he would respond to an invitation to International House, whether he would regard it as too "American" soil; but he showed up exactly on time with another associate, a vice-president named Inoue—a boy of very different quality from the rougher type he'd had with him on the first occasion. We had a formal dinner in a private dining room at International House, with Bob Lifton again present and Kato acting as interpreter.

Knowing that on the previous occasion Iwanuma's associate had hardly said a word, I purposely on this occasion started to direct my questions at Inoue and managed to bring him in so successfully that thereafter he took a very active part in the conversation. I feared indeed that Iwanuma would scold him later for being such an innocent and talking with such naïveté and directness. Inoue had read a novel written by a Communist in the 1920's about a fishing boat and the tribulations and sufferings of the crew and their experience in meeting Russian Communists at one of the Siberian ports—a very dramatic proletarian novel. This book had converted him to Communism and at about fifteen he had joined the Party and started to be active. He told us that he liked jazz but that the Communists were very ascetic and frowned on this; he was only allowed to sing folk songs. But later he had decided that there was no inconsistency between liking jazz and his political ideals—indeed, he felt in jazz the alienation of the Negro consonant with his own alienation and that of his fellows. He finally broke away from the Communists. Bob Lifton asked him then, or later, how he felt about the hot rods, the so-called "thunder tribe" of motorcyclists who terrorize people on the Japanese highways; since the Zengakuren students are sometimes called the Red thunder tribe, and resent this very much, Bob thought that the two young men would reject the label. But they didn't; they expressed sympathy for the hot rodders, much as somebody like Paul Goodman might express sympathy for juvenile delinquents and half identify with them.

Inoue has an appealing, open, sensitive face, and his whole personal quality seemed to me quite different from that of some of the hard agitators of his own movement. There was something about him that kept saying: you see what an honest, humane fellow I am, I keep nothing back from you, I intend no harm. And I had the feeling, which may be mistaken, that Iwanuma sometimes impatiently and irritably wished he would get finished.

At the beginning, in fact, Iwanuma was much the same as he had been before. He came with "answers" to all the questions I had raised on the earlier occasion. I decided to shift the ground and asked him what he thought he would do and what Japan would do if China got nuclear weapons. He said he recognized that this was a possibility and that he could do little to prevent it. If China got such weapons, it would be clear that it was not a socialist country. Already he felt China was almost as bureaucratic and hence as reactionary as the Soviet Union. Then he put a question to me that seemed to grow out of his reading of C. Wright Mills and Huberman and Sweezy. My first reaction—not so much to the details of the question, legitimate on its face, but to its tone—was that we were back where we had started the first time and that there was really no point in talking further with him; his position was closed, it was articulate, and it was defended by his whole stake in his position in the movement of which he is one of the leading figures. I tried, however, to answer Iwanuma on the merits, as if he were open, even while I felt he probably wasn't.

And then—I could almost feel it physically—he relaxed a bit and listened, rather than waiting as he had done hitherto for his chance to talk and come back at me. I'm sure it made all the difference to have Kato there whom Iwanuma knew and respected and who could share with Inoue a great liking for jazz and a feeling that this would not in any way detract from one's intellectual or revolutionary standing.

Thus, "the silent language" worked in my favor on this occasion—but I still realize how close I was to giving up.

Iwanuma started to ask me about the student peace movement in America. Earlier, I think he would have implied that there could have been no such thing in so warlike a country (while his associate seemed to feel that there would be nice people everywhere). I spoke about the Student Peace Union, with its headquarters in Chicago, and about Tocsin at Harvard and about the Slate political party at Berkeley. I said I thought that while the American student peace movement was very small in comparison with the Japanese, it had a sophistication and a universality that might be helpful in Japan—I had said much the same thing in my lecture that afternoon.

Just because it took, on most campuses in the United States, a fair amount of hardihood and dedication to be concerned with peace, the student activists were often exceptional young people who had had to find their way in an inhospitable intellectual climate. I mentioned to Iwanuma that Robert Weil, one of the founders of the Tocsin group, was at I.C.U. and that he might like to talk with him. He wanted to very much and wrote out his own address in English for me to pass on to any Americans, and Inoue did also. The thought occurred to both Bob Lifton and me that Iwanuma conceived of the American student peace movement as a possible captive for his own organization.

In this connection I'm reminded of the argument renewed on this occasion as to whether I was right to give peace priority over social change on the home front. I said that since peace in the nuclear age was essential for assuring continued life and hence essential for any change, I would make any necessary alliances that could guarantee peace and certainly would not reject alliances with conservatives. Iwanuma said, "I cannot ally myself with Prime Minister Ikeda since he does not really want peace."

When Iwanuma arrived, he said that he and Inoue had just come from the police station with their lawyer, where they had gone because a number of Zengakuren students had been arrested, some apparently for picketing at the Soviet Embassy and others for collecting petitions against nuclear testing (addressed to both powers) at railroad stations. I asked what was wrong about that and was told that the police charged them with obstructing traffic. Iwanuma is even now out on bail from a similar charge in Kyoto based on a scene at court as the result of a demonstration last spring. All this is in the day's work for him—but it should be recalled that he is an elegant young man of distinguished samurai family, with a clean white shirt and a carefully knotted tie, a very handsome knitted sweater under his coat, and delicate hands; he is perhaps twenty-three years old, and Inoue about the same age, though he seems much younger.

Iwanuma, like many Japanese, had the impression that the Communist Party was completely outlawed in America. How could that be in a free country, he asked. I was oppressed by the difficulty of explaining the complicated legal situation of the Smith Act and its sequels, just as I had found it difficult to explain my objections to this legislation to many Americans, though for different reasons. What I did do was to indicate that not all Americans were agreed about the matter. I pointed out that the American Communist Party should not be judged on the basis simply of knowledge of the Japanese Communist Party. We talked a bit about the fragmentation of the latter: there is the old core that looks to Moscow, a new younger group that looks to Peking, still another group that looks to Togliatti—just as does one fraction of the Japanese Socialist Party. Inoue and Iwanuma, like other students, seemed to feel there should be no such squabbling and "factionalism"; in a way, they are opposed to politics, while they talk constantly of struggle—as the left-wing labor unions also do. They act as if there should be no differences, certainly no intra-party struggles; thus they combine at the same time anarchic and totalistic tendencies.

When we began, as I've indicated, Inoue was chatty and appealing while Iwanuma was didactic and relentless. But as time went on, the latter softened, though he still listened to Inoue with some impatience. It is possible that the shift was partly tactical, that he saw a chance to make use of the American student movement or even of me. But I doubt if that is the whole story. Rather I think that, like so many less articulate young people in Japan, he too is searching even while he must appear firm to himself and even more so to his followers. I was glad I hadn't given way to my moment of despair earlier in the evening.

Another reason, I suspect, why this encounter with Iwanuma went better was that my article with Maccoby from the *New Left Review* had meanwhile appeared in *Chuo Koron* and of course he had read it. I think this helped to allay the feeling some Left Wingers might well have had that I was an American agent, only cleverer than the others, pretending to be on the side of progress and peace, the better to serve American interests. Even though that article spoke of my identification with the Liberal Project, and the word "liberal" in Japan has even more conservative and middle-class implications than with us, still it gave some reality to who I was and what I thought, some place to take hold.

Tokyo, November 26

This morning, Nat Glazer, Bob Lifton, and I chatted over coffee. Among other things, we talked about the auto-accident rate in Japan. Osaka, a city about the size of Chicago, has well over a thousand auto deaths a year: far above the number in New York, with about a tenth as many automobiles. One element is the enormous speed with which auto culture has hit Japan. The police are still "footmen," who have never been in a car and don't know how it works; they wear glasses and look like professors; there are virtually no motorized police. Moreover, if an unlicensed drunken driver is arrested after killing somebody, there is an even greater feeling here than in America that after all he was drunk, didn't know what he was doing, and so we should be generous with him. The Japanese government is "soft," despite momentary campaigns to crack down on the many traffic violators. But not all the drivers are drunk. On the road to Hakone, Evey and I have twice seen overturned trucks; the truck drivers have a wildness and ruthlessness that one finds only rarely in Japan. They are very young and there is a story in the papers about their persecuting a bevy of girl drivers who, as part of an advertising stunt, drove some cars from Nagoya to Tokyo—the truck drivers frightened and even pushed some of the girls off the road.

Depending so much on an almost tribal social conformity, the Japanese have few inner or internalized restraints when they come into a new situation, whether this is the novelty of the highway culture or the invasion of Manchuria. To be sure, it is hard to find anywhere a culture that has succeeded in incorporating the automobile or in humanizing colonial conquest.

It was arranged that Professor Isobe should come to lunch and that Kato would act as interpreter. Isobe is a sociologist at Tokyo Institute of Technology, close to the students, a sort of advisor to them, and apparently much beloved by them; he is also deeply concerned about peace. As we talked, he seemed a most thoughtful and sensitive person. There were many things we might have talked about, but we happened at first to get onto the subject of the student movement.

He summed things up as follows. In the *demo* of last year, there were three streams: (1) those wanting to preserve democracy, (2) the Communists, and (3) a radical minority of students wanting to make a revolution. The Communists and the Zengakuren idealists joined ranks in the *demo*, but when the Zengakuren girl was killed, the Communists criticized her as being too extreme, a Trotskyist, and this apparent callousness lost them much support. It was one of the elements leading to the popular front's breakup, which began before the *demo* were over and was completed afterward, and is one source of the fragmentation of the student movement today. Since the Communist Party in Japan furnishes much of the organizational energy, social reform cannot get far without its help. The Communist Party has strength in some of the unions and of course helps organize various small groups.

At the same time, there are pressures against the Communist Party in the unions. Partly these are pressures for "radical" outcomes. The "sit-in" by Socialists when Kishi was trying to put through the Security Treaty had seemed to me an unparliamentary and undemocratic tactic, not excused by the fact that Kishi's tactics also were ruthless and disingenuous. Professor Isobe said that such sit-ins were often used to demonstrate to their union leaders that the Socialist deputies were alert, courageous, and were doing something. For instance, just now the Anti-violence Bill, to which all the Left is opposed, was shelved. "It is to be considered at some later time." In fact, everyone agrees that this later time will never come and this way of putting it was to save face for the Conservative Party. But neither the students nor the radical union members are satisfied with this: they want obvious signs of victory. They want something dramatic, not the shelving of a bill.

At our Gamagori meeting, the point had been made that while from the outside Japanese society appears to be gerontocratic, mutually conciliatory tendencies operate and indeed youth and especially students possess considerable moral hegemony over their seniors. In fact, I met older conservative men whose offspring had been active in the 1960 demonstrations and who sympathized with their young people emotionally despite the ideological gap; correspondingly, the student leaders whom we met, far from cutting their ties to their "bourgeois" parents, remain very close to them (Japanese universities are not residential, so that students commute or sometimes live with Tokyo relatives when they come to the metropolis to attend a university). Isobe also commented on the way in which faculty members had been influenced by their students at the time of the *demo*. "Leaders" changed their attitudes when making speeches to students (or to union members) to meet the expectations of the latter.

Isobe said that the radical students have a completely unauthoritarian way of thinking. This is true of the newly formed Socialist League. They have no leader and unlike the Communists do not look for a model outside Japan. They admire the writer Yoshimoto, but no professor can influence them. Their tendencies are anarchistic. However, professors try to put them in contact with others, with workers, with women who are concerned with peace, with farmers, and so on.

At the same time, he said, there is no clear core to the peace movement in Japan. There are the intellectuals, the professors, the students, the artists, and each of these groups is internally subdivided. Many were thrown into confusion by Soviet testing, but what this should lead to is a more universalistic peace movement, not tied to either bloc in the cold war. He went on to say that many Americans who come to Japan to talk about peace seem to be pro-Communist and alienated from the United States. Why couldn't people come who were more truly representative of American opinion? I pointed out that representative American opinion is quite a long distance from world opinion and that our peace movement is extremely tiny. The more sophisticated Americans, I said, regarded Gensuikyo as Communist-controlled, so that only a Communist—or an old-line pacifist—would be likely to come. However, were a meeting held under more neutral auspices, like that called by Canon Collins in London last September, people like Erich Fromm, A. J. Muste, and Homer Jack might come, and I suggested that they should be brought to Japan.

Isobe replied that the fear of Communism is so much less than the fear of war that, since the reverse is true in America, there are enormous problems for mutual discourse. I added that the Committee for a Sane Nuclear Policy had had to face this problem, and that Communists created rather different problems for socialist and liberal or pacifist movements in America than they seemed to do in Japan.

In the *demo* last year (1960) the Communist Party took a low posture and minimized its role. (They did their best to avoid anti-American incidents and emphasized the domestic rather than the international aspect of the protest.) At the recent Gensuikyo Congress, (1961), however, the Communists actively supported Soviet testing. The result was to split the Congress. It is natural for the Japanese to be against testing, and the Communists could not have hoped to prevail against this sentiment. Isobe seemed to be implying that it was unfortunate the movement was split since the rearmament of Japan now in progress also needed to be opposed and the peace movement needed larger goals than merely anti-testing, such as opposition to nuclear arms for Japan itself.

I asked why there didn't seem to be any substantial number of right-wing or conservative students to counter-picket or demonstrate against the Zengakuren-led demonstrations. Isobe responded that these students, who come from well-to-do families and believe that they will get good jobs, are too comfortable to make trouble. Moreover, they believe that the conservative government will remain in power. At Meiji and several other universities, there are traditions of right-wing leadership and an interest in sports such as *karate*; big business supports the sports clubs in these institutions.

I asked Isobe where the Communist Party is recruiting. He said that its potential mass base was in the lowest strata of the double-decker economy. These had not yet joined the party. The Democratic Youth League, consisting of high-school graduates in small white-collar jobs who had not been able to get into universities, was acting as an intermediate power between the Communist Party intellectuals and leaders and this lowest group of would-be recruits.

We talked a little about intercultural exchange. Isobe said that an influential person may lose his influence if he goes to the United States (especially of course if he becomes "too friendly" to America). This situation has gotten worse as more and more exchanges are being arranged at the government level rather than on a private basis: even if in fact a State Department grant does not require a "pro-American" attitude, it will be more difficult for a Japanese to go if he wants to retain his reputation within Japan. All in all, between the pro-Communists who come to the Japanese Gensuikyo from America and the anti-Communists who go to America, Isobe didn't feel that exchange was working in an optimal way!

Isobe is a modest man, with none of the quality of the Japanese big-shot—one reason, no doubt, that the students can talk with him. As he left, a number of police came up the driveway, and I was told that the Crown Prince was coming to a wedding; I think I got a glimpse of him but he is so undistinguished-looking that I couldn't be sure (people are sorry for Princess Michiko, who is married to such a stiff and stultifying man—but then, they add, how can he help it, having been brought up in the palace).

This evening we met after dinner in the conference room at International House with four "white collar" young men, recent graduates from Tokyo University, with whom we were to discuss the problem of the shift from being Zengakuren activists to being organization men. The leader and organizer of the group was Kaneshiro, a young man originally from Hokkaido who had studied jurisprudence and was now working for Sony, an enormous electronic combine. On first impression, Kaneshiro seemed a very smooth but not very exciting person, flawlessly dressed and speaking excellent English. But as the evening wore on, his quality emerged strikingly—so much so, in fact, that after we adjourned I felt troubled that I had talked too much with him and too little with the others. (They themselves would not feel this way, Bob Lifton thought, because Kaneshiro was their spokesman; only an American like me concerned with equalitarianism might be troubled.) Kaneshiro said he thought it would be best if people introduced themselves. He began, saying he himself, since he came from the country, didn't know that the exams for Tokyo University were hard, and so he took them and passed without spending the usual year or more in extra preparation. (This meant that he was younger than most graduates.) Now he was working in the technical department of Sony, apparently concerned also with foreign trade. I asked him if he made any use of his legal training, remarking that very few law graduates seemed to do so; he replied that he did and that indeed he felt he had been well prepared for what he was actually doing in the company.

Next to him was a very vivacious and talkative man, Fuwa. Originally from Nagasaki, he was now in the government. He said that his work at the university had no direct connection with what he was doing now, and the legal training he had gotten was traditional and impractical. In contrast, he praised American education as practical, pointing to the fact that one could learn hotel management at Cornell, where he himself had studied labor relations at the School of Industrial and Labor Relations.

The third was Matsumura, born in Nagoya; he spent one year as a *ronin* before passing his exams and then majored in American Studies at the Komaba campus of Tokyo University. He said he had done so because he felt that a Japan which the Americans had occupied was an American Japan, and that in order to know his own country he should study America. Now he was working at Matsushita, another large electronics company, where his job is to read articles in American magazines and select them for management's attention. (I'm not sure whether he translates any of these or not himself; perhaps a few.)

The fourth and most quiet of the group was Kobayashi, who graduated a few years ago from Tokyo University and is now in the Labor Standards Bureau concerned with social welfare and security. He began in Kyushu and then was moved to Tokyo. As we opened the discussion, Kaneshiro said that he wanted to help provide me with the information I sought concerning what happened to student activists as they went on in their careers.

Fuwa added that the change occurred even before graduation. He had been president of the student government of the law school, and when the Anti-Security *demo* began last year he had to be careful not to get involved, because he was already planning to go to America. He added that he knew some of the leaders of the National Student Association and that it was hard for them to understand the *demo* or why he should fear visa trouble if he took part in them. I asked him whether his Japanese friends were critical of him for wanting to go to America. He said yes, his friends in the student movement thought he'd sold out and didn't want him to go to America, but his professor encouraged him and said it would be good to see another country: the student leaders are less flexible in their thinking than the faculty members.

I asked him if he had written to his friends while he was in America, and he said no. But on returning they thought he had been "wash brained" in the United States, but he himself didn't think so. "I made up my mind myself." He had concluded from his American experience that student leaders were inflexible, and he had begun to criticize Marxism, so that his friends had then criticized him. "I see now another way of developing Japanese society, not through revolution but in a democratic way." On the other hand, the Americans had thought he was a Communist because he criticized America in the *Cornell Daily Sun*, for which he wrote frequent letters. He had been invited to join a fraternity but his fellow students were worried that they wouldn't be able to get jobs because they had been associated with him, and they asked the F.B.I. about this. He wrote about individualism in America for the *Daily Sun*, trying to find the cause of it. When he was interviewed by the paper, the students decided he was okay; American students are much more concerned about right-wing opinion than Japanese students are; there are a great many opinions in America. (His implication seemed to be that there was a far greater spread than in Japan.)

Kaneshiro wanted to qualify what had just been said or implied concerning differences between Japanese and American students. He stated that the Zengakuren students want to be leaders in the realm of ideas rather than in organization, whereas in America the opposite is true. He had been a delegate of his own class to the executive committee of Zengakuren and took part in the *demo*, becoming aware of the gap between the leaders and the students. He felt that the leaders didn't represent the students but constituted themselves a propaganda party; hence he resigned his office. I asked if he wasn't denounced for this as a petty bourgeois and so on, and he said he was openly denounced in the general assembly of students. Yet his resignation gave him satisfaction because it was an act of conscience.

Kobayashi said he was a "standby" during the *demo* and not a member of Zengakuren. His father was an officer. Indeed, Kobayashi tried to get into the Defense Academy, but had failed the physical. However, he didn't want to become a Rightist and when he entered Todai his ideology changed and now he considered himself left of center. "I have no ideological problems." (In fact, both Bob Lifton and I were struck by the truth of this statement: having worked his way from a rightist background, he was now the only one of the quartet who was directly devoting himself to the labor movement in his work; there was something very solid and reliable about him.)

Matsumura, a good-looking young man but without the forcefulness of Kobayashi or Kaneshiro, said he hadn't been radical as a student but rather in the middle of the road. However, in his present job he felt in no position to express his own opinion and he felt a heavy pressure on him to conform. He was automatically a member of the white collar union in the company, but took no part in its affairs.

I then raised the question whether students viewed all companies, all organizations, as similarly constricting. Would any of them examine the details in order to discover whether one might have more freedom in one company than in another—for example, wasn't I right in thinking that Toshiba was more conservative than Matsushita, or did they believe that all big companies would give them the same sort of life ten years from now? I got the impression that Matsumura had made no such judgment, but, like many Japanese "junior executives," planned to live his "real life" outside of his work.

Kaneshiro, however, had turned down the first company to which his professor had recommended him. And when he went to Sony he told them he would resign if they began to manufacture nuclear weapons and that he hoped to retain his freedom to do what he wanted outside of work. They accepted him on this basis and he doesn't now feel any incompatibility between his ideals and his work. Given the lifetime employment pattern in Japan, resignation is so unheard of that I asked him whether he wasn't worried about what would happen if he resigned. He replied that he had decided to save enough money so as to tide him over and then to go to work for the Red Cross, with whom he had already spoken about this. Presently his work included surveying investments to make choices about assistance to underdeveloped countries, and he felt the importance and relevance of this work, since the company can look thirty years ahead and see if technical assistance would be creative over that span.

Fuwa said that there are few student leaders who cannot adjust to the society; and I responded that Kaneshiro is asking the company to adjust to him and that he can do this because he has the courage to quit. The latter continued that he hasn't yet seen the limits on his freedom of action in the company. Most students try to adjust to what they *think* are the rules when they enter a company but they may not test the limits. Bob Lifton pointed out that companies don't want people who are totally submissive and that some young people are smart enough to realize this but are still overwhelmed or dissolved in the company.

I felt that several of the others were somewhat threatened by Kaneshiro's courage and were trying in different ways to show how such courage wasn't possible for them. One said that Kaneshiro was an agile type and another that Kaneshiro's company was different from those where every employee "is a cog in the wheel, and we are told immediately after entering that they don't want individualists." Kaneshiro responded that perhaps he'd been lucky but that he at first refused a bank where he felt he would be a cog, even though it paid more than Sony. Kobayashi, less threatened, said that due to the wage and promotion system by age, mobility was very low. He continued that the wage system should be changed because it provides no incentive for anyone to show initiative, and he thought it would be changed as a shortage of labor appeared in special fields. There were still many regional differentials in pay, and these, too, would be forced to change as shortages developed. Matsumura observed that Kaneshiro had special skills, so that he could afford to be outspoken.

I brought up figures I had seen, that 25 per cent of the students identify themselves as sympathizers with the Socialist Party while 35 per cent sympathized with the Conservatives, and I asked why the latter group of students were so inactive politically. Fuwa said that the Conservatives suffer from an inferiority complex vis-à-vis the Communist Party. The left-wing students have a feeling of irritation about the society and a mission to do something about it, while the students oriented to the Right Wing have no such mission. Kato added that the left-wing students in a profounder sense are "conservative" since their aim is to preserve present prosperity and peace and the pleasures and opportunities that go with these; but they realized that in order to preserve them they must act politically, while the Conservatives don't think it's necessary to do anything. I asked whether conservative professors didn't influence students in the conservative direction. It was said that dissatisfaction felt in the university situation itself—overcrowding, poorly prepared lectures, general anomie—robbed these professors of influence and gave additional fuel to the Left Wing. Kobayashi said that those who support the Conservative Party are totally without ideas, so that they cannot even lead the Conservative students, let alone obtain decisive influence among students generally. Matsumura added that he didn't encounter activist conservative people but rather political apathy—he implied that this was the mark of the conservative.

Kaneshiro said that being "progressive" appeals to students, who recognize that they will change when they graduate: this is their last chance. They feel the difficulty of being free because of the image of society that they have and they don't see any way out. I asked Kaneshiro how his political interest began. He replied that he grew up in a small village where his father was a landlord, and there were few books and no movies. There was, however, one storehouse of books he found, where he read a great deal. He read *War and Peace* but couldn't understand it. Much of his time he played basketball. Later in high school he read the novelists Akutagawa and Soseki. Whenever he took a train ride, he read books, especially in math and the natural sciences, but there were no books on Marxism in the library. This interest began when he came to the Komaba campus, where he talked a great deal with his roommates. This was decisive for his development.

When I said that there was something to be said in favor of this self-education, Fuwa said that while in high school the students work very hard, but not in the university. They just read Marx and metaphysical books and don't know anything about society, so they get still further from reality. They don't study Tocqueville or Max Weber. He added that there were not so many radical students as was generally thought. When he was head of Student Government, there were about three radicals, who could bring four or five other students along with them, so that they would carry some votes by eight to seven, since most people were inactive. (He seemed to think there was something wrong with this, that it was undemocratic, but it seemed to me normal that a minority within a minority is the active ingredient in any institution.) He said that they might get 300 students out of 1,200 at most, but 150 was a quorum and that was enough to get out. Sometimes they would have to postpone the meeting because they didn't have a quorum.

Kobayashi commented that the great inactive majority of students sympathized with the active socialists. Bob Lifton added that the students who are outstanding in their academic work and their personal qualities are also the politically progressive ones and their qualities provide moral authority for the Left. Moreover, the Zengakuren leaders are admired for their authority, even if not for their views.

Kato said that when he was a student, about twenty out of every thousand were politically active. They all devoured Engels' *Socialism: Utopian or Scientific*, and became devoted to the socialist cause. The famous "conversion" (*tenko*) after graduation is largely based on a better knowledge of the world, of what things are like and what is possible.

Fuwa suggested that while Kaneshiro was lucky in his corporate job, those lawyers who were free professionals can do what they want to—he was referring here to the unusual person who goes from law school into the practice of law, developing a trade-union clientele, for example, or serving as a trade-union secretary. But most law graduates have no such freedom.

Matsumura said that there are many students who are progressive, especially among the highbrows, and the others want to follow their lead, although in reality they are petty bourgeois. I asked whether he meant that they follow the fashions, whether in the university or in the country as a whole, when they get out. He replied that they change their views between the time they finish the university and the time they enter their first job.

Bob Lifton said that students seem to disappear as activists once they go out into society, and we asked whether they continued to meet each other. Kaneshiro replied that he had organized a group—not the group tonight—that meets once a month. He wanted this to be an intellectual organization in which "we could go back to the university" and talk freely. Last summer they had taken up Zen as a study. They were also interested in the Roon movement and in other working-class activities. One of the members was a graduate student in psychology working in the field of education. Another had spent eight years in a monastery. One woman, a university graduate, was a practising Zen Buddhist. Another girl was a graduate of International Christian University. Bob asked whether the group had any political goals. Kaneshiro replied that its goals were only intellectual. And he continued that when he was a student he thought about what he would be doing when he was forty years old and he saw this group as a way to build up a fund of fundamental knowledge for later on. "I want to go down to the bottom of our being, to cultivate something in myself and others."

I urged him to write up his views—this hadn't occurred to him—because I felt other students or young graduates might respond to his approach. He said he had avoided any sense of discontinuity between the university and his work both because his work was interesting and because of this group.

Matsumura said that he himself found his work already frustrating and that in ten years he was afraid he wouldn't have any time for his own studies. Now, of course, he enjoyed reading the articles which he had to select and digest, but he agreed with my own comment that top management might not read anything he recommended to them, or, for that matter, read anything at all. Indeed, I raised the question of what would happen to these young graduates when and if they succeeded: wouldn't they at that time have to join the golf-playing, mah-jongg-playing life, the round of pleasure mixed with business and vice versa of the business big-shot? Kaneshiro was prepared to combat this by resigning if need be. Matsumura could not envisage such radical possibilities for himself.

Through the latter part of this discussion, Fuwa had been silent and I was troubled about his being left out. I asked him whether there was any resemblance between the paper work in his office and that which I had seen in *Ikiru*. He said his work, because it dealt with labor, was in terms of content directly linked to his ideals as a university student, but in terms of what he was ordered to do, it often contradicted his goals. The trial of Eichmann illustrated the type of choice he confronts. Now he is at the bottom of the hierarchy and can resist doing things he disagrees with by sabotage, but he wonders what would be his choices once he became a section chief.

Kaneshiro took up the same theme, asking himself what he would do in a society where there was no choice, for instance if he was ordered to go to war. In the "open society" there is a choice and there is space, but in twenty years Japan might go back to its pre-war condition, just as America might become like Russia, and in that case one would at best have the choice of prison or death. I asked Kaneshiro whether there were other students who thought concretely about how they would behave as conscientious objectors. I added that I had found most political thinking in Japan rather abstract and wondered if this was a real question. Kaneshiro replied that he didn't have the sort of faith he wished he had, but that he could envisage two or three people who would understand his life and might help society even after he was dead: it was difficult to express oneself and to be understood—and perhaps this was especially a problem in the Japanese language, which is an emotional language between two people facing each other, exchanging feelings rather than ideas and principles. "I'm trying to train myself to express myself correctly." (By this time the seemingly smooth Kaneshiro had given way in my mind to a much more emotional and of course much more unusual person, with a touch of mysticism and even fanaticism.)

Kaneshiro said that he was watching his company, which was already making electronic equipment that could be used for armaments, and was wondering where the limits are when it could be said that they were in fact making nuclear weapons. Matsumura replied that if he stayed in the company and opposed from within, wouldn't this be better than resigning? Sure that he had heard that plea all too often, which tried to tailor his heroics to normal size, I answered that that was the voice of the devil. Kaneshiro said his limit hadn't been reached yet.

I suggested that Kaneshiro and the others might profit from reading Tolstoy's *The Death of Ivan Ilyitch*; and Bob added that the students, once they get out into society, may have more leverage than they think they do and that much of the problem is internal.

I brought up my impression that even those left-wing students who are ideologically inclined toward anarchism tend to listen to the boss among them: they do not feel free even in their "free" student period. Fuwa added that the Left Wing in Japan behaves in the identical hierarchical way as the Right Wing and that this is very different from America, where strong feelings of equality prevail. In Zengakuren meetings, only the leaders would speak and all decisions would be taken unanimously. Kaneshiro added that in underdeveloped countries a Castro may be needed because changes are occurring faster than the ordinary speed of discussion, but that in Japan this wasn't necessary.

I was moved to ask Kaneshiro about his boyhood and how he had first met the boss problem. He said that in primary school in his village the strongest boy was the boss of the class—and he meant boss in a formal sense. He spoke of his experience, when he was perhaps twelve, of opposing the boss. Not only was he beaten up by the boss, but the boss told every boy in the class to hit him and he, Kaneshiro, had to submit to this, to his humiliation and sorrow as well as physical hurt. He said he hardly ever came home without some hurt. I said that this surprised me, because we hadn't seen fighting among school children. He said he could remember three fights, all involving the boss or a struggle of who was to be boss. The teacher didn't know—one was in a washroom, the others were in back of the school. But ordinarily there weren't fights because it was clear who was boss and the Japanese knew always who was the stronger. (As Matsumura said, it was the

Japanese character: "You roll with the big thing.") But when he got to middle school, the boss in primary school wasn't bright enough for basketball, which needs at least a little intellect for cooperation, and since Kaneshiro was good at basketball, this became the leading factor so that the more cooperative and intelligent boy could be a leader. This made him think that democracy might develop in a society where people realized that cooperation is necessary.

Fuwa pointed out that in Japan there must be unity and this minimizes aggression, whereas in the more mobile American society there is much more aggression and much more fighting in school. I said that I knew some people in America of exemplary courage who could now face verbal battles because they had been boxers and had discovered in school that they could live in spite of being hurt; I added that I wished I had learned it in school and that I had suffered because I hadn't. Fuwa said that he had been oppressed in primary school but that in the university his intelligence allowed him to express what he wanted to and that perhaps his left-wing views to some extent reflected his earlier oppression. (I felt this was rather glib—the kind of thing he might have learned in an American social psychology class.)

Bob Lifton said that he thought, from his own experience, that boys had to fight in the United States up to the age of fourteen or so. And if they didn't they were sissies—unlike Japanese, they had to fight even if they knew they wouldn't win. He compared *The Seven Samurai* with *The Magnificent Seven.* In the former, the samurai didn't have to fight to prove their courage—they were samurai by definition—but only to prove their class; whereas the Americans had to fight in order to show their courage.

Kaneshiro said that in secondary school any fighting at all is regarded as shameful. One tried to conceal that one had fought. It is also shameful to show one's physical power, so that the boss doesn't want to fight and usually doesn't have to. Fuwa said that through games one could tell who was stronger, so that fights weren't necessary.

It was clear as the meeting went on that Kaneshiro was the strong person in this group. His interest in Zen is for a Japanese not strange, though also not common. There was something perhaps a bit obsessive and purist in the way in which he watched the Sony Corporation and speculated about future possibilities. Still, this concern with personal commitment is so rare that I found his stand very significant and in later discussions tried to suggest to people that there need not be a precipitous drop in commitment when one goes from the university to the corporation, especially if one is preoccupied with genuine issues of nonconformity such as whether or not to participate in making nuclear weapons.

As usual on such occasions, it was hard for me to know how to bring the evening to a close. Such matters cannot be settled in a matter-of-fact way: as the senior person present, I would have to decide. I ended the conversation at ten, fearing that I had kept them too long; but much later, going down to the bar for a drink with Bob Lifton, we saw them still talking with each other in the lobby; apparently this discussion had served as a catalyst to bring them together.

Tokyo, November 27

We have crowded our last days with appointments at International House, thus saving the time it would otherwise take to journey about Tokyo. This morning I had a long discussion with Professor Kawakami, a young political scientist who had come up from Kyoto for a visit. Evey sat with us at a table in the lobby and took notes of our discussion. Kawakami began by talking about game theory. He had been fascinated by Thomas Schelling's ideas and was amazed to discover that I was not an expert on this way of looking at international relations. Did I prefer Anatol Rapoport's *Fights, Games, and Debates* to Schelling's *The Strategy of Conflict*? I had to confess that while I had read some of the former book and some articles by Schelling, I had only a marginal familiarity with the work of either man. Kawakami continued by asking me what my theoretical interests and orientations were. As on another occasion when I had talked with young political scientists (it happens in America also), I felt cramped by this somewhat formal mode of approach and yet wanted to be as helpful and hospitable as I could. I raised the possibility that game theory can be used in both good and bad ways: either with an awareness of the human stakes involved, or without this awareness. Where the cold war itself is sometimes looked upon as a football game, it might have different political implications than the application of the same ideas in Japan, where the academic political scientists are combatting irrationality and vagueness and where game theory would not be used (as sometimes in the United States) to disguise from oneself the human stakes involved.

Kawakami's reaction to this, I am inclined to think, was that I was somehow defending irrationality, a problem perhaps especially serious in Japan where intellectuals feel they must vigilantly combat vague and affect-laden ideas. He regarded game theory as a way of getting at rational solutions, as against mere belief and superstition, and said that game theory doesn't concern problems of belief. He said that rationality is important but its relation to belief is important also: the question is how to approach this problem. He said that in America rationalism prevails, but in Japan there is great spiritual frustration because of the irrational factors and the diversity of Japanese life. I asked whether he meant that this was because of the embedded irrationality or "feudalism" against which students hardened themselves. I suggested that what Communism might be for the modern Chinese, "rationality" might be for the modern Japanese.

Kawakami responded that this view was not reactionary, although it could become so, and that to appreciate it the Japanese must first rationalize their life and separate the rational from the irrational.

I tried to shift our terms by raising a concrete question. Think of Japan, I suggested, as a society with a very thin top layer of intellectual rationalists and another top layer of businessmen and bosses who may pursue rational ends but are not rationalists; what would be the prospects for rationality in ten years? Would the victory of socialism be regarded as a victory for rationality? To so abstract and difficult a question, an older man would simply have sighed and thrown up his hands. But Kawakami, in line with the tough-mindedness he favored, was willing to face questions, even the most unexpected ones. He singled out the deeper meaning of rationalism about which we were talking on several levels. He said he looked at the future not in terms of political regimes but in terms of the social character of the young. But he himself couldn't define their attitudes and turned the question around to me. What would be the social character when there is affluence in Japan? Would it be the same all over the world?

I replied that I thought there would be differences because of the combination of traditional elements with modernization. I pointed out that Japanese women in the labor force were different from Russian women in the labor force and different from American women. I said that I was struck with the combination of "rationality" in Japanese industry with much traditionalism both in the corporate familism and the position of working women, and I suggested that the ability of the Japanese traditions to absorb and blend with modernization should not be underestimated. It seemed to me this was especially true because, as compared with other industrializing countries, Japan was a highly literate society where a certain amount of rationality already existed; it was also a fairly homogeneous society—unlike either the United States or the Soviet Union—again allowing for industrialization to be absorbed in a different way.

Kawakami was inclined to deny the homogeneity, saying that people lived in small communities and that people from one clique couldn't understand people from other cliques. There is a warm feeling only within the clique and communication only within the clique. But to my probing he admitted that there are common elements among these groups, at least to some degree. I raised with him the question that I kept raising with others: How in spite of cliques and in spite of "feudalism" so much got done? What were the sources of enterprise? He responded that the new elements coming up the social ladder strengthened the society. Still, while subordinates appreciated the efforts of a boss, the boss didn't like subordinates who were too creative or went in for too much innovation. The relation between boss and subordinates at times permitted innovation; that is, the boss might have a human and warm relation to a younger man, to whom he allowed a certain measure of freedom.

At this point Professor Ichikawa, a leading physicist much concerned with nuclear matters, turned up for my next appointment; he wanted to discuss with me the Committee of Correspondence Newsletter on civil defense. I suggested to Kawakami that he stay if he wished to, and he said he would like to very much. Ichikawa was deeply troubled because of the possible impact on Japan of Dr. Willard Libby's series on fall-out and shelters which had been running in the *Asahi Evening News*. And that very day there had been an article in *Asahi* by a Japanese physicist who had just visited the United States, which chastised the Japanese by saying that the Americans were much more concerned with civil defense; in contrast, the Japanese had taken an all or nothing attitude: they would either all die or all be saved. Ichikawa wondered to whom this man might have talked since he seemed to present only the pro-shelter side of the story. The information available in Japan on civil defense was not reliable and it was necessary to fight this kind of tendentious reporting. Furthermore, it was understandable if a military man talked this way, but for scientists to do so was incomprehensible. The overall impression had been given that the United States was seeking through shelters to survive a nuclear war, while the Japanese were being criticized for fatalism.

Beyond that, Ichikawa was disturbed at the apparent attitude of the American scientists who had been quoted in the paper, for it meant that scientists opposed to nuclear war must be timid and silent and that the fears held in Japan of the imposed uniformity of American opinion would be borne out. Hence he was eager to discover whether there were intellectuals in America of a different view. What could

I tell him about the *War/Peace Report*? About the Committee of Correspondence and its Newsletter? What about my colleague, Paul Doty; where did he stand? I said he was a very dedicated man, that I was sure his voice would be heard; Ichikawa agreed. Where did Jerome Wiesner stand? We talked about these and other scientists whom he knew or knew of and about Eugene Rabinowitch, editor of *The Bulletin of the Atomic Scientists*, whom Ichikawa had met at a Pugwash conference.

Perhaps the physicist who had written in favor of shelters for *Asahi* and who had spent a year in America had not met many intellectuals—was there a gap in America between scientists and intellectuals? He himself had asked a number of leading American nuclear scientists whether they had shelters and none of them had any or were preparing any. I responded that a number of scientists had been fighting on this front since before the first bombs were dropped. Some had grown tired and some had grown "realistic" but a number still carried on, and it was time for new people to come to their aid.

I then asked why the newspapers had taken the line that *Asahi* was taking. Ichikawa said that they had become more conservative. The Japanese people had been frightened by a movie—I think *The Last War*—which assumed that there would be a nuclear war. The newspapers didn't want them to get too excited. There is now tremendous pressure on *Asahi* not to print material on peace. Our interpreter interjected that the Leftists think that the advertisers are the source of this pressure. But, in fact, before there is any overt pressure the papers exercise their own self-restraint. I asked why in the absence of direct pressure the journalists didn't have more pride in their craft. The interpreter replied that they are strongly opportunistic, as intellectuals generally are in Japan.

Ichikawa said that he had written an article for *Asahi* which had been refused. All he could hope to do now was write a report, quoting American intellectual opinion from our newsletter and from what I had said, in the form of a letter to *Asahi*, which he felt they would be obliged to print. (In defense of *Asahi*, Ichikawa said that he had first heard of the Committee of Correspondence from an article in that paper.)

At one point it was suggested that there was no apparent relation between the decency of individuals and the policy of their governments: Ichikawa said that the French people were very nice but their government policy whether in testing or in Algeria was not; the

Japanese people were nice, too, but that didn't mean their policy would be.

Ichikawa said that after the resumption of tests the Japanese scientists got together and discussed this from all angles—scientific, psychological, political—and sent a message to President Kennedy urging him not to resume tests. Ichikawa had expected that Teller would lose power after Kennedy's election but apparently he hasn't. I suggested that Teller was a very powerful witness before congressional committees and that President Kennedy didn't have things all his own way, even if he should know what that way was.

I realized in talking with Ichikawa how enormously persuasive the American example is, even for the most highly educated and peace-concerned Japanese nuclear scientists; what he wanted was to increase the range of American scientists whose voices could be heard on the shelter issue in Japan. Naturally the Japanese are vulnerable to charges that, in comparison with the Americans, they are irresolute or given to all-or-none thinking—for indeed they are.

At this point Ichikawa had to leave. Kawakami had waited all this out with interest and then returned to his themes. He said that America was the most developed country and one where informal relations among people were very easy. He proposed that the American emphases on human relations were rational for our fully developed society, but wouldn't they be less so for developing countries? I didn't catch all his implications here, and I responded indirectly by saying that I didn't think that industrial development was necessarily unilinear. There might be other roads to development.

This troubled Kawakami, who felt that if all societies were different, it would be impossible to communicate. What would be the means of communication? I replied that I did not think similarity of social organization necessarily meant ease of communication, let alone friendship. It was possible to imagine the United States and the Soviet Union becoming more alike and yet finding it even harder to communicate. However, I agreed that it was extremely difficult for the rich and the poor to understand each other within a single society or among societies. What one might hope for was a world religion which could be shared—a very unevangelical and unfanatical religion based on the fact that we are all human and that we require peace to survive.

It occurred to me how much Japanese intellectual life would be enriched by a greater awareness of cultural anthropology. I said that an anthropologist had no doubt of his or her ability to communicate even within an entirely alien society, so that affluence need not necessarily cut him off; or if he had doubts about the completeness of communication, he might try to make use of these very limitations.

Kawakami said that within a traditional society communication between different groups is impossible. But in developed societies professional people in one society can communicate with professional people in another, although he wondered why social scientists find this more difficult than physical scientists. I responded that not all social scientists were alike: anthropologists had an easier time than, say, political scientists or perhaps economists because their field itself was less culturally bound. Kawakami could see that and could see that Keynesian economics might not mean the same thing everywhere. Still, he hoped that science would provide means of communication between peoples.

I pointed out that even in his own field of interest, namely game theory, science had an ideological quality. (And I was surprised to have to point this out to a Japanese familiar with Marxism.) The only cure for this, I thought, was better science. But science as such did not necessarily bridge cultural gaps. Game theory, I suggested, brought by the Americans to the previous Pugwash Conference in Moscow might well seem a kind of paranoid activity to the Russians, while Americans came back and said "the Russians haven't done their homework"—a somewhat ethnocentric view.

The interpreter tried to mediate between us, asking whether a scientist who applies game theory becomes himself more rational? He said that Kawakami seemed to be interested in the theory itself while I was interested in its context and in who handled it. I said I thought there was indeed a mutual attraction between theories and people, although not in a one to one relation, and I said to Kawakami as we parted that I was sorry I couldn't speak with more authority on the subject of game theory.

We were still talking when my luncheon guest came. He was Professor Nakada, who teaches literature at Todai, a man of whom I'd already heard a good deal as someone close to the students who could tell us more about their attitudes and values. I could see why the students were fond of him; he seemed to be a generous, sensitive, and secure person with great poise. Bob Lifton joined us in the private dining room.

Nakada told us about a book, *Listen to the Sound of the Ocean*, a collection of poems written by Japanese students drafted in the war;

in writing these poems they were following the example of German students. These students had died, and the poems became one of the stimuli for the first post-war peace movement. So, too, a film of Imai's, *Till We Meet Again*, had had an impact. It was about a boy who goes off to war and is killed; afterward his girl gets comfort from reading the poetry he wrote. He also spoke of a film, *Japan's Night and Fog*, dealing critically with Japanese war atrocities—of which many in Japan had been unaware till after the war. (Our friend, the film critic Richie, has written about this film and the response to it and has suggested that somewhat less noble motives of curiosity and interest mixed with shame and horror may be involved.)

I told Nakada that we had seen the exhibits at the Komaba campus festival and some of the prizes had seemed to us to go to the less interesting exhibits, to the obvious ones and not to the ironical or sardonic ones. He responded that the prize committee would be guided by the general conservatism of the student majority and would temper their prizes accordingly. But I replied that there hadn't been any conservative exhibits, at least we hadn't seen any. Why was that?

Nakada told us that the previous year some students had in fact put on some reactionary exhibits in the wake of the demonstrations. One group of conservative students had paraded with banners of rice and grass, traditional symbols of peasant riots against their overlords, but in this case deriding the protests and apparently also carrying sexual overtones. Another group of conservative students exhibited a supposed Imperial Rescript, saying that a student must live according to his nature, that is, his impulse life of sex, drink, and so on. Nakada had called these students in this year and told them that he thought they should restrain themselves from these more extreme posters and exhibits which reflected badly on students and the student movement. I expressed surprise that they were so easily persuaded and he said that they were simple and good-natured and hadn't realized that they were doing harm. They were only poking fun, and the very fact that they were Rightists meant that they had weak resistance to authority and were obedient to him and easily persuaded over glasses of *sake*. They agreed that the fame of Todai is important and their exhibits would give a bad impression that the students lived in a riotous way. The exhibits should be an expression of dormitory life and not of individual student life.

I asked what the students had done instead. He said they hadn't done anything. There were not so many of them and they were mostly non-political anyway. The athletes among them, the *karate* players, are under the influence of alumni and business groups who finance them.

I was struck by this example of mild faculty censorship, by the willingness of conservative students to accept policing by a man of the Left, though of the moderate Left.

In the *demo* the positions of the Association of War-Killed Students, that is, the students identified with those poems, had become distorted, for that association had been a very peaceful rather than a demonstrative one. All the student organizations had collapsed after the *demo*. Students wondered why live, why study, and they divided into small quarreling groups. There is a bitter distrust of politics in the student groups. When there was a recent meeting, held in the dormitory, of students from all over the world, the Japanese students seemed more skeptical than those from elsewhere. The North Koreans were full of enthusiasm for contributing to their country, and the Japanese students envied the Koreans, who seemed to have no doubts.

I said I was still puzzled why the students had been so disillusioned after the *demo* and lost their momentum. Lifton responded that many students were afraid of the possibility of chaos and violence; their very success, their ability to arouse the society, had sobered them. Nakada added that, as many had told him, the splits in the Socialist and Communist parties after the demonstrations had increased the ideological confusion of the students and their already considerable distrust of the Communists. They had now become extremely distrustful of the Soviet Union. Lacking any party organization anywhere with which they could identify, they felt no support for their outlook and felt out of step with the rest of the world. Had they, I asked, envied the North Koreans because of the latter's simple purposes or because of their fanaticism? Nakada said that the Japanese students in a way are simple also and that their envy was understandable. They feel frustrated in their own society because they are not recognized, and they look ahead to a future when they must serve big business, with their fate decided the moment they enter a company.

Returning to the *demo*, Nakada said that the invasion of China and Korea had left a sense of guilt, so that when a war criminal—Kishi—became Prime Minister, the students felt aggrieved. Nakada could envisage a clash between the students and intellectuals on the one side and a new military regime based on the defense forces and supported by ties to the United States and South Korea on the other.

Turning to another topic, but not an unrelated one, Nakada gently suggested that in my published interview with Suzuki I had been too uncritical of Japanese life. I said I had not wanted to sponsor complacency and did not agree in every particular with Suzuki's optimism, but that I would be glad to trade the Japanese Right for the American Right. After all, there were ten million Socialist votes in Japan, which were not so easily overcome. Nakada admitted that he had hope in the younger generation. They might even be able to do something about the problem of authority and innovation in big business. On this score Bob did not agree, repeating that when student leaders get immersed in a big firm they feel powerless. The students do not realize that the growing labor shortage would give them greater leverage ten years hence. Nakada agreed with me that students like Kaneshiro could accomplish more if they wanted to; he himself often told students this. And perhaps a sense of solidarity might develop among those young people who are excluded from the universities and who go to night high schools. Town and city politics might provide a chance to train these people. But on the whole he was not hopeful.

To our regret, Evey and I had to interrupt our meeting with Nakada, when it seemed we had hardly begun, as we had an appointment to renew our registration permits. We were accompanied to the Alien Registration Office by a young graduate of International Christian University who is working here at International House at his first, and presumably, by Japanese tradition, his lifelong job.

We went by bus and chatted on the way. He said he had attended International Christian University because Christianity seemed to provide a system of belief in the post-war world where it was difficult if not impossible for young Japanese to find their bearings—he made clear that it was reading of the Bible rather than the desire to learn English that had drawn him there. Three units of study of Christianity are required for graduation, and of course some of the Japanese students just go through this as a routine. Since I.C.U. is Protestant nondenominational, he felt close to the non-church Christian group here.

Like many of the young men at International House, he is educated far beyond the work he is doing, which is often simply being at the desk as a kind of clerk, or running errands; two of the older, more outstanding men would in the United States already perhaps have tenure in a college or university, while here, in their early thirties, though they have done serious scholarly work, they are in the service of foreigners, largely Americans.

In thinking about this, it seems to me that the Japanese "accept the universe"; I find it hard to imagine a Japanese, other than a right-wing fanatic, harboring the kind of long-term grudges and vindictiveness of, let us say, a South Italian peasant. There is both a feeling of live and let live and of die and let die. Perhaps this is one reason for the great preoccupation with suicide, which one finds not only among desperately unhappy people, but also among many who might be thought of as fellow travelers of the cult of suicide. The methods are often dramatic —throwing oneself in front of a railway train or into a volcano, or the famous double suicides of ill-starred lovers—and the practitioners are numerous, so that suicide is one of the principal causes of death of young people. I do not mean that there is the same kind of callousness toward death that I found in the Soviet Union thirty years ago, when it was still in some respects an "Oriental" society. Rather, the individual doesn't have quite the spin on him that he does in the Protestant countries, quite the feeling that his fate is up to him; indeed, many Japanese intellectuals and young people feel that they lack a sense of self; and it is this that attracts many of them to Christianity, more than its religious content, which is alien to the Japanese type of secularism and syncretism.

This afternoon I went with Bob Lifton (Evey still wasn't well enough to go out) to Ochanomizu University, formerly Tokyo Women's Educational College or Normal School—it is said to be the one university for women that is on a parity with the government universities for men. They were having their festival, and Bob's assistant, an attractive and intelligent young woman, went with us. In the cab going out, the assistant, who had been to my lecture day before yesterday, said two very interesting things. In the first place, she commented that my statement that "the countries having the atomic bomb had more fear and anxiety than those without it" would not be understood in Japan: it would be assumed that I was unaware of the enormous fear in Japan at present about fall-out and about nuclear weapons in general. She, however, thought she had been one of the few in the audience who got the point and thereby realized the extent of fear in America; it had occurred to her that her own relative lack of fear, despite her awareness of the danger, was due to her anger, mobilized against the nuclear powers and against testing—an anger that she thought was not present in the United States. She went on to suggest that this might be the case generally in Japan: there was so much indignation that it drove out fear. She said that therefore she had understood my remark on a profounder level than the audience, which had rejected it.

There was another comment of mine she thought had made an impression on the audience, namely, when I said that the urgency of the problem of peace in the nuclear age was so great that every vested ideological or other interest had to be subordinated to it, no matter how appealing that interest was in its own right. I had said that Japanese revolutionaries had to subordinate their aim for revolution to the aim of peace. I also had said that many Americans would have to subordinate their aim for "liberation" to the aim of peace, that is, that the evangelical desire to roll back the Iron Curtain and to expand the boundaries of the Free World had to give way to the aim of peace.

To return to the festival, it was done on a basis entirely different from that of the Tokyo University students. Most characteristic and striking was the room in which the German Club was having its exhibit. No one in the German Club had ever had the opportunity to go to Germany—indeed, that seemed a remote possibility to them. They had borrowed a group of color slides and they had used geography and a bit of German history to arrange the slides and to make their own tape recording. One of the club leaders explained to me in German that the club was selling potato wine (allegedly German but concededly Japanese) and sausages to raise a little money. The slides illustrated only a romantic, almost Wilhelminian Germany: the Rhine, people drinking beer, cathedrals and universities, the empty Parliament building in Bonn, farmers in the field, happy faces in the street. I suppose American third- or fourth-grade children would stare silently and raptly at the showing of such slides; older children and certainly college students would consider it in a class with home movies —and this reaction would not be mitigated by the postcard beauty of some of the slides.

One could say much the same about the Mountaineering Club exhibit. In that room there were route maps on the walls by which the girls showed how one could get to one or another mountain in the Japan Alps or elsewhere. There were some ski boots and some photographs and travel posters. That was about all. Mountaineering is a big thing here among young people. It gives girls a chance to be on their own and perhaps to meet boys. Sports, in fact, are taken like everything else with great seriousness as a kind of education—nothing is done casually. This is true of the golfers, who get themselves up elegantly with every possible club or else don't play at all.

There was also a room at the festival devoted to physical exercise or physical condition, where one could test one's grip or the power of one's lungs as well as weight and height, quickness of reaction, and so on. Young men and women were laughing and giggling as they vied with one another. Bob's assistant commented that this was the one girls' college she'd seen in Japan where the girls had the same free and easy spirit as the boys; we had the same impression—it was very different from the conventlike quality we had sensed at the other women's colleges.

In another room arranged by the Child Study Group was the most popular of the exhibits: here were charts of the Picture Frustration Test which had been administered to a group of fifth- and sixth-grade children—the test had been adapted to deal with the problems of Japanese domestic life. Children had been asked, for instance, what their mothers would say when the children reported that they had borrowed some books from friends: many of the mothers would say, "Please don't tear them," or "Return them quickly," or simply shrug and make no comment at what the caption spoke of as the child's effort to communicate with the mother via the announcement. Indeed, many of the children seemed to see their mothers as indifferent or warding them off. There was an effort to compare responses from working mothers and from housewives and some slight indication that the children thought more of mothers who worked than of mothers who didn't work. There was one chart which indicated that children of working mothers saw men and women as more alike than children of housewives (though the difference was something like 78 per cent as against 66 per cent), and Bob commented that in the United States there was now an effort to "restore the difference" between man and woman, implying that children should be encouraged to view the sexes as different and not as the same. In the local context this was, of course, a "reactionary" remark and our interim guide was somewhat taken aback.

We went to visit the student lounge, brand-new, handsome, and modernistic. Our local guide told us that for a month it had failed to open because the student government and the administration were at odds as to who should run it; finally, "in typical Japanese fashion," there was a compromise.

One of the groups studying Chinese literature had done an exhibit of modern Communist China. There were photographs on the wall of smiling farmers, of health services in a village, of a young pretty girl teaching an older man to read—all the rather rosy things about which we in America have become cynical. Postcards were being sold here, some very nice ones, made in Japan. (Incidentally, we were never asked to buy anything, and this is characteristic of the complete lack of sales pressure here, an attractive aspect of Japan.) The Communist China exhibit had the pastoral quality of the German one, except that it also had some propaganda on the condition of the working woman; but on the whole it was a very mild exhibit, more lyrical than agit-prop.

This evening Evey and I had dinner with two young men from the Foreign Office whom we had met on several occasions; both spoke English easily and well so that we did not need an interpreter. Mr. Otani (who had taken part in an earlier discussion) had training at the University of Tokyo in anthropology and mass communications, while Mr. Michida, though sharing similar orientations, is more of a specialist in international relations.

We had a table in a quiet private dining room at International House. They wanted to begin by discussing cultural exchange, in which they had both been involved for a number of years. What did it mean to bring the Bolshoi Theater to Japan or Kabuki to Moscow? Did it always import friendship? When the Chinese Communists had brought a theater group to Japan, some Japanese Rightists had pulled down the Chinese flag and burned it. The Chinese ended their performance at once and went back. Here cultural exchange had brought conflict, not the promotion of understanding. I responded to this by saying that if one didn't expect too much of cultural exchange—and of course it couldn't substitute for political relations—it could accomplish something. The Russians who applauded Van Cliburn in Moscow or the New Yorkers who applauded the Bolshoi were expressing approbation not only for artistry but for peace, for people on the opposite side of the Iron Curtain. I said I wished there could be many more such "hostage" arrangements. All cultural exchange seemed to me today to have a hostage element, making military attack at least a little less likely.

Otani said that much communication between Japan and the United States was pseudo-communication. He added that the Japanese had also been disillusioned with their cultural exchanges with the Soviet Union.

Otani discussed his study of the image of foreign countries in Japan since the last century; for example, a girl might write to a newspaper that she wanted to go to Yokohama and become the mistress of some foreigner—one way of learning the language and breaking down the barrier. In the post-war years, a Japanese girl might be willing to do menial work for an American family in Tokyo in order to learn English and get to the United States; he spoke of two young ladies of excellent family who had come to consult about being placed in such a family—again an indication of the strength of the desire to learn and to break down barriers. In the pre-war period, views were always hierarchical: another country was always either higher or lower than one's own, and knowing a (higher) foreign language could raise one's status.

Since the war the sense of nationalism has been reduced. Otani gave the example of response to the shooting by an American corporal of an old Japanese woman foraging in a field. A very active Communist leader tried to stir up the Zengakuren on this case. But the students said it was just a murder, and there were murders all the time, lots of them. They weren't thinking in terms of the country but in terms of individuals.

Michida returned to the theme of pessimism about cultural exchange. He said that the students and others weren't interested in every country and thus weren't truly international. The hierarchical tendency to rank some countries above others continued.

I said that one might make a test case here by looking at Communist China, a country almost without cultural exchange. The incident at Nagasaki, where the flag was burned, showed their inexperience. They could have turned the incident much to their advantage by continuing the show and shaming the flag burners; but, as it was, the Japanese were irritated both with the insulters and with the insulted. The trade missions from China seemed to have acted in the same way. I said that what mattered in cultural exchange was who met whom and what was their importance in their own country. As an example, I pointed out that to have equal exchange between the United States and the Soviet Union, since the former was a democracy, a thousand Americans should go to the U.S.S.R. for every few Russians brought to the United States.

Otani asked what I thought was the cause of Chinese isolation. It was not exactly like Japan in the Tokugawa period. There didn't seem to be the same inferiority complex that the Japanese had. I replied that on the contrary it might be Chinese "purity" and a sense of superiority, a feeling that outsiders might corrupt this purity, as well as, of course, *our* anti-Communist isolation of them.

Returning again to his theme, Michida asked whether I thought Khrushchev's last trip to the United States, when he traveled across the country, had had any effect on his view of America. I said it was hard to tell, although possibly his encounter with the labor leaders might convince him that not all that his "Marxist" training had told him about American capitalism was correct. Michida agreed with me that Khrushchev and his colleagues might get along better with big businessmen than with anti-authoritarian working men.

I asked Otani about the study he had done with Bill Caudill in 1954 of the impact of an American base on a Japanese village. Many Koreans came to set up small businesses in a boom-town area between the base and the village itself. This town was a go-between, or neutral zone, for the soldiers and the village people. The boom town seemed like part of American culture to the villagers, with its neon signs, its bars, its jazz and American soldiers and their girls. But the town seemed "Japan" to the GI's, since the girls were Japanese, since they could buy Japanese things there, though in fact it looked very much like an American frontier town and it furnished not Japanese culture but souvenirs and sukiyaki. Sometimes frustrated girls became mistresses of Negroes, with whom they identified as frustrated also.

I said I was surprised how little resentment there was about girls living with American men. Michida said that the girls were looked down on, but also were envied in a way because they could act so freely in the "American" town. Otani added that there were selfish motives: so long as there are prostitutes around the Army, there won't be rapes or other trouble from the GI's. The prostitutes will keep them in hand.

Michida added that after the surrender the golf courses were requisitioned and Japanese were not supposed to play unless they were friends of American officers. Many Japanese golfers were envious of the privileged ones. His father was unusual in refusing to play, though he could have, until all could play.

I asked about the bombings and why there wasn't more resentment of them. Michida said that this was because there was no distinction in Japan between soldiers and people. All had suffered. Otani added that the Japanese were surprised by the gentlemanliness of the Occupation: the Japanese respond to direct experience more than to abstractions. But during the Korean War the American soldiers were very tough and unpleasant and that was one of the worst periods. I suggested that perhaps the political polarization tinctured by racism of the Americans in Korea carried over to the Japanese.

I brought up Nakada's criticism of my discussion with Suzuki published in one of the monthlies, saying that I realized that many Japanese felt the lack of elbowroom in their own society and regarded me as insufficiently critical of that society. I said I had ample exposure in the United States to intellectuals who, like many in Japan, were critical of contemporary society on the ground that it was inauthentic and were deadly serious about it; and that what I liked in Suzuki was his playfulness, even though like other playful intellectuals he enjoys pushing his views to the extreme.

Otani said that the post-war Japanese identify both with Japan and with America. American movies introduce fads by showing the American way. But wasn't it true that the Americans were being Japanized? He spoke of a cowboy television show which had come to Japan and had been hugely popular. When the show returned to America, they had taken some Japanese stories back and had put them on American television, using a gun instead of judo in some particular play. I pointed out that the "Japanization" of America was a much more limited affair than the "Americanization" of Japan.

I suggested that cultural compatibilities depend on the way people see each other and what is visible in each culture. Were the Japanese as conscious of size as Americans? I said Americans notice looks very much. Was the size of Americans something that was highly visible to the Japanese? I spoke of studies of the Truk Islands and how the Trukese had impressed the Americans because they were good at handling machines and at baseball, and were obedient—much as some of the Japanese must have struck Americans. I suggested that some cultures were more fragile, some more permeable than others. Caudill's study of the Nisei and how they appeared to middle-class Americans was a good example of the sort of research I meant. Michida asked about the compatibility of blood types, and I laughed and said that it seemed to me that the Japanese, avoiding anthropological and psychoanalytic explanations, translated everything into biology. Otani said he was interested in Sheldon's work. I said that the culture defined the relevance of certain physiognomic characteristics and that I thought Sheldon, although stimulating, failed to see this. Some cultures are sensitive to the way people look, while other cultures are more sensitive to tone of voice or manner. Otani added that the GI's during the Occupation saw the girls they got as Japanese, but to the Japanese the girls appeared American—they were a kind of buffer between the GI's and the Japanese.

I agreed that Japan was much more visible to Americans than before the war and wondered what the feedback to Japan would be of the "Japan boom" in the United States. Otani replied that when Japanese see Americans enjoying Japanese food they are surprised. Their first reaction is that they can't *really* appreciate it. Japanese believe that foreigners won't like it. They're surprised when a foreigner speaks Japanese, both reactions being based of course on their experience with foreigners. They are not surprised when Chinese or Koreans speak Japanese. But it's not exactly a racial matter. They are somewhat surprised when Indians speak Japanese; they regard India as halfway between East and West.

Along the same line, Michida asked rather poignantly whether Westerners can really appreciate Japanese culture and art. For example, there had been a calligraphy exhibit in Paris. People had thought it wouldn't go over, but it had had an enthusiastic reception. Could the viewers really understand it? Evey responded that they wouldn't necessarily appreciate it in terms of its meaning but in other terms—as form, as abstract art, for instance. Michida continued that if the Japanese people have trouble understanding their own culture, they don't see how foreigners can understand it. He himself was fond of jazz, but how could he really understand it, when it wasn't his culture that created it. (This comment helped us realize the intensity of Japanese feelings of uniqueness and cultural distance, even the response to our liking for Japanese food, such as raw fish and seaweed which, as Otani said, they expect us to dislike.) I said I knew that many Japanese felt they couldn't really play jazz because it was American, and recalled that in Osaka, when we praised the jazz concert, people thought we must be flattering them. Again I said that cultural anthropology would be of great profit to Japan since it would indicate that in principle no culture is incomprehensible to a person who wants to get through the blockages. I added that Japanese might never really get over this "colonial" feeling, in which they were receptive to other cultures but didn't try to penetrate them, until they sent teams to study America, not to copy it but to understand it. (We had met anthropologists who had gone to Mongolia or Tonga or Afghanistan, but that isn't quite the same thing as going to study America or Britain or France.)

One of us pointed out that, unlike America, Japan has never assimilated its many foreigners, nor do the Japanese abroad assimilate very readily.

Again I feared that I was detaining a captive audience. It was after ten. Michida took his little car home and I walked with Otani over to the corner where he could get a cab to the station. He thought I must be walking there for some reason. He couldn't believe that I had come just to accompany him. He spoke again of the sense of uniqueness the Japanese have. And yet it seems to me there is ambivalence about their uniqueness: they are never sure whether they are inferior or superior. I had the feeling that Michida and Otani had tried to cross the barrier and are in a sense quite at home in America or talking with an Ameri-

DR

can, but still feel that they haven't fully made it—perhaps feel this all the more because they know what is involved. I would guess that they must defend America to their Japanese friends and colleagues who are less sympathetic and hold more simplistic views. Though they, too, are critical, they scan the American skies, as do some of the older men we have met, both for intellectual and for moral leadership.

ETR

Tokyo, November 28

The Liftons came up from Kyoto to hear Dave's lecture Saturday and to be with us these last days. I was especially glad that they were here for the lecture since I was not well enough to go. However, today I ventured out with Betty. She and Bob are staying at the old Imperial Hotel built by Frank Lloyd Wright, which I had only glimpsed driving by. I was enchanted to see it again. It is low and spread out, its several wings forming courtyards with pools, sculptures, flowers, and trees, giving the impression of an Oriental palace. The detail is fabulous in its almost archaic splendor, with carvings in the yellowish stone over the doorways and porte-cochere. Betty said that when she first saw it in 1952 there were almost no cars; the hotel looked across the quiet open space to the big park in front of the Imperial Palace; now high buildings are going up on three sides of it, and in front the traffic roars by. In all its jungle richness, it looks marooned.

After going to their room and wandering around the hotel to see all the nooks and crannies, we had lunch in one of its elegant restaurants. Then we walked a few blocks through the Ginza to a small art gallery that Betty is familiar with. We spent several fascinating hours looking through portfolios of prints by contemporary artists. The more we saw, the more I became aware of the variety of Japanese elements in this art: in Saito's work there is the sturdy stylization of traditional Japanese gardens, houses, lanterns, geisha—done in black, deep greens, browns, and sometimes a touch of lacquer red; Hodaka Yoshida's scratched-over black and red splotches have an almost abstract complexity, suggestive of lanterns and toys, festivals and rickshaws; the work of Masaji Yoshida conveys a Zenlike emptiness and delicacy in the shapes of three stones, or a stone and smooth egg-shaped object on wood. Some of these prints bring out the grain of the wood and the strong cut lines of the wood block; others have the soft quality of the brush, others the effect of spilled ink and the pen, which seems to be sometimes superimposed on the print.

DR

This evening, we had dinner with three young political scientists from the University of Tokyo, Professor Fujimoto, whom we had already met, Professor Shishido, and Professor Kozai, whom we were especially anxious to meet, as a student of Professor Nagano and as one of the greatly admired younger men in political science.

We got into a discussion, as so often, of the student movement and the *demo*. Shishido said that the Japanese thought there weren't any Americans who sympathized with or understood the *demo*. He felt that in each country reactions to the *demo* had depended on that country's internal politics. The French seemed to have admired them; the British thought them rather disorderly; the Americans thought them Communist; and so on.

I asked why the students had been so affected by criticism from outside and why they were so convinced that the *demo* had failed. Shishido replied that the leaders felt that the *demo* had failed because in their own ideology they saw them as the road to revolution. The followers had had no such ambition but were disillusioned with their leaders. Fujimoto added that while the ordinary students felt that the *demo* had failed to stop the Security Pact, yet they felt some satisfaction that they could participate in the political process.

Shishido, returning to the theme of American misunderstanding, said that no Americans were in personal danger during the *demo*. He recalled a Zengakuren student who had said "I'm sorry" when he stepped by accident on the toes of an American photographer. There were many such incidents.

I asked whether the "progressive" camp had a monopoly of intellectuals. Weren't there any in the Conservative Party? Kozai replied that it had intellectuals only in the field of economics, where it had the best or at least the most practical ones.

What about trade unions, I asked; are intellectuals welcome there? Shishido said that during the Korean War all the trade unions were broken up and reorganized because at American insistence the Communists were purged—indeed, I got the impression that some of the later radical posture of the unions was due precisely to this purge. Now, however, a reorganization is underway and there is some demand for intellectuals in the unions. (The purge allowed much malice to operate. People got rid of personal foes by accusing them of being Communists.)

I said I was impressed by the strong white-collar unions in Japan; people who in America would be junior-management men seemed active in the unions. Shishido spoke of a former student of his who had entered Hitachi, Ltd., and wanted to be active in the union there. However, the company had put him in the industrial-relations department, depriving him in this way of the opportunity to enter the union, so he had decided to leave the company—he had hoped to be in a branch which would allow him to participate in union affairs, but the company had outsmarted him; of course, leaving was a big step. I spoke of the student we'd seen the night before last who planned to leave his company if they manufactured nuclear arms. Kozai said it was rare to maintain idealism and in most jobs not possible.

We got onto the subject of American attitudes toward nuclear weapons. Visiting in America five or six years ago, Kozai had met some Americans who were sympathetic to his own feelings about nuclear weapons, but he hadn't come across any active organizations. He had only discovered from me that there were groups like SANE or the Committee of Correspondence, and he complained that in Japan it was impossible to learn such things because one found out about America through such governmental channels as NHK or such commercial ones as the Associated Press or *Time*. In the same vein, he asked about I. F. Stone, about whom he had heard through reading Arthur Schlesinger, Jr.'s White Paper on Cuba, where Stone's disillusionment with Castro was referred to. I recommended to him that he read I. F. Stone's *Newsletter*, which appears not to be known at all in Japan. Fujimoto asked about the Liberal Project, which he had read about in *Chuo Koron*; that there were such liberal congressmen seemed to be little known even among well-informed Japanese.

We moved from this to a discussion of the British Campaign for Nuclear Disarmament and Bertrand Russell's position. What would be the effect on other countries if Britain did follow this road? I expressed my own view in favor of the minimum deterrent as a kind of insurance and referred the group to Etzioni's work.

It was then suggested that if Britain disarmed, France and Germany would demand nuclear weapons from the United States and the United States would supply them. On the other hand, British nuclear disarmament might set a good example. I pointed out that the discussion of such matters among people concerned with disarmament in the United States oscillated between the moral and the political, the hortatory and the practical.

In contrast, I mentioned the exhibits at the Komaba campus, which had seemed to me to show concern only with the bomb and not with world politics; the students had a stereotyped image of the world situation. Shishido said that they were fatalistic and in that sense unpolitical. Fujimoto said that the Komaba students were mostly freshmen and sophomores and that the students at the main Hongo campus had more political sense. But, Shishido replied, the latter were less politically conscious, just because they had more political acumen—they were nearer to the realistic world. They had to confront the prospect of doom, whereas their fathers could drive forward with simplistic convictions.

Both Shishido and Kozai had been guest speakers at the Komaba festival. The former spoke about the problem of the constitution. Many students feel that the government is changing the constitution (both *de facto* and seeking to do so legally as well) and they rally round the constitution as the guarantor of freedom and democracy. Kozai had debated with a Communist on the meaning of neutralism in Marxist thinking. The Communist position has been that there is no such thing as neutralism, but now their theory is being revised. The students themselves think neutralism is possible—of course, Kozai was speaking here of professional Communists and not of the many who follow the Party either within the Socialist Party or elsewhere. (Another speaker had been the head of the Anti-Security Pact bureau, a kind of coordinator between the labor movement and the activist students.)

I said I was disappointed to find that some of the student leaders seem to care more for revolution than for peace. Some of the more honest ones had recognized this after the Russian tests had pried them loose from believing that they could have both peace and revolution by following the Communist line. Shishido responded that the logic of the peace movement differs from the logic of revolution in theory but that in practice there could be a common front, especially since the Japanese peace movement has a tradition that is independent of Marxism. This was because the Japanese intellectuals had said that peace must be with *all* countries and the Marxists had attacked this, denying the possibility of neutralism and taking a position like that later taken by John Foster Dulles. Kozai added that one of the basic troubles with the Japanese Communists is that they refuse to recognize the facts of world power politics and believe that anything and everything can be justified in Marxist terms; this is a kind of intellectual laziness.

Shishido said that while intellectuals had left the Communist Party, the Party had increased its power very much since the Anti-Security Pact *demo*. I asked where they recruited and he said from young, inexperienced, idealistic, frustrated people who couldn't get into the universities: girls in business, clerks, the failures; many of the people active in the Roon movement who haven't much chance for promotion and who seek both culture and politics outside the system. But the Communists were still focused on the Soviet Union, whereas they should be studying Communist China.

This led Shishido to ask me why, in the *Chuo Koron* article, Maccoby and I had said that Communist China was a danger. I explained at length that the Communist Chinese were fanatical and menacing, that Stalin had tried to destroy them, and that they felt hostile not only to the United States but also to all the "colonial" powers, including Russia, and were very provincial. In addition, citing Lifton's book, I said that they were puritanically religious: unlike the Russians, they wanted to convert everyone, to uproot filial piety and other Chinese traditions. I spoke of the competition between the Chinese and the Russians in Latin America, especially Cuba, and in Africa, and said that this was a threat to peaceful coexistence of which the Japanese seemed entirely unaware. I was told again that the Japanese had a sense of guilt about China. I stressed my view that the Chinese Communists were repeating with a vengeance some of the mistakes of Soviet collectivization and of Stalin's totalitarian policies, that many intellectuals had fled or had been put into thought-reform camps, while the new generation knew almost nothing of the outside world.

These critical judgments troubled some of my interlocutors. I was asked whether American policy toward mainland China and Taiwan didn't increase the evils I was describing. I said probably it did. It was denied that the Chinese were religious; on the contrary, they had been a highly secular society. I said this was changing. Fujimoto asked whether I meant that they were spreading a new civilization—it seemed difficult for them to grasp what I meant by "religion." Again I referred them to Lifton's study of thought reform, and also to the exhibit of the China study group at Ochanomizu Women's College, which was full of piety about the happy peasants and the health and education movements in China but lacked any sense of the Chinese undercutting of Khrushchev's attempts at peaceful coexistence or any awareness of what would happen when the Chinese gained nuclear weapons. I think it was possible for me to be listened to in talking this way only because the group had previously been convinced of my good will and that I wasn't selling any particular American line. My own knowledge of China is limited, yet I did not feel that these talented men, at home in many ways in the world, had much idea as to what was happening in China, other than that a great Asiatic power was arising from a long period of humiliation, including humiliation by the Japanese.

I have condensed matters here, and I'm afraid I have not adequately conveyed either the brilliance or the human qualities of these men, nor have I sufficiently indicated the differences I sensed among them which there was no opportunity fully to explore.

Tokyo, November 29

This afternoon we went out to one of the suburbs to meet with Mr. Katayama, a well-known Zengakuren leader. We had expected to find him in some kind of graduate-student digs and found him instead in a new suburban house, hovered over by an attentive mother and sister. His pleasant study was lined with books in Japanese and English. Though Katayama speaks English, Miss Yamamoto was present to act as interpreter. A slight man with glasses, he looks like many Japanese student intellectuals: attractive, in a clean white shirt, well groomed, and soft of voice. He is the scholar and editor, whereas Iwanuma is more the activist, but I have the impression that oratory and perhaps personal presence play less of a part in leadership in Japan than elsewhere. Diet members are spoken of as "big stomachs," and I was told there are no orators in the Diet; people have even said that print matters more than personal appearance and that the Japanese language doesn't lend itself to eloquence—of all this, of course, I can make no independent judgment.

Katayama began by describing the movement represented by the journal of which he is an editor, *Political Thought*. In 1956, student criticism of Stalinism had begun. After the *demo* of last year the fetishism of the infallibility of the Communist Party had been further destroyed because of political criticism of the Party. His group had been organized, following the *demo*, to look into the causes of the breakdown of Communism, not only in the political sphere but in the sphere of ideas, and to develop a weapon for criticism of the historical defects of Marxism in Japan, whether Stalinist or Trotskyist. The Japanese Communists are tradition-directed and it was time to change that and to develop one's own theory rather than to accept the given rigid ones. Among the older generation of intellectuals influenced by the Party there was a great vacuum between reality and theory.

I referred to Erich Fromm's book on the early writings of Marx (Katayama was familiar with these) and raised the question whether a more humanistic Marxism might repel rather than attract those eager for a dogmatic "answer." Katayama agreed that dogmatism makes Marxism attractive to the older generation but that among the younger generation just this dogmatism was the target of criticism. European Marxism was rooted in European reality, but when transferred to Japan, the transplanted thought had no connection with the Japanese reality, although just such transplantation was commonplace with Japanese intellectuals. The latter thought the "solution" lay in bringing the realities of Japan in line with the Western experience—this was wishful thinking. Katayama had realized this and awakened to these weaknesses through the criticisms of Stalinism, but even these criticisms were simply opposing one ideology against another and not touching Japanese reality. I suggested that Marxist theories might be out of line in Europe also with the change of time and tradition, and that it would be interesting to study the different Communist parties in each country in terms of the coloration given to Marxism by that country's own particular culture.

I spoke of my disappointment that so few involved with the peace movement in Japan had any feeling for political realities and, despite the worry over fall-out, any sense of urgency. Katayama agreed, saying that the immediate danger of fall-out blurred the analysis of the international situation. In 1955 Zengakuren was active in establishing the Gensuikyo movement. The shock of Soviet resumption of testing had jarred Gensuikyo. But the slogan of "American imperialism" also clouded discussion at last year's Gensuikyo meeting. Katayama said nobody knows what the phrase "American imperialism" means but it circulates in the atmosphere and helps, along with the Soviet tests, to give rise to apathy. While pro-Russian organizations tried to defend the Soviet tests, some Zengakuren members protested against "Russian imperialism," and this phrase also clouded their objective view of the international situation. Katayama argued that the Japanese are close to their own sensory experience and that since Hiroshima they have had a deep awareness of the dangers of fall-out.

While we continued talking, Mrs. Katayama brought in tea and a kind of custard sundae with fruit and whipped cream; and later a different tea, this time with fruitcake. The sister who helped serve us looked familiar. It turned out that she had been in the Child Study Group at Ochanomizu and that we had talked with her there. She was plainly proud of her brother.

I returned to my question as to the priority of peace and asked how he himself felt, not how the movement felt. He said that in his own concept of revolution there wasn't an either-or as between peace and revolution, but of course peace had priority. He went on to say that lots of things had been done in the name of peace under Stalin and this prejudiced the Zengakuren movement about the use of the word. The Hungarian Revolution was suppressed by the Soviet Union in the name of peace, just as France is suppressing the Algerian Revolution in the name of peace. For him the concept of peace is included in the concept of revolution—and this latter concept seemed to be based on the problem of alienation of the self and of the search for selfhood in Japanese life. He went on to say that individuals have been oppressed in the name of peace and that therefore one really couldn't distinguish between peace and revolution. The peace movement in Japan was itself an "other-dependent" movement in which people look to others to achieve their wishes. The first Gensuikyo is dependent on the U.S.S.R., the second (a newer non-Communist peace movement) on the United States. What is necessary now is a third autonomous peace party which would try to influence the government.

All this was truncated, and necessarily delayed by the need for translation, and it was also highly theoretical (even when criticizing excessive theorizing). What was astonishing to me was how confident some prominent university students are who, despite their defeatism, expect to play an important part in the political and intellectual life of their time. Presently, to be sure, there is a period of regrouping and even further splitting of student forces, although there is general agreement that the model of the Russian revolution (and certainly the leadership of Soviet Communism) isn't for them. In the face of the fragmentation of the movement, these students nevertheless have no doubt about the national relevance of their own positions.

By this time a student had come who was to take us to Yokohama; if I could have cancelled the trip then and gone on with Katayama I would have done so, for I felt we had barely made contact and were still really talking past each other.

We had been invited for dinner by Mr. Kawai of the Teachers Union and some of his colleagues. Searching for an interpreter to go with us, International House recruited a senior at Keio University, Mr. Hagiwara, a good-looking, crew-cut young man wearing a tweed jacket over the invariable heavy sweater. In the course of the two hours it took us to get to Yokohama and despite the crowding in the trains, we had some interesting talks. Hagiwara told us that he had entered the chain of interconnecting schools that leads to Keio Senior High School and then on into Keio University itself. He said he had been drawn there in part by his admiration for its founder, Fukuzawa, although Hagiwara commented that most of the students enrolled either because their fathers had gone there or because they had failed to get into Todai or other leading government universities. Like many people with whom we have talked, he was inclined to see present-day Keio—sometimes called the Stanford of Japan—as a comedown from Fukuzawa's exalted ideals. He spoke of friends of his who spent all their time playing golf or in other extracurricular activities. (Extracurricular activities have a far greater importance in Japan than they do, let us say, in the Big Ten, for like much else in Japan they are taken with the utmost seriousness as quasi-educational.) Hagiwara spoke of a friend of his who had done graduate work at Michigan State and found himself woefully unprepared; for example, he had never learned to use a library, and he was now spending six hours a day on his studies, which, as Hagiwara said half jokingly, was more than he had spent in a year at Keio; he then continued, saying that the university student in Japan spent about 50 per cent of his life in his club and 50 per cent at most in his studies. Keio students would say that they were going to their "social studies" when they were going to their golf clubs or mah-jongg class—mah-jongg is their favorite indoor game.

What about the coeds, I asked. Hagiwara said it was entirely different from America. Women comprise about 20 per cent of the Keio student body and they are concentrated in literature, sociology, and art—all "impractical" ways of wasting time before they got married; he didn't see why they didn't go to junior college, as most girls do, since two years of general education was all they needed or could profit from. He said that the Keio boys looked down on the Keio girls, while of course the girls did not expect that they would marry any of these boys, but expected arranged marriages. There is almost no dating, he said, although of course boys and girls share in certain activities, especially those dealing with literature. Most of the Keio boys are there to get a good job in a good company and make a good marriage—or have it made for them. And thus they don't bother with the girls.

Hagiwara had started to learn English in primary school. Then two summers ago he had gone to Stanford Summer School, his only visit to the United States; nevertheless, he seemed quite fluent in English—and, in his energy and go-getter quality and social ease, very "American." This is a quality that affects appearance as well as speech and manner, so that Evey and I often feel we can tell which of the people we meet has been in the United States (going to Great Britain seems to work much less change, and Britain is seen as much closer to Japanese ways). I asked Hagiwara whether what he was doing in taking us to Yokohama was "Arbeit," but he scornfully rejected the idea; he did this because he was eager to meet me; he had a copy of *The Lonely Crowd* with him which he asked me to autograph.

Many, perhaps most, Japanese are characteristically hesitant to express criticism, at least personal criticism or criticism that might be taken as personal—thus, when I have talked with Leftists, even though they know I myself am critical of America, they have modulated what they said, out of fear of offending my "American" sensibilities. If in a meeting I express criticism in very strong terms and say, for example, that so-and-so's work is pedantic or obscurantist, or even make a criticism of some reactionary common enemy, the women present will laugh embarrassedly and hide their faces in their hands and even the men will sometimes do this or an approximation of it. It is as if one had made some grave social error, somewhat amusing but even more embarrassing. Other Japanese who have been "Americanized" in personality (whatever their ideological view of America) aren't like that at all. Hagiwara is frank and direct in criticism. In the course of the evening he said many extremely critical things about Stanford, and only at the end he said that he hoped he hadn't sounded too critical of Stanford, that he was indeed critical, but that if I could see him among his Japanese friends who were always criticizing America, I would see how strongly he opposed them and stood up for America. (I was sure this was true, before he said it.)

Hagiwara has been studying international economic development, and plans to enter a small trading company with a few hundred employees engaged in export-import trade with Great Britain and other countries. He said he prefers to enter this small company, where he has the possibility of getting ahead, rather than one of the huge trading companies like Mitsubishi or Sumitomo which offers great security and, in the minds of most students, the top jobs.

He told a remarkable story of his interview with the company where he has now decided to go. Along with other Keio seniors, he had been screened first by the university and then had taken the exam for this company and had passed it and then gone up for an interview with ten of the directors or leading officials, including the president. As is the custom, all the applicants wore their uniforms, which are stiff and hot. But as it was a July day, Hagiwara decided to appear in a perfectly clean white buttoned-down shirt but not his heavy, sweaty uniform. He knew this might offend people but he wanted to show his independence. It was an unheard-of thing to do (there is such prestige attached to being a university student that the students always wear their uniforms on any formal occasions or on any occasion when they want to impress people—there is here something of the French attitude toward the student as a privileged person, as a member of the elite). The president criticized him at the interview for not wearing a uniform, and Hagiwara explained his position and said that what he wore was cleaner and much cooler than a uniform and made more sense. Other directors also criticized him. For three days he heard nothing and then he got a telegram asking him to come back for an interview with the president. He said that the ten people who had interviewed him had split five to five on whether to take him on. The appointment was for three and he was there at three but was made to wait until 6:30. When he was finally shown into the president's office, the latter apologized for keeping him waiting and Hagiwara said that he could make his apology good by hiring him. The president responded that when Hagiwara came into the firm he would have to serve tea like everyone else (hitherto I'd thought only girls served tea but young men apparently do it too). Hagiwara had the feeling that this was an effort to break his will. He wasn't sure he could take it—yet in Japan if one is fired from a company or leaves, in the system of lifelong employment, one condemns oneself, no matter what the reason and no matter what one's references.

I had been hesitant to ask Hagiwara his attitude toward the *demo*, for Keio students are notoriously conservative and some are Rightist; and he knew, of course, that he had picked us up at the home of one of the Zengakuren leaders. But when I found I could talk freely I did ask him what he had done during the *demo*. He said that less than 3 per cent of the Keio students had taken part in them. Todai students had come over to their campus with handbills and petitions to ask them to turn out for the *demo*. He had stood at the gate and argued with them, telling them that he was against the Kishi government but not against America and not against the Security Treaty, which he thought essential for Japan. They had responded with slogans, and when he had invited them into the campus for more discussion, they had declined. He felt that most of the students had no idea what they were talking about. He had contempt for them as a mob. And he was deeply ashamed over the Haggerty incident, which violated not only Japanese "guest culture" but his sense of orderly democratic process and his deep if ambivalent ties to the United States. At the same time, he felt as many did that the Kishi government had behaved unlawfully or undemocratically in the way it had pushed the Treaty through the Diet, and thus he had some sympathy with the *demo* in spite of his severe criticisms.

I showed him an issue of *New Left Thought* Katayama had given us, and Hagiwara said he was familiar with it. He reads *Chuo Koron* regularly; "everybody" in fact reads *Chuo Koron.* (We have been told that this liberal journal has probably been more cautious politically since the attempt by a right-wing seventeen-year-old boy to assassinate its editor—the boy succeeded in killing a maid at his house and wounding the editor's wife. The fear of assassination operates as a restraint on the Left and is an element in the fear many have of a right-wing resurgence.)

Hagiwara spoke with the greatest distress about the younger generation, whom he defined as those who have grown up since the war and who take for granted all the economic and political advances of contemporary Japan. He referred with dismay to his nephew, aged thirteen. Hagiwara asked him what he wanted to do, and the boy said he wanted to go to America. "That's a fine idea. Why do you want to go?" "So that I can listen to rock and roll." Hagiwara reported this disgustedly. (Evey pointed out that there was lots of rock and roll in Tokyo.) Hagiwara shares the general bewilderment and discouragement about the growing juvenile delinquency in Japan, the lack of traditional values that is sometimes blamed on "Americanization."

He told of an experience he had had on this same crowded railway line between Yokohama and Tokyo when a somewhat drunken American GI pulled a Japanese flag out of his pocket and proceeded with much noise to light it with a cigarette lighter, burn it, and stamp on it. Hagiwara said he went up to him and asked him to consider that he was a soldier on duty for America and that he was harming America; he pleaded with him not to do it, but the GI didn't listen. Then he had to try to protect the GI from being mobbed by the many students on the train. Hagiwara fought with them and pleaded with them not to dishonor Japan but to arrest the soldier. He got off with him and the aroused students at the next station, put him in the hands of the police, who in turn notified the American authorities, who eventually sent him back to the United States.

When Hagiwara translated for us during our dinner discussion, he took no notes but was able to recall considerable stretches without apparent difficulty, though he had had little prior experience; when he was interpreting my comments into Japanese, he spoke vivaciously and forcefully and I felt he was interpreting me, as well as what I said.

Unlike many interpreters, who are understandably nervous and pay close attention to every word, he managed to eat a good dinner as well as to take full part in the translation. On the way back, he said that of course he hadn't admitted he was a Keio student or the occasion would have been difficult, not only I suspect because of Keio's conservative cast but also because it is one of the elite private universities, while most of the men in the room had attended nothing "higher" than a normal college or school. I told him I was reminded of Yoshida's comment that after having gone to America, contacts within Japan were much easier for him; and Hagiwara agreed that that had been his own experience. I've found that when I ask many eminent intellectual and academic Japanese a question that they haven't thought of before and that they can't readily answer, their response is a long sigh, sometimes they put their face in their hands, refusing really to grapple with the question. But that is not at all Hagiwara's pattern: here again he is very direct and responsive. As is obvious, my attitude toward him shifted in the course of the evening. When he first appeared, with his "Joe College" Keio student style, I was troubled about how we would get along, but the more I talked with him, the more impressed I was by a certain dauntlessness coupled with a strong dose of social responsibility in the Japanese tradition.

To the outsider and the Westernized insider, this cohesive sense of social responsibility must appear as one of the many drags upon Japanese efficiency. Actually, however, I'm not so sure that this is in the long run inefficient or that I know what efficiency is. While it takes time to touch all the bases in any Japanese situation—I am astonished at the intellectuals who manage to lead a life as hectic as my own without violating Japanese canons of politeness—it would also seem that these canons provide a certain cushion against pressure. I think of this when we are taking leave after any gathering. We say goodbye at least three or four times, shaking hands in Western style and bowing in Japanese style; we say goodbye in the room and again at the door; then we say goodbye again when the taxi comes, and when we turn around we see everyone bowing and waving to us. And these are men who, to make a living, must hold down three to four jobs, if not more, and who have a deadline to meet, yet they are total prisoners of the ritual—perhaps if they were less than total prisoners they would mind it more and chafe at the endless delays.

Our trip to Yokohama was in fact our first real experience of the Tokyo transit rush hour of which we had read and heard so much. We got on a train at a suburban terminal near I.C.U., where as many people were pouring into the terminal to go toward the city as were coming out from it. The stampede to get aboard the trains and through the long shuttlelike passageways that connect one railroad line with another was rather murderous. To get on the trains, people wait at the car-door stops—sometimes there would be 2,000 waiting for a 400-capacity train. When the train starts, the many people who could not reach straphangers lurch in a solid mass and are kept from falling by the very fact that they are a solid mass—a solider mass than even in our subways. (This sort of nightmare reminds me of the earthquake we experienced night before last about two o'clock in the morning. I thought I must be having a nightmare, and woke up to find the whole house shaking. It was terrifying, though Evey found it more frightening than I did, for, as she said, one never knew when it would stop or whether it would get worse. Actually, it was probably over in less than a minute, and surprisingly no damage was done. We're glad in a way to have experienced that too.)

As we went in toward Tokyo, people left the train but it filled up again by the time we got to the terminal. We took a local for Yokohama because the express was too jammed, and this delayed our ride so that we were nearly an hour late. In spite of the crowding, many people managed to read magazines and books. There were all ages and types: young school girls with their briefcases, holding hands; many university and high-school students in their uniforms; women with babies who were sleeping or wriggling; professional men and office workers with their briefcases—many of whom would certainly not be home before 7:30, after three changes and two hours of commuting. Over the loud-speaker system the conductor not only announced each station several times but also advised passengers not to leave their belongings—wherever one goes in Japan, one is surrounded by a kind of politeness-talk like that of an airline hostess, only more so—a slight oil in the wheels that grind. There is even orderliness in the rush for taxis at the end of the line—very different from many experiences we've had at stations or airports in America.

Let me turn now to the evening itself. Yokohama is the foreign port of Tokyo, a city of warehouses and piers and factories, and a Chinese section, where we saw American sailors and which has a rather ominous air. Our taxi took us over some terribly rough roads that are being dug up for construction and past a huge building project which is the prefectural government's effort to bring culture to Yokohama with a public library and museum and concert hall—really a civic center of enormous proportions; work, as usual, was going on at night. We stopped in a dimly lit street at a dimly lit building which was the headquarters of the local Teachers Union that looks after the affairs of 16,000 teachers in the prefecture; it was not much drearier than other public or semipublic buildings.

Kawai, who had met us in Tokyo, made the introductions of the other four men. One man wore a dark plaid shirt with an open collar, while several others had the standard garb of a white shirt, sober tie, and black or near black suit. We made apologies for our delay; and they then asked whether we would mind having a Chinese dinner, that they had wondered what we would like in the way of dinner and had decided on this. We said it was fine, and so went off in two cabs to the restaurant, located in a very noisy Chinatown, full of tourist traps. In the room next to ours was a loud and hilarious party of Japanese men.

To my surprise, Kawai put Evey on his right and the rest of us were grouped around a circular table with a Lazy Susan in the center. In addition to our interpreter and a public-relations man from the union who ran the tape recorder, there were the three officials of the union, who told us that they had taught for fifteen years before becoming officials—in other words, they had met a payroll—and the journalist from the local paper.

At one point I commented that there didn't seem to be any women officials of the Teachers Union, although an increasing majority of the primary-school teachers now were women. Kawai replied that there was a women's section staffed by older women which aims to counsel the younger women teachers. While the older men did try to understand the problems of a woman teacher, the young male union leaders did not. It seems pretty clear that in Japan a woman cannot boss a man or occupy a position of real leadership save from the leverage of the arts or the mass media—and in the case of the latter, with some tendency to confine women to home-economics programs and things like that. (As already suggested, Kawai himself turned repeatedly to Evey in the course of the evening—something that's never happened before—and asked about American children and what could be done about delinquency, referring here to the movie *The Blackboard Jungle*.)

I asked Kawai about the increase of women schoolteachers and what this portended for the union, since women in America were often politically conservative or apathetic. He explained that teaching was once a well-paid occupation but that now, especially with Ikeda's famous "double income" plan, business jobs pay ever so much better, and men avoid going into teaching, while women, deprived of other opportunities, find their way into teaching. However, the very young girls who are still planning to marry are not much use to the union, while the older unmarried women in their thirties are not close in spirit to these young girls. Thus, it is the task of the leadership to persuade the young teachers that they should be concerned about Japanese society and about improving their own condition so that they can become better teachers.

At one point in the evening I asked the union officials around the table to say what they had done that day, so that I could get an idea of their work. The public-relations man pointed to the tape recorder and said that was his work for the day. One man who came in late said that he was making a survey of crowded classrooms and teacher shortages for presentation to the Ministry of Education. Another man seemed to be a kind of lobbyist and had gone to the Prefectural Education Office to ask for higher pay for the teachers and had taken a deputation of teachers with him as well as arranged for others to go independently.

Kawai and his colleagues brought up two principal concerns of the union. The first was the overcrowded classroom that doesn't allow the teacher to get to know each of her pupils individually, and thus to prepare them for life or prevent them from becoming delinquents. Kawai said that the motto of his local union was: "Without research there can be no education." "Investigation" might be a better translation than "research" which appeared to be the compilation of data to put pressure on the government for more pay or more classrooms or more health care for the children and so on; since education involves practically everything in the society and since these men are dedicated at once to the teaching profession and to social and political change, what they mean by research is partly experimentation and partly propaganda.

As an example of the former they mentioned the innovation of their prefecture concerning examinations for entry into the senior high school, which are the prelude for the even more terrifying examinations to get into the university. Kawai and the man in the open plaid shirt—the most talkative of his colleagues—said that everybody complained in Japan about the examination system but didn't do anything about it. Those who had succeeded by this route felt that it must be all right since they had made it; those who had not succeeded felt helpless to change it. Yet the examination system destroyed the lives of children, interfered with their education, affected their mental health, and even stratified society on the basis of memory work, that is, rote answers to rote questions. The union officials wanted to substitute the school record, the judgment of the school principal, and where necessary a personal interview.

In their prefecture they had also tried to provide a place in high school for every student who wanted it and thus get rid of the examination system altogether for entry into high school; their union maintained that everyone should have a high-school education. However, when it turned out that there were not enough high-school places, the union was in a quandary. They considered admitting a number without examination and then having an examination only for the last few places. But here they were caught between the problem of fairness based on examinations and the damage done by the examinations; they had no ready answer. I could only suggest that America was struggling, though possibly less strenuously, with the same questions and that I sometimes felt that meritocracy seemed to be the only alternative to aristocracy or oligarchy.

While the Teachers Union has the reputation of being one of the most radical of white-collar unions and plays a large role in the union movement in the country at large, this particular group seemed to us to have a genuine interest in pedagogic innovation as well as in larger political change. However, when I raised the question why the Teachers Union was unwilling to employ a University of Tokyo graduate in a staff position, the man in the plaid shirt and several others responded vehemently that a Todai or a Kyodai graduate wasn't necessarily better but that others would defer to them, so that to maintain democracy within the union they could not allow them to come in and dominate it. When I suggested that this protective tariff, though understandable, was not itself democratic—"democratic" is a plus word here, to which constant reference is made—I got no reply.

The man in the plaid shirt said he'd seen figures showing that the average classroom in Japan had fifty-two pupils, whereas in America the number was around thirty. Was this right? I said that the American figure had to be seen as an average and that there were many classrooms which were very overcrowded. American children were more disorderly than Japanese; and therefore the teacher had to spend more time over discipline in many of these classes; having seen and been impressed by *The Blackboard Jungle*, they could understand this. (Kawai told me later that while there was perfect order in the classroom, angry students, bitter because a teacher had failed or "insulted" them, would sometimes waylay him after class and beat him up—

another sign of the degeneration of Japan after the war. Kawai, like so many young Japanese, understandably wants at the same time the insubordination and freedom of America and the national consensus of social responsibility and orderliness of Japan.)

Our hosts and the newspaperman as well were as interested in politics as in pedagogy, and one of the first questions the latter asked me was whether I was anxious about what I had found in Japan. Did I think Japan was headed for disaster? I said, as I had on many occasions, that I didn't want to encourage complacency but that I thought the problems of the big powers were even more grave. (Kawai said later that the problem of peace was one that concerned all of the women teachers and was one form of their political interests that could be developed.)

The newsman then asked whether Japan wouldn't be forced—presumably by America—to accept nuclear weapons. I said I didn't see why it was inevitable and that I thought that Japan was no less safe, and perhaps more so, without nuclear arms than it would be with them. Then it became clear that the newsman's implication was that Japan would have to leave the American alliance if it was to avoid nuclear weapons, and join the camp of the neutrals. (When the Japanese Communist Party in 1955 was so violently opposed to neutralism in Japan, they lost support; for they might in cooperation with socialist and pacifist sentiment have moved Japan away from the American alliance if they had not insisted on the country's joining the Soviet bloc. I'm struck by how many fumbled chances the Japanese Communist Party has had since the war, by the dogmatism and stupidity with which it has thrown these chances away.)

The belief of these men that right-wing groups lurk behind the Liberal Democrats (Conservatives) and the American alliance, only waiting for their chance, seems to me one of the reasons why a peace movement leaning neither toward the Communists nor toward the West has such a difficult time, for many on the Left honestly believe that only by opposition to Ikeda's policies within Japan can they exercise any leverage for peace. Every time Ikeda visits a Southeast Asian country, the feeling grows here that he is building up a military "free world" alliance under the American shadow, and this anxiety is intensified by our growing involvement in South Vietnam. This is so despite the fact that Ikeda is a man, as the Japanese say, of "low posture," who, unlike Kishi, does not seek haughtily to override widespread pacifist or neutralist sentiment.

On the problems of teaching, Kawai emphasized repeatedly the enormous responsibility of the teacher: the teacher must not only help the child get through his exams without failure or distress but must also work with the family to prevent juvenile delinquency and to improve cultural standards. One of the officials trotted out the figures from a recent study I'd read in the paper which showed that more families had television sets than had desks at which children could pursue their studies. As I listened, the thought occurred to me that Japanese children are gay but the adults are sad; in repose these men, like so many others, have sad and lined faces, though when they were talking with us they were extremely animated as well as direct—very alive and appealing in their dedication.

As enormous platter after enormous platter of food was brought in, most of which we couldn't eat, I worried about the bill and how this apparently impecunious union was going to pay it. I had great misgivings about this, feeling on the one hand that they would want to entertain us, but on the other that they had done so too lavishly for their own resources; and so I said toward the end of the discussion that I would like to share the expenses of the evening which we had so much enjoyed. I'm afraid that I made a dreadful mistake: they insisted that it was their pleasure and their party and that they had invited us—and this included the taxis as well as the extravagant meal. Hagiwara said later that I needn't have worried, that the Socialist Party gives the Teachers Union money and that they have a fund for entertaining, that it would not come out of the pockets of the men. He also agreed with me that the teachers on very low salaries would probably resent their union leaders, who were (in the American phrase) "pork choppers" living better than they.

This reminds me that early in the discussion I asked the group about the turnover of union leadership in Japan, pointing out that in the United States only a despot was without threat from factions building on resentments within the rank and file or simply on a desire for a change. Kawai said that there was a good deal of turnover—I pointed to the public-relations man and asked if he was there to prevent it, but got no reply. Kawai went on to say that the turnover of officials was per se not so bad since they usually promised to obey the same platform that had been followed by their predecessors, but that new men, in spite of themselves, always meant new policies and there was a great waste here. If I understood him correctly, he was sufficiently idealistic to want to rely on education and public agitation to retain office.

During the discussion on the examination problem, I realized that as long as some positions are much better than others, are paid better and treated better, some way must be found to select the people for those positions, and there will be feelings of inadequacy on the part of those who haven't made it. Only in a truly equal society would it be possible to play down the examination system, for it would not finally locate people either at the top or at the bottom: there would in that sense be no top or bottom. All work on examinations in a meritocracy is a kind of tinkering.

As we rose to go, the group shifted quickly from serious to courteous and friendly, wishing us a good voyage back to America. When we got into the station in Tokyo, we told Hagiwara that he could put us in a cab and didn't have to take us out to International House; but he vehemently shook his head, saying that it was his "social responsibility" to see that we got home. What would happen if we got in an accident? Anyway, he didn't live too far off, so that he could combine his individualism with responsibility.

Tokyo, November 30

This morning I had breakfast with an economist who works for one of the leading trading companies, Mr. Ishimoto. His name and work are well known not only in Japan but among economists elsewhere interested in international questions. He turned out to be an extremely alert, graying, handsome man, who speaks excellent English. He had been a banker before the war, and in the hazards and chances of the Occupation, he had been purged. But this had been turned to his advantage, because he spent his time of exile reading economics and reflecting on world economy. Thus, he has had in effect a second career and now he travels all over, talking with bankers and government officials and businessmen.

Recently he had visited Czechoslovakia, Poland, Hungary, and Yugoslavia. He was dismayed by the Czechs, who had tumbled from among the freest people to among the most servile, and whose standard of living had also fallen drastically. The Yugoslavs are much freer.

Mainly, however, we discussed his fears of a possible world crash based on credit inflation and the widespread dependence on American gold reserves. As to Japan itself, he felt Prime Minister Ikeda's policy was inflationary, the more so since his prestige depended on his "ten-year income-doubling plan," a pointless and misleading (though widely accepted) slogan which forbade the necessary deflationary measures.

Ishimoto made criticisms I've also heard from American economists against Gross National Product as a measure of the size and strength of an economy, pointing out that it includes television sets and other expenditures in the private sector which do nothing to build up the economy as a whole. Given the general weakness of the public sector in Japan, money would go for consumer—or, for that matter, producer—luxuries rather than, let us say, to develop ports and harbors. No Galbraith, but rather a conservative economist, Ishimoto wanted taxes to sop up consumer and corporate buying power. Government loans should also be used to this end, although the latter are hated because they are reminiscent of the war economy. Furthermore, interest rates should be allowed to rise in order to cut down corporate and private indebtedness. Instead of this, Ikeda was absurdly planning on a tax cut, which of course would be popular.

Ishimoto believes Japanese businessmen to be misled by their experience in the years immediately following the war. Then Japan was poor and starving and could export its products without raising grave objections, particularly as the amounts were still relatively small. But in the future, with a huge output and a rich country, there will be no such readiness in the United States or elsewhere to accept Japanese products, which in any case will cost more with the high wages the expansionist policy is bringing about. It was one thing for the Japanese economy to start from nothing and grow in a clear direction simply by meeting the tremendous shortages. But now the greatest shortages had been made up, and the direction the economy was to take was no longer clear and required thought and planning. Yet politicians and businessmen alike assumed with confidence that the economy could continue to rise at the same high rate. Most big businessmen go right ahead borrowing, in the happy belief that no one will allow them to go bankrupt, although (as I know from the papers) many small businesses are going bankrupt now. This means that the businessmen believe that there is no penalty for failure or overexpansion if one is big enough, but the lack of market pressure to weed out failures must mean eventually the collapse of the whole economy. (Ishimoto noted that a bill which would have made the Bank of Japan independent of the government and hence more of a stabilizing force had failed to pass.)

None of this seemed totally unfamiliar to an American. Ishimoto was scathing about the way in which Ikeda and the politicians soothed people and made glamorous promises while the people go on believing that all will come out right. When I questioned him on the possibly dangerous social consequences of deflation, this seemed not to trouble him. He is something of an aristocrat, and strikes me as rather "British" in his feeling about austerity. As I've already made clear, he shares the contempt for politicians that we've met on all sides. When I asked him where, outside what he would regard as a salutary crash, he saw any hope for his policies, he said that the press was the most important force shaping the Japanese political economy and the only leverage for an effort to redress imbalances. And in the bureaucracy there are people who understand these matters. But there are no political leaders who do.

As I write these lines, the cook and some of the waiters and other boys employed at International House are playing baseball in the driveway where half an hour ago were parked the enormous cars and the attentive chauffeurs of the Rotary Club's weekly meeting. And the other day, when we were down at the Imperial Hotel, white-collar employees from the nearby Toshiba building were playing toss and catch in a vacant lot; it was a striking sight to see these bespectacled and studious-looking young men throwing balls with exceptional speed and force, with all the motions of a big-league star warming up; they took off their coats but kept their ties tightly knotted over their standard white shirts.

We got into a terrible traffic jam this afternoon when several officials of the Nippon Management Association were taking me by cab to the discussion we were to have downtown. It was drizzling slightly, and when I jumped out of our cab to walk the few remaining blocks, they followed me but with reluctance—a reluctance which, as I realized later with a pang, was based on fear of the fall-out that would be brought down by rain; they would, of course, much rather have been late than endure this risk, which leads many people when they have been out in a downpour to go home and take a bath (in water which, as the newspapers point out, is not necessarily any less contaminated).

Our meeting was in a new and handsome office building in which the Association occupies several floors. Although it was 5:30, people were still busily working, or rather looking busy, and they would be here at least two more hours—until the boss goes home, no one else wants to leave. The walls were lined with management journals, mostly American, and there was a large library of books on management, many of them translations from the American. The conference room where we sat and had tea while waiting for others to arrive had the usual overstuffed chairs with antimacassars that lend incongruity to the most modern design; perhaps Japan needs Frank Lloyd Wright-type architects able to insist on designing every item of furniture. These chairs, which every big-shot puts into the conference room as an appurtenance of his position, have a kind of standardized impersonal ugliness.

My host (who was to interpret for me) was a graduate of one of the government universities who had also studied at Massachusetts Institute of Technology. He had done something almost unheard of, quitting another job to come to the NMA. He was one of the organizers of the group interested in consumer behavior whom I was to address. They had instituted some cooperative research, and I asked him how rivalries among competing companies could be overcome sufficiently to allow such research, recalling how difficult it is in the United States to do any pooling, let us say, of research done by NBC and CBS and McCann-Erickson. He told me that cooperative research is possible among companies since in any case they divide up the markets among themselves.

Finally everyone had arrived and had taken his place around the long U-shaped table where each had his name and title written in English on one side of a place card and in Japanese on the other. People went around the room introducing themselves and their work to me. There was an epidemiologist from one of the government agencies who was interested in the relation between protein foods and cancer or heart disease. His presence and that of one or two others reminded me of how Japanese interdisciplinary work often cuts across the line between biology and the social sciences—in the absence of psychoanalytic thinking, there is a tendency to give biological explanations for differences we would be more apt to interpret as cultural. There were also an anthropologist, a demographer, a statistician; most of the perhaps twenty-five others seemed to be in systems analysis, market research, industrial engineering, etc. I was not introduced to a dozen people who were staff people and editors of technical bulletins, etc., at NMA, and all but one of these—one of the chief editors—took no part in the later discussion.

The chairman of the meeting was Mr. Nakamura, an official in one of the governmental research agencies. To my surprise, I found that I was expected to make a speech rather than lead a discussion. He asked me to talk about trends in the behavioral sciences in the United States and what was happening to interdisciplinary work in America. Since he had stood up, I stood up, leading my translator also to stand up; but after a while I sat down so that he could sit down and take notes. Pauses for translation gave me a chance to think of the next things to say. I talked about differences in America between academic research and applied research, discussed briefly the Bureau of Applied Social Research, the Survey Research Center, the National Opinion Research Center, etc., and mentioned Stanford Research Institute, which one of the members of the group had visited while he was at Stanford. I spoke of the relatively greater freedom, it seemed to me, that Japanese academicians had to roam about, as compared with their American counterparts, who tended to specialize, but Mr. Ishii, an older, talkative man, said later that he thought the Japanese situation wasn't so different and that the disciplines were territories in Japan, much as in America.

When I had finished, Nakamura called in turn on various members, who had apparently already received their assignments. After several rather formalistic points had been made about models and methods, Ishii took off on an illuminating discussion of a study of consumer behavior vis-à-vis powdered milk.

In the traditional Japanese family, referred to as Type 1, the pattern is of course patriarchal, which means in practice that the wife is in charge of the kitchen and the husband never enters this sphere either physically or in terms of authority. The wife is not to be thought of as a "wife" or spouse in the American sense, but rather as a daughter or daughter-in-law who shares many functions with the other women in the household; in deciding for or against powdered milk, she will take account of judgments in the family at large as purveyed through this female network. Thus, while as a traditionalist she is unlikely to accept powdered milk, if she does accept it the decision is largely hers and is unaffected by her menfolk.

The Type 2 family is more modern. It is a nuclear (non-extended) family and the husband shares many decisions with his spouse. He is the one to decide the brand name if there is to be a joint decision in favor of powdered milk. The Type 2 family is of course more likely to be familiar with powdered milk, but the wife doesn't have the same complete authority within her sphere; there is a breakdown of the sharp boundaries between spheres, though purchases under 1,000 yen (around $3.00) are likely to be made by the wife without consultation, unless they involve electronic or technical gadgets, where the wife may turn to her husband even for something as inexpensive as an electric-light socket. In these nuclear families, of course, the wife doesn't have to take account of a whole set of kinfolk and how they would regard a purchase. But apparently both in Type 1 and in Type 2 families, if the husband's boss at the office considers powdered milk a bad thing, it is not likely to be bought even if there is considerable need for it within the family. There was also a Type 3 family—and all sorts of variations among the types—but it was decided to try to simplify matters by concentrating on two types.

(I asked later how in a Type 1 family the husband would even know it was being bought and how in any case men at the office would have an occasion to discuss such household questions. I got no satisfactory answer to this. It was agreed that such a "domestic" item would not come up in conversation. I concluded from the lack of an answer that the subordinate would somehow feel the tone of his boss's domestic ménage and would comport himself accordingly—this goes much further than the patterns described by Whyte in *The Organization Man*, where a junior-management man can't have a Cadillac if the boss insists on driving a Buick.)

In the tradition-directed Type 1 family, the kitchen is regarded as demeaning and the husband can't enter it. The housewives, however, need support to feel justified in buying powdered milk—which of course is part of the move away from rice and into dairy products. Thus, if they get together as a group of housewives and decide on powdered milk, that's it. And the housewife can have her way with the support of the other housewives even if the mother-in-law disagrees; but of course the housewife is likely to take account of her mother-in-law as well as brothers, sisters, and so on. In the Type 2 family, there is less clear compartmentalization. The husband is likely to be a salary man or white-collar worker and to take some part in domestic chores and in the children's education. In such a family the mother decides on the type of milk, that is, whether fresh or powdered; the price and brand name are within the father's sphere of intervention. Here, the PTA and the pediatrician, the mass media and advertisements, rather than other housewives, are likely to have a say.

Ishii remarked at one point that this study *wasn't* motivation research, and I realized that the American conflict over MR had been imported; actually what he said did seem to me to take account of motivation, but both he and the interpreter insisted that it was really discussion in terms of where one was located in the family and employment system and not in terms of individual psychology.

Nakamura pointed out that skim milk and powdered milk had had a tremendous increase after the war and that this was the forerunner of other changes everywhere in the rice-eating parts of the world. Those under forty years old were more willing to shift to milk: they were exposed in primary school and in cafeterias to the availability and desirability of milk, while those over forty were not familiar with milk.

I shifted the discussion by asking whether Japanese husbands dictated the voting behavior of their wives and was told that Japanese men were *fathers*, not husbands in the American sense, and that there was no discussion between husbands and wives concerning politics: neither will tell the other whom they will vote for or even whether or not they will vote.

Ishii pointed out that the distinction into types had in turn to be qualified by all sorts of variations. Take the case of a father whose education has been in a rural locality, who has spent two years in Tokyo, while his wife is a Tokyo girl who has graduated from senior high school; in a Type 1 family the man will nevertheless decide on the food to be eaten, the paper to be subscribed to, and so on. But he will not *participate* (rather, I assume, he will dictate), while if the man has more education he can participate.

Mr. Kubo, a labor economist, said he would enter a qualification on what had been said. He pointed out that the new generation living in the *danchi* have views different from the traditional ones about the division of labor between spouses; as in the United States, the man will give his pay check to his wife, who can make decisions about minor purchases in terms of the wants of the whole family and will consult her husband only concerning durables costing 1,000 yen or more, and in terms of brand to be bought rather than quality. Perhaps this should be called Type 3. There are 300,000 *danchi* "tribes," and these are the first "husbands" in the American sense in Japan.

I had raised the question in my opening remarks about the trend in the United States in the educated classes away from conspicuous consumption toward what might be called conspicuous underconsumption and asked whether such a trend was conceivable in Japan. Mr. Niki, a demographer working for the government, said that conspicuous consumption itself was relatively recent in Japan. (Before World War II, as in the case of Chinese merchants, well-to-do Japanese hid their wealth behind ordinary-looking fences: their homes were of the same sort as those of the poor, save that they were bigger and had more mats and more beautiful scrolls or pottery but nothing flaunted on the outside.) Niki agreed with me that the Japanese rich now behave with respect to food and health in the way Westerners did in the late nineteenth and early twentieth centuries. In this sense of belated and combined development, Japan today is a "mixed economy." The very complexities of development were one reason this group had been formed, and it seemed to me that the complete borrowing of American theory and techniques was an effort to gain the magical power of looking directly at other people's consumer behavior—a look previously warded off by Japanese patterns of concealed consumption.

The variety of concerns of the group was illustrated by the fact that the next speaker was a physician in the National Public Sanitation Center who pointed out that the shift away from rice toward milk would minimize stomach cancer. He had come to this conclusion after studying the Nisei in the United States and in Hawaii: as these move away from a rice diet, they have less stomach cancer. He added that in Hawaii Japanese eating patterns change faster than within Japan itself, partly because electricity is more easily available, partly because they learn about milk in the American schools and link milk with being "American."

Nakamura asked me how Americans had put over their anti-animal fat campaign in terms of the dangers of heart disease. I was reminded by his question that, with one exception, the larger and stouter men sat nearer me at the head of the table—people of more "weight" carry more weight in Japan. I answered that I didn't know about this but I wished I could think of a way to put over an anti-fall-out campaign in the United States. (Thinking about weight, I am reminded of the danger of pomposity engendered by the deference big-shots receive, whether in America or in Japan. While Mr. Matsushita, head of the electric company, is the largest income tax payer in Japan, followed by one or two movie stars, these in turn are followed by writers who have a large popular audience—men of the type, perhaps, of J. P. Marquand, who play golf with prime ministers and leading businessmen. The status of writers in Japan is rather like that in the Soviet Union, and the status of pundits is dangerously high!)

On the drive down to the meeting, I had said to Nakamura that I was interested in the way Zengakuren activists changed into organization men as soon as they went into business. Turning away from powdered milk and animal fats, he now asked Mr. Morimoto, a systems engineer, why he thought this occurred. The latter replied that in school students were still dependent on parents and could therefore be free, while on the job they were on their own and had to think of their future, of marriage, and so on. Moreover, employers insist on conformity to the company pattern. His own superior, however, had employed a Zengakuren leader and this had taken courage.

Mr. Hori, who teaches sociology at one of the private women's colleges, commented that a small number of his students had become active in the demonstrations. He thought that they would continue to be active, for the real activists get jobs in the movement itself. It is the sympathizers who change, depending on the environment they are in: they may be active in college, but quiescent in their careers. I asked him about Ochanomizu, and he said that since this was a government school before the war, it was free and it attracted lower-class girls. Now, however, as at the University of Tokyo, it is so hard to get in that students take their exams over and over and attend cram schools; and as they need money for that, it is difficult for a lower-class person to enter. Generally speaking, the Departments of Law, Economics, and Engineering are conservative, and so is Psychology (perhaps this is because many graduates go into industrial psychology), while Leftists are to be found in the fields of Chinese studies, Classics, Government, and Agriculture. Literature in general is pursued by girls and steered away from by boys. The fields of Government and Agriculture may be conservative in periods of prosperity but they are dependent on job prospects and will be radical if job prospects are poor.

At this point the chairman called on Mr. Itabashi, formerly a member of the staff of NMA and presently a director of Sony, a forceful and attractive man who had come in late. He introduced himself as an alumnus of the group and the only employer in the room. He explained the sudden change from the student attitude to the corporation attitude as being due to the Japanese lack of individual selfhood in the Western sense, so that Japanese were permeable to the value systems around them. Student society and employee society are entirely different: in the student society the climbers, the go-getters, are overtly despised; yet since the larger society is competitive, everyone has anxiety and fear for the future, and so the student attitude toward the go-getter is mixed. Moreover, in engineering school or other "applied" departments, teaching is theoretical. Thus, ideological matters tend to be emphasized, and students even in engineering tend to devote their student life to the political angle. Once outside, since people are easily contaminated by the value system around them, they soon learn to be timid and not to speak up. However, one or two brave men who speak up in the employee society can have enormous influence because of this susceptibility of others to any standards that are set, and he has seen cases of such impact.

I was asked whether I had any comments on Itabashi's remarks, and I said that I wished students could get a clearer view while in the university of the climate of business, so that they would suffer less what Everett Hughes calls "reality shock" and might therefore preserve their independence more. I went on to raise questions about the nature of work itself and my impression that employees surrendered not only their right to continue their political activities but also their right to enjoy their work; they were prepared for boredom and, while

DR

they appreciated the improving perquisites of their job as they moved up on the escalator, they did not expect the work itself to become in any way challenging or interesting.

Itabashi replied that the Japanese employee has an emotional outlet for his meaningless work: after the work is done, the men adjourn to a bar where they talk and gripe about their bosses. Indeed, he spoke of one management consultant who goes to a bar frequented by employees the night before he is to meet the employer, in order to find what the climate is and thus to anticipate the problems he will be presented with the next day. Furthermore, there is no clear job description in Japan, unlike the situation in the United States, so that an individual does not own his job in the way he does in America. This means that when he is promoted and becomes a boss he can intervene in his subordinates' work much more than he can in America, while his wife can boss other wives of employees of lower status. This, too, is an outlet for energies displaced from the work itself.

The meeting adjourned, and everybody came down to see us off in our hired car, with the usual three stages of goodbyes. Since it was raining and cold outside while the room had been heated, this last goodbye meant a shift from a temperature of about 85° to something like 45°. Often, of course, there is no heat indoors, but where there is, it is sometimes stiflingly hot, as if the warmth itself were a physical comfort like a hot bath. And people will sit in this warmth wearing long winter underwear and a heavy sweater underneath their suit coats, while Evey and I would always be, to the amusement of our hosts, pulling on or taking off things in a vain effort to keep up with the thermometer.

ETR

A representative from the express company, a dapper young man in neat suit and white shirt who spoke fluent English, came this morning to see about shipping our things home. After he had looked over everything and written it down and given an estimate, he asked for the name. When I told him, he immediately recognized it and said he had read an article in the morning's paper about Mr. Riesman and his visit in Japan; the article had said Mr. Riesman was a "people seer rather than a sight seer," and that Mr. Riesman approved of the *danchi* and preferred Tokyo to Kyoto. He finally left, pleased with himself, and I of course was impressed—but in this highly literate society perhaps this is not so remarkable.

Mrs. Matsumoto and I had arranged to go together to the National

Art Gallery, an immense, gloomy brick building among other museums in Ueno Park. While we were looking at some prehistoric pots and sculpture, the curator joined us. He was a scholarly and brilliant man and told us about the history and the techniques of the arts as he showed us around. When we came to the scrolls, he told us that the calligraphers were very particular about the weight of the paper they used—there were many different qualities and the paper was chosen to suit the poem's meaning and length; the poem was recorded in exquisite calligraphy and pasted in the center of the scroll. The "story" scrolls, which the "reader" unrolls in one hand and rolls up in the other, were made by monks for converting people to Buddhism. We saw a section of such a scroll telling the story of building a temple; there is always a happy ending in which Buddha appears in a cloud when the temple is finished. Another group of scrolls consisted of ink paintings of lively frolicking animals: these were simply exercises in painting done by young priests. The Zen priests did not paint Buddha but made remarkable portraits of the Zen teachers they admired. In some of the story scrolls, one has a bird's-eye view looking down between clouds or between roofs into a scene in a garden. The convention of perspective is the opposite of ours, that is, the parallel lines diverge and the figures become larger in the distance.

On the way home we drove through some very old, narrow streets of the Akasaka district, not far from the Diet buildings. There were lovely old inns and houses with high wooden fences, and also many little shops. Mrs. Matsumoto told me that the Diet members frequented these places—I imagine she meant kept their mistresses here—and so when there is an attempt to raise the taxes to a much needed level, the innkeepers raise a howl, and nothing happens. She said that Tokyo has no fashionable districts and no slum districts, the wealthy and poor live side by side all over the city.

Tokyo, December 1

Not wanting to go out today I had lunch at International House by chance with Nat Glazer and Mrs. Hidaka, who is doing some work with him in city planning. We began talking about women and marriage and careers. Mrs. Hidaka said her mother is a social worker, and so in her family it is acceptable for the wife to have a profession. She said that her husband has liberal ideas about marriage and approves of her working. Japanese houses are so small that women can easily have a career and do their own housekeeping. The women of her generation keep on with their jobs even after having children (she has one very

ETR

young child); but, she thought, the women of the younger generation (I supposed she meant the twenty-year-olds, for she is about thirty) are more likely to stop working when they have children, and then in their spare time join clubs to see movies and so forth to fill up their time.

At this point Nat was called away to the phone and Mrs. Hidaka asked about my impressions of Japan. I got on the subject of the Zengakuren and our discussions with the student leaders. She thought we had gotten a false picture of the Zengakuren because the intellectuals admired them so much, saw their own youth in them, and helped and encouraged them. She didn't think the Zengakuren were constructive, but were simply out for their own glory. When the trade unions and Communists wanted them to cooperate, they always refused; they wanted to be independent and go their own way, do big things, overthrow the government; they were more anarchistic than helpful. She said the *demo* were really the work of the trade unions and workers, but the Zengakuren were the violent ones and got all the publicity and credit. She felt the Communists were constructive and sober people and had been the only ones with the courage to resist the militarists before the war. She wanted to know about the Communist Party in the United States. I told her that the situation was different in our country, that there was not the same sort of frustration as here, that the Communist Party was dead in the United States, and where it was not dead it was destructive. She could not believe that our workers did not desire a revolution. I said on the contrary our workers hated Communism, partly for the wrong reasons, because they are so nationalistic and anti-Russian.

I liked her seriousness and concern and what she said fitted in with what others had said about the moderation of the Communists in Japan in comparison with the extreme Left. Because these far Leftists have no name that we recognize, we do not think they are as dangerous as the Communists, whose name we think we know all too well.

Nat came back and we talked about city planning during the rest of lunch, discussing Nat's article, which described Tokyo as an unplanned city and related it to Jane Jacobs's views in *The Death and Life of Great American Cities.*

DR

This morning Murata and Yoshida brought Mr. Ohashi to breakfast. He is an outspoken journalist who had refused to compromise himself during the war. He struck me as a combination John Gunther, Will

Rogers, and Elmer Davis—twinkly, robust, and stocky. He has a whimsical bent for inventing terms and categories. One example was his division of countries into those that emphasize the animal, those that emphasize the mineral, and those that emphasize the vegetable kingdoms. The less human a country, the better it fared with the mineral kingdom: this was the case of the Soviet Union, which did well in oil but badly in agriculture, while turning men into "animals," that is, into dogs in the Pavlovian sense. As a monologuist, given to witty sallies, Ohashi made one broad and amusing generalization after the other.

Beneath the banter could be glimpsed his general outlook that the Soviet Union and the United States were two quite similar managerial societies in which one could exchange the managerial strata without discomfiture to either, although he admitted that the Russians were somewhat slower and more backward.

I asked Ohashi about his visit to the United States. He said that he'd waited for a year for a visa and had finally started out on one of his round-the-world tours without it. He kept being promised a visa in various places en route, and when he finally got to Havana and it hadn't arrived he wired his publisher, who was supporting the tour, and said that if his visa didn't come in the next day or so, his next book would be entitled, "Round the World Except the United States." The publisher wired back that that was an even better title than "Round the World." He took the exchange of cables to the American Embassy in Havana—this was long before we cut off relations—and had his visa within twenty-four hours; all this was another source of amusement for him. (In general over the course of our stay I received many complaints concerning this matter of whom the United States recognizes and allows to visit America. Many Leftists do not apply because they fear the humiliation of being turned down. I should add that many of the Leftists are ambivalent at best about coming to America: they may use the risk of turn-down as an excuse not to apply. Murata told Evey on another occasion that the Japanese university students most eager to come to the United States and apparently most welcome are rather crass types who admire American opulence and want big cars and the Hollywood style of life in general; when they return to Japan, which they reluctantly do, they are hardly the best reporters on America or mediators between the two cultures. It is sometimes said that Zengakuren activists and other "progressives" wouldn't come to America even if invited; and while this may be true in some cases, I am inclined to think that many would be eager to come and that it would make sense to have them come, provided, of course, that we were prepared to see them return and make many criticisms of America in order to retain both their own sense of self and their position as proper Leftists; still, such a trip might possibly alter the simplicities of their view of America and might also be illuminating for Americans.)

To return to Ohashi, the latter was very fond of his image of Pavlov's dogs as a description of the Russian society. None of this, it should be clear, was said with any harshness; it is hard to imagine America's sarcastic or "sick" comics making a hit with the Japanese. In earlier periods of oppression they had had satiric short verses, a "subversive" form of haiku, but these died out, and the freedom of the press following the war was not conducive to those forms of satire that flourish under oppression. Furthermore, there is no tiny minority that regards itself as especially alienated and unable to communicate with the society as a whole; to be sure, the left-wing students say that they are alienated but they hope to carry the rest of society and certainly the labor movement and the Socialist Party along with them. Thus, the sort of sad intramural sarcasm that appeals to a small minority of the American counter-elite is not for them. (To be sure, as I later learned from Lewis Feuer, copies of *The New Yorker* were extremely popular in Japan right after the war and would circulate from avid hand to avid hand; but as I've noted no such journal has been created among the plethora of new journals in post-war Japan.)

I found Ohashi charming, but almost too conscious of his charm. To my Japanese friends, he seemed a singularly unillusioned man, with a rare kind of political ribaldry and insouciance. I too found him observant, though not very penetrating, and enjoyed his amused and gentle detachment from the prejudices of his time and place. In appearance and style he has some of Thurber's wistful, mildly humorous appeal, without the sadness of Thurber.

Now I've come across Evey's notes on the meeting with Ohashi and see I've left out a number of things. He said that both Russians and Americans wanted to be loved by their neighbors and that this lay behind the ideological struggle of the cold war. From his talks with ordinary people in Russia, he had become convinced that the Russians are more patriotic than Americans: they are less belligerent, having suffered more through war, but they are very proud of the achievements of their society. The Russians adore jazz and can't get enough American records: the government is completely impotent to control aesthetic tastes. However, since the Cuban revolution a compromise between government and people has been attained: while jazz is still damned as "American," the mambo and the rumba are regarded as *both* patriotic and jazzy and have become even more popular than American jazz.

He observed that Chinese students in Moscow live in the Embassy so as not to be contaminated by a corrupt "capitalist" society around them. He had talked to a number of the Japanese studying in Moscow. I asked why they had gone there, since it could hardly be to study technology; he said they went to get socialist or Communist "atmosphere," but they were greatly disappointed to find that at the Afro-Asian University there were no classes on Marxism and that the engineering students from the underdeveloped countries were distinctly unideological.

I asked Ohashi about the Japanese students and their Marxism. He said that the struggle before the war between Trotskyists and Stalinists had been a struggle over which was the perfect orthodoxy—a struggle now altered to one between the Soviet and Chinese versions of Communism as well as between socialists and Communists. The Chinese Communists are in the position today of a graduate student without tenure who will soon be an assistant professor, whereas the Russians have tenure—that's why they still have some authority in Japan despite the dislike of Russians.

The British, he said, let their colonies go slowly and admirably, but neither America nor the U.S.S.R. is able to do this with their satellites, whether in Latin America or in Central Europe.

I asked Ohashi if there were any heroes for the Japanese young. He said that while there are writers they admire, there are no political heroes; as a rule the youth and the Japanese generally since the war have wanted to destroy hero worship, which they regarded as part of the cult of the Emperor.

Growing more serious as I raised serious questions, Ohashi spoke of America's sweet, human, and optimistic attitude; but a succession of failures after World War II had somewhat soured American sweetness. Now America must make a real effort to change and grasp the mind of the world. He feels Kennedy is trying to bring about change in foreign policy. Ohashi said that as a graduate student he was enamored of America and wanted to go there because there was no emperor, but the immigration laws of America prevented his going. Even during the war he remained pro-American. But his experiences with the visa disappointed him. When he finally got to the United States after the war, I think he felt hurt that no Americans had heard of him or knew of his position in Japanese journalism, or of the Friendship Organization he had founded.

Ohashi felt that the best thing the United States could do vis-à-vis the Communists was to send millions of tourists to the Communist bloc, because the Russians all want to copy America and each tourist acts as a lure for the American objects the Russians desire. I think it wasn't only the material possessions of American tourists that Ohashi thought would appeal to the Russians, but also the greater liveliness and sense of freedom. They carry these as an aura. The Americans, he said, are more imaginative than the Russians, more creative. The Russians are only trying to do better in their own immediate family life. That is as far as they can see.

The official of the Finance Ministry whom we had met earlier in our stay, Mr. Koremitsu, had felt sorry that on our first meeting he had not had sufficient time to do justice to the occasion, and he asked his friend Matsumoto to make a return engagement possible. The result was a luncheon at a guest house on a former estate of a noble or very rich man—an estate with a magnificent garden (beautiful even in the rain) and many rooms, each heated by a gas stove. We met first in a Western-style room where we had tea and where the usual photographs were taken, and we were then joined by several additional officials. Evey had been expected but was not feeling well enough to come.

During lunch we began by discussing the views of those economists who feel that an austerity policy is absolutely essential if Japan is to survive economically. I must say I felt that there was something a bit paradoxical in our talking this way as we looked out on the enormous garden in crowded Tokyo, where the lavish conference rooms and offices of the financial and industrial elite seemed by contrast even more conspicuous than offices of comparable eminences in Manhattan. Yet, as also with some of our patrician leaders, austerity appeared to some of the officials to have non-economic value as a spiritual matter. Thus, Koremitsu and one of his colleagues complained about the loss of a sense of purpose and national coherence since the war, a breakdown of values. He asked me what could be done to restore communication with the younger generation, which he feels cares for nothing but personal and selfish aims, such as quick material gain.

I said that this was a world-wide complaint of the older against the younger generation; here again I felt that the Japanese were somewhat parochial in thinking that their problems were peculiar, even though I also admitted that the reversals of the war and post-war period had produced perhaps a somewhat greater generational gap in Japan than in other industrial countries. Still, I felt that the same conversation we were having could be carried on in any conservative men's club in London or in the United States. And I heard again the complaint that there were no leaders in post-war Japan, or at any rate the sort of traditional elite leaders on whom Japan had depended during the Meiji period. Where were the public-spirited men with a sense of conviction, able to stand up against their own group and to take a larger view? Here again I felt the comparability of attitudes to those in the United States, where many talk about the lack of national purpose and look back nostalgically to an alleged earlier spirit of dedication.

This older, austere-type Japanese sees the Liberal Democratic politicians in the same light in which men like Theodore Roosevelt or Henry Adams viewed the politicians who did the will of the big businessmen in the United States in the post-Civil War period. Such politicians appear both weak and reckless, unable to cope with Japan's grave economic crisis, or even to understand it.

Koremitsu asked me if I had met any people in Japan whom I considered to be authentic leaders. I said I thought I had but that he wouldn't like my reply, for I felt that some of the Zengakuren activists were indeed leaders with genuine idealism, dedication, and personal forcefulness. But, I added, these men are self-excluded as well as boycotted from any posts in Japanese business or financial life; nevertheless, they wished Japan well after their fashion, and if Koremitsu really wanted to communicate with youth, as he repeatedly said he did, he could do worse than try not only to talk with but to listen to some of these leaders. Perhaps, I added, he needed go-betweens—people close to the students but of an older generation, such as some of the young faculty members I had been meeting. Koremitsu immediately asked about the latter, and I mentioned several names, which he took down. His inquiry is another illustration of the respect for "culture" endemic among some businessmen and government officials. The latter are as eager to meet professors as their counterparts in the United States.

While we talked, we worked our way through a meal whose printed menu didn't tell the half of it: lobster and soup and chicken and beef and salad and shrimp with rice and fruit and sweet: it was enough to put to sleep even the most intrepid gourmet.

When the talk recurred to the need for austerity to meet the immediate foreign-exchange crisis, I mentioned that I had talked the night before at the Nippon Management Association about the possibility of starting a fad of underconsumption in Japan. What would be the effect, I maliciously asked, if the large golf clubs inside Tokyo gave up their land for parks, or if this handsome mansion and its garden were turned into a public park? I got in answer a reference to Prime Minister Ikeda's having given up golf and taken to living simply.

Early in the discussion, Koremitsu complained that there were no capitalists in Japan. I asked whether Matsushita wasn't a capitalist. Koremitsu's reply made plain that what he meant by "capitalist" was somebody who himself had a great deal of money which he invested with a sense of business and perhaps also civic responsibility. Matsushita was one of a number of men who had become rich in post-war Japan, but the pre-war fortunes had been destroyed and in that sense there were no capitalists. Koremitsu seemed to think that the United States was full of the more classic type of capitalists, for instance John D. Rockefeller III. What he admired was the Rockefeller family's sense of the responsibilities of venture capital as well as civic responsibilities, and this he felt didn't exist in Japan. He said all the businessmen are employees and have the mentality of clerks.

I commented that I had heard this criticism on all sides, but still the foreign visitor couldn't help but see many accomplishments of industrial development: who then were the entrepreneurs? In general I said it had been easier for the Japanese to explain why things failed and didn't work than why they did work. I got the sense from the comments of Matsumoto and others that the next level under the boss was the creative one in Japanese life, whether in the universities or in the government or in business. Murata and other friends had said much the same thing earlier. And I was led to ponder whether in the United States the same thing wasn't true—as in many of our large corporations where the president is a front man who can be sent to Washington for a dollar a year without costing the company anything: on the contrary.

After dinner tonight I walked out, as I often have, to Roppongi and had the pang of realizing what a wrench it would be to leave here. It was about ten o'clock, traffic was heavy, and many shops were still open or were just closing; and at the vegetable and fruit stand on the corner the man was taking in his bicycle and putting away some oranges preparatory to closing for the night. Many people were still on the streets. It was a mild night—these last days have been the most beautiful of all, with little rain, and quite clear and brisk like fall days in Vermont, though sometimes with high winds that stir up the dust. While undoubtedly there are streets in Tokyo where one would not want to walk late at night, and while indifference to public as distinguished from private enterprise means that there are hardly any street lights and lighting must therefore depend on the stores and their neon signs, I felt quite safe. And in this ever changing scene, I still see new things and new faces even on familiar walks.

Tokyo, December 2

We had an early lunch, which turned out to be a farewell party with Japanese red wine and toasts for our return to Japan. At this lunch there were just the Matsumotos, Professor Kawasaki, Professor Hayakawa, the three young International House assistants, Kato, and us. After lunch a group gathered to go with us to the airport, where we discovered our plane would be an hour or so late. We all went to the coffee shop and had a gay, pleasant time discussing novels and movies. Kato told me quietly how much Dave's visit had meant to him—I often feel, being the wife, that people can say things to me that they would hesitate to say to Dave.

Finally, our plane was called. We went downstairs and down the ramp. When we turned back and waved goodbye, I thought how much had happened in these two months, how my view of the world had changed, and how I had come to love Japan, "the end of the world"—its misty mountains, abstract paintings, modern cities, and most of all, the people we have learned to know—and especially these people waving to us.

Index